*Other books by Michael Harrington*

THE OTHER AMERICA

THE ACCIDENTAL CENTURY

TOWARD A DEMOCRATIC LEFT

# SOCIALISM

# SOCIALISM

## MICHAEL HARRINGTON

Saturday Review Press / E.P. Dutton & Co., Inc.

New York

A portion of this book first appeared in *Dissent* magazine, May, 1970, Volume XVII, Number 3.

*Published simultaneously in Canada by Doubleday Canada Ltd., Toronto.*

*Library of Congress Catalog Card Number: 76–154260*

*ISBN 0–8415–0141–6*

*Saturday Review Press*

PRINTED IN THE UNITED STATES OF AMERICA

*Design by Tere LoPrete*

*Third Printing*

*To the memory of Norman Thomas*
*And the future of his ideals*

I OWE THIS BOOK to Norman Thomas and to all the other comrades of the socialist movement, the living and the dead, who were, and are, both my inspiration and my postgraduate university.

In particular I want to acknowledge the contributions of two socialists. Even though I have some serious disagreements with him on issues of socialist strategy, I am permanently and deeply indebted to Max Shachtman, who first introduced me to the vision of democratic Marxism and whose theory of bureaucratic collectivism is so important to my analysis. In the course of writing the last chapters on the future of socialism I received the most generous, and brilliant, political and literary help of my friend Irving Howe. As the editor of *Dissent* he has accomplished Herculean labors; he is certainly one of the most important men of the Left in his generation.

Finally, Stephanie Gervis Harrington played a critical role in the intellectual and literary genesis of this book. Her editorial judgment made a decisive contribution to my work.

# Contents

| | | |
|---|---|---|
| I | *The Future of the Past* | 3 |
| II | *The Preconditions of the Dream* | 11 |
| III | *The Democratic Essence* | 36 |
| IV | *The Unknown Karl Marx* | 55 |
| V | *Das Kapital* | 77 |
| VI | *The American Exception* | 109 |
| VII | *Socialism Discovers the World* | 134 |
| VIII | *Revolution from Above* | 154 |
| IX | *Socialist Capitalism* | 187 |
| X | *The Substitute Proletariats* | 216 |
| XI | *The Invisible Mass Movement* | 250 |
| XII | *Beyond the Welfare State* | 270 |
| XIII | *Beyond the World Market* | 308 |
| XIV | *Socialism* | 344 |
| | Notes | 375 |
| | Index | 407 |

# SOCIALISM

# I

## The Future of the Past

SOCIALISM HAS KNOWN increments of success, basic failure and massive betrayal. Yet it is more relevant to the humane construction of the twenty-first century than any other idea.

This book is about the future of the socialist past. It is not a narrative or a chronology, but a search for a living tradition, and it will therefore dwell on what has been only insofar as it touches on what might be. That, however, does not mean that I approach history like a fundamentalist preacher rummaging through scripture to find authority for his own favorite apocalypse. Such a moralistic account of socialism would not in the least help in changing the world. So it is in the interest of my intense partisanship to be as ruthlessly honest as possible: my subjectivity forces me to be as objective as I can.

I begin, like every student of the past and future, with a conviction about the present. Man has socialized everything except himself. He has rationalized his work and nature and the very planet in every respect save one: with regard to their underlying purpose. And, just as the socialists predicted more than a century ago, he is in conflict with an environment that he himself has brilliantly, and thoughtlessly, created. His genius threatens to overwhelm him.

Under capitalism, an intricate system of antagonistic cooperation makes a single individual more productive than a thousand once were. Science, the community of human knowledge, is casually employed for private purposes with revolutionary public consequences. This creates the highest living standard ever known, rots the great cities, befouls the air and water, and embitters classes, generations and races. Under Communism, these contradictions are collectivized, not resolved. The state owns the means of production, and a bureaucratic elite owns the state. Its interests, which are every bit as egotistic as those of corporations, are imposed upon the system by totalitarian command. The anti-social is thus consciously planned rather than being dictated by the "will" of the market.

Unfortunately, most of the people of the world do not even have the luxury of suffering from such sophisticated ironies. In the age of space exploration they struggle to satisfy primordial needs for food and shelter. More often than not the unification of mankind has made them more miserable. Trade more effectively than ever exacts a tribute from the poor nations to the rich, both capitalist and Communist; medicine saves a baby from an ancient plague only to deliver him up to a new kind of hunger; a miraculous seed threatens rural unemployment and even starvation because only elite farmers can use it.

The ultimate in these contradictions is both unprecedented and obvious to the point of banality. Nuclear science has penetrated the innermost secrets of our world and discovered there the possibility of annihilating it. It is as if the human race had persevered through the millennia only to reenact the drama of Adam and Eve. In the goodness of the fruit of the tree of knowledge there is the taste of evil.

These things need not be. Even the most superficial critic of society now realizes that it is not our knowledge, but the way in which it is organized, that menaces us. But beyond that humanist cliché there must be the specifics of a tough-minded, socialist solution: exactly how are we going to socialize the already social means of production? For one need not any longer ask whether the future is going to be collective—if we do not blow ourselves to smithereens, that issue has already been settled by a technology of such complex interdependence that it demands conscious regulation and control. The question is: What form will twenty-first-century collectivism take? Will it be a totalitarian, a bureaucratic or a democratic collectivism?

Socialism answers: Our technology could indeed be the instrument of enslavement; or it could, for the first time ever, provide the material base for a genuine human community that would democratize economic and social as well as political power. That socialist possibility, which will be detailed in the last three chapters, is not the insight of some radical prophets. It is, as the next chapter will show, either an observable tendency of social reality or it is a delusion. The history of socialism, then, is not simply the accumulation of a certain wisdom; it is the process whereby men and women have themselves defined what socialism is in the course of struggle. The past I am concerned with here is, in short, alive.

Indeed, I have often been struck by the way in which the theorists of some of the most daring and vanguard ideas of the contemporary Left are only faint and unwitting echoes of some long-dead socialist giant. Among the college-educated and upper-middle-class American activists of the sixties and early seventies, I have glimpsed the wraith of that most proletarian of French revolutionaries, Auguste Blanqui. He, too, thought that the working class had been so stupefied by the capitalist system that it would have to be saved from itself by an elite conspiracy which could only permit democratic freedoms once the people had been properly reeducated. Or, to take an even more remarkable anticipation, in the debates of Gracchus Babeuf and his Conspiracy of Equals in the 1790s, one glimpses Stalin and Mao waiting in the wings.

So the early socialists asked the questions that still bedevil us, and that is one of the many reasons they deserve our attention. But I do not propose to people this book with a race of prophetic supermen. On the contrary. It is important to root out every bit of messianism from the socialist vision, to reject the notion of a secular redemption that, like the incarnation of Christ, claims to make all things new. Every time men have acted upon that kind of chiliastic definition, the result has been totalitarian. Therefore the rich history of socialist tragedy and error is as important as the record of its profundity. Marx and Engels, to cite a single, spectacular instance, mistook the rise of capitalism for its decline. Only if socialists learn a chastened empiricism from such facts is there any hope for the plans and projects outlined in the last chapters of this book.

More generally, the demystification of Marx and Engels will be a central theme in this analysis. Their words are now used to

justify theories and practices they would abominate. They are
seen by most people as the fathers of totalitarianism and as materialistic simpletons who taught that economic interests neatly
determine the entire course of society. As long as that falsification of the socialist past prevails—and it is a state religion in
Russia, China and other Communist countries—the graven images
of Marx and Engels are among the greatest obstacles to the socialist future.

There also are socialist classics that must be recovered if the
next century is to be decently created. In 1914 Lenin wrote that,
since they had not studied Hegel's *Logic*, for almost half a
century "none of the Marxists understood Marx."* My attitude
is almost as extreme and arrogant. I believe, as Chapter V will
document, that *Das Kapital* has been barbarously treated by its
contemporary academic critics, like Paul Samuelson, and even
unfairly handled by sympathetic thinkers, like Joan Robinson. As
a result, there is much in that magnificent book that, despite the
fact that it was published more than one hundred years ago, is
new. I propose to rescue it from the distortions of the professors
and the rigidities of the keepers of holy writ. For it could help
us, not simply to understand the world, but to change it.

An overview of socialist history also illuminates an idea that
is crucial for understanding what is happening today under Communism, in the Third World and within the welfare state. This
is the concept of anti-socialist "socialism."

Bismarck was, as will be seen later on in greater detail, the
first of the anti-socialist "socialists." In 1878 he outlawed any
organization that even advocated socialism. By 1882 he was telling the Reichstag, "Many of the measures that we have adopted
for the welfare of the land are socialistic and we need more socialism in our state. . . ." Clearly, the Junker leader had not
undergone a sudden conversion between 1878 and 1882, moving
from the Right to the Left. He had shrewdly understood that
the socialists had mass appeal, and he was determined to use
socialist slogans in order to fight socialism.

Even before Bismarck attempted to co-opt the socialist appeal,

---

* In order not to clutter up the text, the references to notes for each section of a
chapter will be grouped under a single numeral at the end of that section. Since
this introduction is so brief, all of its references will be found in note 1. In the
lengthier chapters, there will be a note for each substantial section. The notes
themselves will be found at the back of the book.

Marx had understood the potential of anti-socialist "socialism." In the 1850s he analyzed the Crédit Mobilier under Napoleon III in France as "Bonapartist" or "imperial" "socialism." And in an attack on Proudhon he used an even more telling phrase. "Communism," Marx wrote, "must free itself from all the 'false brothers'" of the fashionable socialisms of the time. He did not realize that in the twentieth century the "false brothers" were to become world powers, and worse, that they would call themselves Marxist.

Early on, then, a sophisticated conservative understood that socialism had accurately anticipated two of the most important tendencies of the modern age. Technology was indeed making economic, social and political life more collective, even when it operated under the auspices of laissez-faire; and millions dreamed that this process could be made the instrument of their emancipation from poverty and servility. The collectivizing trend meant that the state would have to take a role in directing the economy. The socialist aspirations among the people could be used to provide popular support for such policies—even when they were in the service of some new, or more efficient, form of exploitation.

Thus from Bismarck to the present moment, dictators and charlatans as well as democratic socialists have fought for the possession of the word "socialism." Joseph Stalin invoked it to justify psychopathic purges and the totalitarian accumulation of capital; Clement Attlee used it to help build a democratic welfare state in Britain after World War II. But the most monstrous single definition of the term was unquestionably the "National Socialism" of the Nazis. Gregor Straser, the "Left-wing" Nazi, said that Hitler was responding to the "anti-capitalist yearnings" of the masses.

If, then, socialism is to have any meaning—past, present or future—a way must be found to distinguish between the various, and often murderously hostile, claimants to its name. And this is particularly important in the 1970s when one is confronted by Russian, Chinese, Yugoslavian, Israeli, African, Cuban, Chilean, Indian, Arab and other "socialisms." In the Tower of Babel that is the Left, is there any empirical test that can establish the difference between the authentic and the spurious socialisms?

It was one of the many accomplishments of Karl Marx and Friedrich Engels to demonstrate how this can be done. One must, they said, go behind the socialist rhetoric of a given movement and discover who is making the decisions and what interests are being served. Using those criteria, they realized as young men in the 1840s that the times were giving birth to two new movements: to socialism and to "socialist" anti-socialism. In *The Communist Manifesto* they pointed out that there were reactionary and conservative "socialisms." They told of aristocrats who hated capitalism because it was anti-feudal and wanted to march back to medievalism in the name of "socialism." And there were small businessmen who wanted the capitalist giants who threatened them to be controlled; intellectuals with blueprinted panaceas; and even utopians among the bourgeoisie itself who dreamed of a harmonious capitalism free of conflict. They all called themselves "socialists."

The hallmark of these "socialisms" was that they were the creations of self-seeking minorities, ruses whereby feudalists or shopkeepers or businessmen sought to cloak their special interests in soaring universals. But capitalism, Marx and Engels said—and they were, as will be seen, both right and wrong—was creating a new and vast majority which owned no means of production and whose common good required nothing more than the democratization of the economy and society. A genuine socialist movement was one that led the struggles and articulated the needs of these people.

Marx died in 1883 and thus did not have the opportunity to see how Bismarck would turn the anti-socialist "socialism" described in the *Manifesto* into a state policy. But Engels lived long enough to see through this trick and his disciple, Karl Kautsky, the famous "pope" of Marxism before the First World War, even gave it a new name. He called it "state socialism," a strategy of government intervention into the economy, including the nationalization of certain enterprises, for the purpose of shoring up capitalism.

These distinctions from the socialist past must be carefully explored for they are crucial to the present and future. In 1917 a socialist revolution triumphed in a Russia that lacked the preconditions for socialism. Eventually, most of the revolutionists were murdered in the name of the Revolution and a new form of class society, anti-capitalist and anti-socialist, came into being. Variants of this bureaucratic collectivism have now appeared in Eastern Europe, China and, in new and unexpected mutations, throughout the Third World. Do these cases then prove that the socialist vision of the people emancipating themselves is a hoax?

The welfare state poses a similar problem in a radically different context. The reform of capitalism was achieved largely because of the presence of a mass socialist movement (or, in the United States, of the unions) and over the outraged protests of businessmen, who gained enormously from the change. The advances that were thus made are quite real and the result of a democratic struggle. They are the very opposite of those "revolutions from above" carried out by a Bismarck or a Stalin. But the danger is that the welfare state is then equated with socialism itself. In their daily battle to make capitalism more tolerable, socialists could lose their vision of a fundamental transformation of social relationships. The classes would remain and the domination of private, minority priorities would take on much more sophisticated forms. With the unwitting cooperation of the socialists themselves, their dream would become the new facade of an old order.

So it is possible that, in quite different but parallel ways, the socialist ideal will be expropriated under Communism and the welfare state and in the Third World. That would mark the corruption of the future.

Class societies have, of course, always justified themselves in the name of the highest values of religion or honor or freedom. But if socialism were to be effectively turned into a rationale for new modes of exploitation, then there would be no hope of a just order of things. That has not yet happened, for despite the monstrous crimes committed in its name, the socialist vision still speaks to the majority of mankind. In the Communist sphere, for instance, every movement of opposition and protest—the East German general strike of 1953, the Polish and Hungarian uprisings of October, 1956, the Czechoslovakian spring of 1968 and the Polish strikes in the winter of 1970–1971—was trying to create the "human face of socialism," not to return to capitalism. Paradoxically, as Zbigniew Brzezinski has noted, in Eastern Europe, "socialism has wide popular support whereas Communism as an institutionalized belief has not." Thus the distinction between the socialist ideal and its manipulation, first formulated by Marx and Engels, has enormous practical significance for the present and future.

But if the people were to accept the anti-socialist "socialisms" as genuine, then one of the most crucial elements of the socialist possibility—a conscious mass movement—would disappear. The millions would have internalized the definition of dictators or bureaucrats that the people cannot rule and must passively accept orders from on high. That would be the death of socialism. And that is why I will take such pains in this book to understand anti-socialist "socialism."

Finally, this book describes the necessity of socialism, not its inevitability.

I am not at all sure that there will be a socialist alternative to Communism and the welfare state. It is certainly quite possible that the twenty-first century will belong to bureaucratic collectivism and that the dream of human self-emancipation will turn out to have been mankind's noblest deception. But I am sure that if men are to master their own genius—if the fantastically productive and destructive and interdependent technological society we have blundered into is to be our homeland and not our prison —then they must socialize themselves along with everything else. So after so many failures and betrayals the socialism defined here does not pretend to be the wave of the future. It is simply our only hope.[1]

# II

# *The Preconditions of the Dream*

UTOPIA WAS A FANTASTIC VOYAGE into the present, which was disguised as the future, and sometimes even an idealization of the past. Its details were almost always reactionary, and yet its effect was enormously progressive. For as it changed and developed within history, the people increasingly listened not to its authoritarianism, but to its central premise that men can consciously shape their future. In this mood they made brilliant misreadings of the classic utopian texts which helped them change reality.

Utopia began in the theology of the Hebrews in the desert and the speculation of the Greeks in their cities. After the fall of the Roman Empire, it disappeared for about seven centuries and suddenly emerged during the breakdown of feudalism as a movement of militant holiness. And then after four hundred years of defeats, it finally became a political force on the Left wing of the capitalist revolution. At every point in this process, it was the child of the present, not the father of the future. For the ideal, even as pure theory, cannot escape the limitations of its own age.

So even mankind's dreams of justice had their historic preconditions. And that applies with even greater force to the attempt to actually realize them. It is one of the most basic of contemporary socialist truths that the good society only becomes possible when there is a technology of abundance and a mass movement capable of mastering it.

Indeed, much of the tragedy of this century derives from massive efforts to ignore this fundamental proposition. From the Russian Revolution of 1917 through the Great Leap in the China of the fifties to the Cuban sugar harvest of 1970, men have tried to force their way into the future with an iron fist. They often succeeded in transforming the conditions of social life, yet they did not, and could not, create socialism in the absence of its preconditions. So, ultimately, the leaders of these movements were armed Platonists, totalitarian utopians who tried to impose a millennium upon the people.

However, I do not want to discuss the preconditions of socialism solely in terms of the Communist experience. This idea is, after all, not an afterthought designed to explain away some recent and current dictators, but a matter of the socialist essence. I will go back to the beginning and show how socialism, even as dream, could never be very much better than the actual, historic possibilities of human life, and how, in the nineteenth century, those possibilities for the first time became utopian.

Karl Marx was the first socialist thinker to become conscious of these things and to formulate them systematically. He did so in the midst of a philosophic debate about the meaning of meaning.

The abstractions of Western man, like his utopias, are suffused with the reality of their time and place whether the men who think them know it or not. By the seventeenth century, capitalism was not simply destroying the medieval social structure in the advanced countries of Europe, it was shattering a world view as well. All the hierarchies—the animal, vegetable and mineral, the political, economic and social—had been links in a great chain of being which departed from, and returned to, God. But once man began to create reality in his own image, he could no longer pretend that it was a reflection of divinity and ruled by a providence. Norms and values were deprived of their heavenly foundation. Science could prove itself in practice, but what basis was there now for ethics and philosophic truth?

There was, the nineteen-year-old Karl Marx wrote to his father, a basic contradiction in German philosophy between "what is and what should be." It could not be resolved, he came to realize, in the mind of some thinker, for he would be locked within the limitations of his own consciousness. But there was, Marx eventually said, a social class that was forced by the conditions of its daily life to fight for a self-interest which was also the common interest of mankind. Therefore, that which should be—utopia, socialism, the highest values of the West—was no longer the construct of a professor's imagination. Rather it was a living, breathing tendency of social reality itself, incarnated in the struggle of the proletariat. Thus there were temporal preconditions to the eternal truth about what man should be, and now they were actually being fulfilled.

The importance of this insight to socialism—past, present or future—cannot be exaggerated. Marx's own hope that the working class would rapidly turn the values of German classical philosophy into social reality has, of course, been long since disappointed. Nevertheless, there is either a trend toward socialism among the people as they are—not the people as they should be—or else socialism is a fraud and a delusion. In this chapter I will probe these preconditions as they appeared historically in dreams and abstractions, in utopia and philosophy. Then, in the final chapter, I will show that they still may be fulfilled in reality, even though in ways not imagined in the philosophy of Karl Marx.[1]

# I

The hope of a truly just society has been universal. It can be located in Buddha's ascetic communism which appealed to the masses as against the Brahmins (although, like another revolutionary creed, Christianity, it, too, became a bulwark of the status quo). There were Chinese utopias in the first years of the Christian era, and in eleventh-century China there was even a brief experiment with the welfare state under the Emperor Shen Tsung.

But the Western utopian tradition that was the profound influence upon European socialism begins with the Hebrews and the Greeks. It was simultaneously revolutionary and conservative, basically other-worldly, and yet perceived one of the most crucial aspects of socialism—the relationship between abundance and the new society.

A nomadic people who lived in between the two highly developed cultures of Egypt and Babylon, the Israelites made an extraordinary intellectual leap to monotheism, in part because they were so backward. Their life in the desert was, as Max Weber has pointed out, so primitive that they did not even have the tools and the artistic tradition to make an icon of their deity. So when they came into contact with the learning and sophistication of their neighbors, their God was able to skip over the stage of polytheism precisely because he was imageless. Then when the tribes settled down, they acquired a parasitic court, a new business class and an impoverished peasantry and proletariat.

So in the crisis of the eighth century B.C. the prophets emerged to summon the people back to the simpler virtues of the desert faith, denouncing the capitulation to riches and privileges that had estranged Israel from its God. "Woe to those who decree unrighteous decrees," Isaiah thundered, "and the recorders who make mischievous records, to thrust aside the needy from their rights and to rob my poor ones of justice." Out of this essentially conservative desire to recall Israel to the old ways there came a magnificent messianic—and utopian—vision of the future: "Then the wolf will lodge with the lamb, and the leopard will lie down with the kid; the calf and the young lion will graze together." Thus the idealized past became the future, the simplicity of the nomadic years in the wilderness inspired the description of the golden age to come. After the time of the prophets there was a long silence, yet the utopian spirit they had articulated lived on, particularly among the manual laborers and the backwoodsmen, inspiring radical sects like the Essenes and the Men of the Land. And that was the aspect of the Jewish tradition that prepared the way for Christ.

The revolutionary creed of the Christians, as Ernst Bloch has said, looked toward a "new heaven and a new earth," and, of all the texts of the Old Testament, it based itself most of all upon Isaiah. They, too, believed that their saviour would see to it that the lowly would inherit the earth. And yet there was still a deeply conservative element in this break with Judaism. Saint Peter was so convinced that he was a reformer of the old law rather than the leader of a new church that, according to the Acts of the Apostles, it took a special visitation from God to persuade him to speak to the Gentiles. When he did, his appeal went far beyond the messianism of the Jews and spoke to all the dispossessed of the Mediterranean world.

That most convinced of atheists, Friedrich Engels, put it this way: "The history of early Christianity offers noteworthy points of similarity with the modern labor movement. Like it, Christianity was in the beginning a movement of the oppressed. It appears first as a religion of slave and freedman, of the poor without rights and of peoples dominated or dispersed by the Romans." But this utopian appeal could not, of course, survive the political triumph of the Christians. When Catholicism became imperial under Constantine, it turned into a religion of the rulers rather than of the ruled. Similarly, there are those, to pursue Engels' analogy, who argue that the workers were corrupted by their reformist victories and therefore abandoned the revolution, but I disagree with this interpretation, as Chapter XIV will show.

And yet, a crucial theological event with enormous implications for the socialist future had taken place. For the Greeks and the Eastern religions, time was usually an endless cycle and prophecy was the foretelling of inevitable facts, as in the tragic theater. For the Hebrews, the world was moving toward a Messiah, and the prophet, even as he looked back toward the idealized nomadic past, called upon the people to act differently so as to persuade God to make a righteous future. The Christian version of the eternal was even more humanistic: their God had become man.

The ambiguity in all of this can best be seen in Saint Augustine's *City of God*. On the one hand, it is a deeply pessimistic book, reflecting the imminent breakdown of the Roman Empire. The faithful are summoned to turn their back upon all the secular cities—Cain, Augustine recalls, was a builder of cities—and to look only to God for salvation. And yet, the faithful were themselves a city—the city of God. Once that idea was introduced into history, there was a religious basis for trying to build that heavenly community on earth.

What was important about these Judeo-Christian images of the messianic age was not their explicit content—which was often a conservative plea to turn one's back on the world and trust only to the Lord—and indeed, these religions often functioned to rationalize injustice, or at least to make it tolerable. Rather their importance lay in creating powerful metaphors and symbols that could be read—or even misread—as promises of an earthly paradise. And it is therefore their resonance, their connotations, that, as will be seen, were to seize the imaginations of generations that were to come centuries later.[2]

This is obviously even truer of Plato's *Republic* than it is of the scripture. His version of the ideal commonwealth is frankly conservative, a ruling-class utopia conceived by a partisan of the party of order at a time of great social change. It is, Marx quite rightly said, "an Athenian idealization of the Egyptian class system." But then, elitism and authoritarianism are a recurring motif in utopias precisely because those visions are elaborated when the material and human preconditions for socialism are utterly lacking. The people were engaged in an often bitter struggle for scarce goods and, in the case of Plato's Athens, most of them were enslaved. Under such circumstances, harmony does not come voluntarily, even in an imaginary state; it has to be forced, particularly if the injustices of class domination are to be maintained.

But Plato's aristocratic utopia—and the Rightist political ideas of Lycurgus, the founder of Sparta, or of Pythagoras, another member of the conservative movement in Greece—was not the only expression of the utopian impulse in those times. There was also Iambulos' Island of the Sun, which was based upon a crucial socialist insight: that abundance makes new men.

The Island of the Sun (some say it is based on Madagascar, others on Indonesia) is temperate and there is enough food, little work and much leisure. It is not democratic in the modern sense of the word, since each organ of power is presided over by a hegemon who rules for life. But neither is it caste-ridden or a slave society. Its description does not have, of course, the philosophic depth of Plato's commonwealth, and yet it was considered an important enough document during the Renaissance and may well have influenced Thomas More. But the most important thing about it is that it asserts how abundance might change human nature, making man more peaceful and cooperative. Twenty-three centuries later, the notion is quite pertinent.

The idea of Cockaigne—a paradise in which there are "rivers of soup, jets of wine, cheese cakes falling down from red skies, self-frying fish and roast thrushes flying ready made into one's mouth" —dates back at least to the fourth century before the Christian era, when the Old Attic comedy was already making parodies of it. But by the third century, when Iambulos wrote, it had become more serious. The conquests of Alexander the Great and the discoveries of his admirals had lifted men's eyes from the city to the world. The future could now be conceived of as a distant marvelous island at the end of a fantastic voyage. And in Iambulos' version of it, which was much more realistic than those that preceded his, there was a crucial point: that a surfeit of goods would make the division of labor progressively less oppressive and permit free time to become the normal condition of human life.

So the Greek utopia was not simply authoritarian, like Plato's Republic, even though there were major historical forces driving it in that direction. And there were those, like Iambulos, who understood how abundance could revolutionize human existence. But even Plato, for all his elitism, was to have an honorable place in the pantheon of the militant utopianism to come. The Middle Ages, as Ernst Bloch remarked, have a "productive misunderstanding" of him, and he, like the Hebrew prophets and Christ, was turned into a forerunner of the Left. Thus in Germany in the sixteenth century, the Anabaptists invoked the name of this champion of law and order to justify a rebellion.[3]

But before those highly selective readings of Plato and the scripture could be made, utopia disappeared from the consciousness of ordinary men and women for some centuries. From Saint Augustine to the twelfth century there were no major manifestations of its spirit in Europe. The monastic movement had, to be sure, provided a refuge for the ideal of the community and reformers periodically tried to recapture its original commitment. But the monks were threatened by their own success. The cloisters, almost alone in the Middle Ages, enjoyed the economies of large-scale production and therefore, as the most efficient economic units, came to dominate their areas. As Karl Kautsky said of them, "they went from producers' cooperatives to exploitation cooperatives."

But in the twelfth century utopia revived. Ironically, the reason was the burgeoning of capitalism. Feudalism had begun to crumble but the capitalists were not yet triumphant. The old order was losing its hold upon the people, but it was not at all clear what the new order would be. Under such circumstances, people began once again to dream of the good society. Now, however, that reverie was less an impossibility than it had been in the desert of the Hebrews or the cities of the Greeks. And men actually took up arms for the dream.

There is a strange factor in this development, one that will be encountered quite often in the history of socialism: that good times make people rebellious. For the areas in which the most militant movements emerged—northern Italy, southern France, Flanders, Brabant and England—were also the places where the greatest economic advances had been made and, more often than not, the living standards of the people had risen. In Émile Durkheim's classic study of suicide there is an insight that helps explain how prosperity can radicalize people: "In obliging us to exercise a constant discipline, poverty prepares us to accept the collective discipline docilely, while wealth, in exalting the individual, always runs the risk of waking that spirit of rebellion which is the source of immorality." So it was that between the twelfth and the sixteenth centuries, utopia made its first contact with the most important of its material preconditions: capitalism.

More often that not, this new utopianism took a religious form. On the one hand, it was directed against a crucial institution of the down-going order, the Church, and proposals for ecclesiastical reform usually cloaked seditious demands to make a new future for the entire society. On the other hand, this opposition to the established clergy took a religious form and utopia was imagined as the Kingdom of God upon the earth. Francis of Assisi, with his passionate dedication to early Christian poverty, was one expression of this new unrest, but the papacy disarmed his movement by assimilating its conservative elements and excommunicating its radicals. But with Joachim de Floris in the late twelfth century the mood became explicitly political. His prophecies were to inspire the holy militants throughout the next three centuries. There were, Joachim said, three ages of human history: the age of the Father, of discipline and law, represented by the Old Testament; the age of the Son, of love, but of love institutionalized in the Church; and the age of the Holy Spirit, which was to come, the age of consecrated anarchy.

This vision reverberated throughout Europe for at least the next three hundred years. If one did not know better, it would almost seem as if there were a gigantic conspiracy. Just below the surface of the Middle Ages, Michael Freund writes, there was "a mystic-heretical movement of sects which grew out of the ancient heresies and which was almost as foreign to Protestantism as to Catholicism. . . ." This was the tradition that leads not to Martin Luther and the other Protestant reformers who made their peace with the princes, but to Thomas Münzer, the communist prophet and leader of the German peasant revolution in the sixteenth century. Consider just a few of its interconnections.

In the twelfth century in southern France the Poor Men of Lyons followed Pierre Wald, a merchant who had given away all of his wealth to the poor (his followers were sometimes called Waldensians). They preached their Christian communism with such vigor that their doctrine spread to northern France and into Germany and Bohemia. The Waldensians, and a similar group, the Albigensians, were finally exterminated by a bloody papal crusade in the early decades of the thirteenth century. But the spirit had taken root in northern Europe, in France and the Lowlands, and it grew. The Brothers and Sisters of the Free Spirit attacked both private property and the traditional family structure, and they spoke of the coming of a Joachim-like Kingdom of the Holy Ghost.

In the fourteenth century the radical theology spread from Holland to England where the reform theologian, John Wycliffe, took up the attack against Rome and the property of the Church. His ideas inspired the Lollard movement, which arose in 1381 under Wat Tyler. It was defeated—Richard II tricked Tyler into letting himself be taken by promising the abolition of feudalism— but the news of Wycliffe's ideas had by then traveled to Prague where Jan Hus took up the cause. Hus, like Wycliffe, had the support of some powerful interests in his country, including Queen Sophia and Emperor Wenceslaus, but his teachings were so subversive that he was eventually executed as a heretic.

There were two wings of the movement that followed Hus. The more conservative contented itself with demanding a national church and the secularization of the episcopal lands. But even that tendency had its social aspect, for it demanded that communion be given to the faithful as both bread and wine. This was a democratic point, for it attacked the ritual dominance of the clergy over the laity (the latter took communion only under the form of bread). But the revolutionary wing, the Taborites (named after the south Bohemian city of Tabor, the center of their strength), were for the abolition of the entire feudal order. When Tabor was taken, their agitation subsided, but it had already had its effect throughout all of Europe.

"We are all Hussites," Martin Luther was to say in the sixteenth century. But the Hussites, as we have just seen, were split in two, and Luther clearly identified with their conservative wing. It was Thomas Münzer, the leader of the German peasant uprising, who continued the radical vision of the Taborites. He was, Karl Kautsky was to remark, one of the two men who stand at the beginning of the modern socialistic movement (the other was Thomas More). Luther, Münzer charged, had given a "Bohemian gift" of the cloisters to the nobility. This attack found responsive listeners among the peasants who, after having made some gains when commerce first developed, now saw their living standard decline.

Münzer preached a sort of atheistic humanism in the guise of prophetic religiosity. He said the Bible was not the final authority, for the Holy Ghost was still alive among the people. (The echo of Joachim is no accident; he was one of the official patrons of Münzer's movement.) So men must make themselves godly in the here and now by building the Kingdom of Heaven upon earth in which all property would be held in common; they must not think of Hell, which was a doctrine designed to divert them from their worldly tasks. These ideas, the utopian patrimony of all the medieval movements going back to Joachim, could not, however, inspire an effective political movement. In 1525 Münzer established himself in Mühlhausen and attempted to institute a communist regime, but within a few years the entire rebellion had been crushed and thousands, including Münzer, had been executed.

In the period of the emergence of capitalism, then, the breakdown of the feudal order gave rise to a remarkable utopian spirit which swept through almost all of Europe. It could not possibly create a new socialist society, for, as Münzer, the most militant of the prophets, discovered, what the peasantry essentially wanted was private property in the form of land for each man. There was a prophetic pathos to his failure, which Friedrich Engels caught in a brilliant insight. It obviously applies to Münzer in the sixteenth century, but it also might have been written of V. I. Lenin during the last year of his life, or of some of the Third World leaders today.

"The worst thing that the leader of an extreme party can experience," Engels wrote, "is being forced to take power when the moment is not yet ripe for the rule of the class he represents and for the carrying out of those measures that the rule of that class requires. What he *can* do does not depend upon his will but upon how far the conflict of classes has been driven and how highly developed those relations of production and exchange are which provide the basis of the class struggle. But what he *should* do . . . is bound up with his previous doctrines and demands. . . . What he *can* do contradicts all of his previous principles and positions and the immediate interest of his party; and what he *should* do is impossible. He is, in a word, forced to represent not his own party and class, but that class for whose rule the movement is really ripe."

So the great peasant movements that accompanied the end of feudalism, including those, like Münzer's, with communist aims,

served the cause of the capitalism they despised, for socialism was not yet possible. And this fact, which can be seen so vividly in the history of reawakened utopianism between the twelfth and sixteenth centuries, obviously applies to the Communist, and other, attempts to build socialism in the impoverished lands of the twentieth century. For the dream still had its preconditions.[4]

# II

The rise of capitalism in the late Middle Ages had reawakened utopia. The capitalist triumph turned it into a realistic possibility.

Between the sixteenth and nineteenth centuries the utopian impulse emerged as the Left wing of the capitalist revolution which was to create the basis for socialism: a technology of abundance and a working-class movement driven to democratize it. So the utopias of this period develop within mighty political parties in England and France and pose modern problems that persist to this very day: whether wealth shall be divided or shared, whether it is possible for a new bureaucratic ruling class to take over from the bourgeoisie, and so on. There are also the first glimpses of anti-socialist "socialism" in action as French bankers seize upon the ideal for their own purposes.

In what follows, then, the dream makes contact with reality, the cry of the Hebrews in the wilderness becomes relevant in the industrial cities of Europe.

In the English Revolution of the seventeenth century politics and theology were inextricably mingled. The Royalists believed in bishops; the more conservative anti-Royalists, the Presbyterians, in a church ruled by elders; and among the Independents were people who stood for congregational control of religion as well as the sects on the Left. There was a distinct link with that religious communism of the previous four centuries. For it is possible that three of Cromwell's generals and seven of his colonels were Anabaptists, followers of that revolutionary doctrine that had inspired Münzer and his men. Thus there was a continuity on the Left wing of the movement which goes back as least as far as Joachim de Floris.

It was small wonder that such teachings took root in England. In the fourteenth and fifteenth centuries the peasantry had done fairly well, but in the sixteenth century there was a tremendous commercialization of agriculture. Thomas More expressed it vividly: sheep were eating men. In the first part of *Utopia*—which is a critique of the England of More's time that is hardly disguised at all—Raphael (More's alter ego) says, "Those placid creatures which used to require so little food have now apparently developed a raging appetite and turned into man-eaters. Fields, houses, towns, everything goes down their throats." This was, of course, a direct result of the importance of wool to the growing English commerce. As a consequence, Raphael continues, "Each greedy individual preys on his native land like a malignant growth, absorbing field after field, and enclosing thousands of acres with a single fence."

"Sir Thomas More's bitter joke about sheep eating men turned out to be truer than he knew," Christopher Hill wrote recently. "For in the sixteenth century, whilst the living standards of men and women of the lower classes fell catastrophically, the living standards of sheep improved remarkably."

The German peasants who followed Münzer had many of the same griefs and believed in the same theology, and yet they did not have the impact of the English revolutionaries. The reason is that economic development in seventeenth-century England had reached a much higher level than in sixteenth-century Germany. Therefore the discontents of the people at the bottom converged with the need for radical change that was being felt in the middle reaches of the society. The Presbyterians, Congregationalists and Anabaptists were united in the common cause of doing away with the old order. So Utopia, paradoxically, benefited from the enormous energy generated by capitalism. It may even be, as Michael Walzer has argued, that the new and educated middle class was a driving force in this development.

But that meant that the moment of victory for such a revolutionary movement signaled conflicts within the triumphant, but quite diverse, coalition. "Communist parties," Marx wrote, "first appear inside the bourgeois revolution when the constitutional monarchy is done away with. The most single-minded republicans —in England, the Levelers, in France, Babeuf, Buonarrotti, etc.— are the first who proclaimed the 'social question.'" In Marx's analysis, it is only after the kings were pushed aside that the people could confront the limits of the emerging bourgeois system itself. As long as feudalism prevailed, men thought that all evils, all oppression, would vanish with it. Now they were forced to recognize the profound antagonisms within the revolution itself.

The socialist tendency which thus appeared in the English Revolution defined itself in terms of a question that was to divide the Left throughout its history and which is still on the agenda in the Third World today. Will the good society be based upon a division of the wealth taken over from the old order or upon the common ownership of it? That issue is quite important today in the developing nations, which must choose between a land reform creating a class of individual proprietors and collective farming (it will be analyzed in that context in Chapter XIII). It was first debated by the Levelers, who were often thought to have been radical egalitarians to a man.

In fact, as more recent research has demonstrated, many of the Levelers were small property owners who tenaciously defended their plots against the wealthy but actually proposed to exclude servants and beggars from the vote. The socialists were the Diggers. Under their magnificent leader, Gerrard Winstanley, they held that there must be the right of access to common land, not a division of it. In *The New Law of Righteousness* (it has been called "a *Communist Manifesto* written in the dialect of its day") Winstanley proclaimed his basic principles, which came to him by a direct revelation from God:

"Work together; eat bread together; declare this all abroad,

"Israel shall never take hire, nor give hire.

"Whosoever labours the earth for any person or persons, that are lifted up to rule over others, and doth not look upon themselves as equal to others in the creation: the hand of the Lord shall be upon that labourer: I the Lord have spoken it and I will do it."[5]

Significantly, the debate between the Levelers and the Diggers also took place on the left wing of the French Revolution, but in more secular terms. In seventeenth-century England the utopian spirit had taken its first step into modernity but it still had strong ties to medieval communism. Therefore political radicalism was still masked in religious rhetoric and a Winstanley presented his excellent position as emanating from God. But in the French Revolution generally, and on this issue in particular, the discussion was straightforward and secular. As the dream came closer and closer to reality, it lost its fantastic trappings and based itself upon reason rather than revelation.

In the course of the Revolution, poor peasants and their allies

had demanded the passage of an "agrarian law" that would effectively parcel out the land. But, said Gracchus Babeuf, the leader
of the socialist Left wing of the Revolution, "the day after the
establishment of the agrarian law, inequality will begin again." In
the society of the future, the "association" (Babeuf's term for the
socialist ruling body, a word that was to have a fateful history, as
will be seen) "will always know what each one does, so that he will
not produce too much, or too little, but the right thing. It will
determine how many citizens will be employed in each speciality
and how many young people will take up each speciality. Everything will be appropriated and proportioned in terms of present
and predicted needs and according to the probable growth, and
ability, of the community."

So the *Manifesto of the Equals*, published by Babeuf's group,
stated, "We demand the communal enjoyments of the fruits of the
earth: the fruits are for all." Thus, with Babeuf and Winstanley,
utopia began to face the concrete problems of the social organization of the future and developed the idea of not simply dividing
up wealth or protecting small peasant property, but of creating a
society based on new principles of communal cooperation.

On another question Babeuf's movement was even more prescient: the role of democracy. In the France of the Revolution there
was not yet a developed working class but rather a plebian mass
of artisans and poor in the cities and land-hungry peasants in the
countryside. Since there was not—and could not be—a cohesive
socialist and labor movement, Babeuf and his comrades turned to
conspiracy. Buonarroti, whose account of their activity was one of
the most influential radical books in the nineteenth century, described one of their debates which anticipated anti-socialist "socialism" of the twentieth century.

"A very delicate point was carefully discussed in the insurrectionary committee," Buonarroti wrote. "It was a question of determining what part its members would play in exercising the new
authority. One considered that the conversion of the insurrectionary initiative into a permanent power, which would necessarily
be quite extensive, would make the people suspect that the
members of the committee were ambitious and self-seeking. Such
accusations would be easily spread and found credible since
nothing would impede them, and they could keep the committee
from doing what it proposed. . . .

"On the other hand, the insurrectionary committee did not see

many men in whom the purity of principles was joined to the
courage and firmness and intelligence required to put its proposals
into practice. They knew how dangerous it was if they did not
give the job of carrying out the program to those who had the
strength to begin it. And they feared the duplicity of certain
persons with whom they found themselves in competition. After
having hesitated for a long time, our conspirators were about to
decide to ask the people for a decree which would exclusively
confide the initiative and execution of the laws to them."

But that, the conspirators realized, posed the danger that there
would be "a class which is exclusively concerned with the principles of the social art, with laws and administration, which
would find in the superiority of its own spirit, and above all, in
the ignorance of its compatriots, the source for creating distinctions and privileges. Exaggerating the importance of its services,
it would easily come to think of itself as the necessary protector of
the nation. And clothing its own audacious enterprises in the
public good, it would still speak of liberty and equality to its
unperceptive fellow citizens, who would be subjected to a servitude all the more harsh because it seemed legal and voluntary."

This was a stunning presentiment of Joseph Stalin and the new
ruling class he was to bring to power. The Babouvists had decided
to chance that danger, but they were arrested before they could
carry out a coup. Their conspiratorial tradition, as will be seen,
traveled east to Petrograd where it reappeared in 1917. And in a
few short years in Russia the worst of Babeuf's fears of what would
happen if the insurrectionary committee substituted itself for the
masses were confirmed.

There was one other count on which Babeuf's conspirators were
shrewdly prophetic. "The French Revolution," Sylvan Maréchal
wrote in the *Manifesto of the Equals,* "is only the forerunner of
another revolution which will be much greater and more profound.
It will be the last revolution." There were a number of reasons
why Maréchal accurately foretold a new revolution even before the
old one had ended. The French Revolution had almost promised
utopia. The Enlightenment was to be rationally enacted into law;
Liberty, Equality and Fraternity were promised for all. Moreover,
in its more radical period the government had intervened actively
into the economy, dividing up supplies, regulating prices, and thus
turning the idea of an activist, socially concerned state into reality.
The gap between the utopian dream and practical politics seemed

to be closing before the very eyes of the conspirators. But, they realized, the ideals of the Revolution could not possibly be fulfilled within the framework of a bourgeois society.

It was, in short, disillusionment with the capitalist revolution that was to be the immediate prelude to the mass movement for a socialist revolution. Thus man consciously arrived at the point of transition betweeen utopia and reality, a moment that has been widely misunderstood due to a simplistic reading of Karl Marx. It is therefore worth examining in brief detail.

By 1800 it was clear that the extravagant predictions of liberty, fraternity and equality really signaled the triumph of capitalism over the entire society. But that does not mean that the French Revolution was a deception staged by capitalists in order to achieve their selfish aims. In the popular, mechanistic notion of Marxism something like this simple determinsim is usually asserted. Even a distinguished economic historian like Alexander Gershenkron erects this straw man as a description of Marx's analysis. There was, Gershenkron argues as against his imagined Marx, no revolution "directed against feudalism and carried out by the bourgeoisie in the interests of the bourgeoisie to further the development of capitalism." Of course not. If history were so straightforward and dominated by conscious economic interests, it would hardly require a Marx to decipher it.

For Marx, the French Revolution was led by petty-bourgeois democrats who believed sincerely and passionately in the values they proclaimed and were the unwitting agents of a social order many of them despised. They, like Thomas Münzer, suffered from a contradiction between what they honestly wanted to do and what they actually could do. It was for this reason Marx was, as Shlomo Avineri has rightly pointed out, so critical of the Jacobin terror. Robespierre, Marx wrote, "sees in great poverty and great richness only a stumbling-block to pure democracy. He wants therefore to establish a universal Spartan frugality. According to him, will is the principle of politics. The more one-sided and hence the more accomplished is the political reason, the more does it believe in the omnipotence of the will, the more blind it is to the natural and spiritual limits of the will, and thus is incapable of discovering the roots of social evil." (The passage might stand as Lenin's epitaph; on that, more later.) But will, however ferocious, cannot escape the preconditions of the dream.

The radicals of the French Revolution, Marx wrote in 1848, did not know that "each time they opposed the bourgeoisie, as during 1793–94 in France, they actually fought for the implementation of the interests of the bourgeoisie, even if not in the manner of the bourgeoisie. The whole of French terrorism was nothing else than a plebian manner to put an end to the enemies of the bourgeoisie." Thus, for Marx, terrorism was a kind of bloody utopianism, an attempt to substitute will for historic process. Therefore he was profoundly anti-terrorist, for the very need to go to such extremes was an indication that the revolution could not possibly fulfill its announced aims.[6]

It was not too long after the French Revolution that more and more Europeans began to understand these limitations upon it. So the utopian tradition culminated in the first decade of the nineteenth century in a reaction to that disappointment. Two of the most important figures of that moment were Claude Henri de Saint-Simon and Robert Owen. Their ideas were significant in and of themselves, but the reason that they changed history was that a new social force heard, and distinctively interpreted, them: the working class. Capitalism had not only created the economic preconditions of socialism, but also as a result, that class which was its human precondition.

Saint-Simon was a planner and a technocrat. He objected to capitalism because it allowed parasitic coupon-clippers to share in the wealth of the actual producers and he proposed a rational allocation of investment funds through a central bank. Given this emphasis, Saint-Simon was not particularly concerned about democratic participation or a mass movement. He himself tried to win both Napoleon and Louis XVIII to his ideas, and after his death in 1825 his disciples attempted to convert Louis Philippe when he came to power in 1830. In this elitist aspect Saint-Simon's ideas became the ideology of the most prominent bankers and entrepreneurs around Napoleon III. One of them, the banker Isaac Pereire, has been described by Alexander Gershenkron as having "contributed so much, perhaps more to the spread of the modern capitalist system in France" than anyone else, and yet he remained "an ardent admirer of the Saint-Simonian doctrine" until his death.

This vignette is more than a curiosity for it illustrates an important tendency in socialist history. In many of the original definitions of socialism—certainly in Saint-Simon's and even in Marx's—there was an analysis of the inefficiency and waste of

capitalist society and an insistence upon how much more productive socialism would be. It was quite possible for a French
banker—or a Russian or a Chinese dictator—to abstract this element and turn it into *the* definition of socialism. So what becomes
crucial, in regard to Saint-Simon and to socialism in general, is not
simply the abstract socialist scheme, but who reads it, and for
what purpose.

The French working class read Saint-Simon in a completely
different way than the bankers. It seized upon his use of the
word "association," the notion that the producers themselves
would run the enterprise, and took up his hatred of the unearned
income of passive capitalists. So an essentially technocratic theory
was converted by the workers into an authentic socialist perspective. Like the German Anabaptists with their revolutionary Plato,
they had made an extremely perceptive misreading of Saint-
Simon's ideas. They ignored his elitism and emphasis upon efficiency; they embraced his hatred of parasites who did not work
but received profits; and they translated his vision of an "association" under the tutelage of bankers and planners into an argument
for ownership of the means of production by the direct producers.
In the process they turned a humane technocrat into a quasi-
anarchist.

The fate of Robert Owen, the great British utopian, was similar
to Saint-Simon's. He was a most effective businessman who by
providing various benefits for the workers in his factory at New
Lanark made a profit of £160,000 in four years. Owen taught that
a bad environment—like that found in all the plants in the
England of his day—resulted in bad character. He wanted to have
cooperation in model factories, rather than the competition of the
existing system. Since he himself had proved that such a course
was not only moral but good business, he sought to interest
capitalists, bishops and politicians in his ideas, with some early
success.

It was a strange accident that forced Owen to turn to the working class. He made the mistake of speaking openly of his skeptical
views on religion. Polite society, which could tolerate talk of a
profitable cooperation between workers and management, would
not permit godlessness. At that point, the only audience open to
him was at the bottom of society, and so this essentially conservative man became the founding father of British trade unionism
and socialism. In part, that happened because he changed his

point of view; in part, because the workers changed it for him in the reading they made of his views.

Thus in *The Report to the County of Lanark* in 1821 Owen described how the productivity of capitalist society was advancing more rapidly than the workers' means of subsistence. The producers, he said, drawing upon the labor theory of value found in the great classical economist, David Ricardo, were the source of wealth in the society and it was therefore necessary to have a new system of exchange. Labor seized upon these notions and adapted them to its own needs in the bitter class struggle of the time. And Owen, who detested class war and always stressed harmony, became the presiding spirit of the Grand National Trade Union.

And yet, he never really did outgrow his conservative views. He exalted the old days when the landed proprietor was seen as having a mutual interest with "even the lowest peasant" and the latter considered himself as being "somewhat of a member of a respectable family." Under such circumstances, he argued, the "lower orders" were content and it was one of capitalism's greatest crimes that it had disturbed this equilibrium. The workers, however, picked and chose from among the parts of Owen's theory, ignoring his romantic version of the past, taking up the cry that labor, as the source of wealth, deserved the full product of its toil.

So the decisive moment for utopia occurred when the masses saw in it a program for the transformation of their daily lives. In the process they had to creatively misread both Saint-Simon and Owen. But not Karl Marx, for he was the first thinker to realize what was happening and to make it explicit; he was the consciousness of the dream, the moment when it awoke to itself.[7]

## III

All previous revolutions, Marx said, had "taken over limited instruments of production and thus broke through only to new limitations." But now the "two practical preconditions" of socialism were at hand. The powers of production were becoming so developed that they made abundance for all a real possibility. That, Marx insisted, was an "absolutely necessary practical precondition, for without it one can only generalize *want,* and with such pressing needs the struggle for necessities would begin again and all the old crap would come back again." That is the bitter truth that still haunts the Third World: that the socialization of poverty is only a new form of poverty.

The second precondition came about because the very development of those means of production "had made the mass of mankind 'propertyless,' " and since the might of its own social productivity loomed over it like an alien power, revolutionary.

The details of this analysis, particularly as they concerned the rapidity with which the workers would become conscious of their plight and transform it, have to be drastically revised. (Marx himself, as will be seen, did exactly that to these formulations of 1845–1846.) But the essential point remains valid to this day. If socialism is ever to become a reality, it will not be because some prophet has a vision in his mind's eye or because there is some providence unfolding in history. It is a possibility based upon the unprecedented development of technology and it can become an actuality only when there is a conscious majority that masters that productivity and puts it to the service of human need.

Marx became aware of these things as a philosopher. At first glance, that is a surprising way for such eminently practical and political truths to emerge. But just as utopia developed in the midst of actual events, the abstractions of Western man were worldly, too. The turmoil of the capitalist revolution invaded the farthest reaches of metaphysics and that was—if one speaks very carefully, since theories are never a mere "reflection" of reality—a precondition of Marx's discovery. Intellectual history had to evolve and, as it were, prepare the way for the insights of that profound and unique individual, Karl Marx. In outlining that process a basic contradiction of social thought based upon capitalist assumptions becomes apparent. It has been transformed somewhat in the more than a century since Marx identified it, but it still remains. Capitalism can rationalize all the departments of production and their related sciences. It is just its own totality that it cannot understand.

John Donne had posed the issue in vivid poetic imagery in the early seventeenth century:

> And new philosophy calls all in doubt
> 'Tis all in pieces, all coherence gone . . .

And in philosophy one hears that same anguished cry in the writings of a contemporary of Donne's, the English philosopher,

Thomas Hobbes. In the Hobbesian world there is a constant war of each against all, for man is predatory, egotistic and competitive. Where, under such conditions, Hobbes asked, was the basis for the loyalty of the citizen to some superior authority? Each member of society, he answered, had a self-interest in limiting the unbridled egotism of his neighbors. Therefore one accepted political community for the most anti-communitarian of reasons: it was the only way to protect the individual from an anarchy that would be the ruin of all.

But the human nature that Hobbes thus described was not eternal but a product of the new capitalist order. As C. B. Macpherson points out in his brilliant reinterpretation of the Hobbesian analysis, in traditional societies, like feudalism, most people are content with the social rank to which they are born, and competition is usually confined to the nobles and the clerics. So Hobbes was really speaking about the "new man" being created by capitalism in the seventeenth century. Moreover, for all his *Realpolitik,* Hobbes evaded a crucial issue. That political authority which ruled over society as a sort of referee was seen in his theory as impartial, a neutral in the war of each against all. In fact, of course, it was dominated by an elite and served as its weapon against the majority.

However, it was not just the medieval theory of society that had broken down. For as science advanced, it threatened all of metaphysics. It brought with it the assumption that only those propositions that can be verified empirically are true. This assumption worked brilliantly with physics and chemistry, but it was utterly subversive of traditional ethics and epistemology. So in the eighteenth century when David Hume rigorously applied this scientific criterion to the traditional categories of thought, he undermined some of the most perennial ideas, like the law of cause and effect. One could, he said, describe how one event followed another, but that did not prove that there was any link between them. As Leszek Kolakowski described the event, "Intended to provide science with unshakable foundations, Hume's analysis deprived it of any possible foundation."

Where, then, was a principle of coherence? Political man and economic man in the Hobbesian vision were engaged in a permanent conflict with each other; and philosophic man was, in Hume's analysis, utterly bereft of his old truths. Then, by one of those leaps that do not fit into neat, determinist accounts of history, these intellectual preoccupations of the most advanced of European societies, Britain, suddenly came to obsess one of the most backward, Germany. David Hume, Immanuel Kant wrote, "interrupted my dogmatic slumber."

Kant asked of metaphysics, "If it is a science, how does it come about that it cannot establish itself, like other sciences, in universal and lasting esteem? It seems almost ridiculous, while every other science makes ceaseless progress, to be constantly turning around on the same spot without moving a step forward in the one that claims to be wisdom itself and whose every oracle everyone consults."

Kant never did discover an objective basis so that philosophy, in the words of the title to his *Prolegomena to Any Future Metaphysics*, "will be able to present itself AS A SCIENCE." Mathematics, as the pure intuition of space and time, could make remarkable progress, but men could only know the appearance of the external world. There was a place in this scheme for science and industry since they dealt with tangible experience and their results could be checked. But there was no longer any basis for the philosopher's boast that he had understood the very essence of reality, the thing-in-itself. For as soon as thought "goes beyond the boundary of experience and becomes transcendent, [it] brings forth nothing but illusion."

So Kant, even though he was an Idealist, was aware of the historic circumstances that had led to the crisis of philosophy. But the problem was not simply located in the contrast between scientific success and philosophic uncertainty; it also had roots in the structure of the capitalist system itself. On the one hand, as George Lukacs pointed out in his brilliant Marxian analysis, *History and Class Consciousness*, capitalism was the most rational society that had ever existed, quantifying every aspect of life in order to produce more. On the other hand, the capitalist economy, by its own proud admission, had no conscious directing principle. Rather it put its trust in the invisible hand of the market, which was supposed to vector all private greeds into a common good.

Capitalist intellectual life, then, was particularly schizophrenic. The system was increasingly scientific as to details, but irrational as a totality, and each triumphant period of production was crowned by an inexplicable crisis. Moreover, capitalism idealized its own atomization, asserting that the division of society into isolated, competing individuals was its master stroke. And since, as we will see in a moment, the most abstruse theorems often have a remarkable resemblance to the political and social conditions under which they were defined, it was difficult for a thinker who accepted the premises of such a society to discover any principle of coherence.

Hegel sought a way out of this impasse and his writings vividly illustrate how social and metaphysical thought can be intimately related to each other. In politics, he rejected that "unsocial society" of Kant and Hobbes in which men are limits upon one another's freedom and an individual's rights are circumscribed by those of his neighbor. Similarly, in logic he attacked the Kantian counterposition of the forms of thought and an ultimately unknowable world. In each case, his grievance was the same: that atomistic citizens without organic relationship to a community, or atomistic ideas without a necessary relationship to reality, were the product of a mechanistic way of thinking. In politics and in logic he insisted that there be living connections. Hegel, the great system-maker, was also an existentialist.

As a young man he saw the French Revolution as a great victory: "At a stroke, new ideas and concepts of right proved their validity and the old framework of injustice was powerless to resist. . . . Now man has realized that ideas must rule spiritual reality. This was a magnificent sunrise. All thinking beings celebrated the epoch. An exalted emotion ruled the world, the enthusiasm of the spirit was everywhere as the reconciliation of God and the world now took place for the first time." By 1794 the Terror had turned Hegel against the Revolution; then, by applying the very same principles that had once made him its enthusiastic advocate, he switched his allegiance to the Prussian monarchy. For he saw the monarchy as the force that would forge a unity out of the dispersed German states: it, too, was the historic agency of community.

Any philosophic system that could thus successively defend the French Revolution and the Prussian royal house had to be profoundly ambiguous. On the one hand, Hegel's thought is suffused with the motion of change, and new times coming: "It is not difficult," he wrote in the *Phenomenology of Spirit,* "to understand that ours is a time of birth and transition to a new period." It was this consciousness that made him celebrate the living interconnections of ideas and reality and of men with one another. But on the other hand, even in his youthful radicalism, he perceived the

French Revolution as the triumph of its Idea rather than of its revolutionaries. And as he grew older and more conservative, this thesis became all the more pronounced. There is a "cunning of reason" within history that uses the passions of men and women to work out a design that is unknown to them. This Absolute, which has its way with history, can only be known when it has completed its mission, and the role of the philosopher therefore is to look back upon events, not to change the world.

So even though Hegel fought against the atomization of so much of the life and thought of the capitalist era, he, too, ultimately believed in an invisible hand. Indeed, it may even be that he quite literally took the notion of the "cunning of reason" from Adam Smith's vision of the miraculous harmony of capitalist competition. It is this issue that separates him from Karl Marx.

Marx, of course, owed a great debt to his conservative precursor. In contrast to the utopians, this first completely modern socialist did not project his ideas upon reality and then try to persuade God, or various and assorted princes, churchmen and bankers, to put them into practice. In the Hegelian tradition, he insisted that socialism must be an observable and actual tendency of social development if it is to be taken seriously. But he differed most profoundly from Hegel—and this difference is of infinitely greater moment than the contrast between the materialism of the one and the idealism of the other—in that he held "it is man—actual, living man—who acts, possesses, struggles—and not 'history' which needs men as a means to accomplish *its* end—as if it were a separate person." To be sure, Marx agreed with Hegel that the historic actors regularly served ends other than the ones they intended. But he did not glory in the fact, as Hegel did; he proposed to change it, to help men to become, for the first time, truly conscious and thereby the masters of their own destiny.

In the process, Marx claimed to have solved that contradiction between "what is and what should be" which he had first confronted as a young philosophy student. The question of justice, of ethics—of utopia, if you will—was no longer a matter of theory for scholars to discuss. It had become a tendency within reality and men now, for the first time in history, had the opportunity, and the obligation, freely to determine the content of their own human nature. The truth was not to be discovered in a Hegelian retrospect upon the past; it was to be created by means of a social revolution which would make the future.

So it was that in a philosophic debate that reverberated with the sounds of revolution Marx came to understand not only the preconditions of the dream, but also the necessity to act upon them. He thus defined a possibility, not an inevitability (even though he—and much more, Engels—sometimes talked as if the latter were the case). For him, it was not ordained that history be socialist, but men could now struggle to make it so.

The possibility Marx defined had been more than two thousand years in the making. And in understanding how utopia journeyed through the centuries from the deserts of Palestine to the industrial cities of Europe, a basic criterion of the socialist future emerges. The good society cannot be willed into being by prophets or holy men or philosophers, but requires a certain level of economic development and, above all, the conscious activity of the millions before it can come true.[8]

# I I I

## *The Democratic Essence*

IT IS ALMOST NINETY YEARS since the death of Karl Marx. In that period his memory has become one of the principal obstacles to socialism.

Right-wing anti-Communists have supported the orthodox Communist interpretation of Marx. Joseph Stalin and J. Edgar Hoover have both argued that he was the father of totalitarianism and taught that the ideal society could only be achieved through a brutal dictatorship. In this Communist-Rightist reading of him, Marx is against all civil liberties and has no use for bourgeois sentimentalities about truth and justice because he holds that material, and particularly economic, self-interest is the secret of all ideals. Since he is thus supposed to have founded a science of society, a dictator acting in his name can claim to serve the objective interests of the masses over their dead bodies.

The orthodox Communists interpreted Marx in this way so that he could provide a rationalization for their totalitarian practices. The reactionary anti-Communists gleefully accepted these theories because they rightly thought that such a vision of socialism would discredit it and also permit them to defend the status quo, even when it was fascist, in the name of anti-Communist freedom. And in recent years there have been authoritarian militarists in the Third World who, having heard the good news that Marxian socialism resembles a barracks organized to promote economic development, have suddenly discovered that they are men of the Left.

So a return to the original Karl Marx is not simply a matter of scholarship. It is a contemporary political act, an attempt to restore his genuine memory to the future.

This chapter, and the two that follow it, will try to do that by way of a Marxist analysis of Karl Marx. He will be sketched at the intersection of his freedom and necessity as the child of one age and the father of another, transforming the historical conditions that helped form him. Above all, he will be seen as a man who changed his mind, or had it changed for him, since he himself regarded the process by which men and events move one another as central to his theory. The god of the various Marxist churches is almost never seen in the fullness of his errors, which obscures the humanity and depth of many of his truths.

And yet there is a constant in the life of Karl Marx. As a political tactician, a philosopher and an economist, he regarded democracy as the essence of socialism. This was not a pretty moral tacked on to his system. It was, as these chapters will show, the rigorous conclusion of a realistic analysis of economic and social power. And it is a more urgent truth today than when Marx first uttered it.

# I

The young Karl Marx, and that lesser giant, Friedrich Engels, were distinguished from all the other radical theorists of their time precisely by their insistence upon the democratic character of socialism. This fact is well over a hundred years old and quite new. Those seeking freedom under Communism in recent years have rediscovered this historic reality and made it an incitement to change within a system claiming to be Marxist. So the guardians of the Communist status quo must dismiss the democratic passions of Marx and Engels as the youthful indiscretions of men who were to become sincere totalitarians. That, as the next chapter will show, is simply not true; but for now the focus is upon their political beginnings.

In his monumental *History of Socialist Thought*, G. D. H. Cole defined an important aspect of the life of the young Marx and Engels: "It needs to be borne in mind that, in the controversies of the 1840s which preceded the publication of the *Communist Manifesto*, Marx and Engels had the appearance of moderates, setting themselves in opposition to socialists who were taking a more extremist line." On their Left were the Blanquists, who advocated that a revolutionary elite take power in the name of the people; the utopians, who wanted to withdraw totally from a corrupt system; and the millenarians, like Weitling, who saw the lumpenproletariat, including criminals, as an important force for the good society. On their Right were the Tory socialists, who wanted to go back to an imaginary, egalitarian feudalism; the Christian socialists and the simple cooperators, who counted on the good will of the powerful; and the state socialists, like Louis Blanc, who thought that the bourgeois government could be the instrument of revolutionary construction.

What distinguished Marx and Engels from all of these thinkers was their insistence that socialism could only develop through a democratic mass movement. This can be seen most vividly in their opposition to the French revolutionary Auguste Blanqui.

Blanqui was one of the most courageous, and even appealing, men in the history of socialism. But with an indomitable spirit and the best will in the world, he nevertheless inspired an authoritarian Leftism that still survives. He became a conspirator in 1824 at the age of nineteen and was arrested for the first time in 1828 after a street fight with the police. When he was again brought before a court in 1832 (he spent much of his adult life in jail), he was asked his occupation and replied proudly: Proletarian. And yet, for all the suffering and commitment of a militant lifetime, Blanqui could never go beyond a conspiratorial version of socialism. This man whose compassion for the proletariat is beyond question did not, however, think that the proletarians could emancipate themselves.

"The poor," Blanqui wrote in 1834, "do not know the source of their miseries. Ignorance, the daughter of bondage, makes them a docile instrument of the privileged. . . . Alas! Humanity marches with a bandage over its eyes and rarely rises up to gain a confused view of its path." Given this analysis, it was quite logical that Blanqui would denounce universal suffrage as a "betrayal." "To ask the vote for these subject populations," he said in his critique of the Revolution of 1848, "is to demand it for their masters." Therefore, in the name of a most genuine commitment to the working class, Blanqui could not trust the workers.

In a sense, his position was quite understandable. The workers of the first half of the nineteenth century had been subjected to indescribable brutalities. In his *Situation of the Working Classes in England* Engels himself had given a vivid picture of the hunger, child labor, slums and moral degradation that were the lot of the proletariat. There have been recent scholarly attempts to challenge his descriptions, but, as E. J. Hobsbawm argues quite convincingly, the mills of those times in England were indeed dark and satanic and the standard of living of the masses fell as capitalism triumphed. It was Marx's and Engels' genius to see that within this dehumanized mass there was nevertheless the potential for men and women to master their society.

So Marx and Engels never gave in to that revolutionary indignation that drove Blanqui to despair that the workers could emancipate themselves. They therefore rejected the conspiratorial proposals to save mankind in secret. As Marx wrote in 1850, "It goes without saying that the conspirators never bestir themselves to organize the proletariat in general. Rather their function is to anticipate the revolution, to speed up the crisis by artificial means, to make a revolution on the spur of the moment when the conditions for it do not exist." And Engels said some time later, "Blanqui is essentially a political revolutionist, an emotional socialist who sympathizes with the suffering of the people, but he has neither a socialist theory nor specific socialist proposals for solutions to social problems. In his political activity, he was essentially a 'man of the deed' who believed that a small, well-organized minority which made a revolutionary coup at the right moment could, by some initial successes, bring the popular masses along and make a victorious revolution."

Marx and Engels, then, rejected Blanqui's conspiracy, as well as the feudalists, shopkeepers and other minorities on the Right who attempted to use socialist rhetoric to cover their own purposes. In each case they counterposed the idea of a democratic movement to proposals that would make some elite the salvation of the people. This attitude was not simply based upon political considerations. It was also the core of Marx's philosophy. He defined the issue quite explicitly as early as 1845, and even though the crucial passage is extremely compressed, it is very much worth examining in detail.

In his *Theses on Feuerbach* Marx commented on "the materialistic doctrine of the changing of circumstances and upbringing," that is, the theory that if the conditions of men's lives and their schooling are transformed, then their character will be altered too. Marx argues that this view "forgets that the circumstances must

be changed by men and that the educator must himself be educated. So it must split the society into two parts, the one rising
above the other." In such a materialist philosophy, as in Blanqui's
politics, the great masses of the people are inert, the object of
forces beyond their control. Their conditions are changed for
them by educators, or conspirators, who somehow have escaped
the determinations that afflict ordinary mortals and are therefore
able to alter institutions from on high.

Marx contrasts his own view to this vulgar materialism (which
is now widely called "Marxism"): "The convergence of the changing of the circumstances and human activity, or self-changing,
can only be conceived and rationally understood as *revolutionary*
praxis." Men transform the circumstances that form them; socialism cannot be decreed for the masses, it must be won by them.
It is a matter of people changing both themselves and their
environment.* Given this basic analysis, Marx posed the role of
his own ideas in a completely democratic way. As he wrote in
1843, "material power can only be overthrown by material power,
and theory becomes a material power only when it takes hold
of the masses. Theory is capable of taking hold of the masses as
soon as it proves itself to men, and it can prove itself when it is
radical. To be radical is to grasp the matter at the root. But for
man, the root is man himself." This did not simply mean that the
people would, having been inspired by Marx's ideas, win their own
freedom. It also meant that they would become different kinds of
human beings in the process. "When the Communist artisans come
together," he wrote in the *Economic-Philosophic Manuscripts* of
1844, "the original purpose is to forward education, propaganda,
etc. But at the same time, a new need appears, the need for society, and what begins as a means becomes an end." The socialist
movement is itself the embryo of socialism.

Therefore the aim of communism could not be defined as the
mere abolition of private property. That could only lead to a "raw
communism" where "community is only the community of work

---

* The *Theses* were written by Marx in 1845 but were not published until after
his death, in 1888. Engels' version of them was slightly revised and in general
easier to understand than Marx's. But in his editing of Thesis 3, which is quoted
above, Engels dropped the reference to self-change (*Selbstveränderung*). This did
not change the meaning of Marx's comment, but I have translated the original
text because it puts an even greater emphasis on that democratic vision that was
at the heart of his philosophy. The original can be found in *MEW*, III, pp. 5ff;
Engels' revised text is printed in the same volume, p. 533; and n. 1, p. 547, gives
a summary of the history of the text.

and the equality of salaries that the common capital, the *community* as general capitalist, pays." The point of communism was much more radical than that. Under all previous systems men had produced "only under the domination of immediate physical needs." As a result, the producer had only felt free when he was most like an animal: in eating, drinking and sex. The specifically human—free, conscious activity—was denied him, and even his sensuality was degraded. "The formation of the five senses," the young Marx wrote in one of his most lyrical passages, "is the work of all previous history. The senses that were confined to raw, practical needs were limited. The human form of food did not exist for the hungry man, only its abstract character as food." So man can only become man when his very senses also become human and these various alienations are abolished. "The richness of human need," Marx concluded, "is a precondition of socialism."

Such an analysis, it is obvious, is quite subversive of the gray Communist societies of today with their priority on heavy industry and their stern limits on individual consumption. Therefore the orthodox Communists must dismiss, or ignore, the young Marx. Thus Louis Althusser, perhaps the leading theorist of the more Stalinist wing of French Communism, builds a Chinese wall between the theories of the 1840s and *Das Kapital*. The latter, Althusser says, has nothing to do with the "idealistic aspirations" of the early writing. For Althusser, Marxism is a science, and just as in mathematics, once the basic postulates are established, their logical implications can be worked out without reference to the world outside the window. This "Marxism" has little to do with Marx's insights in the 1840s and much to do with justifying a dictatorship that fulfills the "objective" needs of its passive subjects.

Sadly enough, some of Marx's democratic critics have, for different reasons, agreed with the orthodox Communist interpretation on this question. In a sense, what they have in common with the totalitarians whom they oppose is that they, too, would be embarrassed by the democratic Marx because he undermines neo-capitalism as well as neo-Stalinism. Consequently, Daniel Bell, who is in political sympathy with the anti-Stalinist movement in Eastern Europe, nevertheless essentially agrees with the scholarship of their armed opponents. Bell writes that "in the last few years in Europe, a whole school of neo-Marxists . . . have gone back to the early doctrines of alienation in order to find the basis for a new, humanistic interpretation of Marx. To the extent that this is an effort to find a new, radical critique of society, the effort is an encouraging one. But to the extent—and this seems as much to be the case—that it is a form of new myth-making in order to cling to the symbol of Marx, it is wrong. For while it is the early Marx, it is not the *historical* Marx. The historical Marx had in effect repudiated the idea of alienation."

That, as I will demonstrate in some detail in Chapter V, is not true. There is, to be sure, no question that Marx changed many of his ideas between the 1840s and *Das Kapital*. In the early years, as will be seen in a moment, Marx and Engels were unquestionably much too enthusiastic in their anticipation of the imminence of socialist revolution. As a result, their emphasis is upon revolutionary politics, will and subjectivity. The latter writings, *Das Kapital* above all, are the work of a philosopher-revolutionary who is also a profound economist. The prophetic spirit is still very much present—the idea of alienation is utterly central to *Das Kapital*—but now it speaks from within a complicated world of statistics and analysis. So one can say with Karl Korsch that between the *Manifesto* and *Kapital* there is a shift of accent from "the subjective rebellion of the workers to the objective rebellion of the forces of production." But, as this book will show, even in describing this momentous transition, the commitment to democracy and the self-emancipation of the working class is central to all of Marx's writings, both youthful and mature.

In the 1840s, then, Marx and Engels became socialists and what set them off from all other radicals of the time was their insistence upon the democratic character of the coming revolution. This fact is sometimes conceded by the Communist inventors of the totalitarian Marx, but it is explained away as a youthful exuberance and naiveté. That is not true.

The commitment to democracy dominates Marx's whole life; it can be found in *The Communist Manifesto* and, above all, in *Das Kapital*, and not just in the early writings.[1]

## II

Between 1848 and 1850 Marx and Engels changed their minds about their basic political orientation no less than three times. *The Communist Manifesto* was a great, and contradictory, document which advocated an alliance with the very bourgeoisie whose death sentence it pronounced. When the course of action derived from this ambiguous analysis proved a failure, Marx became a disillusioned and bitter ultra-Leftist. But then in 1850 reality forced itself upon him and he once more turned to the work of elaborating a tactic for the mass movement.

The two years between 1848 and 1850 were the period of Marx's anti-democratic temptation, and the dictatorial Marxists have celebrated them ever since. In fact, he never did become a partisan of revolution from above, even in his angriest hours, and by late 1850 he had begun to deepen his democratic strategy for socialist revolution. So if Marx's memory is to be saved from the totalitarians and restored to the future, these developments must be seen in detail.

The opening sentence of the preface of the *Manifesto*—"A spectre is haunting Europe, the spectre of Communism"—was wrong.

England, the most industrialized nation of the time, had a mass working-class movement in Chartism, but this movement did not go beyond the struggle for democratic freedoms. In France there were indeed socialist political groupings, but the country was overwhelmingly peasant and those rural millions were to applaud the bloody suppression of the proletariat in June, 1848.

In Germany the bourgeois revolution had not even taken place and the bourgeoisie itself was already giving signs of the timidity it was to show in the coming upheavals. On the rest of the continent conditions were, politically and economically, even more backward than in these three countries.

In one mood—but not in all their moods, for they contradicted themselves on this count—Marx and Engels pictured reality as much more radical than it was. *"Democracy is today Communism,"* Engels proclaimed at a London meeting in 1845. "Democracy has become the proletarian principle, the principle of the masses. The masses may be more or less clear about the unique and true significance of democracy, but there is still a feeling that the basis of social equality is in democracy. . . . With insignificant exceptions, all European democrats in 1846 are more or less clear Communists." This is in the all-or-nothing spirit of Marx's view in 1843 that the bourgeoisie no longer had a role to play and that the proletariat and the philosophers would soon jointly realize the millennium.

But in another mood Marx and Engels knew the truth: that in most of the countries of Europe it was only the conquest of bourgeois freedoms, not socialism, that was on the agenda. In 1847 Marx wrote with considerable realism, ". . . the aristocracy can only be overthrown when the bourgeoisie and the people join together. To advocate the rule of the people in a land in which the aristocracy and the bourgeoisie are still allies is sheer madness." And in the same year Engels took much the same line: "The Communists are far from starting useless fights with the democrats under present circumstances. Moreover, in all practical party questions the Communists appear as democrats. . . . So long as the democracy has not yet conquered, so long do the Communists and democrats struggle together, so long are the interests of the democrats also those of the Communists."

This contradiction between a sense of imminent proletarian revolution on the one hand, and the sober knowledge that the coming battle would seek only democratic freedoms on the other, can be found within the *Manifesto* itself.

The first two sections are a magnificent sweeping summary of a history that culminated in the struggle of the bourgeoisie and the proletariat. Socialism, before Marx and Engels defined it, was a nebulous idea. It meant, G. D. H. Cole writes, "collective regulation of men's affairs on a cooperative basis with the happiness and welfare of all as the end in view and with the emphasis, not on 'politics' but on the production and distribution of wealth and the strengthening of 'socializing' influences in the life-long education of the citizens in cooperative, as against competitive, patterns of behaviour and social attitudes and beliefs."

Some workers had been attracted to the movement for conservative reasons. In England, for example, it was not the poor who were first attracted to the socialist ideal, but the labor elite of the artisans. They were the ones who felt themselves directly threatened by the growth of a system that would degrade them to the level of "ordinary" workers. There were others who responded to this new word not because it summoned them to a struggle against capitalism, but because they defined it as a means of fighting the emerging time-clock rationality of industrial society. This was to be the source of important confusions. For if socialism were opposed to economic calculation rather than to capitalism itself, then the good society would be unable to plan or to create wealth with modern methods and lay the material basis for a system of genuine equality.

It was in these years when "socialism" appealed to philanthropic businessmen, conservative artisans fearful of industrial progress, opponents of industrialism itself, feudal aristocrats, bankers, preachers, revolutionary conspirators and gentle co-operators that Marx and Engels made the idea precise. They located socialism in the future, not in the idealized medieval past; they based it upon the unprecedented productivity of means of production centralized by the bourgeoisie rather than upon utopian colonies; they therefore insisted that the revolution would not divvy up the social wealth but rather subject it to democratic ownership and put it to social use. And they saw that this trans-formation would come about not through the charity and rea-sonableness of the rulers, but as a result of the class struggles of the vast majority.

These things are brilliantly defined in the first two sections of the *Manifesto*. The third section described the various anti-socialist "socialisms." Then the final section—which is only eleven paragraphs long, but deals with the critical problem of tactics —advocates a united front with the very bourgeoisie whose funeral has just been announced. In England, Marx says, the Communists will ally with the Chartists, a working-class move-ment seeking a more perfect bourgeois democracy. In the United States they are to back the agrarian reformers whose key demand was free land, i.e., private property, in the West. In France the Communists are to march with the petty-bourgeois radicals, and in Germany with the bourgeoisie itself. At no point are they to form their own completely independent movement for social-ist revolution.

Thus Jean Jaurès was too harsh, but basically right, when he held that "what the *Manifesto* proposes is not the revolutionary method of a class sure of itself; it is the expedient revolution of a weak, impatient class that seeks to speed up events by trickery." The trick that Jaurès alleges is a tactic of promoting Communism by means of an alliance with the bourgeoisie. G. D. H. Cole takes somewhat the same view. The revolutionaries of the period, he wrote, "found it difficult to reconcile Marx's ferocious denunciations of the bourgeoisie with his insistence upon helping them to power." Therefore, says Cole, Marx adopted a radical phraseology in the *Manifesto* to "win the ears of the revolutionary groundlings."

The Machiavellian explanations of Jaurès and Cole go too far. In this period Marx and Engels changed their minds and tactics so often that they were anything but wily strategists. Indeed, their chief fault was the *ad hoc* way in which they responded to changing political circumstances. But if they were not engaged in trickery, one of their central assumptions about the period— that proletarian revolution was on the agenda—was simply not true. Engels himself admitted as much retrospectively. In an 1893 preface to an Italian edition of the *Manifesto* he wrote, "Though the workers of Paris had become conscious of the inevitable antagonism between their class and the bourgeoisie, neither the economic development of the country nor the spiritual development of the French laboring masses had reached the point which would have made the transition to socialism possible. In the other countries, in Italy, Germany and Austria, the workers from the very first only acted so as to bring the bourgeoisie to power."

This false evaluation of the strength of the working class in the *Manifesto* was linked to another, more surprising, error: the overestimation of capitalism itself.

The *Manifesto* is, of course, lavish in its praise of the capitalist past, and even present—too lavish. It asserts that "in scarcely a hundred years of class domination, the bourgeoisie has created greater, more colossal forces of production than all the preceding generations put together. Mastering the powers of nature and of machinery, applying chemistry to industry and agriculture, with steamships, railroads, electric telegraphs cultivating the entire world. . . ." But that was much too positive an assessment of the capitalism of the period. As Franz Mehring, the German Marxist historian, wrote during World War I, "When they drew up the *Communist Manifesto,* they regarded capitalism as having reached a level which it has hardly reached in our day."

Simultaneous with this excessive admiration for capitalist accomplishments, the *Manifesto* overstates capitalist tendencies toward misery. For the *Manifesto* was written at the end of the "Hungry Forties," that time of mass malnutrition in England when the theory that wages would, at best, provide only "for the maintenance of the worker and the continuation of his race" seemed quite true. If, however, it had been drafted in 1857, the perception of social reality would have been quite different. But an even more serious error was the *Manifesto's* assumption that "the previously existing middle classes, the small industrialists, merchants and rentiers, the artisans and peasants" were becoming proletarian. Within ten years of 1848, the numbers of the petty bourgeoisie were to increase and Marx was to recognize and analyze that fact.

Thus the *Manifesto* is a schizophrenic statement. Its dialectical and historical method, its definition of socialism and identification of the historic tendencies of capitalism, represented an incomparable advance for a confused socialist movement. Its overestimation of both capitalism and Communism and its assertion that society was rapidly polarizing into two, and only two, significant classes were misleading. And, as it turned out, its tactics were much too soft on bourgeois democracy. This last, rather bizarre, fact is worth examining for two reasons: it emphasizes that Marx and Engels' democratic commitment was so serious that, far from being crypto-totalitarians, they were too uncritical of the bourgeois democrats; and it helps us to understand the bitterness of their disillusionment which came at the end of this tumultuous period.

Perhaps the most telling summary of their participation in these events was made by David Riazanov, a great Communist scholar who was purged by Stalin. In 1848, Riazanov points out, Marx and Engels refused to organize a separate proletarian party. Basing himself upon the experience of the French Revolution with its long, drawn-out movement to the Left, Marx wanted the workers to fight as a part of the bourgeois democratic forces. Indeed, when Stephen Born, a member of the Communist League, actually organized the workers in Berlin on a class basis during that period, Marx and Engels turned on him bitterly.

So it is incredible, but true, that Karl Marx's *Neue Rheinische Zeitung* was attacked during the Revolution of 1848 for not paying enough attention to economics and to the working class. Marx admitted the charge: "From all sides people reproach us that we have not described the *economic relations* that form the basis of the current class and national struggles. We purposely only touched on those relations when they actually intruded immediately into the political battle." But by March–April, 1848, Marx continued, the bourgeoisie had triumphed in France and feudalism was victorious everywhere in Europe. In a sharp *volte face* he drew a conclusion diametrically opposed to the theory he had been acting upon for several years: "any social reform remains a utopia until the proletarian revolution and the feudal counterrevolution take each other's measure in a world war."

These events are important for both scholarly and political reasons. In the last, tactical section of the *Manifesto*, even as Marx advocated an alliance with the bourgeois democrats, he warned the workers of their basic hostility to the capitalists alongside of whom they were to fight. In Germany, he comments, "the bourgeois revolution can only be the immediate prelude to a proletarian revolution." So E. H. Carr can argue that the *Manifesto* had "announced the prospect in Germany of an immediate transition from bourgeois revolution to proletarian revolution without the intervening period of bourgeois rule." But if that is indeed the case, then the *Manifesto* also anticipated, and legitimated, the Marxism of both V. I. Lenin and Joseph Stalin, for that is exactly the kind of revolution they claimed to make in Russia (the details of their theory and practice will be treated in Chapter VIII). Carr's reading of a seemingly abstruse point of history and doctrine has the very political result "that the Russian Revolution can claim to be a legitimate child of *The Communist Manifesto*." And that is an important step in making Marx the father of totalitarianism.

Carr is wrong. Insofar as the *Manifesto* was interpreted by Marx and Engels themselves, they read it as committing them to a long-term alliance with bourgeois democracy, not as urging a Bolshevik-like leap from an unripe capitalism to a revolutionary socialism. This is clearly the premise of their actions in 1848. It was only when Marx turned his back on the strategy of the *Manifesto* in late 1848 that there is even a hint of the view that Carr ascribes to the *Manifesto* itself. For two bitter disillusioned years after that turning point, Marx was indeed in a sullen, ultra-Leftist mood, and this period is a classic source for the Bolshevik, and then the Stalinist, version of Marxism. Even then, however, Marx never became dictatorial, much less totalitarian. But in any case, the crucial moment in that period was his decisive rejection of anti-democratic politics.

Marx had known even before the revolutionary events that the German bourgeoisie was hardly radical. That fact was explained by the uneven development of the country: the capitalists "find themselves already in a conflict with the proletariat before they have even constituted themselves as a class." If their country's backwardness had been, in part, an advantage for the German socialists by making their political consciousness more revolutionary than the society itself, it had made the bourgeoisie more reactionary. They could not possibly envision a revolution in the French manner, for the armed masses might refuse to stop at the overthrow of feudalism and go on to attack private property itself.

By late 1848 the treachery of the bourgeoisie had exceeded even Marx's anticipation of it. He wrote of that class, "Its light is like the light of a star which first appears to people on earth after the body which is its source has been dead for 100,000 years. The March Revolution in Prussia was such a star for Europe. Its light was the light of a long-rotting social corpse."

This new analysis required a new strategy. By March of 1850 Marx and Engels, who had refused to build a workers' party only two years before, were calling upon the proletarians to set up their own fiercely independent organizations. When it was necessary, they were to march together with the petty-bourgeois democrats, but in any case, they must form secret, armed groups. And then, in a passage that prefigures some of the tactics of the Russian Revolution of 1917, Marx and Engels wrote, "The workers must set up their own revolutionary proletarian regime alongside the new official government, whether in the form of local boards, councils, clubs, or committees of workers. . . .

"From the very first moment of the victory, the workers must distrust not only the defeated reactionary party, but its former comrades as well, and fight that party which will try to exploit the common victory on its own." And the conclusion—which clearly echoed in the mind of Leon Trotsky in the Petrograd Soviet of 1917: "The battle cry must be: Permanent Revolution." (*Die Revolution in Permanenz*)

This mood lasted for about two years, from the fall of 1848 to the middle of 1850. It brought Marx as close to anti-democracy as he ever came.[2]

## III

It was during this ultra-Leftist period that Marx used the fateful phrase "dictatorship of the proletariat."

It is, alas, of little political moment that it can be demonstrated that when Marx wrote this phrase, he did not mean "dictatorship," at least as the word is now commonly employed. Nor does it matter to posterity that the phrase is used only a few times in the writings of Marx and Engels and at one point describes anarchist libertarianism rather than violent suppression. Nevertheless, the phrase provided a certain semantic legitimacy for the anti-socialist totalitarians who were to inscribe the slogan on their banners. But even if the truth is not a political defense against history, it is important to anyone who would understand the socialist movement and what Marx and Engels really meant.

It was in April of 1850 that Marx and Engels met with some Blanquists and Left-wing Chartists in London. There they signed the statutes of the World Society of Revolutionary Communists. Article I declared: "The aim of the association is the overthrow of all privileged classes, their subjugation by the dictatorship of the proletariat which will maintain the revolution in permanence until communism, the last organizational form of the human family, will be constructed." The organization was stillborn. The Blanquists sided with the anti-Marxist minority within the Communist League and Marx and Engels (and the Chartist Harney) denounced the statutes in October, 1850. But the phrase "dictatorship of the proletariat" had now been identified with Karl Marx and his ideas.

The problem is Marx did not mean dictatorship when he said dictatorship. Even in his *Class Struggles in France* which was written during the bitter months in early 1850, the term is used so as to be compatible, even identified, with democracy. *"The constitutional republic,"* Marx wrote of the peasants, "is the dictatorship of their united exploiters; the *social democratic* red republic is the dictatorship of their allies." In each case, it is possible to have a republic, and in the latter instance, a social democratic republic, which is also a dictatorship.

Such a paradoxical definition makes no sense in contemporary vocabulary. It makes, however, a good deal of sense when it is understood within the framework of Marx's thought. Sidney Hook brilliantly clarified this point in *Towards the Understanding of Karl Marx*. In Marx, Hook writes, "wherever we find a state we find a dictatorship." In the Marxian analysis, the state is necessary only in a class society of inequality where the struggle over scarce resources is organized—by force, if necessary—to favor the ruling class. Therefore the most libertarian of bourgeois democracies is a dictatorship in the sense that the economic wealth and power of the rich contradicts the theoretical political equality of all citizens. For economic power is political power, and under capitalism, the means of production are always concentrating and falling under the control of an ever smaller elite. "Dictatorship" then defined the class basis of a society, not its political forms, and it did not necessarily imply the repression of civil liberties.

Thus it was that Engels, who also proclaimed his belief in the dictatorship of the proletariat, was against any form of minority rule. In 1874 he analyzed the French ultra-Leftists: "Given Blanqui's conception of the revolution as the work of a small, revolutionary minority, it followed necessarily that there would be a dictatorship after the revolution; *not, to be sure, the dictatorship of the entire class of the proletariat*, but of that small number who made the surprise attack and who are themselves organized under the dictatorship of one individual or of a few members of a small group." ( Emphasis added.)

But it was in Marx's and Engels' description of the Paris Commune as a dictatorship that the uniqueness of their definition is most apparent. As Engels put it, "In opposition to the changes that had taken place under all previous forms of the state, where the servants of the society become its master, the Commune had two weapons. First of all, every position, be it administrative, judicial or educational, was filled by universal suffrage of the people and was subject to immediate recall by the same people. And secondly, all official jobs, high or low, were paid at the same wages as the workers received." Thus "dictatorship" equals universal suffrage, immediate recallability of all officials and a working-class wage for the bureaucracy. What is "dictatorial" about the situation is that the property forms of the society now systematically favor the workers as they once—even in democratic republics—discriminated on behalf of the bourgeoisie.

So "dictatorship" does not mean dictatorship but the fulfillment of democracy. The tragic problem is that the scholar can follow the subtlety of the Marxian analysis, but the activist in the street—and the dictator occupying the seat of power—tend to take the word at its most obvious, and brutal, meaning. It is in this way that Marxism has become identified with anti-democratic repression.

But then, what is involved is not a scholarly gloss on some canonical text. For Marx and Engels, as these chapters show, define socialism in its very essence as a movement of the overwhelming majority which would smash a "democratic" state apparatus that had been designed to exclude the people from participation. It is not just that the creation of dictatorships in their name rests upon a misreading of their specific ideas on the subject of political freedom. It subverts their entire conception of socialism as well.[3]

## IV

It was in the fall of 1850 that events forced Marx and Engels to reverse themselves once again. They abandoned that ultra-Leftist intransigence that had led them to their brief flirtation with Blanqui's conspiratorial ideas. But even more important, they had made a decisive turn toward deepening their democratic vision of socialism.

The Revolution of 1848, Marx argued, had been created by the depression of 1837–1842, the speculative crisis of 1846 and the failure of the potato harvest and the consequent hunger in Ireland. Prosperity had returned to England in 1848, and in 1849 there was a great spurt in the cotton industry. This helped the Germans and the French as well as the English, and the discovery of gold in California gave even more encouragement to the system. Marx concluded, "Given this general prosperity in which the productive power of bourgeois society develops itself as much as it can within the framework of bourgeois relations, there can be no talk of revolution."

The Communist League split over Marx's new analysis. Two leaders of the organization, Willich and Schapper, continued to defend the old position. Marx charged, "In the place of critical analysis, the minority is dogmatic. It is idealist, not materialist. Instead of making living relationships the driving force of the revolution, they appeal to *pure will*. While we say to the workers, 'You have fifteen, twenty, or fifty years of civil war and popular struggle to carry out, not only to change the relationships but to change yourself and enable yourself to rule politically,' they say, 'We must either come to power or we might as well go to sleep.' "

In March, 1850, Marx had called for insurrection and "permanent revolution." Six months later he stoically contemplated the possibility that it would take half a century of struggle before socialism would triumph and insisted, in profound contrast to the Blanquists and other conspirators, that the workers had to change not only political and economic relationships, but themselves as well. Antonio Gramsci, one of the founders of the Italian Communist Party, brilliantly understood the profundity of the moment, even though he did not see all its implications.*

In a polemic against Trotsky, who had applied the theory of the "permanent revolution" to Russia, Gramsci wrote, "The political concept of the so-called permanent revolution first emerges in 1848 as the scientifically elaborated expression of the Jacobin experience from 1789 to Thermidor. The formula applies in a historic period in which there do not exist large mass political parties and unions, when society was therefore in a more fluid state. The countryside was backward and a few cities exercised an almost total monopoly of political-state efficiency, or else the latter was concentrated in a single city (Paris for France). The state apparatus is relatively undeveloped and there is considerable autonomy for the national economy in relationship to the world economy.

"In the period after 1870, with the colonial expansion of Europe, all these elements change. The internal and international relations of the state become more organized and complex, and the '48 formula of 'permanent revolution' is replaced in political science by the formula 'civil hegemony.' There occurs in the political art that which occurs in the military art: the war of movement becomes increasingly a war of position."

Gramsci's insight is basic. In the years leading up to 1850 Marx was a democrat in the Jacobin sense. He saw the coming revolution as a gigantic popular explosion from below, as a democratic insurrection. But in the 1850s and 1860s he had to revise his most basic strategic notions. The working-class movement was changing, it was organizing itself into unions, and there were possibilities of political action that could not have been even imagined earlier. At that point, Marx's perspective became even more democratic in the modern sense of the term: it increasingly envisioned the nonviolent and electoral conquest of power. It is that momentous change that is the subject of the next chapter.

But even before that transition took place, at the very outset when he first became a socialist, Karl Marx had understood that

---

* Most Communist writers, particularly in the Stalinist era, wrote vulgar political apologetics for totalitarianism annotated with the obligatory citations from Marx. But a few of them—Gramsci, Lukacs, some of the English historians—did serious work.

democracy was of the socialist essence. That knowledge pervaded his economic, philosophic and political analysis of the 1840s, and in *The Communist Manifesto* its application even led him to be too uncritical of the bourgeois democrats. He recoiled bitterly from that error and committed a rhetorical sin which history has not forgiven and which many a totalitarian has celebrated: he used the word "dictatorship" to describe democracy. He recovered from that tragic error within a matter of months and it cannot be allowed to obscure the depth of his democratic commitment.

Most important of all, in the 1850s Marx became the first Marxian revisionist. He analyzed the prevailing situation, developed a new strategy and in the process prepared the way for one of the most decisive events in the history of socialism: its identification with the labor movement.[4]

# I V

# The Unknown Karl Marx

THIS CHAPTER IS ABOUT the unknown Karl Marx.

There are, to be sure, a few scholars who know who he was. But as far as most of the literate public is concerned, the Karl Marx who lived between 1850 and 1883 did not exist. That unknown Karl Marx is so at variance with the totalitarian, or the insurrectionary or the intransigent Marx of popular myth that the meaning of his mature years has either been ignored or distorted. He was, for instance, certainly revolutionary, but also a moderate, and that dialectical combination baffles most of the accepted readings of him. In what follows, I will try to bring that Marxian unity of contraries back in all of its complexity, for the future already demands the same quality: a very thoughtful audacity.

After the defeats and disillusionments of 1848, Marx worked out a new strategy. In the most crucial single turning point in socialist history he succeeded in identifying his ideal with the aspirations of the nascent labor movement, and this identification marked the rise of democratic socialism.

It had been, as the last chapter showed, a tremendous moral and intellectual accomplishment to see the brutalized urban masses of the new capitalism as the agency of their own emancipation. Now Marx made another daring leap. He realized that the un- and even anti-revolutionary unions that had been built in the 1850s and in the early 1860s were the cells of the revolution-to-come. He was, of course, bitterly attacked from the ultra-Left because of this view, most notably by Bakunin. But he rejected the latter's apocalyptic vision of creative destruction and insisted upon the role of a conscious working class. As a result, the democratic character of his final goal became even more precise and profound.

As Marx's tactic began to succeed, it attracted the attention of sophisticated conservatives. Napoleon III was the forerunner, trying to manipulate the labor movement for his own purposes, but it was the Junker Bismarck who came up with the truly bold scheme: he proposed to co-opt socialism itself. This was the first appearance of a phenomenon which is still quite contemporary: anti-socialist "socialism." Marx fought it on democratic grounds, rejecting the idea of a "revolution from above" in terms of his basic theory and his immediate tactics.

Paradoxically, Bismarck's plan promoted the fortunes of the socialists it was supposed to undercut and was a crucial factor in winning German social democrats to Marxism. Thus between Marx's death in 1883 and the outbreak of World War I in 1914 a mighty labor and socialist movement emerged, and it seemed that the Marxian prediction of working-class revolution was being inexorably fulfilled. Then, in the supreme hour of trial in August, 1914, the socialists betrayed their most fundamental principles, as the workers of Europe, who had solemnly pledged to oppose any bourgeois war, joined their various national armies to slaughter one another. European socialism has not yet recovered from that moment and it may never do so, for it raises the most basic questions about the revolutionary potential of the proletariat.

These three aspects of the rise of democratic socialism—the link with the trade unions, the struggle against anti-socialist "socialism" and the partial triumphs that culminated in the basic failure of 1914—are all fascinating in and of themselves. But, like the rest of the history in this book, they are also part of a past that illuminates the future. The question of which class, or classes, will lead in the creation of the good society is still very much on the agenda; there are anti-socialist "socialisms" all over the globe, with the new variants literally developing almost every year; and European social democracy has not yet solved the problems that led it to betray Marxist principles more than half a century ago. The unknown Karl Marx has something to contribute to each of these questions.

# I

It could be plausibly argued that the Karl Marx who is described in these pages is a backward, and wishful, projection of this writer's present politics. Since there is indeed a remarkable convergence between my current attitudes and my version of history, let me cite an authority who cannot be impeached on such grounds. When it suited his purposes, and only but unmistakably then, V. I. Lenin understood the momentousness of the change that took place in the 1850s and led to the emergence of Marx the social democrat.

In 1905 the Russian socialists were debating whether they should take the lead in the coming revolution and whether, if the movement triumphed, they should participate in a Provisional Revolutionary Government that would be based upon the peasantry as well as the working class. Plekhanov, the father of Russian Marxism, was against such a tactic; Lenin was for it (Chapter VIII will treat these matters in greater detail). In the course of their dispute Plekhanov turned back to Marx and Engels' bitter address to the Communist League in 1850. That was the period when they warned against making any concessions to the petty-bourgeois democrats and argued that the workers must arm themselves, form secret societies and even build counter-institutions which would exist alongside of, but opposed to, the official institutions. This precedent was invoked to prove that the Russian revolutionaries should not join with the petty-bourgeois democrats of their day—the radical peasants—but should take a much more intransigent stand.

Lenin countered Plekhanov with a brilliant analysis of the decisive change that took place in the 1850s. When they wrote that address in March, 1850, he said, "Marx believed that capitalism was in a state of senile decay and the socialist revolution seemed to him 'quite near.' Shortly afterward Marx corrected this mistake. . . . The proletariat might still have to face fifteen, twenty or fifty years of civil war and international conflicts 'not only to change the conditions, but to change yourselves [the proletarians] and to render yourselves fit for political rule.'"

Then Lenin describes the history that followed upon Marx's change in mind. Twenty-five years after they had wrongly dismissed the issue, he continues, Marx and Engels were still fighting for democratic freedoms in Germany. And in 1885 Engels hoped that a German revolution would bring power to those very petty-bourgeois democrats he had once written off as being too treacherous. So there was, as Lenin quite rightly emphasizes, a basic change in Marx's and Engels' orientation which took place after 1850 and dominated their actions for the rest of their lives. They realized that in their anger over the betrayals of 1848, they had underestimated the potential of democracy for social change. It is in this context that one must understand their enormous contribution, and commitment, to the creation of a social democratic movement by means of an alliance with essentially reformist trade unionists. In the perspective of *The Communist Manifesto*, and even more so in terms of the ultra-Left analysis of 1850, such a tactic would be a betrayal. For the mature Marx, it was the path to a socialist mass movement.

Lenin is, of course, the sponsor of another Marx who stands in dramatic contrast to the man and the politics he thus described in 1905. In 1917 the issue was not one of sharing power with peasants but of seizing it in the name of the proletariat. Therefore Lenin focused upon the *Manifesto,* Marx's defense of the Paris Commune, and his critique of the obsessive legalism of the German socialists (if one learns the particular texts a Marxist uses, it is usually easy to predict the political conclusions). But if Marx's writings are granted the courtesy of a Marxist interpretation—if they are seen in their actual relationship to their time and place and not treated as a scripture to be ransacked for holy precedents—it is clear that the democratic Marx described by Lenin in 1905 was the mature Marx who existed in reality.

So V. I. Lenin is at least the partial authority for Karl Marx, the democratic socialist, who is described here.

In the years after Marx's dramatic change of mind in 1850, a trade-union movement had emerged in Europe. That was the critical precondition for democratic socialism then; it remains so now. In England the economic expansion that began in 1849 was to last for almost a decade and eliminate the hunger that had given rise to Chartism. At first the new conditions did not radicalize the workers at all. Two million of the most vigorous and independent among them left for the United States, and those who stayed behind found it relatively easy to find jobs. But then there was a crash in 1857–1858 and labor responded by militant protest. In 1859 there was a mass strike that involved sections of industry that had never before been organized. It was in the course of this struggle that the leadership of it declared they were engaged in a conflict between the political economy of labor and the political economy of capital.

Meanwhile the French labor movement was also growing, but under the most ironic of auspices. After the economic downturn in the late fifties, Napoleon III attempted to win support among the workers by allowing them a certain freedom of union organization. The followers of Proudhon took advantage of this imperial concession (and were promptly denounced by the Blanquists for selling out). Then in 1862 Armand Lévy, a journalist on the Right wing of the labor movement, asked the "Red Prince," Jérôme Bonaparte, for financial aid to send a French workers' delegation to the Exposition being held that year in London. The Blanquists once again denounced this contact with the ruling class, but many Proudhonists went along. The resultant meetings between the French and British trade unionists were a major factor in the establishment of the International Workingmen's Association (IWMA), the "First International," in 1864.

It was this most un-Marxian united front of British labor, which was politically oriented toward the bourgeois radicals, and French followers of Proudhon, who traveled with aid from the Bonapartes and were for state aid to decentralized associations of producers, that Marx made the focus of his politics for the next several years. This tactic, which outraged all the purists at the time, laid the basis for the historic identification of socialism and trade unionism that persists in Europe to this day. Marx formulated it most brilliantly and explicitly in the "Inaugural Address" to the IWMA in 1864.

One section of that document gives a particularly vivid measure of how far he had traveled from the bitter days of defeat in 1849 and 1850, but more than that it gives Marx's answer to a perennial problem for radicals: What is the relationship between immediate reform and ultimate revolution?

After describing how all those on the Left had been hounded into silence or exile after 1848, Marx cites two exceptions in the decade of gloom that followed upon the failure of the revolution. One was the rise of a cooperative movement, which proved that wage labor was not necessary and could be, and would be, replaced by "associated work which is performed by willing

hands, hearty spirits and happy hearts." But his second example
of victory in the time of reaction is even more revealing. Marx
hailed the struggle in England for the legal restriction of the
working day to ten hours as "a conflict between the blind rule
of the law of supply and demand, which forms the political
economy of the middle class, and the control of social production
through insight and foresight, which is the political economy of
the working class. So the Ten Hours Bill was not simply a great
practical accomplishment: it was also a triumph of principle.
For the first time in the full light of day the political economy of
the middle class gave way to the political economy of the working class." And in showering his contempt upon the middle
class, Marx denounced the economist Nassau Senior, who had
fought the shortening of the working day on the grounds that
it "would sound the death knell of English industry."

Yet Marx and Engels had themselves come perilously close to
adopting Senior's position in the name of radicalism some years
before. In March of 1850, when both were in their ultra-Left
mood, Engels wrote about the Ten Hours Law for a Chartist publication. It was, he said, "a false step, an unpolitical and even reactionary measure. . . ." Capitalism as capitalism required profits,
and that meant lengthening the working day. Limiting the working day, he argued, did not challenge the system in any basic
way, but only made it less efficient.

To his credit, Engels did not go the whole route and oppose
the bill. But his critique of it was quite in keeping with his
attitude, and Marx's, in 1850. If one believes that revolution is
imminent, then reforms, which ameliorate the contradictions of
the system rather than driving them to the outside limit, impede
the coming upheaval. But by 1864 both Marx and Engels understood that an insurrection of the type of 1848 was no longer
feasible. They therefore devoted their lives to linking the socialist ideal to the struggles of a labor movement that was gradualist,
and thus the Ten Hours Bill was no longer a "false step," but
now "a triumph of the political economy of the working class."
The all-or-nothing radicalism had vanished; the potential of democracy and the value of reform had taken its place.[1]

There are those, however, who argue that Marx's formulation
in the "Inaugural" and other documents of the period were only
tactical in character. These statements, Robert C. Tucker holds,
"*seemed* to sanction gradualism, an electoral orientation and a

belief in a peaceful path of socialist revolution." Later on, Tucker says, they were used by social democrats "to paper over the discrepancy between theoretical revolutionism and practical reforms" and that was "part of the general process of the deradicalization of the social democratic Marxist movement." So powerful is the image of Marx the "radical"—in the extremist, apocalyptic and anti-moderate sense of the word—that even though more than half of his adult life does not conform to it, his actual behavior is dismissed as "seeming" to be what it is not.

In fact, the true radicalism of Marx in this period, as in the 1840s, was that he was courageous enough to be outrageously moderate when that was what the times required. And his attitude on the Ten Hour Law was hardly an afterthought or a rhetorical strategy designed to hold together a coalition of non- and anti-socialist trade unionists. In Marx's masterpiece, *Das Kapital,* an entire historical section is devoted to the progressive historical significance of that struggle over the length of the working day. It is, to be sure, quite true that he returned to some of the revolutionary formulations of *The Communist Manifesto* in the period when he felt obliged to defend the Paris Commune against the near-universal condemnation of it in all of Europe. Yet once the immediate political need of defending the sacrifice of the Communards was past, he became quite blunt and unromantic about the event. In 1881 he wrote of it, "apart from the fact that this was only an insurrection of city workers under exceptional circumstances, the majority of the commune was not at all socialist *nor could it be.* With a modicum of common sense, it could, however, have achieved a compromise with Versailles [the seat of the reactionaries who drowned the Commune in blood] which would have been useful to the whole people—which was all that could have been achieved. The appropriation of the Bank of France would have put a rapid end to the blustering of Versailles."

Indeed a romantic simplification of Marx's attitude on the Commune is crucial to many a contemporary Leftist myth. Lenin had made that event a decisive precedent for his taking power in 1917; it proved that the Marxian revolutionary would, given the chance, "smash" the status apparatus and thus make a single, giant leap from the old order to the new. But before the Commune, Marx was apprehensive, highly critical of his followers in Paris and their Jacobin bombast, concerned because the followers of

Proudhon and Blanqui were in control of the working-class movement. But when the rising took place and he was attacked from
the Right by the bourgeois—and trade-union—critics of its violence and from the Left by Bakunin, who pointed out how de-
centralist and un-Marxian the revolution in Paris was, Marx rallied
rather uncritically to its defense. These are the polemical and
propagandist writings which Lenin, and those who follow in his
tradition, have elevated to the status of Marx's final word on the
subject. They thus ignore his considered opinion, as expressed in
that 1881 letter and other comments: that the Commune was a
botched, and badly led, act of proletarian heroism.

When it was not a question of establishing a precedent for his
own seizure of power, Lenin himself was perfectly aware that
Marx saw the Commune as an inevitable failure. But just as he
conveniently forgot the democratic Marx he had once known
when the insurrection became imminent, so did he also forget
what he knew of the Commune.

But perhaps the best way to understand the sea change in
Marx's views is to see it in the context of his debate with Bakunin
within the First International. That exchange counterposed proletarian and lumpenproletarian socialism, and even more important, concerned the ultimate vision of socialism. Indeed, the
discussion is still going on.

Bakunin championed the revolutionary potential of the lumpenproletariat. This was not the disciplined working-class movement
created by the necessities of struggle against capitalism. It embraced, in his definition, "the millions of the uncivilized, the dis-
inherited, the miserable and the illiterate, this great popular
*canaille* which, being almost totally virgin to all bourgeois civilization, contains within itself, in its passions and instincts, in all of
the necessities and miseries of its collective position, all the germs
of the socialism of the future. . . ." It was "the proletariat in rags,
the wretched." It has been celebrated more recently by Frantz
Fanon, who wrote, "So the pimps, the hooligans, the unemployed
and the petty criminals, urged on from behind, throw themselves
into the struggle for liberation like stout working men. . . . The
prostitutes, too, and the maids who are paid two pounds a month,
all the hopeless dregs of humanity, all who turn in circles between
suicide and madness, will recover their balance and march proudly
in the great procession of the awakened nation." And Herbert
Marcuse, though he speaks as a Marxist, has the same Bakuninist
hopes for "the substratum of the outcasts and outsiders, the ex-

ploited and persecuted of other races and other colors, the unemployed and the unemployable."

Marx had great compassion for the lumpenproletariat—and great suspicion of its political predispositions. In his most systematic analysis of it in the first volume of *Das Kapital*, he saw it as a result of the "overpopulation" and social turmoil that capitalism had created by destroying the old order. It was, he said, the "Lazarus stratum" of the working class, composed of "vagabonds, criminals and prostitutes," of the jobless, the children of poverty and the unemployable. Precisely because the conditions of lumpenproletarian life were so precarious and fluid, its activists tended toward a Bohemian personal life and a politics of conspiracy and insurrection. Therefore, Marx argued in his analysis of the victory of Napoleon III, these adventurists could be mobilized by reaction to serve its purposes. The insight was shrewd: in the 1930s the Nazis in Germany had just such a wing in their movement and one writer even called them the "armed Bohemians."

Therefore Marx rejected Bakunin's faith in the emancipating power of lumpenproletarian destructiveness and the "spontaneous organization" of the people's liberty. Under his leadership, the London Conference of the IWMA in 1871 voted in favor of a tactic that held that "constituting the working class as a political party is essential for the triumph of the social revolution and its ultimate aim, *the abolition of classes.*" It was precisely this insistence upon democratic and political struggle that marked him off from Bakunin, Blanqui and Proudhon in the International. Democracy was, once again, the distinctive and defining element in his position.

But then, what was involved in this debate was much more than a mere question of tactics. It concerned the very essence of socialism itself. In Bakunin's romantic theory (and in practice, the arch-libertarian was a man of conspiracy, fantasy and authoritarianism), there was no need for a disciplined and political self-consciousness on the part of the masses. The revolution was to be an elemental event, an act of tempestuous human nature, and it was necessary to worry about construction only after the work of ruin had been accomplished. In Marx's perspective, it was the democratic self-organization of the proletariat that was the truly radical act—even if it initially took reformist forms. The aim remained utterly revolutionary: *"the abolition of classes."* The strategy was now social democratic.

This does not in the least mean that Marx had become a so-

cialist on the model of the German social democrats just before
World War I, that is, believing in a legalistic, one-way evolution
to the new order. For it must be remembered that in 1871 the
demand for democracy was quite subversive of the status quo in
Europe. In France the generals and the National Assembly were
in control and the Left had been shattered; in Germany the vote
was explicitly weighted in favor of the propertied classes, and the
Reichstag, in any case, had no real power; in Austro-Hungary the
Hapsburgs ruled; and so on. Therefore when Marx insisted on
fighting for thoroughgoing democracy, he was, even as he proposed an alliance with the bourgeois liberals, advocating an extremely radical course of action.

If Marx had any fault in this area it was that he had illusions
about what democracy, in and of itself, could accomplish. In 1852
he had even argued that "the carrying of Universal Suffrage in
England would therefore be a far more socialistic measure than
anything which has been honoured with that name on the Continent. *Its inevitable result here* [in England] *is the political su-
premacy of the working class.*" As it turned out, of course,
universal suffrage did not have that effect in England and Marx's
hopes were disappointed (for reasons that will be examined
shortly).

In any case, if Marx never became a legalistic evolutionary, as
some of his disciples did, he emphasized the self-conscious emancipation of the proletariat at all times and he saw the struggle of
workers' parties for democratic freedoms as a crucial element in
this process. Indeed, the unknown Karl Marx might be reproached
for having been somewhat too naive about the potential of universal suffrage.[2]

## II

In the 1860s and 1870s Marx's tactic was applied in Germany with
increasing success. As a result, Bismarck adopted a fateful plan:
he would defeat the new movement by taking over its slogans,
and even part of its program, and making them serve his own
anti-socialist purposes. This was the first appearance of anti-
socialist "socialism" as a major political force, but certainly not the
last. An analysis of it should therefore provide insights into a
phenomenon that is likely to continue well into the twenty-first
century.

What follows, then, is a brief survey of a distant past which is by no means finished: the origins of anti-socialist "socialism."

In the early 1860s the German liberals had helped create workers' education societies in order to win the proletariat to their reformist cause. One of the architects of this policy, Schulze-Delitzsch, advocated self-help through consumers' cooperatives and credit associations. In 1863 Ferdinand Lassalle was invited by the Berlin and Leipzig workers' societies to address them. He attacked Schulze-Delitzsch and came out for producers' cooperatives which would receive state aid. Lassalle's speech had enormous impact, and on May 23, 1863, the General German Workers' Association (*Allgemeiner Deutscher Arbeitsverein*) was founded on the basis of his program and with a grant of almost dictatorial authority to him.

Lassalle was an extraordinary man—a swashbuckler who died in a duel, a romantic with an aristocratic life-style. Marx thought his downfall came when he fell in with "military adventurers and revolutionaries in kid gloves." There had been bad blood between the two leaders, partly based on politics, partly the result of the fact that Lassalle had once refused to lend Marx some money. It was this hostility that kept Marx from recognizing that Lassalle had brilliant gifts as an organizer, and for all his weakness as a theorist, was therefore one of the founders of the German social democratic movement.

In 1863, when Lassalle succeeded in organizing the General German Workers' Association Marx and Engels greeted the truly historic event with sectarian sullenness. Engels was outraged that Lassalle was building his organization "on the basis of our earlier work," and Marx said that his writings "abound in historic and theoretical blunders." Some years later, in 1868—after Lassalle was dead—Marx's assessment was more generous and more accurate: "After it had slumbered for fifteen years, Lassalle—and this remains his undying service—woke up the German working class."

Indeed, as Franz Mehring has pointed out, some of the theoretical errors committed by Lassalle and excoriated by Marx had their origin in *The Communist Manifesto*. If Lassalle believed that there was an "iron law" holding wages to subsistence levels, he could certainly cite that document as his authority (Engels himself admitted in 1885 that the *Manifesto* was the source of Lassalle's heresy, noting that Marx had changed his mind on this rather crucial point). And the *Manifesto* had called for centralized state credit, another Lassallean plank. The mature Marx, to be sure, went far beyond the Marx of 1848, but if personal factors were not at work, it is hard to see why he was so harsh on an associate whose greatest fault was to have learned too many lessons from the young Karl Marx.

And yet there was one difference between them which was of tremendous importance. It concerned democracy and anti-socialist "socialism."

By the time he organized the Association in 1863 Lassalle had turned sharply against the liberal democrats with whom he, and the German workers, had previously worked. More than that, he looked toward Bismarck and the Prussian royal house as possible allies in the socialist struggle. The Junkers and the throne were, of course, steeped in feudal tradition, and if they felt compelled to make the transition to a modern economy, they were still contemptuous of the bourgeoisie. So there was a historic basis for urging the convergence of the German Right and Left, both of which were anti-bourgeois, against the liberals in the middle.

When Lassalle led a deputation of workers to see the king, he reported back to his followers that the monarch was on their side and that the logic of his position would require him to support universal suffrage. This attempt at revolution from above was in keeping with Lassalle's general outlook. He emphasized the reconciliation of "freedom and authority" and spoke of the "dictatorship of intelligence," attacking the bourgeois liberals for their individualism. The state, he emphasized, must be "the unity of individuals in an ethical whole."

Marx and Engels fought Lassalle's Bismarckian strategy in the name of democracy, and argued for a united front with the capitalists against the feudalists. As Engels wrote in 1865, "It is in the interest of the workers to support the bourgeoisie in its battle against reactionary elements, *so long as the bourgeoisie remains true to itself*. Every victory that the bourgeoisie achieves over reaction is, under this condition, good for the workers. The German workers have instinctively recognized this. They have, quite rightly, voted in all the German states for the most radical candidates they could find."

After Lassalle's death, Marx was even more explicit. In a letter to Lassalle's successor, Johann Baptist von Schweitzer, he criticized the emphasis on unity and authority: "Here, where the workers have been bureaucratically disciplined from the cradle on and believe in established authority, it is necessary above all *to teach them to be independent*." As it turned out, Lassalle's practical political intuition was better than Marx's: German unification did come about through the Prussian throne and Bismarck, not by way of a bourgeois democratic upheaval. However, Marx was not only right, but prophetic, on the principled issue. The absence of a German revolution from below, as Barrington Moore has persuasively demonstrated, prepared the cultural and political way for Adolf Hitler.[3]

More immediately, Lassalle's tactics were the political prelude to the emergence of anti-socialist "socialism." Bismarck had learned that there were gains to be made by appealing to the workers' anti-capitalism from the Right. And the labor movement itself had shown that it contained some who could not distinguish between a democratic and an authoritarian collectivism. As time went on, the difference between these two trends was, as we will see, to take on enormous, even critical proportions. In the 1880s confusion over it allowed Bismarck to carry out his own version of Lassalle's strategy.

In the election of 1874 two German workers' parties—one following Marx, the other Lassalle—shared only 3 percent of the vote, but after they united at the Gotha Congress of 1875, their strength increased to 9 percent in the campaign of 1877. This electoral success was followed in May and June of 1878 by two attacks upon the life of the Kaiser. Using these assassination attempts as a pretext, Bismarck effectively outlawed the institutions of German socialism with an Anti-Socialist law. Paradoxically, this policy strengthened the socialists, for it proved to the people that their agitation had been quite effective and it also had the result of forcing the underground leadership into a radical mood and ultimately to Marxism itself.

So Bismarck could not rely upon the stick alone against the German socialists and their movement; he also employed the carrot. In 1881 he initiated wide-ranging health and accident insurance programs which were designed to draw the workers away from the social democrats. But the people understood that the government had become benevolent primarily because of the socialist mass threat. So they kept on voting for the Marxists, in part precisely because of Bismarck's attempt to co-opt their program. Yet, Bismarck's welfare programs and nationalizations were at such obvious variance with the laissez-faire model of capitalism that the social democrats had to define this new development. They called it "state socialism."

It had long been understood that government ownership of the means of production could be the basis of a new form of oppression. That, of course, had been a crucial point for anarchists like Bakunin and the mutualists (advocates of producers' cooperatives with aid from state subsidies) who followed Proudhon. Even Louis Blanc, who is usually identified as the father of the statist tradition of socialism, was aware of the problem. The socialist *ateliers* which he proposed to set up with government aid were to be regulated, but not run, by the state. Central control of the economy, Blanc said in 1848, could lead to tyranny and the formation of a new social class.

Karl Marx himself was particularly concerned with this problem. As a German, he came from a nation and culture with a long bureaucratic tradition and an authoritarianism that, as he indicated in his letter to Johann Baptist von Schweitzer, pervaded even the working-class milieu. In one of those crucial documents of his own first formulation of Marxism written in 1843, he wrote that "bureaucracy has taken over the state itself, the spiritual essence of the state, as its *private property.*" So state property was not necessarily socialist; it could be the private possession of the bureaucrats who run the state.

In *Anti-Dühring*, which was first published in 1878, Engels had been more precise. As the capitalist economic system became more complex and interdependent, the bourgeois state would have to take over the direction of the economy, precisely in order to maintain capitalist exploitation. This, he continued, would require the nationalization of some industries, and first of all, the means of communication and transportation: the post office, telegraph and railroads. Bismarck soon confirmed this prediction, and in a footnote to a later edition of the book Engels warned that the Junker's nationalizations had given rise to "a certain false socialism . . . that sees *any* statification, even Bismarck's, as socialistic."

It was Karl Kautsky who defined this phenomenon as "state socialism," i.e., a statified, anti-socialist version of capitalism. And Engels commented on Kautsky's theorizing in a letter to Eduard Bernstein in 1881: "It is a purely self-interested falsification of the Manchester bourgeois to see every interference of the state with free competition as 'socialism. . . .' We should *criticize* that, not *believe* in it. This so-called socialism is, on the one hand, nothing more than feudal reaction, and on the other, an excuse for printing money, with the secondary aim of turning as many proletarians as possible into state functionaries. They want to organize a labor army alongside the disciplined ranks of the military and bureaucratic armies. So choices will be imposed by state authorities instead of by factory foremen. What a beautiful socialism! That is where one comes out if one believes in the bourgeois who pretends, but does not really think, the state is equal to socialism."

In another letter, this time to Bebel, Engels remarked that these false views of socialism had developed out of a "one-sided and overriding struggle against the Manchester school." In confronting that pure model of market-economy capitalism, it would seem that any act of state intervention was anti-capitalist; in confronting the real world, that was simply not the case, for the state was regularly used as a tool by the capitalists. This critique of state socialism was to become a commonplace in the Marxist movement at the turn of the century. It was popularized in the United States by Louis Boudin and William English Walling (the latter wrote an entire book, *Socialism As It Is*, about it) and developed by Hilferding, Lenin and Bukharin. Thus Gabriel Kolko, writing from the ultra-Left, is quite wrong to account for the failures of twentieth-century socialism on the grounds that "nothing in socialist theory, much less in laissez-faire and marginal economic theory, prepared socialists for the possibility that a class-oriented integration of the state and economy in many key areas would rationalize and strengthen capitalism. . . ."

It is certainly true that the popular equation of socialism with statification did enormous damage to the movement in this century. It gave a "socialist" legitimacy to Communist totalitarianism, just as it once had to Bismarck's bureaucratic capitalism. And it also helped to justify the confusion of the welfare state with socialism. But this happened in spite of socialist theory, not because of it. And the source of this perversion is not to be found in intellectual analyses—the Marxists were quite perceptive on that count—but in the emergence of anti-socialist "socialist" movements that subverted the definition for very practical and political purposes.

So the socialism defined by the unknown Marx between 1850 and his death in 1883 was political and democratic, refusing the chiliastic vision of Bakunin and the conspiracies of Blanqui. It was reformist with a revolutionary purpose, in that it saw an alliance with trade-union gradualism as a step toward the abolition of classes. It advocated the democratic ownership and control of large-scale means of production, not the distribution of wealth or decentralized production. But it was fearful that bureaucracy would usurp democratic power, and therefore fought tenaciously against the equation of socialism with state ownership pure and simple. As a corollary to that proposition, Marx repudiated any political coalition of the Left and the Right against bourgeois liberalism and advocated instead a united front with the liberal capitalists against the feudalists in the name of democracy. And Marxian socialism based itself not upon the good will of capitalists nor upon the destructive rage of the lumpenproletariat, but upon the democratic self-consciousness of the workers.

On every point history has confirmed the judgment of Marx as against that of his rivals. Yet a little more than a quarter of a century after his death the movement he had inspired turned its back on his principles. He had obviously been very right—and just as obviously, very wrong. The consequences of his errors persist to this day as much as those of his truth. So it is at least as important to understand his failure as it is to appreciate his accomplishment.[4]

## III

The German Social Democracy survived Bismarck's "socialism" and flourished. By the 1912 elections they had won a third of the seats in the Reichstag, made a de facto alliance with the Liberals, and in effect created a *Grossblock,* an electoral united front of the working-class and bourgeois Left. The unions, which had only 300,000 members in 1892, enrolled two and a half million workers in 1913. The party organization and press were the wonder of the socialist world and the Germans were the dominant factor in the Second International. It seemed that history was providing a magnificent confirmation of the Marxian perspective.

Yet when the decisive test came in August, 1914, the German socialists, along with most of their comrades around the globe, betrayed their solemn and repeated anti-war promises. The proletarians turned out to be as patriotic as the bourgeoisie and some of the most fundamental assumptions of Marx and Engels were thus refuted in historic practice. The reasons for this shift are so complex that an entire library could be devoted to analyzing them. What is particularly relevant here is an outline of those factors involved in this fateful moment that throw light on the future of socialism itself.

First of all, the capitalist economies of the second half of the nineteenth century were not as crisis-ridden as Marx and Engels initially thought they would be.

The period in which Marx and Engels became involved in politics—the second quarter of the century—was marked by particularly violent economic crises. And there was tremendous social dislocation as a result of the migration from rural areas and the destruction of handicraft industry. This was the reality that was imperfectly recorded in the *Manifesto*. Yet during the time when Marxist influence spread, in the last quarter of the century, real wages were going up and there was tremendous industrial expansion. So, as Fritz Sternberg formulates the paradox, "in the same period in which Marxism became of primary importance for the European working classes, their conditions of life and, above all, the general trend of development, was not in the least in accordance with the laws of capitalism as analyzed by Marx."

At the very end of his life Engels was quite aware that life was not conforming to theory. "The acute form of periodic processes which previously had a ten-year cycle," he wrote in a brilliant note to the 1894 edition of the third volume of *Das Kapital*, "seems to have become more drawn out. . . . Possibly it is a matter of an extension of the duration of the cycle. In the childhood of the world market one can trace cycles [in the first edition: "crises"] of approximately five years; from 1847 to 1867 the cycle is definitely ten years; do we now find ourselves in the preparatory period of a new world crash of unheard-of intensity? That seems to explain a lot.

"Since the general crisis of 1867," Engels continued, "great changes have taken place. The colossal expansion of the means of commerce—ocean-going steamships, railroad, the electric telegraph, the Suez Canal—has for the first time really created a world market. The previous monopoly position of England in industry has been broken by a number of competing industrial lands. The investment of excess European capital has spread endlessly throughout the globe and opened up new areas, so that capital is now more widely dispersed and can overcome crises due to local speculation more easily."

Then Engels noted the structural changes that had taken place in capitalism: "Through all these developments all of the old crisis tendencies and the occasions for the buildup of a crisis have been greatly weakened or done away with. Competition yields in the domestic market in the face of cartels and trusts and is limited on the external market by protective tariffs with which all the great powers, except England, surround themselves. But these protective tariffs are only weapons for the final campaign, which will decide the domination of the world market. So each element that works against the repetition of the old crisis conceals within itself the seeds of a much more widespread and powerful crisis in the future."

This amounted to an extraordinarily perceptive and realistic revision of the Marxian perspective by way of a Marxian analysis. The intimations of new, and even greater, breakdowns were corroborated by World War I and the Great Depression of 1929. But the confirmation did not come until after the horrors of 1914 had begun. That meant that the new Marxist mass movement, for all its commitment to the rhetoric of revolution, developed under conditions of relative capitalist prosperity, and gains for the working class. Indeed, this fact was understood by socialists quite early: in 1901 the Austrian social democrats, among the most sophisticated Marxists in the world, revised their party program to strike out the references to the immiserization of the proletariat.

This is not to picture a secure and happy working class in those days. In Germany, for instance, real wages did go up between 1890 and 1900 when prices were stable. But with the new military expenditures after the turn of the century there was a rapid rise in the cost of living and wages fell far behind profits. Still, the workers had been given some reason to think that their destiny depended not on socialist revolution, but on capitalist success.

Even if the economy had failed and the workers had been held to subsistence wages, this would not have guaranteed that the socialist movement would have been militant and revolutionary. In general, times of severe privation are fearful and conservative, not radical. Indeed, the very growth of the socialist movement was, in some measure, a result of working-class optimism in a society in which the masses were making some real gains. At the same time, these conditions provided the economic basis for a politics that was increasingly gradualist and incremental. So when World War I broke out and revolutionary tactics against the government itself were required if the anti-war promises were to be redeemed, the movement was utterly unprepared to take to the streets.

On this count, Bismarck prevailed, not Marx. The proletariat had been given a sufficient stake in the society, so that when war came, it felt it had much more to lose than its chains. After the socialists in the parliament had voted for the military budget, the president of the State Insurance Office said, "The approval of the war credit by the Social Democratic Party represents the most beautiful success of German social reform."

But then, it was not just the politics of the social democracy that was affected by these events. Its philosophy was transformed, too, and sad to relate, Friedrich Engels played a significant role in the process.[5]

The first Marxism—that is to say, Karl Marx's ideas as a system, a doctrine—was elaborated between Marx's death in 1883 and Engels' death in 1895. As George Lichtheim has pointed out, it was the work of Engels, Bernstein, Kautsky and Plekhanov, with the assistance of the historians Mehring and Riazanov and the political leaders Liebknecht and Bebel (Germany), Guesde (France) and Victor Adler (Austria). Engels proclaimed its basic tenet at Marx's funeral: "As Darwin discovered the law of development of organic nature," he said, "so Marx discovered the developmental law of human history."

But Marx himself had made no such claim. Indeed, in an analysis of Russian history and possibilities of socialist revolution there, which will be analyzed at length in Chapter VIII, he specifically rejected such a notion. Engels, however, had always been concerned to stress the analogy between the natural and social sciences, the political and the biological processes. Marx, to be sure, approved the text of *Anti-Dühring*, which contained more than a little of the Darwinist interpretation of his method, but that book was regarded by him as a popularization, not a work of theoretical precision. In their division of labor at the time, Engels commented, his own work was more polemical, Marx's scientific.

But Engels' scientistic version of Marxism could not have had such enormous impact if history had not been waiting for it. It coincided perfectly with the inexorable progress of the social democracy within a relatively prosperous capitalism in which change was evolutionary. The masses, as Antonio Gramsci was to point out later, wanted a simple philosophy with the "aroma" of inevitability about it. It gave them a substitute for the religious faith that many of them had lost. At this point, there emerges, from a Marxist point of view, one of the most significant failures of Marxism: that it never became the consciousness of the working class except in its most vulgarized form.

Thus reality had qualified Marx's own enormous confidence in the self-emancipatory potential of the workers. In the years before World War I his principal heirs in the German Social Democracy became aware of this momentous development.

Karl Kautsky wrote to Victor Adler in 1901, "Socialist tendencies or instincts or dispositions or whatever will be naturally created in the masses by their class situation. But when one speaks of *consciousness*, i.e., of scientific knowledge, that comes to the masses from without. The class situation of the proletariat creates a socialist *will*, but not a socialist knowledge." Kautsky was quite right in making this distinction, yet it laid the basis for a Marxian rationalization of anti-socialism. If the workers themselves were no longer the ultimate judge of their own class interest, if a socialist science had to be brought to them "from outside," what was to keep those socialist "scientists" from exercising power over the workers?

In his famous study *What Is To Be Done*, Lenin had followed the Kautskyan analysis: ". . . the working class exclusively by its own effort is able to develop only trade-union consciousness. . . . The theory of socialism, however, grew out of the philosophical, historical and economic theories elaborated by educated representatives of the propertied classes, by intellectuals." This was a fact of enormous significance—and sad to say, it was a fact. There were those, like Rosa Luxemburg, who tried to insist upon the old verities of working-class consciousness, but history did not bear them out, either in her lifetime or after.

The fact that working-class consciousness did not develop as Marx thought it would had enormous consequences for socialist organization.

If the working class itself had been a vast, conscious movement, then control would have remained in the hands of the rank and file. But the admission that intellectuals and professionals had to be the agents of the class provided the basis for a bureaucracy which could develop its own interests and policies. That indeed happened and, strange to relate, the most perceptive of the socialists understood that it was taking place, but felt themselves helpless to do anything about it. This was not only true of a brilliant Left critic of the leadership like Rosa Luxemburg, but of some of those whom she attacked as well.

Thus Kautsky wrote to Victor Adler in 1909, "In Germany, however, the masses have been drilled to always wait for the command from above. The people above are so absorbed in the administrative business of the enormous apparatus that they have lost all wider vision, all interest in anything outside the movement. We saw this first in the unions, and now, since the political organization has grown so, in it, too." And August Bebel wrote to Adler, "One cannot see anything of the old willingness to sacrifice; today every job must be paid for—and well paid."

But perhaps the most devastating and prophetic critique of the German socialists came from a Frenchman, Jean Jaurès. In a dramatic confrontation at the Congress of the Socialist International in Amsterdam in 1904, Jaurès told the Germans, "Between your apparent political power, as it is measured from year to year in the growing number of your votes and mandates, between this apparent strength and the real strength of influence and action, there is a contrast that appears all the more while your electoral strength grows. Oh yes! On the morrow of the elections in June in which you received three million votes our eyes were opened up. You have an admirable strength in propaganda, recruitment and enrolling members, but neither your tradition nor your proletariat nor the mechanisms of your constitution permit you to throw this apparently colossal force into real, effective action."

Then, in a cutting and shrewd observation, Jaurès told his German comrades, "You have disguised your impotence for action in the intransigence of your theoretical formulas."

Was this development, then, inevitable? That was the thesis of a famous study of the social democracy by Robert Michels. There is, Michels argued, an "iron law of oligarchy." Democratic movements therefore inexorably give rise to anti-democratic bureaucracies. But then, Michels went on to say, there would be another wave of democracy from within the movement and the usurpers would be challenged. This difficult, frustrating process would go on and the cause would not progress in a straight line, but by fits and starts, by way of victories and defeats.

This question, and all the other issues posed by the failure of European socialism in 1914, is still unresolved. Now, after the Keynesian "revolution" following World War II, the integrative and assimilative power of capitalism is even greater than it was in

1914. The social democratic movements themselves have lost much of their *élan* and the bureaucracies are therefore even more powerful. It is quite possible that these events announce the doom of the socialist hope; but it is not necessarily so. This chapter has outlined the problems as they were first raised; the rest of the book will try to give some answers to them.[6]

Strangely enough, the secret of the unknown Marx is that he was too optimistic about, too trusting in, democracy. But if he erred in degree in this regard, his achievement is still remarkable: he saw in the ragged proletariat of the mid-nineteenth century the men and women of the good society; he recognized in reformist trade unions the cells of social revolution. If the more extravagant of his hopes have been disappointed, the basic social forces to which he looked have done much to change the world. And, as will be seen, they have the power to change it even more in the future.

# V

## _Das Kapital_

It is men who create wealth. In doing so, at a certain historical point they become so productive that they must create a just society, for the old orders of domination are no longer capable of containing their ingenuity.

These simple profundities are at the center of Karl Marx's work as a political economist. In _Das Kapital,_ they inspired a structure of such complexity and sweep that it is presumptuous to even think of outlining a few of its leading themes within the limits of a single chapter. But I have undertaken this risky enterprise for a number of reasons. First, Marx's analysis of capitalism, even though it is clearly dated in many respects and wrong in others, remains a magnificent summary statement, not simply of the economics of socialism, but of its politics and philosophy as well. Its central truth is huge, obvious and systematically ignored by most scholars to this very moment: that it is not capital or the market or abstention from consumption that produces wealth; it is man. Unless that fact is mastered in all of its ramifications, it will be impossible to build a humane social order.

Secondly, this work of explication requires that one realize how shabby and downright incompetent so many of the contemporary academic treatments of Marx are. There are, to be sure, scholars who have recognized his greatness. Wassily Leontiev cites Marx's predictions of the increasing concentration of wealth, the elimination of small and medium-sized enterprise, technological change, the growth of fixed capital and the business cycle, and comments that they constituted "an unsurpassed series of prognostications fulfilled, against which modern economic theory, with all of its refinements, has little to show indeed."

But Paul Samuelson's performance is, alas, more typical of the academic critics of Marx. In 1957 Samuelson wrote an article that concluded, "A minor post-Ricardian, Marx was an autodidact cut off in his lifetime from competent criticism and stimulus." This contemptuous tone pervades his discussion. For instance, Marx is reproached for having ignored the "patent fact that natural resources are productive." Had he understood this obvious point, Samuelson remarks disdainfully, he would have been in a better position "to explain why some people are very rich indeed and why some countries are more prosperous than others." To say this, Samuelson must ignore one of the most famous of Marx's programmatic statements, the *Critique of the Gotha Program,* where the fact that nature is a source of use value, and therefore of wealth, is described as a truism to be found in children's primers.

What confuses Samuelson is that while Marx insisted on the "patent fact" that natural resources are an element of wealth, he also said that they did not, in his very precise definition of the term, create exchange values. In failing to explore what Marx meant (or in ignoring it), the Nobel laureate followed an interpretive principle that is often encountered in academic essays on the subject: that the proper reading of any given passage by Marx is the one that demonstrates he was a blockhead.

A few years later, a colleague challenged Samuelson, pointing out that his "Marxian economic models" were not at all Marxist. Samuelson casually replied that perhaps Marx did not assert the idea he, Samuelson, had earlier defined as Marx's most basic and distinctive error, and added, "I claim no competence or interest in such doctrinal history." The "doctrinal history" referred to is nothing more, nor less, than what Marx said on such subjects of present-day relevance as economic crises and the impact of technology upon society.

These pages should also demonstrate that Louis Althusser, Daniel Bell and all the others who counterpose the youthful and the mature Marx are quite wrong. In 1843 Marx had concluded that the "essence of all forms of state power" (*das Wesen aller Staatsverfassung*) was "socialized man" (*der sozialisierte Mensch*). And, he said, "only when man has recognized and organized his own powers as *social* powers . . . will human emancipation be complete." *Das Kapital* is nothing other than a magnificent analysis of "socialized man" and, in particular, how productivity grows enormously through the application of science to a cooperative, interdependent process of production. And its conclusion is, of course, that man must recognize, and organize, these powers of his as *social* powers.

The central contradiction that keeps humanity from taking that step is more acute today than when it was described in *Das Kapital*. The economy is infinitely more "social" than it was in the nineteenth century—every branch of production has been rationalized a hundred times over since then—but its control and direction, even if corporate and bureaucratic, are still private. There has been, in Max Adler's phrase, socialization without solidarity. The basic paradox of *Das Kapital* is therefore still very much in force: that it has become a practical necessity, a matter of urgent self-interest, to create a society of social justice. For unless that unprecedented ability to create wealth is consciously directed toward the fulfillment of human needs, we will choke to death on our own unprecedented affluence, while millions in the ex-colonies starve in the ancient way.[1]

# I

When Karl Marx used the word "economics" he did not mean the same thing as the academics of his own time or of today. Many, perhaps most, of the critiques of his work ignore this crucial fact and therefore excoriate him for having given the wrong answer to questions he never asked. So this brief survey of *Das Kapital* will first try to establish its subject matter. For the definition of terms is in this case a political as well as a scholarly act and it even predetermines at the very outset many of the conclusions that appear to be reached through careful impartial study.*

Perhaps the best way to begin is to take up Marx's summary of his method in the third volume of *Das Kapital*.

---

* There will be so many references to *Das Kapital* in this chapter that I have included the citations in the text. In the *Marx-Engels Werke* the first, second and third volumes of *Das Kapital* are found in Volumes XXIII, XXIV and XXV. However, to help readers who may be using another edition or a translation, I will refer to them, respectively, as Volumes I, II and III of *Das Kapital* and will include chapter identifications to further facilitate the location of my references The page numbers will, however, refer to the three volumes of the *Werke*.

It begins *sotto voce* with an analysis of how profits are made from land. The simplest form of ground rent, Marx writes, is labor rent, "where the immediate producer spends a part of the week cultivating his land . . . and the other days of the week labors for the landlord without compensation." In that case, the exploitative relationship is vividly apparent on the very surface of the social reality. The serf—for this is a feudal arrangement—creates his own means of subsistence by working for himself. Then he delivers up a surplus, in the form of unpaid labor time, to the lord, who has control of the conditions of production.

From this deceptively simple example Marx passes to a fundamental generalization: "The specific economic form in which the unpaid surplus labor is pumped out of the actual producer determines the relationships of domination and servitude. . . . It is here that the entire organization of the economic society that arises out of these production relations is based, as well as the specific political form of society. *It is in every case the immediate relationship of the owner of the conditions of production to the immediate producer—a relationship that in every case always corresponds to a given developmental stage of the art and mode of labor and thereby to its social power of production—wherein we find the innermost secret, the hidden basis of the whole social construction and of the political forms of the relationships of sovereignty and dependence.* In short, here is where we find, in every case, the basis of the specific state form. The same economic base, however, can exhibit endless variations and deviations in its appearance as a result of countless empirical circumstances— natural conditions, race relations, outside historic influences, etc. —and these must be carefully analyzed in terms of the empirically given circumstances." (Emphasis added.) (III, Chapter 47, Pt. 2, pp. 798–799)

This passage has an enormous number of ramifications—one of them, Professor Samuelson might note, is that "natural conditions" account for economic differences between nations—but only a few of them can be stressed here.

First of all, there is the concept of the surplus. All societies save the most primitive, Marx argues, create a surplus over what is required to sustain the work force and to reproduce the conditions of production. The secret of the social, political and economic order—of the society as a totality in which these three orders interpenetrate one another—is exactly how the dominant powers extract this surplus from the direct producers. This can be done by force, as under slavery; by traditional relationships of lordship and serfdom, as under feudalism; by tax-gathering, as in various ancient Asiatic societies where the state held title to the land and collected its rent in this form.

This analytic apparatus was developed, of course, to facilitate Marx's analysis of capitalism. It can, however, be quite usefully applied to situations that did not exist during his lifetime. In the thirties in the Soviet Union, as Chapter VIII will detail, the collective farms were required to sell their grain at a fixed price even if this price did not cover the cost of production. In this case, the specific mode of extracting the surplus was the employment of totalitarian force, and it was indeed the "innermost secret" of Communist society, the key to its class system. This Marxian criterion is also particularly valuable in posing the problem that confronts every nation in the Third World today: whether a surplus can be accumulated for investment in industrialization without the brutalities of early capitalism or of Stalinism.

Secondly, the Marxian analysis of surplus shows that in each form of society the direct producers work an unpaid portion of the working day for those who own, or control, the means of production. This can be clearly seen, as Marx indicated, in the feudal system of labor rent where the serf's time is quite literally divided between work for himself and compulsory work for the lord. And, to take a more recent American example, something like this relationship was quite visible in the sharecropping system in the South.

But capitalism is not as straightforward as feudalism. It is, Marx wrote in the *Theories of Surplus Value,* "different from all previous systems in that the capitalist does not rule the worker through his personal qualities, but only insofar as he is 'capital.' . . ." The slave, the serf, the member of the Asiatic community, were all forced to surrender their surplus through extraeconomic means, like force, tradition or taxation. For them, political and economic domination were one and the same. But in the world of Manchester economics, exploitation is much more subtle. The worker is "free" to refuse the wage bargain with the employer, and if he accepts it, he is paid at a market wage. How, then, could there be unpaid labor time and the extraction of a surplus under this system?

This is one of the central issues explored in *Das Kapital.* Marx sought to demonstrate that in the transaction between employee and employer, the latter was, just as much as a feudal lord, able to appropriate unpaid labor.

Thirdly, in the quoted passage one can see how Marx the economist was also a political scientist and a sociologist. The relationship between owners and producers, which corresponds to a certain stage of technology, is the secret of economics, social structure and political forms. And one of the greatest single sources of confusion about Marx's writing arises when academics attempt to reduce his multifaceted ideas to the single dimension of their particular discipline. To stress this crucial idea, it is well worth while to probe a most basic point: that Marx's definition of economics is not at all what contemporary scholars understand by the term.

The labor theory of value had emerged in the seventeenth century as a weapon of the rising capitalist class against aristocratic landlords. In the version of it propounded by William Petty and John Locke, it legitimated the private property of entrepreneurs and celebrated the "labor" of a new producing class which was doing battle with parasites. In the late eighteenth and early nineteenth century the notion was sometimes put to conservative use as an argument that workers should not be paid anything more than their cost of production, i.e., a subsistence wage.

For Marx, this new mode of thinking corresponded to enormous changes in society and the economy. The peasant family producing for its own needs would not see their corn and cows as commodities to be sold on a market; their work would appear, not as an abstraction to be measured in labor time, but as a family function. As social reality changed, so did social consciousness. The Physiocrats responded intellectually to a society that was becoming more commercial but in which agriculture was still dominant by making land the source of value. Adam Smith, from the vantage point of a still more developed economy, saw labor as the measure of equivalence that allowed one to equate a ton of iron and two ounces of gold as being "worth" the same value (he later elaborated a cost of production theory, but that is not relevant here).

This Smithian idea of a generalized labor underlying, and equating, various commodities, Marx said, "corresponds to a society in which individuals pass with ease from one kind of work to another, which makes it immaterial to them what particular kind of work may fall to their lot. Labor has become here, not only in categories but in reality, a means of creating wealth in general and is no longer bound up with an individual in a specific setting." (I, p. 63) In C. B. Macpherson's excellent formulation, under feudalism there is an "authoritative allocation of work or rewards" which is based on custom and status; in capitalism man's labor and skill "are regarded not as integral parts of his personality, but as possessions, the use and disposal of which he is free to hand over to others for a price."

It was, in Marx's view, the great merit of Smith and Ricardo that they analyzed this new historic situation. In a society of increasingly complex production and exchange, there had to be some form of equivalency to facilitate the movement of commodities. Under such conditions, the myriad buyers and sellers of the most variegated goods could hardly mill around until they bumped into someone with whom they could barter. There had to be some way to equate twenty yards of linen and a pair of boots so that each could be sold independently of each other, but yet at a price that accurately measured their relative worth. That equivalent, the classics said, was labor. What the linen and the boots had in common was that their production had required an expenditure of labor time and their value could therefore be determined by the amount of labor time invested in each. And to make matters easy, all of these various relationships could be expressed in terms of the "general equivalent," money. (I, Chapter 1, Pt. 3, pp. 83ff.)

For Marx, this analysis was both revealing and obscurantist. It was absolutely true that in an economy that was increasingly social—in the sense that it required an intricate national, and even international, division of labor—but where the producers operated as independent, private units, there had to be equivalents to facilitate exchange. It therefore made good practical sense to say that a coat was "worth" so many boots or so many dollars. But in precisely that vocabulary all the other things that coats and boots had in common—in particular, that they were produced and exchanged within a gigantic framework of human cooperation and that they satisfied human needs—were obscured. They were "worth" the money they would fetch.

So the classical economists, Marx argued, explained *how* coats and boots related to each other in terms of the universal equivalent of labor time as expressed in money, but they never asked *why* usefulness had to be put in such terms. (I, Chapter 1, Pt. 4, p. 95) As long as one focuses upon the question of how the coats and boots relate to each other, then the traditional academic concerns about prices, wages and supply and demand are obviously paramount. That, however, assumes that the context in which these factors operate is somehow "natural," that it is a given and therefore not even worthy of investigation.

In point of fact, Marx notes, there had already existed economic systems in which capitalist forms of calculation were not at all dominant. Under feudalism, social relationships of personal dependence were much more important than the cash nexus. And, looking toward the future, in "a union of free men working with common means of production and exercising their individual labor powers in a self-conscious way as social labor power" (I, Chapter 1, Pt. 4, p. 93), the categories of capitalism would not apply either. Therefore, for Marx, the crucial question was why, and how, men had eternalized economic terms that had developed out of the specific conditions of capitalist production. The reason why was that this mode of thought gave a transitory system the appearance, and legitimacy, of natural law. This was done by prescinding from underlying class relationships and the decisive role of men in creating wealth. So Marx proposed to go behind these abstractions and investigate the reality they both revealed and concealed.

Marx, then, did not regard the behavior of prices or the schedules of supply and demand as unimportant. And he was quite appreciative of the efforts of classical economists in trying to understand the workings of these categories. But he saw them as dependent variables in a system in which class structure and changes in the productivity of labor were much more basic and decisive. Therefore—and the confusion caused by this fact has reigned for more than a century—Karl Marx's subject matter was different from what was, and what still is, commonly called "economics."

Even as sympathetic and perceptive a critic of Marx as Robert Heilbroner misses the fullness of this point. He writes, "The labor theory of value . . . may be immensely useful in elucidating the mode of transfer of surplus as an historic problem, but it is scarcely useful when it comes to the analysis of the operational problems of a modern state, capitalist or socialist." Of course! At no point did Marx focus his attention upon the "operational" problems of either capitalism or socialism, because he thought that such an emphasis distracted attention from something much more basic. Therefore he developed a macroeconomic analysis of those tendencies of capitalist society that create the framework, the fundamental limits, in which the operations take place. He did not think that microeconomic questions were unimportant. Considerable space is, after all, devoted to the questions of supply and demand and prices under capitalism in the third volume of *Das Kapital.* Marx's historic contribution was not, however, in working out the details of those processes but in describing the factors that determined the very context in which they occur.

These differences between Marx and the academy over the very definition of economics are related to the actual development of capitalist society. In its early phase, economic theory was a weapon of bourgeois enlightenment against feudal obfuscation; and the discipline insisted upon taking on the big issues, like identifying the sources of wealth within a society. The Physiocrats criticized the Mercantilists, Smith the Physiocrats, Ricardo, Smith. Marx is the culmination of this tradition and its turning point. For once capitalism became established, too much candor and inquisitiveness on the part of economists could only play into the hands of the new anti-capitalist movement.

Ben Seligman defined this change quite well: "Orthodox economists have evolved through the years some fairly elegant analytical structures from which, as Joan Robinson has said, it has been possible to derive with great accuracy the value of a cup of tea. This, however, was a little question, not a big one. Marx, although possessing much cruder tools, exhibited a far deeper sense of the meaningful. . . ." Moreover the way in which this split developed made it possible for the academics to depict themselves as scientists while dismissing Marx as a man of political prejudice. For the new orthodoxy concentrated its attention on marginal changes in prices, supply, demand and the like, and that analysis of increments could be concisely expressed in the equations of calculus.

So it was that Alfred Marshall, the giant of the post-Marxian mainstream, inscribed his *Principles* with the motto *"Natura non facit saltus"* (Nature does not make leaps). That phrase, Alexander Gershenkron has remarked, "did triple duty by referring to Marshall's effective use of calculus as a methodological device, to his belief in the general fundamental gradualness of economic structures and processes of social change, and to his rejection of certain economic policies that seemed to involve an unduly high rate of change. *Inevitably* in the minds of readers, the first reference was called upon to lend spiritual support to the other two." (Emphasis added.)

In short, Marshall's political prejudices were every bit as important as Marx's, only he could cloak them with a seeming mathematical objectivity. Similarly today with econometrics. The academicians who are so busy feeding data into machines predetermine much of the result by the way in which they write up their computer programs. But if the little questions can thus be ingeniously quantified, that will still not make the big questions go away. They provided the basis of Marx's definition of economics; they persist to this very day.

So Marx's subject matter is not the play of economic forces within a system which is assumed as given, but the dynamic factors that change the system and all the dependent variables that operate within it. The element he found most crucial, and contradictory, in this process was the growing productivity of labor as it was socialized in the interest of private profit. The resultant "socialized man" was thus not simply an ethical ideal, but an emergent economic trend of decisive importance as well. This is the definition of his discipline that distinguished Marx from the bourgeois economists. They sought to formulate the impersonal laws, inexorable as a mathematical equation, that ruled over the economy. But for Marx, those laws are themselves transitory, the creation of men and women who, once the preconditions of mastering them have been fulfilled, can change them.[2]

## II

*Das Kapital* begins its study of the existential reality behind capitalist economic categories with dry-as-dust definitions and a tightly argued and abstruse analysis of the "fetishism of commodities." This is because the book proceeds from the abstract to the concrete.

On the face of it, that is a preposterous order to follow, since it is obvious that thinking always moves from the concrete to the abstract. But there is a method in Marx's apparent madness and he described it carefully in an introduction to the *Critique of Political Economy* (which was not actually published until 1903, after his death). He wrote, "It seems to be the correct procedure to commence with the real and concrete aspects of conditions as they are; in the case of political economy to commence with population, which is the basis and subject of the entire act of social production. However, this proves to be false when it is examined more closely. Population is an abstraction if we leave out the classes of which it consists. These classes, again, are but an empty word unless we know the elements on which they are based, such as wage-labor, capital, etc. These imply, in turn, exchange, division of labor, prices, etc. Capital, e.g., is nothing without wage-labor, value, money, price, etc. So if I were to start with population, I would begin with a chaotic whole. Then on closer examination I would proceed to increasingly simpler ideas. From the immediate concrete I would move by way of finer and finer abstractions to the very simplest determinations. From there I would start on the return journey until I would eventually return to population, but this time not as the chaotic presence of the whole, but as a rich totality of many conceptions and relationships."

Therefore the reader must be warned that the opening pages of *Das Kapital*—or, for that matter, the entire first volume—contain conscious simplifications. Marx, like everyone else, actually began with the "chaotic whole" of immediate experience, but in his masterpiece he follows a logical rather than an experiential order. So in understanding any part of the Marxian analysis one must carefully ask: Under what simplifying assumptions is it subsumed? Thus even in Joan Robinson's generous reading of Marx, she mistakenly thinks that he first asserts a "purely dogmatic" theory of subsistence wages which he then abandons. Actually that is only one of the many conscious simplifications with which the first volume abounds (it deals with an isolated capitalist economy which is not part of the world market, contains only two classes and is engaged only in perpetuating itself through simple production and reproduction). As *Das Kapital* proceeds from its opening abstractions back toward reality, these simplifying assumptions are progressively dropped once they have helped in the understanding of the social whole as "a rich totality of many conceptions and relationships."

Marx's method is of interest on its own terms but it is stressed here for a special reason. This interpretation of *Das Kapital* will begin with the *conclusion* of Volume I. It is there, in the chapter on the "Historic Tendency of Capitalist Accumulation"— a magnificent historical generalization," Gershenkron calls it—that one finds a statement of the reality that the earlier abstractions explicate. And since there is so much confusion about Marx's meaning in the opening pages, particularly about the definition of that confusing term "value," it is legitimate to begin with the more realistic, and accessible, statement of what he is describing.

Capitalism, Marx writes, begins with an expropriation. The private property of the artisans and the peasants must be destroyed so that they can be turned into wage workers. For as small-scale production develops, so do cooperation and the division of labor and the other elements of Marx's most crucial variable, the social productivity of labor. At a certain point in history, the technical basis is thus laid for large-scale production. So the new capitalist system must destroy the petty producers, turning them into wage workers, in order to take advantage of the gains in social productivity.

Marx continues, "As soon as this upheaval is deep and massive enough to break up the old society; as soon as the worker is turned into a proletarian and the conditions of his labor have become capital; as soon as the capitalist mode of production stands on its own feet, then the wider socialization of labor [*Vergesellschaftung der Arbeit*]—the further transformation of the earth and of the other means of production into socially exploited means of production that are thus worked in common [*in gesellschaftlich ausgebeutete, also gemeinschaftliche Produktionsmittel*]—takes on a new form. What is now to be expropriated is no longer the individual worker, but the capitalist who exploits many workers.

"This expropriation completes itself through the play of the imminent law of capitalist production itself, through the centralization of capital. One capitalist kills many capitalists. Hand in hand with this centralization, or the expropriation of many capitalists by the few, the cooperative form of the labor process develops itself on an ever-increasing scale. There is the conscious, technical use of science, the planned exploitation of the earth, the transformation of the means of work into means that can only be used in common, the economizing of all the means of production by using them as means of production for combined, social labor, the bringing of all people into the net of the world market and through it the international character of the capitalist regimes." (I, Chapter 24, Pt. 7, pp. 790–791)

The labor theory of value is an accurate and fantastic description of this process, a way of thinking that arises because the socialization of labor under capitalism is carried out under private auspices.

If such an essentially social economy were consciously planned, then its participants would be aware of one another as cooperators in the gigantic enterprise of satisfying human needs. Indeed, something like that feeling does emerge when the one form of planned social production under capitalism, the creation of the means of destruction, becomes dominant in the midst of a major war. The planners do not ask how much the weapons cost, but attempt to determine the relative urgency of the need for them. The workers still labor for a wage, but every effort is made to appeal to their patriotism and to give them a sense of being part of a common effort. The system is, to be sure, still capitalist, as profiteering and the black market demonstrate. But in the name of survival it is forced to appeal to socialist emotions and to engage in a kind of production for use.

Such "military socialism" (which dates only from World War I) is tolerable in periods of emergency. But over the long run it is obvious that its definition of the economic process—as deriving its productivity from the social organization of work and satisfying consciously chosen human needs—is subversive. It threatens an economy that rewards money so lavishly on the grounds that private capital is the real source of wealth. And the classical economists did not have the opportunity to observe the economic effects of a twentieth-century war in any case. How, then, could a society whose dynamic was the increasing social productivity of labor—the emergence of "socialized man"—become conscious of itself in a way that would not threaten private ownership of the means of production?

The question was not, of course, posed in such an obviously biased way. The bourgeois economists attempted, honestly and straightforwardly, to explain how the economy worked. But they made the assumption that the capitalism they confronted was an expression of human nature rather than a transitory system. So they were blind to all the issues that became visible when one recognized non- and anti-capitalist alternatives to the existing order. They were thus sincere, and even profound, apologists who could not become conscious of their own limitations. Their science was "bourgeois," not in the sense of having sold itself to capitalist bidders, but because its basic assumption would not permit it to see beyond the bourgeois order.

The basic, and unique, cell of the capitalist economy these men studied was, Marx said, the commodity (we are returning now to the opening section of *Das Kapital*). The commodity is not simply a useful article, although it must also be that. Its historically unprecedented feature is that it is a useful article which is made to be sold on the market. Such products had existed long before capitalism but they had never dominated the economic activity of an entire society. Now, for the first time ever, men were mainly engaged in creating use values in order to exchange them. The commodity, in short, was both a use value and an exchange value. (I, Chapter 1, Pt. 4, pp. 94ff.)

These commodities, Marx showed, were produced in the kind of social labor process described in the chapter on the "Historic Tendency of Capitalist Accumulation." Men worked together in a highly rationalized division of labor in order to satisfy one another's needs, but this was done within a system of seemingly independent producers: "Objects of use become commodities only when they are the product of private labors carried on independently of one another. The complex of these private labors forms the totality of social labor. Here the producers first come into social contact with one another through the exchange of the products of their labor, and thus the specifically social character of their private labors first appears within these exchanges." (I, Chapter 1, Pt. 4, pp. 85-87)

Translated into contemporary terms: An auto worker buys a television set; an electrician buys a car. These two commodities are the result of an intricately organized production process in which coal, steel and other materials are fed into a scientifically based technology and the finished goods are then sold through an international network of distribution. The quality and price of the car and the television set will be affected by innovations within this complex division of labor. And yet, the auto worker and the electrician are probably not even aware of the role their own department plays in the work of their factory. Each one's labor satisfies part of the other's needs, but that is not why they work. They make commodities in order to get paid and to be able to buy someone else's commodities. They do not see each other as members of a social process; they "meet" only when they buy each other's commodities. "The social character of man's own labor is reflected as an objective characteristic of the product of labor itself." The auto worker is "worth" a certain percentage of the cost per hour of the television set; the electrician is "worth" a fraction of the cost per hour of the car. This is their "relationship."

So the membership card in the capitalist economy is money. The human cooperation and planning and science that are its foundation cannot be given their proper importance, for that would deprive capital of its excuse for taking the surplus. Instead, society abstracts from the human and technical variety of the labor process and reduces everything to the universal equivalent of money. This procedure facilitates the central illusion of the system: that it is capital which is productive. For it ascribes to products and dollar bills that creativity which is really exercised by men. It is, Marx says, like the fetishism of the primitives. In the misty world of religion people invested the products of their mind with supernatural powers: their fears and hopes became gods. Now, in the age of scientific technology, the products of men's hands take on a similarly mysterious life: money "creates" value, the stock market is a "bull" or a "bear," the economy "heats up" or "cools down."

One of Marx's current academic critics, Ralf Dahrendorf, gives a perfect example of how the capitalist vocabulary cannot call things by their own names. He tells how industrial sociologists have come to suspect, under conditions of relative affluence, "that in many disputes wages have an indirect and symbolic rather than an immediate function. Money is the lingua franca of the economy; in it one expresses less what one wants than that one wants something; thus workers translate all their wishes and complaints into the vernacular of financial demands." This is not so much new sociology, as Dahrendorf thinks. It is classic Marxism.

The fetishism of the commodity developed historically. The Mercantilists, Marx wrote, saw gold and silver as the source of wealth, the Physiocrats land, the classics, capital. Each theory corresponded to a given stage in the economy when, respectively, trade, agriculture and industry were dominant. All of them ignored the fact that it is men in society who create value. Gold, silver, land and capital are constituents and symbols of value, but the underlying fact, the true creator, is the social productivity of labor. (I, Chapter 1, Pt. 4, p. 97)

At this point one reaches a distinctive, often misunderstood moment in Marx's analysis. Capital, Marx says, is not productive.

But isn't it perfectly obvious that machines play an enormous part in making labor productive and therefore are a source of value? In an early, and rather sympathetic, reading of Marx, Joan Robinson reproached him for oversimplifying this issue. "Whether we choose to say that capital is productive," she wrote, "or that capital is necessary to make labor productive is not a matter of much importance. What is important is to say that *owning* capital is not a productive activity. The academic economists, in treating capital as productive, used to insinuate the suggestion that capitalists deserved well by society and are perfectly justified in drawing incomes from their property."

Marx, Mrs. Robinson argues, obscured his own excellent insight about ownership by insisting on too much, i.e., that capital itself is not productive. "It is more cogent to say that capital, and the application of science to industry, are immensely productive, and that institutions of private property, developing into monopoly, are deleterious precisely because they prevent us from having as much capital, and the kind of capital, as we need. This view is inherent in Marx's analysis. He foresaw the time when the monopoly of capital becomes a fetter upon the mode of production which has sprung up and flourished along with, and under it. Centralization of the means of production and socialization of labor at last reach the point where they become incompatible with the capitalist integument. The substance of Marx's argument is far from being irrelevant to the modern situation, but the argument has become incompatible with its verbal integument."

This is sympathetically put, yet I think Mrs. Robinson misstates Marx's view somewhat and therefore fails to understand why he insisted with such vehemence that capital is not productive. What is involved is not a terminological nicety but, once again, the central role of "socialized man" in the Marxian analysis.

When Marx spoke of capital, he did not mean the actual plant and machines. "Capital is not the sum of the material and producing means of production. Capital is the means of production transformed into capital. *In themselves, these means of production are as little capital as gold and silver are in themselves money.*" (Emphasis added.) (III, Chapter 44, Pt. 1, p. 823) In other words, it is precisely the relationship of *ownership* of the means of production which gives title to a profit that Marx defines as capital. He is quite willing to grant that a functioning entrepreneur should be paid. But his money, Marx notes, comes to him "independent of property in capital and much more as a result of his function as a nonowner, as—a worker." (III, Chapter 23, p. 393)

In making this distinction, Marx anticipated a scholarly discovery of Cambridge economists, including Mrs. Robinson, in the 1960s which has been the spearhead of a radical attack upon current orthodoxy. The two meanings of capital are confused: "finance controlled by capitalists which earns profits is identified with the physical equipment and stocks which assist labor to produce output." When that erroneous equation is made, then one can argue that as the output of the machines increases, so does the "productivity" of the stock certificate. For both are lumped together as "capital." Marx, however, never made this error. He always clearly distinguished between the actual plant and the relationship of ownership which turned it into "capital."

But Mrs. Robinson's basic question still remains. If Marx understood that science and technology are a crucial element in the labor process, why should he deny that capital, in the concrete and physical sense of the term, is productive? The answer to this question is fundamental to Marxian economics for it shows how rigorous Marx was in rejecting the fetishistic method of ascribing spiritual qualities to things. "Living labor," he remarked in the *Theories of Surplus Value*, ". . . is incorporated in capital and appears as an activity belonging to it. . . ." A machine can only "produce" wealth because of the ingenuity and sweat that men put into it. Capitalism, however, could not tolerate such a truth. In its characteristic mode of thought, the productivity with which men endow machines is first imputed to the machine itself, and then transferred to the dollars that bought it or the share of stock that identifies its owner.

Unfortunately one of the most explicit analyses that Marx ever made of this point is found in a somewhat obscure text: a draft of a chapter of *Das Kapital* which was not included in the published work and which did not appear in print until 1933. This "sixth chapter" of Volume I of *Das Kapital* treats of the process of the production of capital and insists upon the distinction between the material means of production, which are not capital, and the economic relations of production, which are crucial for

Marx in determining the system. Marx writes, "Science, the general intellectual product of the development of society, also appears directly incorporated into capital, and its application to the material of the individual worker. The general development of society is exploited by capital through labor and reacts upon labor as if it were the productive power of capital and thus seems to be a result of the development of capital itself. . . ."

So within the conceptual world of capitalism the superstitious proposition that capital or money or "waiting" (abstention from present consumption) is productive seems quite logical. Therefore in the next step of his argument Marx traces the historic process that led men to this sophisticated primitivism which invests machines and markets with wills of their own.

His analysis is complicated but its basic thrust can be summed up in a few propositions. In the first economies men bartered goods and products exchanged against one another. Let C stand for commodity and this process could be described by the simple formula: *

C-C.

As economic life became more complex, money (M) intervenes to facilitate this transaction. A man sells his commodity for money and then buys someone else's commodity with the funds he has received:

C-M-C.

When such exchanges become general, there is a mercantile economy. But even under such conditions of relative development, the idea that money itself is creative seems absurd. During the Middle Ages, for instance, usury—making money from money— was defined by the Catholic Church as a sin.

Money only turns into capital when it becomes the starting point of the entire process. A man has money and wants to make a profit. He invests it in the production of no matter what article, for he is not concerned with the use value to be created but only with the profit to be realized. Now the transaction could be described as:

---

* To be precise in Marxian terms, in barter, products, not commodities, were exchanged, and "commodity" is reserved to describe only goods privately produced for a market. The symbolic notation is simplified here by ignoring this distinction which, in other contexts, is quite crucial.

### M-C-M′.

It is precisely this developed capitalist system that can give rise to the illusion that it is the capital rather than the social process of production that is the source of value. (I, Chapter 4, pp. 161ff.)

Now that seemingly innocuous definition of the commodity as a product with both use and exchange values becomes a key to the understanding of the entire economic system. Its essential characteristic—which differentiates it from the goods of all previous systems—is that the producer of commodities aims, above all, at the realization of exchange value. For him, a warehouse of exquisitely fashioned, but unsellable, use values is, quite literally, worthless. They must at least seem useful to be sold, but the crucial thing is that they *be* sold, for only then do they have a "value." And given that basic bias, capitalism will, as its history so abundantly shows, produce the disastrous and profitable, e.g., the polluting internal combustion engine, and ignore the socially urgent, e.g., housing for the poor, because the latter will not yield a high enough return.

Moreover, these equations have raised the basic issue of the surplus. For in the capitalist formula

### M-C-M′

M′ is greater than M. Somewhere in the process of distribution and exchange, a surplus value has been created over and above the cost of production. Indeed, it is precisely in order to appropriate that surplus that the capitalist makes his investment in the first place. But where does it come from? (I, Chapter 4, p. 165) In the era of merchant capital, when traders tried to sell dear and buy cheap, they tried to explain it as a reward for shrewdness or even sharp practices. Marx quotes Ben Franklin in this mood: "War is plunder, business is swindling." (I, Chapter 4, p. 178) But in the developed capitalist economy, where exchange is rationalized, it is impossible to equate profits and chicanery.

It is at this point in the analysis that Marx presents his famous thesis that labor power is the source of the surplus. (I, Chapter 4, pp. 181ff.) What Marx calls the "constant capital"—the machines, raw material and the like that are used in the production process —imparts a value to the final commodity which is fully paid for as a cost of production. It therefore cannot be the source of an increment in value. But labor power—including the labor power of working entrepreneurs—has a unique characteristic: it is paid according to its costs of production, at value, yet it produces more value than its cost of production. Like the serf, the worker labors part of the day for himself, i.e., to get the wage that permits him to live (it is not, as will be seen, a subsistence wage), and part of the day for the capitalist who, by virtue of *owning* capital, is able to extract the worker's surplus.

Now it might be argued that this whole analysis is simply a matter of definition. Ben Seligman summarized this view with regard to Marx, Marshall and Keynes: "All three agreed that revenue minus wages, material cost and depreciation yielded profit. However, they did not agree on the definition of the elements to be deducted from revenue. As to the remainder, they simply had different names for what the reasonable person called profit. Marshall considered this a great driving force, Marx scorned it, and Keynes was indifferent, believing it fine so long as it did not impede the proper functioning of the economic system."

One could say that there is no empirical way of determining which of these thinkers is right, that their differences are simply a matter of different prejudices. Yet there are objective data that support Marx's analysis as against Marshall's and evidence that it was precisely his way of understanding labor power that permitted him to make one of his most brilliant, and corroborated, prophecies: that capitalism was a system of periodic crisis.

In the actual historical development of capitalism to the present, the elements that were so important to Marshall and the orthodox academics—risk-taking, abstinence from consumption and the other factors said to make capital "productive"—have become less and less important. Investment is more and more a function of retained profits, i.e., of the surplus produced within a corporation by the workers, or else it has been collectivized in huge institutions like insurance companies. Even invention and innovation have been rationalized as scientists and engineers are subjected to a division of labor resembling that in the plant. In all of these aspects, the economy has behaved in a Marxist, rather than a Marshallian, way.

Secondly, it was Marx's insight into the role of labor in the production process that enabled him to understand the tendencies toward crisis within the capitalist system. The orthodox academics created more and more sophisticated models of economic equilibrium in which every increase in supply automatically generated a matching increase in demand. The cyclical breakdowns that took place in reality were then accounted for in a number of ingenious ways, including the assertion that their periodicity was attuned to that of sun spots.

Marx was scornful of this idyll. "Nothing is more absurd," he wrote, "than the dogma that commodity circulation determines a necessary equilibrium of buyers and sellers since every seller is a buyer, and vice versa." (I, Chapter 3, Pt. 2, p. 127) One of the many reasons that Marx saw through this theory was his awareness that labor power created—and increasingly—more value than it received in wages: "The ultimate cause of all actual crises always remains the poverty and limited consumption of the masses in contrast to the drive of capitalist production to develop the forces of production as if the absolute consumption capacity of the society were their only limit." (III, Chapter 30, p. 501)

It is remarkable that Clark Kerr so systematically underestimates the importance of this Marxian insight in a recent comparison of Marx and Marshall. Kerr ascribes to Marx a position which the latter systematically attacked—that there are "iron laws" in the economy. But even more to the point, he freely admits the remarkable limits of the orthodox economic faith. Alfred Marshall, Kerr notes, "neglected depressions and mass unemployment, and had faith that equilibrium at full employment was the natural tendency of capitalism." But those were nothing less than the crucial determinants of the quality of human existence in capitalist society, and Marx, for all of his errors, understood the truth about them because his vision was always focused upon working men and working women rather than upon the differential calculus.

Since this section has dealt with so many definitions, it would be well to put them into perspective before turning to the very heart of *Das Kapital*, the analysis of the "laws of motion" of capitalism.

For Marx, capitalism is an increasingly social process of production—using science and centralization to rationalize the globe itself—which is carried on by private producers. It cannot, therefore, become conscious of the essentially social origins of its growing productivity without casting doubt on the legitimacy of its dominant institutions. So it reduces all the interconnections of cooperation to market relationships: the auto worker and electrician "meet" only in the scale of their products, wages become a "lingua franca" for other emotions. Since men are thus defined in terms of money, money appears to be human, and productive. It is turned into capital and invested primarily to yield a profit, incidentally to turn out something useful. In the process, those who own the means of production are able to appropriate a surplus generated by a unique commodity—labor. For the power of labor creates much more value than it is paid in wages. Yet this marvelous quality, from the point of view of the capitalist, is also a menace, for it contains within it the inherent possibility of overproduction.

At every point in this extraordinarily complex analysis the animating insight is the same: that men create wealth.[3]

# III

Given these basic definitions, Marx sought to describe the "law of motion" of capitalist society. Only when he had dealt with this big question could he turn to the dependent variables, the little questions, like the effect of supply and demand and the determination of prices. The dynamic of the system, he argued, drove the capitalist progressively to socialize labor in his struggle to extract more of a surplus from the direct producers.

Historically, the method that capitalism first used to pump more of a surplus out of the working class was straightforward and brutal: by actually extending the working day and thereby the volume of unpaid labor that the employee contributed to the profits. Marx called this "absolute surplus value." (I, Chapter 15, pp. 192ff.)

Western man has by now become so accustomed to the qualitative change in the conditions of life that capitalism thus brought about that he has quite forgotten that only a few centuries ago it was not thought "natural" to spend most of one's waking hours at work. In 1530, Christopher Hill has pointed out, a man could earn his yearly bread in fourteen or fifteen weeks of labor—and two and a half centuries later he had to toil fifty-two weeks a year. In a richly documented treatment in Chapter 8 of Volume I, Marx describes how the emergent capitalist order fought mightily to lengthen the working day and to force women and children into the labor force. But there was a limit to this process. The day has only twenty-four hours and the body can stand only so much.

At this point, the system became much more ingenious. Instead of simply expanding the hours of labor, the capitalist increased the productivity of labor. Thus, although a man still worked the same period of time, his output increased enormously and so did the surplus value appropriated by the owner of the means of production. Marx called this "relative surplus value" and the search for it is a crucial aspect of the capitalist dynamic. As this process is described in *Das Kapital* in a wealth of historic detail, the machine, the concentration and centralization of capital, the application of science to technology, all tend to make the economy more and more social and productive, but the decision-making and the limits of consumption are still privately determined.

This new technology, Marx writes, could have provided a way to free the factory hand from the degradation of the division of labor, lifting him above the productive process and making him its master. (I, Chapter 13, Pt. 4, p. 442) But when machines are used for capitalist purposes—when they are capital—the point is not to make the labor process more tolerable, or even creative, but to increase profits. So, as Marx analyzed the development of mass production, it destroys skills and turns the workers into semi-skilled tenders of machines. Thus as work becomes more social, it paradoxically becomes even more alienating—routine, impersonal, without initiative. (I, Chapter 13, Pt. 4, pp. 442–444)

*Das Kapital* is quite explicit on this point, but the *Grundrisse der Politische Oekonomie*, Marx's notes from 1857–1858 which essentially constitute a first draft of his masterpiece (they fill a book of more than a thousand pages), are even more precise. The title of a section in that volume is, in a sense, a marvelously compact summary of the Marxian indictment of capitalism: "Contradiction between the basis of bourgeois production (the value measure) and its very development. Machines, etc."

As Marx describes the technological basis of this contradiction, the development of big industry so increases the productivity of the individual worker that output does not depend on how much he works but rather "upon the general state of science and the progress of technology, or the application of science to production. . . . In this transformation, it is neither the immediate labor that man himself performs, nor the time during which he works, but the appropriation of his common productivity . . . in a word, the development of the socialized individual, that appears as the basic source of richness and production. . . . The surplus labor of the

masses has ceased to be the precondition of the development of
the common wealth, and the leisure of the few is no longer the
precondition for the development of the common power of the
human intellect."

In the course of this description Marx clearly recognizes the
trends toward automation: "Labor no longer appears as incorporated within the production process, but rather men become the
overseers and regulators of that process [*Wachter und Regulator*]." All this demonstrates the degree to which "social knowledge"—that development of science which is itself increasingly
the work of a community of scientists—becomes "the immediate
power of production."

But this magnificent accomplishment, Marx argues, is intolerable within a capitalist system. On the one hand, the capitalists
do everything in their power to make production independent of
labor time; "on the other hand, the colossal powers of production
thus created are measured in labor time." Capitalism's capacity—
and drive—to expand production are boundless; but the consumption capacity of a society that constantly seeks to economize on
labor time is not. As Marx put the point in outline form in Volume
II of *Das Kapital,* "Contradiction of the capitalist mode of production: the workers, as buyers, are important for the market.
But as sellers of their own commodity—labor power—the capitalist society has the tendency to keep them to a minimum price."
(II, Chapter 16, Pt. 3, p. 318)

This disparity between production and consumption, Marx
insists, is not to be explained by saying that the worker receives
too little of the product of his own labor. In his analysis wages are
determined by the same economic laws that constrain the capitalist. They may rise over time, and particularly during the boom
that almost always precedes a crash, but as a cost of production
they must be kept to a minimum. If some conscientious employer
would pay his men more, that would require him to raise his
prices or lower his profits. In the first case, he would soon drive
himself out of the market; in the second, he would be less able
to compete with his wealthier antagonists. Moreover, it is a historical fact that depressions occur at moments of high working-
class consumption. The problem, then, is not that the workers
have too little, but that the system has overproduced.

Thus the capitalist crisis, as Marx analyzes it, is unprecedented.
In all previous social systems economic breakdown did indeed

take place where people did not have enough, when a poor harvest or a natural calamity made foods and goods scarce. But now the problem was one of "too much," of glut. There were "too many" shoes, and therefore the shoe workers, whose wages had reached new heights precisely because they were turning out shoes in enormous quantities, had to be laid off, which further reduced the market for everything else. It was, in short, capitalism's necessary obsession with expanding production through socializing labor that, within the confines of the system, turned out to be catastrophic.

Some students of Marx think that this contradiction between production and consumption within capitalist society is only one of a number of Marxist theories of crisis. That, for example, is the thesis of Paul Sweezy's quite lucid exposition of *Das Kapital* in *The Theory of Capitalist Development*. I disagree. Marx's various analyses of breakdown all present the same basic contradiction—between socialized labor and the private uses of it—only from different points of view. It can be seen in terms of the antagonism between production and consumption. It also can be located within the production process itself as an unplanned and inevitable disproportion between the development of capital-goods and consumer-goods industries. (III, Chapter 15, Pt. 3, p. 267)

But the most controversial single statement of the crisis tendency inherent in capitalism is the theory of the falling rate of profit.

The falling rate of profit, a theme Marx inherited from the classical economists, is an obvious deduction from his own analysis. If labor is the source of value and, in their struggle for more and more surplus, the capitalists force one another to increase constant capital (investment in machines) as compared to variable capital (wages), then the element in the production process that is uniquely creative is in relative decline. Then, all other things being equal—*which, for Marx, they never are, except as a simplifying assumption*—the profitability of capitalism, its ability to produce surplus value, will fall precisely as its productivity increases. And this is a most dramatic illustration of the contradiction between social and private purposes, for it makes the capitalists the unwitting agents of their own destruction.

As far as one can tell, the rate of profit has not declined. Therefore, some academics would say, there is no point in following the intricacies of a theory that cannot even describe the real world.

Yet Marx himself was quite aware of this difficulty: "If one looks at the enormous development of the productive powers of social labor," he wrote in Volume III of *Das Kapital,* "then in place of what economics had previously described, namely, the explanation of the fall in the rate of profit, one must tell why, on the contrary, this fall has not been greater and more precipitous than it has." (III, Chapter 14, Pt. 1, p. 242) That, he commented, could only be accounted for on the basis of countertendencies offsetting the trends he had described.

Indeed, Marx comments that "the same causes that create the tendency for the rate of profit to fall also are the source of these countertendencies." (III, Chapter 14, Pt. 4, p. 246) The most important single case in point, and one that has tremendous ramifications for the entire Marxian analysis, is found, as one might expect, in the growth of productivity. Early on, in Volume I, Marx distinguishes between the organic and the technical composition of capital. The organic composition is the ratio of constant to variable capital, i.e., it expresses the tendency for machines to grow relative to the wage bill. The technical composition measures investment per worker and the consequent change in output this brings about. (I, Chapter 23, Pt. 1, p. 640)

So constant capital increases and variable capital declines which would make the rate of profit fall; but at the very same time, and for the very same reason, the productivity of socialized labor increases so much that even if the surplus labor in each unit of production is less, the sum total of units is so great that the mass of surplus, and the mass of profits, rises. (I, Chapter 23, Pt. 2, p. 651) As Marx puts the paradox, there is "on the one hand a tendency to a progressive fall in the rate of profit and on the other hand a progressive increase in the absolute mass of the appropriated surplus value, or profit; so that on the whole a relative decrease in variable capital and profits is accompanied by an absolute increase in both. The twofold effect can express itself only in the growth of the total capital at a rate more rapid than that expressed by the fall in the rate of profit." (III, Chapter 13, p. 233)

Thus Marx sees the growing productivity of labor as a crisis factor—it threatens overproduction—and as a means of overcoming crisis—investments that save on capital or enormously increase output per worker can cheapen goods and therefore create new markets. Paul Samuelson cannot tolerate such indeterminacy. He measures Marx by a non-Marxist standard and finds him wanting: "This does not mean that for him a postulated secular econometric law meant that literally what it prophesized would indeed happen; for, like Malthus and others, he often spoke of 'tendencies,' and in such a way that we hardly know how to decide when he was wrong—and hence when he was right!" Samuelson, in short, wants those mathematical certitudes that anticipate the price of a cup of tea; Marx is concerned with analyzing the historic destiny of the system and therefore must take alternate possibilities into account. And the latter is "right," not because *Das Kapital* contained a prophecy of the crash of 1929, but because it offers a method that allows one to understand such an event and to change the system so that it need never happen again.

Even Mrs. Robinson fails to perceive the dialectical complexity of Marx's analysis. She writes of him that "the argument of *Capital* did not lead him to expect any appreciable upward trend in the level of real wages under capitalism. . . ." Marx, she says, assumed that the rate of exploitation is constant. But that, she continues, would mean that real wages would go up along with productivity. She concludes, "This drastic inconsistency he seems to have overlooked, for when he is discussing the falling tendency of profits he makes no reference to the rising tendency of wages which it entails."

This is inaccurate. There are, to be sure, passages in *Das Kapital* that veer toward an immiserization theory in which wages must fall. Marx remarks at one point that under capitalism "the great majority is always poor and must remain poor," (II, Chapter 16, Pt. 3, p. 318, n. 32) which could be taken to mean that wages will never go up. But the main Marxian analysis points clearly to a rise in real wages accompanying the decline in the rate of profit.

Marx, as was noted earlier, saw the period immediately before a depression as characterized by a boom and rising wages. (II, Chapter 20, Pt. 4, p. 409) Indeed, there is an entire chapter in Volume I devoted to showing how wages increase under certain conditions in capitalist society. (I, Chapter 23, p. 640ff.) But perhaps the clearest statement is found in Volume III: "The compensation of the falling rate of profits through their rising mass is only valid for the total capital of the society and for the big, well-prepared capitalists. The new, independently functioning and rising capitalists [*Zusatzkapital*] find no such conditions of compensation and must create them. Thus the fall of the rate of profit intensifies the competition of the capitalists, not the other way around. This competition is accompanied by a temporary increase in wages and a resultant and further temporary decline in the profit rate." ( III, Chapter 15, Pt. 3, p. 267 )

Marx was not able to develop this point, but his followers did. As far back as 1899 Kautsky commented that "the living conditions of the proletariat are today higher than they were fifteen years ago." He distinguished betweeen absolute poverty, which was not growing but declining in capitalist countries, and "social poverty," the failure of the workers to increase their living standard in proportion to their contribution to the social product. Lenin endorsed Kautsky's thesis, and at their 1901 Congress the Austrian socialists, among the most brilliant theorists of the European movement, took references to immiserization out of the party program. In 1929 Henryk Grossman demonstrated at book length that the idea of rising wages was central to the Marxian analysis and more recently Jürgen Habermas has documented the same point.

So in the complexities of the Marxian analysis, the "law of motion" of capitalist society is discovered through an analysis of the changes in the social labor process. In the search for relative surplus value the capitalist increases investment per worker and thereby enormously expands social productivity. But this triumph is contradictory for he has at the same moment prepared the way for a crisis of overproduction. The basic cause of this breakdown is to be found in the antagonism between social labor and private decision-making and appropriation. Seen in terms of production and consumption, this antagonism is visible in the glut that appears in a booming capitalist economy at a time of high wages; seen within the production process itself, it is the private planlessness of an essentially social system that leads to disproportions between capital and consumer-goods industries; and seen from the vantage point of profits and surplus, it is expressed in the tendency of the rate of profits to fall and for the mass of profits and rate of wages to rise, prior to the crisis.

Thus "socialized man"—the individual who can produce as much as a thousand, or ten thousand, workers once did because of the advances of science and the cooperative organization of production—emerges, but within the framework of a private and anti-social system. Once Marx had made this profound analysis of the fundamental trends and alternatives of capitalism, he could then turn to the issue of prices, which so obsessed academic economics.[4]

First of all, it is made quite clear in *Das Kapital* that the value of a commodity—the socially necessary labor time it contains—does not determine its price: "This is no defect, but on the contrary admirably adapts the price form to a mode of production whose inherent laws impose themselves as the mean of apparently lawless irregularities that compensate one another." (I, Chapter 3, Pt. 1, p. 117) That, you might say, is Marx's own, and characteristic, statement of Adam Smith's theory of the invisible hand. And in a letter to Kugelmann, Marx developed the same point: ". . . daily exchange relations and the value quantities *cannot be immediately identical.* The character of bourgeois society precisely arises out of the fact that there is no conscious social regulation of production. Reason and natural necessity assert themselves only as a blind average."

The theory of value is, in other words, macroeconomic. By examining the changes in the social process of production—the evolution of socially necessary labor time—one understands the basic tendencies of the economy, which in turn set the context for the microeconomic transactions of supply and demand.

For Marx, the demand for goods is a dependent variable, not a given. It is determined "by the relationship of the different classes to one another and by their respective positions, namely, and first, through the relationship of total surplus value to wages, and secondly, through the relationship of the different parts into which the surplus value is divided (profit, interest, rent, taxes, etc.); and so here again it is shown that nothing can be explained on the basis of supply and demand until the basis which that relationship itself reflects is made clear." (III, Chapter 10, p. 191)

In dealing with the supply of goods the crucial point is not, as so many academic economists believe, to pose hypothetical prices and then calculate the supply that will be offered under those conditions. That suggests a rationality about business decisions that even the proponents of this view admit does not exist in the real world. Most executives figure out their cost of production, add a markup and thereby set the price. If they were somehow ruled by an exact knowledge of demand—which is itself, as Marx emphasized, dependent on a number of factors—then there would never be a crisis of overproduction. But that, of course, is simply not the case.

Marx, as on almost every issue, focuses his attention with regard to supply on the production process itself. As Rudolf Hilferding cogently summarized his approach, under capitalism the capitalist "must be able to set the commodity at a price which is equal to cost price plus average profit." This Marxian description, it will be noted, more accurately depicts the real world of business than the theories of supply and demand. "If he is unable to realize this price . . . the process of reproduction is arrested, and the supply is reduced to a point at which the relationship between supply and demand makes it possible to realize this price. Thus the relationship between supply and demand ceases to be a mere matter of chance: we perceive that it is regulated by the price of production, which constitutes the center around which market price fluctuates in directions which are perpetually opposed, so that the fluctuations compensate one another in the long run. . . . In the long run therefore the relationship between supply and demand must be of such a kind that the price of production (brought about independently of this relationship) may be attained which shall yield the capitalist the cost price plus the profit for the sake of which he has undertaken the production. Then we speak of the equilibrium of supply and demand."

In other words, a careful analysis of the process of production as it affects the social classes and their share of output, and as it changes the costs and character of business, must be made prior to the observation of the relationship between supply and demand. For the latter are the function of the former. At any given moment it is quite possible—and often very useful—for academics to take a snapshot of the economy and to analyze the relations of supply and demand that equilibrate cost of production plus profit and price. But Marx was more interested in describing the macro-movements and dynamic trends of the system itself. In the process he made his share of errors and that series of incomparable predictions that Wassily Leontiev enumerated.

This, then, is *Das Kapital* in briefest outline. Its subject matter is not the short-run interaction of supply, demand, prices, wages and other elements. It is, rather, a description of how structural changes in the capitalist system brought about the socialization of labor. In a brilliant historical analysis Marx shows how emergent capitalism expropriates the petty producers and turns them into proletarians working for a wage with privately owned, but socially organized, means of production. As this process proceeds apace, the big capitalists take over the smaller capitalists and the system tends toward increasing centralization and monopoly.

In this entire process, Marx continues, it is not owners virtuously abstaining from consumption who create wealth. It is not even the increasingly complex machines, for they are only as productive as the workers (and in his broadest usage, Marx would include scientists and even functional entrepreneurs in the term) make them. Rather it is men and women who create wealth, and that is an intolerable truth for capitalism since the obvious corollary is that those who create wealth should also enjoy it. And they do not: the surplus extracted from the direct producers is not consumed by them. The market-determined wage they receive is less than the value their labor imparts to the output. They, like the feudal serf, therefore work a portion of the day to earn their keep —and a portion of the day to supply the owner of the means of production with a surplus.

Indeed, the dynamic principle of this system—its law of motion —is precisely the capitalist's effort to increase that surplus. This is first done through lengthening the working day, but that brutal process reaches the limits of human endurance. So the struggle for more surplus now goes forward by means of a never-ending socialization of labor which raises output per man-hour at an unprecedented (in terms of all previous economic systems) rate. This feat is, however, most contradictory. On the one hand, it threatens a glut, since production advances in giant strides but consumption is restricted by the class structure of the system; and it has the potential of reducing the rate of profit, since the unique source of the surplus, labor power, is diminishing in relation to the investment in machines. But these crisis trends do not operate unchecked. For on the other hand, the mass of labor power may be declining relatively, but the rising productivity increases its worth absolutely. And capital-saving innovation and lower unit-labor costs may make it possible to cut prices and expand markets.

*Das Kapital* does not contain econometric prophecies as to how these various, and sometimes compensating, tendencies will work out. But it does propose a method of analysis and focus upon key variables that are valid to this very day. It took the Great Depression to drag the academic economists into the real world and teach them that it is in society's urgent interest to vastly increase the consumption of the masses. And even in the post-Keynesian economics of the 1970s, as Chapters XII and XIV will show, our unheard-of productivity remains the greatest threat to our happiness because it is still under private domination.

In short, Marx's central theme—the changes in productivity

brought about by the socialization of labor and its consequent effect on the rest of the system—is more relevant today than when he wrote *Das Kapital*. Those neat mathematical equations with which academicians described perfect equilibrium served an intellectual purpose, but they are now ready for the museum. Marx's categories, on the other hand, can be used to analyze automation, which he anticipated, economic development in the Third World, the crisis of the environment and so on. Indeed, much of the rest of this book will document how his magnificent insight into the conflict between social means of production, i.e., modern technology, and a private mode of production, ie., capitalism, is one of the most usable truths of the twentieth, and the twenty-first, century.

The conclusion of Marx's analysis is also utterly germane to the present situation. It is, indeed, a matter of economic necessity to create the good society. For as long as the fantastic creator of wealth, socialized man, is trapped within private and anti-social institutions, his cooperatively developed but antagonistically organized genius will threaten him. And the point of socialism, if one can sum up the three volumes of *Das Kapital* in a phrase, is that man, having socialized almost everything else, must now socialize himself.

# V I

# *The American Exception*

MOST OF THE PEOPLE in the world today call the name of their dream "socialism." The word, to be sure, has many, and even contradictory, definitions. Yet its tremendous resonance obviously tells of a deep yearning for fundamental change among hundreds of millions of people.

America is the great exception.

The American worker, unlike his counterpart in all the other advanced nations, thinks and speaks well of capitalism. Even in the 1930s, when the system was in even more of a shambles here than in Europe, there was still no socialist outburst. And though many students and intellectuals in the sixties and early seventies have begun to subject the society to an explicitly radical critique, there is certainly no mass movement in that direction. The United States is thus almost the only country on the face of the globe where "socialism" is a bad word.

Scholars have been explaining this situation for more than a half a century. As early as 1906, when the Socialist Party of Eugene Victor Debs was still in its ascendancy, Werner Sombart developed what was to become the most popular theory to account for it. In the United States, Sombart said, "all the socialist utopias have foundered upon roast beef and apple pie." Sombart himself thought that this phenomenon was temporary and that the moment would eventually come when socialism would be a force among the millions. But those who restated his basic insight usually made it absolute: Because of its enormous wealth, America was in the past, is in the present, and will be in the future, immune to socialism.

In recent years this thesis has been internationalized. While Europeans were debating Marxian subtleties, one is told, Americans were revolutionizing social existence. As a result of the unprecedented affluence of this country the class struggle and its militant myths have begun to disappear and arguments over the division of the social product have become pragmatic and nonviolent. As the countries of the Old World join this wave of the future, their political movements will be Americanized along with everything else. Then there will be, some prestigious intellectuals said, an "end to ideology"—which was a polite way of saying an end to socialism. Thus Sombart's roast beef and apple pie were turning into a global force.

That is bad history and bad sociology. In fact, America was never as well fed as this argument assumes and isn't even today. And, paradoxically, to the limited degree that this country has enjoyed some material advantages as compared to Europe, it has been an incitement to riot. Indeed, it is quite possible that in the coming period a maldistributed and anti-social affluence will radicalize more people than hunger ever did.

This chapter is primarily about the bad history underlying the complacent vision of an unradical America. In reality, socialism in America suffered not from the conservatism of the nation, but from its irrepressible utopianism. Secondly, there were laboristic tendencies of the kind that led to a mass socialist movement in England even in the heyday of that arch anti-socialist, Samuel Gompers. And thirdly, the American living standard, and the politics that it inspired, were—and are—much more complex than Sombart's metaphor of shoals of roast beef and apple pie suggest.

I do not go into these things simply to set the historical record straight but because they prepare the way for understanding the most bizarre fact of all: that there is a mass social democratic movement in America today in a pro-capitalist, anti-socialist disguise. Chapter X will describe it; this chapter will outline some of the circumstances that led to it. For there were precursors to this strange phenomenon and Karl Marx and Friedrich Engels confronted them.

None of this is to deny that American capitalism is exceptional.

Of course it is, which is one of the main reasons that the socialist impulse in this country expressed itself in a bourgeois rhetoric. And the components of that exceptionalism are fairly easy to outline. Phillip Taft, a sympathetic biographer of Gompers, writes about "the absence of feudalism in America, the greater class mobility, the higher standards of living, the right to vote for all male citizens as well as the greater social democracy." That is about the same as Lenin's view of the "long-standing political liberty and the exceptionally favorable conditions, in comparison with other countries, for the deep-going and widespread development of capitalism" in the United States.

The exceptional aspects of the American experience are, in short, so obvious that political foes can agree upon them. These unique elements will be acknowledged here, but the emphasis will be upon that which is new in the American past: that this country has a social democratic tradition that, for good historical reasons, never learned to pronounce its own name. With that understood, we can then turn, later on, in Chapter X, to our invisible mass movement—the American social democracy.[1]

# I

America was too socialistic for socialism. That was the original problem.

In 1824 Robert Owen, the British socialist, came to the United States. He had already become something of a pariah in the polite society of his homeland because of his irreverent views about religion. But on his journey to Harmony, Indiana, the town he had just bought from Father George Rapp for $135,000 for an Owenite community, he received an enthusiastic welcome at every step. On February 25, 1825, Owen spoke in the House of Representatives in Washington before an audience that included the outgoing President, James Monroe, the President-elect, John Quincy Adams (who took time out from working on his inaugural address to attend), many members of the House and Senate, Justices of the Supreme Court and Cabinet officers.

In the course of his remarks, Owen told this distinguished assemblage that it was necessary to build a new society in the United States. In the American future that he evoked "the degrading and pernicious practices in which we are now trained, of buying cheap and selling dear, will be rendered wholly unnecessary: for so long as this principle shall govern the transaction of men nothing really great or noble can be expected from mankind.

"The whole trading system," Owen continued, "is one of deception: one by which one engaged in it is necessarily trained to endeavor to obtain advantages over others, and in which the interest of all is opposed to each, and in consequence, no one can attain the advantages that, under another and better system, might be, with far less labor, and without risk, secured in perpetuity to all.

"The consequence of this inferior trading system is to give a very injurious surplus of wealth and power to the few, and to inflict poverty and subjection on the many."

In the 1820s there was no other nation on the face of the earth where capitalism could be thus denounced, and socialism extolled, in a meeting convened by the political elite. There were many reasons for the remarkable event: the United States was born of revolution, possessed of vast lands where a nation had to be created, and from the Great Awakening of 1734 had been periodically inspired by a religious spirit which sought to build the Kingdom of God upon the North American earth. In such a society it was not at all strange that a British utopian with a scheme for remaking the world should present it to the President and the Congress.

But Owenism in the United States did not survive the 1820s, and in the early 1830s a trade-union movement emerged as the channel for social idealism. So it was that the first workers' parties anywhere in the world were formed in New York and Philadelphia in 1829 and 1830. At a time when none of the working people of Europe had the right to vote, labor elected the president of the Carpenters' Union in New York to the state Assembly. The "free gift" of the ballot in the United States made it possible for the nascent proletariat—actually, its members were artisans because the factory workers at that time were mainly women and therefore voteless—to assert itself very early.

The rhetoric of this development, particularly that of the middle-class reformers like Frances Wright, Robert Dale Owen (Robert Owen's son) and George Henry Evans, often had a strikingly Marxist sound. In November, 1830, Frances Wright wrote, "What distinguishes the present from every other struggle in which the human race has been engaged is that the present is evidently, openly and acknowledgedly, a war of class and this war is universal; it is the ridden people of the earth who are struggling to throw from their backs the 'booted and spurred' riders whose legitimate title to starve as well as to work them to death will no longer pass current; it is labor rising up against idleness, industry against money."

It was small wonder that Marx looked upon this movement with enthusiasm and wrote in 1845 that the Americans "have had their own socialist democratic school since 1829." But paradoxically, it was the very favorable situation, which gave rise to the political, and even socialist, working-class movements of the 1820s and 1830s, that made the organization of the American Left so difficult. In Europe it was precisely the outcast status of the worker, his formal exclusion from the political process, that forced him to that solidarity that expressed itself in socialism. In America, by way of contrast, it was the existence of universal male suffrage that made the non-working-class parties try to co-opt and absorb the workers' demands at a very early moment in the nation's history.

And yet, so pervasive was the utopian spirit that when the crisis of 1837 destroyed the labor organizations, there was a revival of communitarian socialism. The ideas of Owen and Fourier won a new generation of American disciples, among them Horace Greeley, the editor of the New York *Tribune,* who was later to hire Marx as a European correspondent. This was the period when Marx and Engels were themselves moving toward their first definition of socialism, and they reacted to the American events with a giddy joy. The New World, they concluded, offered exceptionally favorable conditions for the growth of a socialist movement.

As Engels saw it in 1845, settlements like New Harmony, Indiana, and Zoar, Ohio, proved that socialism could work because "people who live in community live better and work less, have more reason to improve their minds, and . . . are better and more moral than their neighbors who still have private property." And in 1847 Marx anticipated the argument that the lack of feudalism was central to the American experience but used it to argue that the country would therefore be more socialist, not less: "The question of private property, which is world-historical in our age, has meaning only in a modern, bourgeois society. The more developed such a society, the more the bourgeois dominates the nation and its state power, the more harsh the social question becomes, harsher in France than in Germany, in England than in

France, in the constitutional monarchy than in the absolute monarchy, in the Republic than in the constitutional monarchy. So, e.g., the collusion over the credit system and speculation is nowhere more acute than in North America. Nowhere is *social* inequality more severe as in the Eastern states of North America, since it is not in the least concealed by political inequality."

Indeed, throughout their lifetimes Marx and Engels could never decide whether the exceptional characteristics of American society boded good or evil for the socialist movement. During the Civil War, when they enthusiastically supported the North, their partisanship clearly got the better of their judgment. In congratulating Lincoln on his reelection in 1864, they rightly observed that many European workers had sided with him. But they then went on to say that the workers "were the true bearers of political power in the North" and to describe Lincoln himself as a "single-minded, steely son of the working class." Those propositions are political romance.

However, there were moments during the Civil War when Marx and Engels were much more realistic than in the letter to Lincoln. In 1862 Marx wrote to Engels, "the way in which the North conducts the war is exactly what one would expect from a *bourgeois* republic where fraud is enthroned." In the 1880s in his correspondence with Sorge, Engels often emphasized how untheoretical the Americans were and even held that "the *Manifesto*, like all the shorter works of Marx and myself, is far too difficult for Americans at the present time."

But however much Marx and Engels vacillated on the question of whether America would be particularly receptive or particularly hostile to socialism, they came quite early to a stunning conclusion: that the Left in the United States would first develop as a pro-capitalist movement.

Marx arrived at this most dialectical thesis in 1846. A German socialist, Hermann Kriege, was the editor of a New York paper, *Der Volks-Tribun.* In a short time he had caught the infectious utopianism of his new homeland and was writing that "the *Holy Spirit* of community must develop itself out of the hearts of love." When he became more explicit, he championed the panacea of free land: "Every poor man will be transformed into a useful member of human society as soon as one provides them with the opportunity to be productively active. That is guaranteed as soon as the society gives him a piece of land upon which he can provide for his family. If the enormous land surface (the 1400 million acres of American state property) will be taken away from business and provided, in limited quantities, to labor, that will in a single blow put an end to poverty in America. . . . "

Marx and Engels ridiculed the economic theory behind this proposal. By making the land grant inalienable, they said, Kriege was trying to forbid industrial progress and concentration by fiat and ignored the fact that the farmers with the most productive soil would soon be masters and all the rest serfs. And even if the scheme went into effect, they said, in a matter of forty years population increases would exhaust the land reserve and poverty would start up all over again. Then came the shrewd, and completely anti-sectarian, conclusion: "If Kriege had understood the free-land movement as the first form of the proletarian movement made necessary under certain specific conditions, as a movement based upon the living conditions of a class which necessarily must become communist, then we would have no disagreement with him. If he had demonstrated *how communist tendencies in America must originally appear in this seemingly anti-communist, agrarian form [in dieser scheinbar allem Kommunismus wider-sprechenden agrarischen Form],* there would be no argument."

In the United States socialism would first appear as anti-socialism, and this was a necessity rooted in American conditions! In pointing out that Marx and Engels identified this strange trend, I do not mean to suggest that they prophesied the anti-socialist social democracy that will be described in Chapter X. Both of them clearly expected that in the not-too-long run the exigencies of capitalist production would bring forth a socialist movement in the United States just as in Europe. Yet they were aware that a confused pro-capitalist radicalism was not only possible and progressive in the United States, but inevitable as well. Given the great land mass of America, the workers necessarily would look toward the agrarian West for their salvation.

There they would envisage not a collective system of production, but every man as an independent farmer. As economics, the scheme was preposterous; as politics, it was a vital expression of mass hostility to industrial capitalism. This was the dream that led to the Homestead Act of 1862, and it still gripped the imagination of the masses in 1886 when Henry George ran for mayor of New York on a platform of nationalizing the land (more on that event in the next section).

It did indeed turn out, as Marx expected, that the hope of escaping from the class struggle to free land was a myth. In the 1860s it took $1,000 to make a go of a farm, and the cost increased later in the century. So for every industrial worker who became a farmer, twenty farmers became city dwellers. And for every free farm acquired by a farmer, nine were purchased by railroads, speculators or by the Government itself.

And yet, if free land did not actually fulfill its mythic function, the people did not give up the dream that it would. Instead, of abandoning their panacea and turning to socialism, the workers remained under the spell of agrarian radicalism. The farmers "stood in the forefront of the battle against the control of the society by business" and as Greenbackers and Populists they sought to use Federal power to fight the railroads and the bankers and to provide the economic basis for a society of small producers. And more often than not, it was the militancy of the wheat farmers on the plains, of the metal miners in the West and of poor whites and blacks in the South that dominated the urban movement. Thus, in Richard Hofstadter's brilliant phrase, it was "entrepreneurial radicalism" that held sway in American protest politics from the Jacksonians to the Populists.

As a result of this situation, the American unions could only develop in opposition to middle-class utopians seeking salvation in the fields. As far back as 1829 Frances Wright's insistence on advocating that children be taken away from their parents so that they could get a properly egalitarian education unquestionably hastened the collapse of the Workingmen's Party. From that time on, the visionaries attempted to divert the unions from the actual job of fighting for wages and hours and other mundane gains and to orient them towards this or that panacea. In the National Labor Union after the Civil War the reformers were so effective in driving the workers out of the organization that the First International would not even send a delegate to its convention.

Marx and Engels themselves had a personal confrontation with the exuberance of American reform. In the 1870s Victoria Woodhull and Tennessee Claflin took over a section of the First International in the United States and preached, among a wide variety of doctrines, free love. The movement, Engels wrote, had been "invaded by bourgeois swindlers, free-love advocates, spiritual enthusiasts, Shakers, etc." And, in an outraged mood, he reported that the Woodhull forces held a meeting in New York in May,

1872: "They united all the male and female cranks in America. . . . *And Mrs. Victoria Woodhull was nominated for the Presidency of the United States, and in the name of the International!"*

This encounter with the feminist free-lovers could be seen as a moment of comic relief in the history of socialism if it did not so clearly illustrate the difficulty of building a socialist movement in a country in which so many people were so enthusiastic, but vague, about creating the future. And in the labor movement this meant, ironically, that the Marxists had to line up with those who were to become the most effective "pure and simple" trade unionists—and the most effective anti-Marxists.

At the same time, Marx's American followers had to fight against socialist, as well as agrarian, sectarianism. The German-American followers of Lassalle were, like their master, for state aid to cooperatives as the main solution to the social question. So in the name of socialism they fought the unions, which they regarded as a diversion from the real struggle. During the great strike wave of 1877, for instance, they told the workers of the "futility of planless revolts." The Marxists, on the other hand, fought against premature efforts to establish labor and socialist parties in the 1870s and put their emphasis on building trade unions. The North American Central Committee of the First International reported to Marx and his associates in 1872, "Reform Societies do not understand the labor question, and yet these societies are continually growing and working men are being led astray by them."

With the rise of the American Federation of Labor (AFL) in the 1880s, the Marxist perspective was fulfilled. The Knights of Labor were the last big organization that, in the name of labor, mixed workers and middle-class reformers together in a humanist freemasonry. When it was defeated and the genuine trade unionists prevailed, the Marxists, who had sided with the latter, were promptly classified among the crackpots whom they had helped to vanquish. The unions had moved, in Selig Perlman's analysis, from the political struggle against monopoly characteristic of the reformers to a "stable and job-conscious trade unionism."

In the conventional view the anti-ideological unionism thus defined in the 1880s and 1890s with Marxist support has persisted to this very day. That, as much of this chapter and Chapter X will show, is not the case. But what is particularly relevant at this point in the analysis is that it was not the anti-socialism of the American experience, but rather its amorphous, uncritical utopianism that was a major factor making the organization of a modern socialist movement so difficult. Therefore, even as brilliant a thinker as Joseph Schumpeter must be counted as wrong when he said, ". . . that great sociologist, the man in the street, has been right once more. He said that socialism and socialists were un-American." In some ways the problem was exactly opposite to the one Schumpeter defined: in the nineteenth century America was too socialistic to become socialist.

There is a related aspect to this paradox of an America too radical for socialism. As Leon Samson formulated it, Americanism, the official ideology of the society, became a kind of "substitutive socialism." The European ruling classes, which derived from, or aped, the aristocracy, were open in their contempt for the proletariat. But in the United States equality, and even classlessness, the creation of wealth for all and political liberty were extolled in the public schools. It is, of course, true that this was sincere verbiage which concealed an ugly reality, but nonetheless it had a profound impact upon the national consciousness. "The idea that everyone can be a capitalist," Samson wrote in a perceptive insight, "is an American concept of capitalism. *It is a socialist concept of capitalism.*" And that, Marx had understood in his quarrel with Kriege in 1846, was why socialism would first appear in this country in a capitalist guise. What he could not possibly anticipate was that this dialectical irony would still be in force over a hundred years later.

So it was America's receptivity to utopia, not its hostility, that was a major factor inhibiting the development of a socialist movement. The free gift of the ballot and the early emergence of working-class parties were portents of assimilation, not revolution. The ubiquity of panaceas within the reform movement tended to discredit serious proposals for the future and even forced the Marxists to ally themselves within the early labor movement with the "pure and simple" trade unionists. Finally, the country's image of itself contained so many socialist elements that one did not have to go to a separate movement opposed to the status quo in order to give vent to socialist emotions.[2]

## II

In the last two decades of the nineteenth century the brutal triumph of industrial capitalism and the trusts began to force America out of its agrarian reveries.

In the conventional interpretation of this turning point, an organized labor movement emerged under Samuel Gompers and wisely and decisively rejected socialism in the 1890s. The Socialist Party had a brief moment of Debsian glory between 1901 and 1912, when it reached its electoral high point, and then entered into a process of steady, irreversible decline. The Progressives, who were eclectic and nonideological as befits a genuinely American group, were the real victors as job orientation prevailed over class consciousness, pragmatism over socialism, and Woodrow Wilson prepared the way for Franklin D. Roosevelt.

I read those years differently. The AFL did indeed reject socialism in the nineties and take its stand for "pure and simple" unionism and a "voluntarist" opposition to state intervention. But history would not allow it to act upon that choice, for events pushed labor more and more toward politics and the acceptance of Federal action. By the end of World War I the trade unionists were moving toward acceptance of the socialist immediate program which they had rejected in the 1890s, and in 1922 they took the unprecedented step of formally allying with the Socialist Party in the Conference for Progressive Political Action. In 1924 labor supported the La Follette candidacy, an action that anticipated the political involvements of the Depression years.

Thus the social democratic impulse in American life did not, as the Debsians had thought it would, lead to the growth of a mass socialist movement on the German model, where the party predated and dominated the union. Rather it worked along the same lines as in England, politicalizing the unions, a fact that some of the perceptive socialists had noted by the end of the First World War. In the course of these developments the class struggle in America was more fierce than in any European country. That is one reason, among many, to reject the thesis that the high standards of living in this country—Sombart's roast beef and apple pie—were what kept it from moving Left. For the really unique factor in this period was not the anti-socialist wealth of the society but the immigrant character of its working class.

American history, in short, moved between 1877 and 1937 toward the emergence of a labor and social democratic movement. Because of the special quality of the national experience, it did so in a crabbed, tortured and shamefaced fashion and, just as in the case of the workers fighting for free land, refused to utter the name of socialism even as it lurched to the Left.

It was in 1877 that the "cyclonic force" of the railroad strike appeared as an omen of the turmoil to come. It began after several years of unemployment and centered on the issue of arbitrary wage cuts. Starting in Martinsburg, West Virginia, it immediately caused the authorities to call in Federal troops to restore order. Even so, the movement spread to Baltimore, where the railroad depot was burned down, and then throughout the East. By midsummer, 100,000 men were idle. There was constant violence—thirteen were killed and forty-three wounded in Reading, Pennsylvania, nineteen were killed and more than a hundred wounded in Chicago—and eventually two thirds of the nation's rail mileage was affected.

The nation's capitalist innocence was being destroyed. Between 1877 and 1940 the "United States has the bloodiest and most violent history of any industrial nation in the world." There were Homestead, the great Pullman strike of the nineties, the "Colorado Labor War" of the first decade of the century, the Seattle General Strike of 1919, the Little Steel Massacre of 1937. And in each one of these explosive encounters workers were pitted against the police and soldiers in pitched battle.

There is one important aspect of the pervasive violence of the American class struggle that bears upon the theory that it was the high standard of living in the United States that kept the workers relatively contented. It also subverts the happy expectation of the end-of-ideologists that the rest of this century, and the next, will be unradical because the workers are affluent. In point of fact, to the degree that America was better fed and freer than Europe before World War I—and the figures, as will be seen shortly, are ambiguous on this count—it was a provocation to insurgency. In Europe, as Seymour Martin Lipset has noted, the rigid class structure and relative poverty had the effect of keeping the workers in their "place" over considerable periods of time. In this country the egalitarian ideology and the lack of clearly defined limits to social mobility made for greater individual discontent among the workers.

The unrest exploded in 1877 and the years up to the turn of the century were to be particularly turbulent. After 1877 businessmen became enthusiastic about the National Guard, which they saw as an anti-strike and anti-revolutionary force. And in August, 1882, M. A. Hardacker wrote in the *Atlantic Monthly*, "Our era of prosperity and happy immunity from those social diseases which are the danger and humiliation of Europe is passing away.

Optimistic as we are, we cannot fail to know that the increasing proportion of the incapable among us is repeating here the problem of the Old World . . . every year brings the conditions of American labor into closer likeness to those of the Old World. An American species of socialism is inevitable."

But when the moment of upsurge came, it was like the free-land movement forty years before: the turn to the Left was made in the name of a bourgeois, not a socialist, utopia.

In 1886 the trade unions went through the year of the "Great Upheaval." The membership of the Knights of Labor jumped to one million, the AFL grew rapidly and seventy-three labor parties were formed in twenty-six states. The spearhead of this development was in New York where Henry George, running as a labor candidate, was almost elected mayor. George's principal plank was the "single tax," a proposal to nationalize all land rent and thereby solve the problems of society. That, as Marx had written to Sorge in 1881, was a radical capitalist demand. "It is," he said (quoting an earlier polemic against Proudhon), "a frank expression of the hatred felt by the industrial capitalist against the landlord, who appears to him useless and functionless within the totality of bourgeois production." Under such a scheme, Marx argued, big business would not have to pay taxes, the means of production would remain in private hands and capitalism would be strengthened, not attacked.

So in 1886 the American urban workers were still obsessed with the notion that their emancipation was tied to the land and they backed a candidate who stood for a more efficient capitalism, not socialism. Even though Engels shared Marx's critique of George's theories and therefore of his party's program, he supported the campaign enthusiastically. The crucial fact, he wrote Sorge, "is always the constituting of the workers as an independent party. That the first program of this party is still confused and explicitly defective, that Henry George carries its banner, is an unavoidable inconvenience, but also only temporary." Thus Engels lashed out at the German-American socialists who refused to support the George movement simply because it had an anti-Marxist program.

As it turned out, the independent labor parties faded almost as rapidly as they appeared and Engels' enthusiasm, as so often was the case, was disappointed. But there are two very important facts about this incident that bear upon the central themes of this chapter. First, as late as 1886 Engels understood that the process he and Marx had identified in 1846—a tendency toward socialism with capitalist slogans—was still dominant. And secondly, a decisive moment had arrived in American working-class history. After 1886 the Knights of Labor, a sort of Masonic order for workers and middle-class reformers that often opposed strikes, lost their influence and Samuel Gompers came to the fore. He had, as we have seen, the support of the Marxists in his struggle against the utopians. One of the main reasons he turned on his old allies was that they, unlike Engels, were unwilling to tolerate the dialectical complexities of the American Left.

The great and abiding sin of American socialism has been sectarianism: the tendency to counterpose the socialist vision of a complete transformation to the partial demands and ideological imprecisions of men and women engaged in a struggle for their daily bread. In the early years in particular, this sectarian attitude was a reflection of the actual living experience of the socialists. Between 1850 and 1890 almost all of the socialists in America— and they rarely numbered more than a few thousand—were German. They "lived in the penumbra of society, confined in their own neighborhoods in the cities, spoke their own language, published their own newspapers, organized their own parties and carried on their own disputes—all quite remote from the concerns of native Americans."

Those among them who followed Lasalle had no use for pure and simple trade unionism, disparaged strikes and dogmatically insisted that the political movement was the only one that counted. Even the Marxists, who had a sound position in theory, often tended to look contemptuously upon the untheoretical Americans. As Engels wrote in a bitter letter to Sorge in 1890, "The anti-Socialist laws [Bismarck's illegalization of the German social democracy which forced many of its activists to flee to the United States] were a misfortune, not for Germany but for America, to which the last of the louts were consigned."

These German socialists were "louts" [Knoten] to Engels because of their rigidity, their mechanical application of Marxian principles to American society. They did not understand, he said, that America was "without a feudal past and therefore proud of bourgeois organization and will escape from the old, traditional categories of thought only through praxis." Americans would not, as the German emigrés thought, be won to socialism ideologically;

they would come to it as a practical necessity. They thus sometimes moved toward socialism with capitalist banners.

A little before Engels wrote to Sorge an event occurred which
clearly had a role in turning Gompers against the socialists. In
1888 a dispute arose as to whether the Socialist Labor Party
could be affiliated to an AFL body. Gompers, who had gone
through so much agony establishing the principle that labor
organizations were unions, understandably opposed the idea. But
the SLPers were as obdurate as Engels pictured them and forced
a day-and-a-half debate of the question at the next convention
of the AFL. "The conflict was an important one," Henry Pelling
writes, "partly because it threw Gompers, who was as yet by no
means an anti-Socialist, into a defensive attitude against the
Socialist movement; but also because, owing to the uncompromis-
ing tactics of their leaders it alienated a substantial section of the
Socialists altogether from the AF of L." Gompers was so upset
by the incident that he wrote Engels a very respectful letter in
which he described himself as a "student of your writings and
those of Marx," and told Sorge that he would abide by Engels'
judgment in the matter. Engels, unfortunately, never answered
him.

It was in this context of doctrinaire, sectarian socialists quarrel-
ing with an AFL leader who had good reason to be suspicious of
reformers within the labor movement that one must understand
the fateful debates that took place in 1893 and 1894. At the 1893
Convention of the Federation, Thomas J. Morgan, a socialist delegate from the Machinists in Chicago, introduced a "Political
Programme" based on the eleven planks of the Independent
Labour Party in England. The American movement was particularly susceptible to British examples since the AFL had modeled
itself on the Trades Union Congress in that country. The tenth of
the eleven points endorsed "the collective ownership by all the
people of all the means of production and consumption." (The
other demands included compulsory education, the eight-hour
day, the nationalization of the telegraphs, telephones, railroads
and mines.) The Convention refused to recommend the program
"favorably" for membership discussion—by a vote of 1,253 to
1,182—but did propose that the trade unionists discuss it in
anticipation of a vote at the 1894 convention.

In 1894 all the planks other than the tenth were easily endorsed,
and there are scholars who feel that the workers in the AFL were

for the entire program, including collective ownership. But the Gompers leadership maneuvered a defeat for Plank Ten and then argued that the whole program had been defeated. Typically, Gompers attacked the collective ownership proposition, not on its merits, but on the grounds that its adoption would drive workers away from, and even out of, the AFL. But whatever his motives, the event signified a major defeat for the socialists in the organized labor movement.

The effect of this setback was then compounded by Daniel De Leon. A brilliant, utterly intransigent Marxist, De Leon had joined the Socialist Labor Party in 1890 and rapidly become its leading spokesman. After the 1894 rejection of the political program, De Leon led his followers in the establishment of a Socialist Trades and Labor Alliance, a dual union competitive with the AFL. Had he become an employer and chained his workers to the machine, he could have done nothing to more effectively outrage the leaders of the AFL. From that time on, Gompers became increasingly hostile to socialism.

So the sectarianism of the American socialists had more than a little to do with their own early failure. Yet, is it then true, as Howard Quint has suggested, that had they "triumphed over Gompers in 1894, conceivably the whole course of American labor and political history might have been altered?" I think not. For the faults of the socialists were not simply individual and psychological. They were the almost inevitable consequence of an attempt to apply European categories to a country in which, for more than half a century, the effective anti-capitalist mass movement had defined its goals in capitalist terms. But even more to the point, the AFL reversed its 1894 decision over the next thirty years, only it never mentioned that somewhat embarrassing fact publicly. The needs of the American workers forced them to organize politically as a class, and that, as Engels had so well understood, was the decisive criterion marking a move to the Left.[3]

That transformation did not occur quickly. When Gompers turned against the socialists in 1894, he went to the opposite extreme, advocating a laborite version of the pure laissez-faire ideology. His philosophy was "voluntarist": hostile to all social legislation on the part of government; friendly toward the more sophisticated employers who would give some kind of acceptance to trade unionism. It is this phase in the history of the American labor movement that the scholars think of when they stress the enormous qualitative difference between the European and American experience. Unfortunately, most of them do not notice that it didn't last very long.

Gompers' voluntarism contained curious elements of Marxism and syndicalism. One of the few propositions the AFL president retained from his socialistic youth was the thesis that the capitalist state was necessarily an instrument of the bourgeoisie. Therefore —and on this count he agreed with the ultra-Leftists in the Debsian Socialist Party who fought against the endorsement of any immediate demands upon the existing order—it was dangerous for the workers to rely on the government for social legislation. It was from this point of view that the AFL opposed health and unemployment insurance as well as old-age pensions. Indeed, Gompers once went out to three Pacific coast states and helped defeat referenda in favor of the eight-hour day.

But this opposition to social legislation was not simply based on Gompers' youthful memories of the Marxian theory of the state. In part, it represented a profoundly, and understandably, American distrust of a government that had so often been used to break strikes. And in part, it was a shrewd organizer's policy not to divert the workers' attention from collective bargaining, where the AFL was their representative, toward political action. Therefore when laws were proposed that did not compete with the union, i.e., dealt with matters beyond the reach of collective bargaining, the AFL was for them: legislation for women limiting hours of work, child labor laws, the eight-hour day for Government workers, and so on.

And yet, however explicable it is in retrospect, it was of considerable consequence that the chief spokesman for organized labor in the United States was for a period of time a champion of laissez-faire economics and, in the National Civic Federation, the co-worker of shrewd corporate leaders like Mark Hanna, J. P. Morgan and August Belmont. But this voluntarism and class collaboration could not prevail very long because the problems confronting the AFL membership would simply not allow it. The Federation had already begun to move tentatively toward the Democratic Party in 1908, and in 1912, when Woodrow Wilson was elected, the unions involved themselves in mainstream politics and worked for a labor reform program. Wilson signed the Clayton Act which officially said that labor was not a commodity (and therefore, the AFL leaders wrongly thought, protected unions from anti-trust prosecutions); he appointed a union man Secretary of Labor; and he gave the AFL the feeling that it had a friend in the White House. So by the election of 1916, the voluntarist philosophy notwithstanding, the unions were becoming much more deeply involved in politics. And in 1917, as Thomas Brooks has noted, Wilson became the first American President to ever address a labor convention when he appeared before the AFL.

After World War I the politicalization of the American workers proceeded at an even faster pace. A majority of the rank and file, Phillip Taft has written, had come to reject the classic Gompers position and favor much more forthright political and legislative action. The railroad unions became the focus of an opposition to Gompers which extended far beyond his traditional socialist rivals. It was a sign of the power of this movement that the Federation overrode Gompers' opposition and came out in favor of the nationalization of the railroads after the end of the war.

In 1919 there was a vast strike wave followed by a vigorous open-shop campaign on the part of American business under the euphemistic title of the "American Plan." But as unemployment rose to five million in 1921, and there were wage cuts throughout the nation, labor found it difficult to fight back. When a boom began in 1922 the unions were combative, particularly because the Harding Administration had so often used the injunction against workers. It was during this period that the Mineworkers came out in favor of public ownership of the mines. The Federation itself responded in 1920 by adopting a reconstruction program that put it on record as favoring "industrial democracy" and a fairly wide-ranging number of legislative reforms.

During these years there was also growing sentiment for a new party. The Chicago Federation of Labor started an Independent Labor Party in 1918, New York followed suit in 1919 and a National Labor Party was formed in November of that year. The Socialist Party was generally hostile to these developments—it regarded itself as the only center of authentic working-class independence—but there were some members who were sympathetic to it. The Labor Party vote in 1920 was disappointing —about a fourth of Debs' total—yet the movement continued to grow.

Hence in 1922 the AFL unions joined in the Conference on Progressive Political Action and allowed the Socialist Party to affiliate formally with it. This was, as Taft has recognized, a "major change" in AFL strategy. One might even argue that it amounted to a repeal of the 1894 decision against independent labor political action. And, in fact, the CPPA led to the La Follette campaign of 1924, again with the socialists as a publicly acknowledged component of the coalition.

The significance of this development has been obscured by a number of factors. The unions were disappointed by their 1924 venture in political independence; the Socialist Party was split over the Russian Revolution; and employers became more subtle in their anti-unionism in the twenties. So from 1924 to the Great Depression the AFL reverted back to Gompers' voluntarism. But as the subsequent history of the movement was to show, this was only an episode. The main trend, which emerged so strongly in the thirties, was toward labor political action.

Thus American workers had to organize unions on a class basis in order to defend their economic interests, for agrarian utopias provided no real solution to their problems. Then, even though Samuel Gompers labored valiantly that it might be otherwise, they were forced to involve themselves in politics on that same class basis. In the process, they were not at all like German unions, which were founded by socialists and were political from the outset, but rather followed the English pattern in which pragmatic anti-socialists were dragged toward socialism by the press of events.

So the basic drive of working people in this country was the same as in Europe: capitalism did not satisfy their fundamental needs and they had to struggle as a class, both economically and politically, against the system. What was exceptional was that this essentially social democratic development was carried out in the name of capitalist, rather than of socialist, utopias, a fact with roots in the American past and, as will be seen in a moment, in the immigrant character of the working class before World War I. For several generations now scholars—and not a few socialists—have been mesmerized by the bourgeois surface of these events and did not notice their socialist core. That is one of the main reasons why the mass American social democracy, which will be described in Chapter X, is still invisible.[4]

### III

But what, then, of those shoals of apple pie and roast beef?

One answer is that they did not exist, at least not to the extent that Sombart and his devotees believed. This point is worth emphasizing in some detail because it relates to a crucial contempory misunderstanding: that the America of the 1970s has given an adequate standard of living to the majority of its people. That, as Chapter X will show, is simply not the case: and, as this section will demonstrate, it never was. Secondly, to the extent that the United States did enjoy some material advantages as against Europe, it is psychologically simplistic to assume that this would automatically make the citizen here more content. This is an important reality to examine historically since it is so relevant to all the end-of-ideology theories which claim that affluence is now rendering both the class struggle and socialism obsolete.

Finally, there are two key factors that do account for what is unquestionably exceptional in American socialist history. Friedrich Engels was one of the first to state them, simply but cogently: "There are two circumstances that have, for many years, kept the full consequences of the capitalist system in America from coming to the light of day. These are the easy availability of cheap land and the huge immigrations." The first of these has already been analyzed, the second will figure prominently in what follows.

To begin with a fundamental fact: The typical American never did gorge himself on roast beef and apple pie. He still doesn't.

John R. Commons, the great labor historian, was the author of the theory that the American worker was job-oriented rather than class-conscious like his European counterpart. Yet in Volume I of the *History of Labor in the United States,* which Commons edited, Don D. Lescohier commented, "Undergoing the vicissitudes of repeated periods of unemployment, experiencing in many occupations a less rapid rise of wages than of living costs, they [the wage workers] could see that while some groups, like the building mechanics, had made distinct progress, other groups, like the iron and steel workers, employees in meat packing plants, cotton mills, saw mills, tobacco and clothing factories, had not held their own against the rapidly rising cost of living."

Suggesting that life in those days was lived on a treadmill, Lescohier writes, "From 1899 to 1915, gains in real wages were slight, the gains of good years being about canceled out by the losses of bad years." There were advances during the war—the railroad unions thrived when the government took over the industry, which was one reason why they favored nationalization after the Armistice—but then came the post-war recession and the employer offensive. In comparative terms, the average American factory hand in 1909 worked a little less than his British similar, received 2.3 times the wages, but paid out 2.08 times the rent. America was, in short, not that much better situated than the country that was witnessing the simultaneous rise of Liberal radicalism and Labour Partyism.

But in one important respect being a worker was much more difficult in the United States than in Europe during much of this period. In the absence of social legislation, "conditions of work were allowed in the United States that would not have been tolerated in other industrial countries. This was because the workers who suffered most were usually immigrants who could make little protest and rarely possessed the vote." In 1893 one out of every ten operating employees on the railroads was injured in some way, and one out of every 115 was killed. Conditions improved somewhat in the years before the war, but the United States was still well behind European countries in safety and social legislation.

So the first problem with the abundance interpretation of American labor history—and the supposed contentment that made the workers impervious to socialist appeals—is that the facts do not support it, or do so only when the theory is so qualified as to be almost useless for explaining anything. Secondly, even to the limited extent that wages in the United States were better than in Europe—mainly for the relatively small minority of skilled, organized workers—there is no reason to believe that a higher standard of living necessarily makes for docile workers.

Under feudalism and in the early days of capitalism economic crisis took a brutally obvious form: recession and starvation went together. In the Hungry Forties of the nineteenth century in England Chartist protest increased in bad times and all but disappeared when prosperity returned in 1850. In those days a depression usually began in the agricultural sector as a result of a poor harvest. That made food in short supply, and by contracting the domestic market, threw men in the cities out of work at the same time. But after the 1850s, extreme hunger and economic crisis no longer necessarily went together since the industrial sector was becoming dominant and high unemployment was sometimes even accompanied by a fall in the cost of living. At this point the modern, specifically capitalist kind of radicalization began to appear: the insurgency took place after the dark days, not during them, for "the long-term depression factors . . . helped to accumulate inflammable material rather than to set it alight."

Indeed, the only evidence in recent times that it is low living standards that make people rebellious derives from a very special case: when a rising standard of living is interrupted by a sudden downturn. And even in this situation it is the good times that are the breeding grounds of radicalism, not the bad. In short, a sense of relative deprivation, of not getting a fair share of society's wealth, is much more provocative than straightforward misery: American industrial unions were organized in 1936 and 1937 when there was hope, not in the pit of the Depression in 1932, when there was despair.

So the data contradict the simplistic assumption that high living standards, where they did in fact exist, made America less Leftist than Europe. Indeed, the rise of the German Social Democratic Party took place under conditions that were relatively better than those in the United States (they were documented in Chapter IV). In Germany the nineties saw a rise in real wages, while these were bad times in the United States. And from the turn of the century until World War I conditions in the two countries were quite similar as workers raced on a treadmill to keep pace with inflation. It is this latter reality of uneven, insecure good times that helps explain why the AFL in that period broke with Gompersism, but not with Gompers.

There was, however, one mitigating factor in the American experience, and it, rather than the abundance of the society, was responsible for the slow, exceptional development of a social democracy. That was the impact of immigration upon the politics and social structure of the nation.

Around the mid-nineteenth century the immigrants were mainly poor Irish, who spoke English, and fairly skilled and sophisticated Germans and Scandinavians, who adapted rapidly to American life. But toward the end of the century the newcomers were South and East Europeans, who generally came from backward economies and peasant cultures, did not speak English and lacked urban skills. The Italians are a particularly rich example of what this meant. The first emigrants from Italy came from the more advanced areas of Rome and the north and went to South America where, in the developing areas of Brazil, Argentina and Uruguay, they played an important role as traders and merchants. But around 1900 those who came to the United States were from the poverty-stricken south and from Sicily.

Having left a pre-modern culture, they huddled together in the

American cities where they reestablished the old village loyalties. So the Italian workers in the construction industry were hired as crews and were under the control of *padroni*. Their ethnic consciousness thus made it extremely difficult to identify, much less resist, their exploiters, since the middleman with whom they dealt was one of their own countrymen. It was this pattern, repeated in different ways among the East Europeans, that made it so difficult for the AFL—or even the Industrial Workers of the World—to unionize the mass production hands. And the Socialist Party, as Morris Hillquit wrote in 1909, was "compelled to address the workers of this country in more than twenty different languages."

For Selig Perlman, the immigrant character of the American working class was one of the main reasons for the failure of socialism: "American labor remains one of the most heterogeneous laboring classes in existence—ethnically, linguistically, religiously and culturally. With a working class of such composition, to make socialism or communism the official 'ism' of the movement, would mean, even if other conditions permitted it, deliberately driving the Catholics, who are perhaps a majority in the American Federation of Labor, out of the labor movement, since with them an irreconcilable opposition to socialism is a matter of religious principle. Consequently, the only acceptable 'consciousness' for American labor as a whole is a 'job consciousness' with a 'limited' objective of 'wage and job control.' . . ."

Perlman's deductions are, if the previous analysis is correct, much too sweeping since, even in the Gompers period, American labor went far beyond mere job consciousness. Yet the religious aspect of the immigrant phenomenon did play a significant role. It was not so much the conscious, organized anti-socialism of the Catholic Church which was important—the Militia of Christ, the main Catholic anti-socialist group in the labor movement before World War I, never had more than seven hundred members and only a few functioning chapters—but the fact that the working class in this country was not alienated from religion, as in Italy and France, and belonged to a church that lacked the socialistic tradition of British dissenting Protestantism. And this was, of course, particularly true of the Irish, one of the most important nationalities in the AFL.

It was not just socialism that suffered from this situation. The AFL itself never reached out to the great mass of industrial workers, most of them participants in the later immigrations. In the 1910 census, for instance, the skilled workers numbered four million, the semi-skilled and the laborers almost seventeen million. The IWW made valiant attempts to organize the latter groups but they never achieved more than sporadic, episodic victories.

It is only when the Sombart thesis about American wealth subverting socialism is placed in this immigrant context, where the crucial factor is foreign birth rather than abundance, that it makes any sense. For it is true that many of the immigrants, even though living under objectively degrading conditions, saw their lot as improved compared to the old country. They thus had an impression of relative betterment, not relative deprivation. Indeed, this pattern can be observed in nineteenth-century Europe, where in the formative period of the working class the labor force was recruited from the rural areas and the "new recruits were often attracted by the prospect of better earnings, and other incentives, and consequently, for a time, were better contented." So in America, where between 1880 and 1920 the workers hailed from the countryside of the world, this effect was pronounced.

Finally, ethnic differences turned worker against worker. Isaac Hourwich made a shrewd assessment of this hostility at the time: "Though the introduction of machinery has had the tendency to reduce the relative number of skilled mechanics, yet the rapid pace of industrial expansion has increased the number of skilled and supervisory positions so fast that the English-speaking employees have had the opportunity to rise on the scale of occupations. This opportunity, however, was conditioned upon a corresponding increase of the total work force. It is only because the new immigrants had furnished the class of unskilled laborers that native workmen and older immigrants have risen to the place of an aristocracy of labor.

"The primary cause which has determined the movement of wages in the United States during the past thirty years has been the introduction of labor-saving machinery. The effect of the substitution of mechanical devices for human skill is the displacement of the skilled mechanic by the unskilled laborer." Therefore "the fact that most of these unskilled workers were immigrants disguised the substance of the change—the substitution of unskilled for skilled labor—and made it appear as the displacement of highly paid by cheap immigrant labor."

Thus in both the AFL and the Socialist Party there was hostility to the immigrants based on the mistaken impression that they were the cause of those displacements which, in fact, capitalism had created. Given this deep split in the working class and the fact that the mainly immigrant industrial workers stood outside of the organized labor movement, it is not at all surprising that the American social democracy developed one generation later than the European and in a unique way. Indeed, what is surprising in American history is the degree to which, despite the enormous differences between this country and the Continent, a class and political consciousness did emerge, even in the time of Gompers. Our past testifies not to the feebleness of the impulse to resist capitalism through economic and political organization, but to its extraordinary strength under the most adverse conditions.

In short, American history was exceptional, but that fact has been exaggerated out of all proportion by most students of our history. It does, indeed, account for why the social democratic movement in this country could not call itself by its proper name. That happened in part because the ubiquitous American utopianism, based on a vision of egalitarian and homesteading capitalism, tended to discredit the serious socialist attack upon the centers of modern industrial power. It also was a result of an immigrant working class which, for ethnic and religious reasons, could not unite behind a socialist banner, or even in trade unions. And paradoxically, to the extent that the vaunted wealth of the society did provide higher living standards for the minority in the AFL, it created the basis for a class political movement even under Gompers. The roast beef and apple pie were a radical factor in our past.

And all of these complexities were precursors of that present reality which will be analyzed in Chapter X: of a mass social democracy in the United States which is invisible because, in typically American fashion, its socialistic aims are phrased in capitalistic rhetoric.[5]

# VII

## Socialism Discovers the World

ONE OF THE RICHEST chapters in the history of the Left, which is by no means finished, began when socialism discovered the world.

The utopian dream can be found in almost every culture. Yet the preconditions for acting on it—a technology of abundance and a conscious mass movement—first appeared in Europe and the lands of European settlement as a result of the capitalist revolution. What, then, was to be the attitude of socialists toward that majority of mankind who had not yet even reached the capitalist stage and the possibility of the good society? Were the non-Europeans destined to go through the same brutal process of capital accumulation that afflicted Europe and America—or were they to cram those miseries into an even more intense period of industrialization?

In trying to answer such questions the socialists took up themes so basic that they remain at the center of political discussion today. Marx first thought that capitalism was the wave of the future in the colonies, an idea that animated the liberal hopes of the Alliance for Progress a century later. He then changed his mind and suggested the possibility that those countries might skip the capitalist stage altogether, and that notion inspired Lenin, Stalin and Mao and motivates most of the leaders of the Third World at the present time.

After Marx's death the socialists won electoral battles and faced these questions as practical political problems. In the process they confronted a dilemma which has yet to be resolved: How do socialists act when they have enough power to influence, but not to basically change, capitalism? Must they either righteously, and ineffectively, abstain from exerting this influence, or should they use it and thus strengthen the system they hate by making its exploitation more rational and tolerable? V. I. Lenin did not even recognize that this was an issue, for he was in the underground, not in the parliamentary opposition. But his contribution to the debate over colonialism in which these questions were posed was momentous. In a theory that is now widely accepted throughout Asia, Africa and Latin America he said that capitalism in its advanced stage is necessarily imperialist and that socialists should therefore not concern themselves with making it more livable, but only with overthrowing it.

This chapter, then, is about a distant history which will probably not be finished until well into the twenty-first century.

# I

One of the most important questions in the Third World today is whether capitalism offers a way out of economic backwardness. Karl Marx was one of the first thinkers to face up to the issue and he erred by being much too pro-capitalist.

In *The Communist Manifesto* Marx had described a tidy, inevitable historical progress. Ancient society produced feudalism, feudalism produced capitalism, and capitalism was in the process of producing socialism. The internal development and class struggles of each system were seen as preparing the way for its successor until socialism would put an end to classes altogether. Applying this schema to the colonies, they would not be ready for a socialist revolution until they had first gone through a capitalist stage.

"The difficult question," Marx wrote to Engels in 1858, "is this: On the Continent the revolution is imminent and will immediately take on a socialist character. But will it not necessarily be crushed in this little corner, since in a much greater area the bourgeois society is still ascendant?" Thus socialism was still a possibility only for the European minority; the rest of the world was heading toward capitalism. And something like that view seems to be implied in a much-quoted remark from Marx's 1867 introduction to *Das Kapital,* that "the industrially developed lands show the less developed image of their future." That comment is usually taken out of context and used to prove that Marx thought that Asia, Africa and Latin America would follow in the very footsteps of Europe and America. Actually, the "less developed" country to which Marx referred in this passage was Germany, not India, and when he wrote it he had completely abandoned the simple progressions of *The Communist Manifesto*.

But even though the 1867 remark has been carelessly misread, there are authentic pages in the earlier Marx that lay out a linear version of history. These are the statements that allow Paul Samuelson to say that Marx saw history as "a one-way evolution" and E. H. Carr to write, "Marx believed that bourgeois capitalism, once established, would everywhere run its full course and that, when it began to decay through its own inherent contradictions, then and only then would it be overthrown by socialist revolution." Gunnar Myrdal even thinks that it was Marx who convinced both capitalist and Communist economists that the developing nations are simply at a different "stage" of the same process which the advanced economies passed through earlier.

On the economic level this youthful Marxian theory of a capitalist road for colonial development can be dealt with rather easily, since its major predictions obviously did not come true. But on a political and moral level Marx's analysis must be approached with great respect for its tensions and nuances, since it poses one of the most critical questions in the modern world: To what extent is violence "progressive" if it clears the way for economic advance and a higher form of society? A careless reading of Marx on this point can be, and has been, used to justify the crimes of both British imperialism and Joseph Stalin. In fact, it is only the younger—more schematic—Marx who offers any warrant for such a view, and what has been ascribed to him as a central insight was was really a youthful error. As his research progressed, as we shall see, what struck him was the way in which the non-European nations deviated from the pattern he described in the *Manifesto*. He therefore searched for alternatives to capitalist modernization in the economically backward countries and considered the possibility that entire historical stages might be skipped. Among other things, that allowed him to reject the rather bizarre conclusion that followed quite logically from his earlier theories. For if history had ordained that the colonies must go through a capitalist phase, then in them the Marxist must first look to the businessman, not the worker, as his hero. That, as the next chapter will show, is precisely what some of Marx's disciples, who had not understood their master's change of mind, decided. Consequently, Antonio Gramsci, writing against such an interpretation in 1917–1918, could argue that in Russia and Italy, *Das Kapital* "is the book of the bourgeoisie, not the proletariat."

In a series of articles in the New York *Daily Tribune* in 1853 Marx analyzed British rule in India. The English, he wrote, have "dissolved these semi-barbarian, semi-civilized communities, by blowing up their commercial basis, and thus produced the greatest, and to speak the truth, the only *social* revolution ever heard of in Asia. Now sickening as it must be to human feeling to witness these myriads of industrious patriarchal and inoffensive social organizations disorganized, and dissolved into their units, thrown into a sea of woes, and their individual members losing at the same time their ancient form of civilization and their hereditary means of subsistence, we must not forget that these idyllic village communities, inoffensive though they may appear, had always been the solid foundation of Oriental despotism. . . . The question is, can mankind fulfill its destiny without a fundamental revolution in the social state of Asia? If not, whatever had been the crimes of England, she was the unconscious tool of history in bringing about the revolution."

Does this mean, then, that Marx supports the British in their unwittingly progressive enterprise? On the contrary, Marx regards these events as unveiling "the inherent barbarism of bourgeois civilization" and he is obviously concerned with defeating colonialism as rapidly as possible: "The Indians will not reap the fruits of the new elements of society scattered among them by the British bourgeoisie, till in Great Britain the new ruling classes shall have been supplanted by the industrial proletariat, or till the Hindoos themselves shall have grown strong enough to throw off the English yoke altogether." For "the devastating effects of English industry are only the organic results of that whole system of production as it is now constituted."

Those on the Left who came after Marx and defended British imperialism or Stalin's terror on the grounds that they carried out a progressive economic task ignored the fact that Marx detested the revolution from above which he described and was seeking an alternative to it, by means of a democratic revolution from below, even as he was recording its devastations. "When a great social revolution shall have mastered the results of the bourgeois epoch," he wrote, ". . . and subjected them to the common control of the most advanced peoples, only then will human progress cease to resemble that hideous pagan idol who would not drink nectar but from the skulls of the slain." There were, alas, those who attempted to worship that idol in the name of Marx, and they will be heard from later on.

In short, when Marx held that history was advancing by monstrous means, he did not become a critical supporter of that wave of the future, but rather sought a revolutionary alternative to it. If I may anticipate, he would not have supported the totalitarian accumulation of capital by the Stalinists or Maoists on the grounds that it prepared the industrial preconditions for socialism any more than he would have backed Japanese capitalism, Spanish fascism or South African racism, all of which experienced considerable economic growth after World War II. To him, as he wrote in his polemic against Proudhon, "of all the means of production, the most productive power is the revolutionary class itself." To suppress that class in the name of an "objective" progress measured in tons of steel or kilowatt hours was therefore profoundly antisocialist. And that is why Marx strove to organize the British and Indian masses against British colonialism even though it was, by his definition, an unwitting agent of progress.

But Marx did not simply define a complex attitude toward what the British were doing in India; he also made predictions on the basis of his analysis. In understanding why he was wrong, one must focus on a crucial aspect of the problems of the developing countries in the modern world. Marx held that "modern industry, resulting from the railway system, will dissolve the hereditary divisions of labour, upon which rest the Indian castes." The colonialists would, he said, bring political unity, the telegraph, the free press and that "great desideratum of Asiatic society," "private property in the land." There would be, in other words, vast economic "spread effects" (I use a contemporary phrase) from the colonialist crimes.

In fact, the great mass of Indian society was not affected as Marx thought—and even after formal independence much of the old system prevailed. As Gunnar Myrdal puts it, Marx "exaggerated the effectiveness of railroads in bringing about industrialization in India, and also the power of spurts of industrialization to induce changes in attitudes and institutions." For capitalist investment in colonial lands (aside from those colonies settled by Europeans, i.e., the United States, Canada, Australia and New

Zealand) have, from Marx's day to the present, created enclaves of modernity within backward societies rather than transforming the entire society.

So capitalism did not live up to Marx's high expectations for it. In part, as will be seen, this was because the world market was structured so as to make it difficult for any non-European nation to become capitalist. But there was another factor that helped to falsify his predictions, one which he himself began to perceive in the late 1850s: that the colonial societies had gone through a completely different evolution (or lack of evolution) from the European. This not only suggested that capitalism was not an internal necessity in those lands; it also opened up the possibility that, under very specific conditions, they might skip the stage of capitalism altogether.[1]

Thus one turns from the Marx who was too optimistic about capitalism to the Marx who was too optimistic about socialism.

His theories, Marx came to understand, generalized the experience of the European minority of the globe and did not even begin to account for the conditions of life for that majority which never got beyond the very first stage in the *Manifesto*'s progression. Whether the ancient societies of Asia and Africa would have to repeat the European pattern in the course of modernization was a question he could not answer but, if socialism were victorious in Europe, there was a very good chance, he thought, that some of them could skip the capitalist stage altogether.

In a note to the 1888 English edition of *The Communist Manifesto* Engels hinted at a powerful criticism of that famous document. At the time of the *Manifesto*, he said, scholars had not yet discovered "that common ownership of the land by the village commune which was the original form of society from India to Ireland." But, as he and Marx were to learn after writing the *Manifesto*, most of mankind never progressed beyond the very first stage of the supposedly universal evolution they had described. Indeed, even in the nineteenth century tens of millions in India and China (and perhaps Russia) were living under conditions that were neither Roman, feudal, capitalist nor socialist, the four types of society in the *Manifesto*'s schema.

It was during the 1850s that Marx realized that most of the world did not fit into the framework of the *Manifesto*. He did so in the course of analyzing what he called the Asiatic (or Oriental) mode of production. His comments about it hardly add up to a rounded theory, yet they do completely subvert the notion that he stuck to the simplifications of his youth all his life. In large areas of Asia and the Middle East, Marx came to understand, the absence of private property in land was a crucial component of stagnant, despotic societies. Sometimes Marx—and Engels almost always—stressed the importance of the public irrigation works the state maintains in those countries; sometimes he emphasized the parochialism of isolated communes with primitive manufacture and land owned in common.

In either case, the result was a form of social life without internal movement: "Indian society has no history at all," Marx wrote in 1853, "at least no known history. What we call its history is but the history of successive intruders who founded their empire on the passive basis of that unresisting and unchanging society." And Engels wrote to Marx in 1853 that "the key to the whole Orient is the absence of private property in land."

There were two consequences to this intellectual discovery. The *Manifesto*'s schema was shattered; and so was the notion that the colonies must pass through a capitalist stage on the way to socialism. For if most of the people of the world lived under a system that had never gone beyond the first stage of social evolution, and lacked any internal source of change, they clearly could not repeat the European pattern in which capitalism developed out of the contradictions of feudalism.

This point is not only crucial for an understanding of Marx; it also is basic to any contemporary analysis of the problems of economic development. As George Lichtheim put it, "What occurred in the Western world between the middle of the eighteenth and the middle of the nineteenth century was unique and unprecedented." But if this is the case—if the European evolution was a deviation from the rule that holds for most of mankind— then modernization becomes all the more problematic. For then the colonies of Marx's day and the ex-colonies of the present do not simply lack the economic preconditions for industrialization, but the historical and cultural preconditions as well. Marx himself was aware of this complexity.

In a letter that he prepared in 1877 for the editors of a Russian journal, *Otetschestwennyje Sapiski*, Marx wrote, "The chapter on primitive accumulation [in *Das Kapital*] does not pretend to do more than trace the path by which, in Western Europe, the capitalist order of economy emerged from the womb of the feudal order of economy." He then accused his critic, N. K. Michailowski, one of the editors of the periodical, of turning "my historical sketch of the genesis of capitalism in Western Europe into an historic-philosophic theory of the general path every people is fated to tread, whatever the historic circumstances. . . ." That, Marx said, was not his point at all. He had merely wanted to say that if Russia took the capitalist path, then a good part of its peasantry would be turned into proletarians. But actually, he concluded, if there were a victorious socialist revolution in Western Europe, it could provide its Russian comrades with many of the material preconditions of the good society and therefore they might be able to skip the miseries of capitalism altogether.

This most emphatically does not mean that Marx had been converted to peasant socialism. That was the theory that developed as the socialist idea traveled east to countries where the oppressed masses were rural, not proletarian. In Russia, as early as 1850, Alexander Herzen, the spiritual father of the populist *Narodniks,* had argued that the survival of common peasant property in the land provided the point of departure for a new, higher order of society. Thus Russia would proceed from feudalism to socialism by way of peasant communes and without passing through capitalism. Marx's great opponent Bakunin took up this vision and advocated a great transformation based in the Slavic countryside.

That idea was, Marx said with characteristic vehemence, "Schoolboy's asininity! A radical social revolution is bound up with historic conditions; the latter are its preconditions. It is thus only possible where there is capitalist production and the proletariat has at least an important role. . . ." Thus Russia could not leap over the capitalist stage on the basis of its own meager resources, but only if it had massive aid from a triumphant European socialist revolution which had taken place in a country where the preconditions had been fulfilled. Marx was, I hope to show, quite right on this count. That is why the leaders who have tried to base socialism on the peasantry—from Lenin in the last years of his life to Mao—have indeed changed history, but not in the way they intended. Yet if this strategy has not worked, still it has inspired mass movements and great revolutions in Russia and China. And so in mid-nineteenth-century Russia there appeared a solution to the problem of backwardness that endures to this moment: that the impoverished nation, perhaps because it is poor, can leap into the future and avoid the corruptions of an advanced economy.

Even though Marx was vigorously opposed to the champions of

peasant socialism in Russia, he took them quite seriously. Between 1868 and 1870 his letters show him learning Russian so that he can pursue his research in greater depth. And this line of investigation raised the question of Asiatic despotism in a new context. For the very communes that the *Narodniks* idealized, Engels wrote in a polemic in 1875, were so isolated that they created "the very opposite of a common interest" and were "the material basis of *Oriental despotism*." In this, he said, Russia resembled India. But there was an outside hope: the commune "could make the transition to the higher form of society without the Russian peasant passing through the intermediate stage of bourgeois land division. This, however, can happen only if, before the destruction of the commune, a proletarian revolution is victorious in Western Europe and provides the Russian peasant with the preconditions for such a transition. . . ."

Throughout the 1870s Marx and Engels repeated this idea, and in an eerie anticipation of the events of 1917 speculated that the European socialist revolution might well begin in the most backward of capitalist nations, in Russia. They did not for a moment believe, as Stalin was to claim, that a peasant nation could create socialism on its own. But they did think it quite possible, as they wrote in 1882, that "the Russian Revolution would give the signal to a proletarian revolution in the West." If that were the case, and the Russian and Western European revolutions could complement each other, "then the present Russian common property in the land could serve as the point of departure for a communist development."

There are those—Eduard Bernstein and E. H. Carr among them—who think that Marx and Engels put forth this analysis simply to improve their relations with the Russian radicals. Yet it is hard to believe that two such serious thinkers would have stated and restated a perspective on the European socialist revolution just to curry favor with a handful of Russian intellectuals. Engels was certainly aware of the growth of capitalism in Russia in the 1890s and was therefore somewhat less sanguine about the commune making a transition to socialist agriculture. But he reiterated the possibility that Russia would initiate the European socialist revolution the year before he died, in 1894.

For a few years between 1917 and 1921 it seemed that Marx and Engels' audacious scenario was coming to pass. There was a socialist conquest of power in Russia and the German working class seemed to be on the verge of revolution. If those two events had indeed converged, then German socialism could have, just as Marx suggested, provided the fraternal aid that might have saved the Bolsheviks from the consequences of their country's economic backwardness. History was not, however, so obliging: the German revolution failed, the Russian Revolution was fatally isolated. And yet, as Chapter XIII will show, the basic theory in Marx's speculations about Russia is still quite relevant. For if socialists in the advanced countries could really transform their societies, that would make it possible for them to give the kind of help that would allow Third World nations to skip many of the miseries of capital accumulation.

But even if socialists were to succeed in creating such an alternative, economic development in the ex-colonies would still not be simple. Engels was quite blunt about the complexities involved. In a letter to Karl Kautsky in 1882 he hypothesized that socialists had triumphed in Europe, set the colonies free and started to help them in their quest for socialism. Even under these circumstances, however, what would happen was not at all clear: "But what social and political phases those countries will pass through before they come to socialist organization, on that I believe that we can today pose only muddling, speculative theories. Only one thing is sure: the victorious proletariat cannot force its blessings upon any foreign people."

So the mature Marx and Engels had not only abandoned the schematic analysis of historic stages in *The Communist Manifesto*, but also saw much that was indeterminate and even ambiguous in their analysis of colonialism. The capitalist road to modernity which they had first predicted did not turn out to be as effective as they had thought it would be. But that did not mean that the colonies could, on their own, simply skip capitalism and proceed to socialism, for they lacked the material and cultural preconditions for such a gigantic advance. There was, they said, one best hope: If socialism won in the advanced countries, it could then provide the material basis for a difficult and as yet unchartered leap from the past into the future. And that is still the best hope.[2]

## II

In 1896, the year after Engels died, these issues moved from theory to politics. The London Congress of the Socialist International—the "Second International," which claimed direct descent from Marx's International Workingmen's Association—took a straightforward position on colonialism. It favored the "full right of self-determination for all nations" and held that "whatever manner of religious or civilizing pretext colonial policy might have, it is always only in the interest of the capitalists." That was the last time the issue was ever to seem so uncomplicated.

Between 1896 and World War I socialists appeared as enthusiastic champions, and bitter opponents, of capitalist imperialism. There were those who declared socialism had no place in the colonies; those who, in the name of the Left, supported imperialism; and those who were revolutionary and intransigent foes of colonialism. Yet no one had any solution to the basic problem: how to find a democratic and humane way to industrialize economically backward countries. Even so, every one of the positions the socialists took was to have an influence on history, and most of them still inspire millions today.

One approach to colonialism was simplicity itself: it held that socialism has nothing to say to the majority of mankind.

It was in 1909 that Enrico Ferri, the Italian criminologist and a member of the Italian Socialist Party, went to Argentina. He lost little time in telling his comrades there that they had no business being socialists. Socialism, he said, was a European importation in Argentina, not an indigenous phenomenon. Only when "machines and steam" created a working class could such a movement have a right to develop. Juan B. Justo, the father of Argentinian socialism who had translated *Das Kapital* into Spanish, replied on behalf of his countrymen. The ruling class in Argentina, Justo argued, faced the problem of how to create a proletariat in a country with vast areas of free land. It had consciously sought to form a rural proletariat and it had filled the towns with a population of half-starving people. So there was a mass basis for socialism, even though it did not resemble the European model.

Justo's argument in some ways prefigured themes that were to be taken up by men like Mao, Fidel Castro and Frantz Fanon. But Ferri, despite the quietism of his mechanistic reading of the young Marx, was also a precursor. Within a few years the theory of history as a succession of ordered and inevitable stages was, as the next chapter will detail, to become a major factor in the politics of the Russian Left. For like Ferri, most of the Russian socialists were to place their faith in the triumph of capitalism.

Another socialist attitude was defined in 1899 when the Boer

War broke out. It was urged in the name of a most reformist socialism; it was blatantly pro-imperialist; and if its essentials are understood, it was a polite British anticipation of Joseph Stalin.

Britain's Independent Labour Party and Social Democratic Federation stood by the principles of the Socialist International and opposed the war. But the Fabians and George Bernard Shaw were in favor of annexing the Boer Republic. Their argument in favor of this colonialist policy was based on humanitarianism. The Boers, Shaw quite rightly observed, would enslave the natives in South Africa if they won. Therefore the British had to take over that country in the name of its defenseless majority. Ideally, he said, South Africa and its gold should be internationalized and owned by a federated world state. But ". . . until the Federation of the World becomes an accomplished fact, we must accept the most responsible Imperial Federation available as a substitute for it. . . ." And for Shaw, "the most responsible Imperial Federation" was, of course, the British Empire.

Shaw's conclusions were, as usual, outrageous, yet his points cannot be dismissed out of hand. The fate of the natives in South Africa during the past three quarters of a century has been a matter of some moment and Shaw's worst fears have certainly been borne out. But to pose the question in terms of this single issue is to miss the historical importance of what Shaw and the Fabians were doing. They were in all matters technocratic, proposing to save society and institute socialism from the top down by "permeating" the Liberal and/or Labour Party with their ideas. It was this consistent support for revolution from above that led Shaw to be sympathetic to both Mussolini and Stalin and turned Beatrice and Sidney Webb into admirers of the Russian Revolution only when it entered its Stalinist phase.

There was, as we have seen, a certain authority for this view if Marx's writings on British colonialism were misread. He had, after all, argued that the imperialists would make an unwitting contribution to the future of the Indian people. But he did not— and the distinction is as important now as it was then—praise history for operating with such cruel cunning and therefore give his political support to the unconscious and bloody agents of social change. In fact, he excoriated British colonialism as showing the "inherent barbarism" of capitalist society and sought alternatives to it, both among the British and the Indian masses. Social democrats like Shaw or Eduard Bernstein, who supported German expansionism because "high culture has a higher right," had utterly distorted Marx. In this manner the socialist argument for revolution from above entered the movement by way of its colonialist Right wing. In rather short order, as the next chapter will detail, it was to become the central rationale for the totalitarian pseudo-Left of Joseph Stalin.

It was at the Stuttgart Congress of the Socialist International in 1907 that the issue came out into the open. Two of the questions debated there are still being asked: Has the revolutionary spirit of the working class been corrupted by a living standard based on colonial exploitation? How do anti-capitalists use their political power *within* capitalist society?

At the Amsterdam Congress of the International in 1904 Van Kol of Holland said that "in a socialist state there would also be colonies but the socialist party will stop the exploitation and torture of the natives and will protect them against the hypocritical action of various religions." But he and his co-thinkers did not really push their political point of view. Then in 1906 political developments in Germany made them decide to take the offensive. The social democrats had voted in that year against credit for carrying out a colonialist war in Southwest Africa. For its own reasons the Center joined with them, and the government's defeat led to the dissolution of the Reichstag. In the campaign that followed—that which came to be known as the Hottentot Election—the socialists suffered their first setback since 1884, losing one half of their seats and dropping from 32.6 to 29.5 percent of the vote. Meanwhile in Belgium the issue of what to do with the Congo had become a major political question. What was now at stake was not an exercise in Marxian theory but the question of how socialist parties would relate to a colonialism that seemed to have considerable popular backing.

At the Stuttgart Congress a majority of the Colonial Commission voted out a resolution by Van Kol that said, "The Congress . . . does not condemn all colonial policy on principle and for all times, because under a socialist regime, it could have a civilizing effect. . . ." Van Kol was supported by Bernstein and David from the German party but bitterly opposed by Karl Kautsky. In a passage that might have been written to corroborate Lenin's bitter, scornful judgment against the "sham socialists" who held such views, Bernstein said, "The modern working class is not a remnant of the feudal 'Third Estate' which is detached from society and which one can counterpose to it as an isolated body. The working class is, in its economic situation, tightly bound to society and has an interest in its development; it is false to pretend that the possession of colonies runs counter to the interests of the proletariat, except when it acts as a fetter on economic development."

It was Karl Kautsky who took the lead in attacking Bernstein and Van Kol at Stuttgart. Colonial policy, he argued, was not beneficial to the natives or the workers, but an instrument of monopoly expansion. Moreover, he said, foreign rule is no way to raise the culture of a subject people. They must fight for their independence and socialists must support them.

At Stuttgart Kautsky's position carried by a vote of 128 to 108. But, as Lenin noted at the time, this victory occurred only because the delegates from countries without colonies voted in favor of the anti-colonial position. Therefore, Lenin was forced to conclude (and in this he seconds Bernstein), ". . . as a result of the extensive colonial policy, the European proletarian *partly* finds himself in a position where it is not his labor but the labor of the practically enslaved natives in the colonies that maintains the whole of society." But, he reassured himself, ". . . this may be only a temporary phenomenon."

Thus Lenin introduced an idea that was to become basic to his analysis of the world: that imperialism had created a labor aristocracy in the West, a small minority of privileged workers who sometimes corrupted their entire class through opportunistic accommodations to capitalism. But was it indeed true—as Bernstein declared enthusiastically from the Right and Lenin admitted ruefully on the Left—that the living standard of the European working class was artificially high because of superprofits made in the colonies? And was this a major factor in dampening the revolutionary ardor of the proletariat in the early years of this century?

The kernel of Lenin's theory was not new. As early as the 1850s Marx had argued that it was Britain's foreign trade that created vast new markets and thereby offset the natural tendency of the capitalist system to overproduction. And in 1858 Engels wrote to Marx that "the English proletariat is fast becoming more and more bourgeois. The most bourgeois of all nations seems to have finally reached a point where it has a bourgeois aristocracy and a bourgeois proletariat alongside the bourgeoisie. In a nation which exploits the whole world that is, to certain degree, understandable."

In 1885 Engels saw this colonial fact as the decisive explanation for the failure of the Left in Britain. He wrote, "The truth is this. So long as England's industrial monopoly lasted, the English working class to a certain degree participated in the profits of this monopoly. These profits were divided up most unequally; the privileged minority took the largest part, but the great mass itself now and then got a share of some overlooked portion. And that is why, since the death of Owenism, there has been no socialism in England. With the breakdown of this monopoly the English working class will lose its privileged position. All the workers—the privileged, leading minority not excluded—will see themselves reduced to the same level as the foreign workers. And that is why there will once again be socialism in England."

Lenin's argument was much more pessimistic than Engels', though it, too, was based on the effect of colonialism upon the metropolitan proletariat. Where Engels saw the end of the British trade monopoly as a signal for the immiserization, and radicalization, of the workers in that country, Lenin held that the same event had "Anglicized" labor in all of the advanced capitalist economies. Now the Germans and the Americans were to enjoy the corruptions of colonial exploitation, too. Thus the enormous profits of imperialism defined a new epoch of capitalism. Strangely, we are not sure that those imperial superprofits really existed. Colonialism, as Marx realized in the 1850s, is a costly affair: it requires large military and administrative expenditures. If these are seen as debits, then colonialism was a subsidy to those industries involved directly in it, which did not have to pay the costs, of the colonial infrastructure that allowed them to make profits. In this context, it would seem that the objective basis of Lenin's theory is probably inaccurate.

But there is another, and more sophisticated, way of drawing up this balance sheet, which was suggested by a Dutch socialist named Wiedijk in 1904. All the expenditures for the colonies, he pointed out, went to the imperial bourgeoisie: they were the ones who built the ships, uniformed the troops and in general profiteered on the "loss" side of the state budget. In this argument, however, the crucial factor in colonialism is not so much superexploitation as it is the fact that it provided the political rationale for a kind of pre-Keynesian pump priming. The distinction is an important one. For if Lenin (and Engels, who anticipated him in this line of reasoning) was right, then the disappearance of the colonial markets would be a mortal blow for capitalism. But if the side effects of colonial intervention were more important than the trade itself, then capitalism could evade crisis even when colonial expansion was no longer possible so long as it found some new form of government spending to take up the slack. The latter explanation is, as Chapter XIII will discuss, the more persuasive of the two.

The second element in Lenin's analysis—that imperialist living standards made for labor reformism—is also dubious. It was before the end of empire, in the years right before World War I, that the English working class carried out some of its most militant actions and even developed a syndicalist movement, which was about as revolutionary as English politics ever got (this was also the period of extreme feminist activism, which employed non-violent revolutionary tactics). And indeed, as Lenin himself realized at one point, the labor aristocrats of Europe and Russia were precisely the ones most open to, and convinced by, socialist ideas. The poorest, and least "corrupted," workers were politically debilitated and sometimes conservative (or, later on, fascist).

It was not, then, simply colonialism that dulled the ardor of the European workers. It was, rather, the unforeseen and complex development of capitalism itself, a process in which colonialism played a role, but not necessarily a decisive one (all the ramifications of this analysis will not become apparent until later chapters dealing with the Third World).

The second issue the socialists confronted in this debate arose out of a discussion of the Belgian Congo. It involved nothing less than defining a political stance for which there was no precedent in Marxian thought or any other socialist theory. Today, almost three quarters of a century later, social democrats are still struggling with the problem.

In the classic Marxist scenario the socialists were to move quickly from powerlessness to power. The wretched of the earth would win the final conflict and abruptly transform the entire social order, from bottom to top. As time went on, Marx and Engels moved away from this insurrectionary vision and considered the possibility of a peaceful democratic road to socialism in England, the United States, France and Holland. But they never analyzed what their followers should do when they won not power, but an increment of power within a system that still remained capitalist. This, as Chapter XI will document, was to be the central problem for the social democrats when they tried to deal with the Great Depression of the thirties, and it plagued the Wilson Government in the England of the sixties. The question of what the Belgian socialists should do about the Congo was the first time it was put as a practical political issue.

In 1885 Leopold II received the Congo as his private property, not as a colony of the Belgian state, from an international conference in Berlin. By the 1890s he was losing so much money in the enterprise that he had to turn to the government for financial aid.

The Belgian socialists opposed this financial aid on the grounds that the funds being spent to help Leopold would be much better used in dealing with social problems at home. It was, they said, time to treat the blacks as equals with the whites—and to stop treating whites in Belgium like blacks. So the Belgian Workers' Party and most of the public were against annexation of the Congo because they viewed it as a drain on the budget. When Leopold's fortunes in Africa improved a bit and the Parliament voted him a loan, the socialist deputies left the chamber because they did not want to even be present for such a scandalous vote.

Between 1899 and 1903 Leopold put down tribal insurrections with bloody violence and an international anti-colonial campaign was launched against him. In Belgium itself it was the socialist Émile Vandervelde who courageously took up this cause even though his comrades did not believe that it was politic. It was, Vandervelde remembered later on, his "Dreyfus Affair." By 1906 the agitation against Leopold was so effective that the Parliament took up the question of the status of the Congo.

The problem posed for the socialists did not look anything like the situation Engels had imagined in that famous letter to Kautsky. It was not a socialist Belgium that had to decide on the form of its fraternal aid to a Congo it was leading to independence. Rather, socialist parliamentarians had a voice in deciding how a capitalist Belgium would, in the midst of the capitalist world, deal with a country that had been suffering for years as the "private property" of Leopold II.

The options were all unacceptable. There was no possibility of

establishing an international regime in the Congo for, as Vandervelde pointed out, that would simply set up a multinational form
of capitalist exploitation which would not be responsible to any
elected parliament. There was no nationalist movement within
the Congo to take over the direction of the country, and there was
a very good possibility that if the Congo were given independence,
the Arabs, who were better organized than the blacks, might
reintroduce slavery. But if the socialists were to favor Belgium
taking over the Congo, it would mean voting in favor of turning
their own country into an imperialist power.

Vandervelde came to the reluctant conclusion that from the
point of view of his long-time and courageous defense of the blacks
in the Congo, the least evil course was for Belgium to annex the
country. But within his own party he was in the minority, attacked
by advocates of "socialist" colonialism on the one side and by
intransigent opponents of annexation (who had no solution to the
problem) on the other. Eventually, the Belgian socialists were to
patch up a unity of sorts. In 1908 the party campaigned against
the actual annexation proposal before the Parliament (Vandervelde himself opposed its terms) but their hostility was based on
the domestic social consequences of the policy rather than on
opposition to colonialism itself. When the issue came before Parliament, the socialist deputies once again left the chamber, this
time because they did not want to reopen the crisis in their party
by debating the matter publicly. By 1920, however, all these
doubts and hesitations had been forgotten. The Belgian socialists
campaigned by talking of "our fine Congo colony."

Lenin, needless to say, was extremely sharp with any socialist
who made the slightest concession to colonialism. But, it must be
emphasized, he was able to take this position primarily because he
did not face the dilemmas that confronted Vandervelde and the
Belgian socialists. In 1916, for instance, Lenin was attacked for his
insistence on socialist support for the right of national self-determination. His critics, who were attacking from the Left, pointed
out that as long as capitalism existed, it was impossible for the
colonies to be given their freedom.

Under the imperialist system, Lenin replied, the colonies
"cannot be extricated from dependence on European finance
capital. From the military standpoint as well as from the standpoint of expansion, the separation of the colonies is practicable,
as a general rule, only under socialism; under capitalism it is

practicable only by way of exception or at the cost of a series of revolts both in the colonies and the metropolitan countries." But this only means, he argued, that "these demands must be formulated and put through in a revolutionary and not a reformist manner. . . ." So Lenin himself knew that there were no socialist alternatives to imperialism within capitalism. The reason he could be so pure about the question was that czarist despotism never asked him, as Belgian capitalism demanded of Vandervelde, to choose from among impossible options.

In other words, Lenin remained true to *The Communist Manifesto* scenario, which projects a sharp break in continuity, a rising of the powerless to seize power. Under the conditions of czarist autocracy, which resembled mid-nineteenth-century Europe more than early twentieth, that was understandable. But the impossible demand raised by a leader of a semi-legal movement looking forward to an insurrection could hardly guide a socialist deputy who, as a result of an unexpected historical evolution, found himself compelled to take a position on a specific colonial issue within a capitalist parliament. And in this contrast between Lenin and Vandervelde is symbolized the split that was to take place in the socialist movement: the Western Europeans on the one side, trying to cope with the political and moral complexities of life within capitalist society; the Eastern Europeans, and later the Asians and the Africans, on the other, for whom capitalism was not really a possibility, and revolution was the only alternative.

So socialists had discovered the world. They responded to the experience in contradictory and ambiguous ways, and the problems they found there have yet to be solved.

The hopes of the young Marx that capitalism, by utterly transforming the colonies, would lay the basis for a socialist revolution were never fulfilled. The spread effects of imperialism were much more modest than he had expected: the railroads did not subvert immemorial and anti-modern cultures, but turned out to be only slivers of modernity. But Marx's dream of advanced socialist powers saving the developing countries from the agonies of industrialization by massive fraternal aid was more realistic, and even though this has not yet happened, it is central to the perspective of present-day socialism. The first attempt to act on this possibility, however, the Russian Revolution of 1917, led to the skipping of a stage in a way never dreamed of by Marx: Russia jumped from feudalism to anti-socialist "socialism."

Finally, in the debates among the socialists of over fifty years ago basic themes were defined which must run like a red thread through any analysis of the Third World in the closing years of the twentieth century. Is there a capitalist road to modernization? Is it possible for a nation to skip the stage of capitalism altogether and build a just order on the basis of a peasant mass movement? For decades now there have been intensely practical, and bloody, disputes over these theoretical issues posed at the Second International, before World War I.[3]

# VIII

## *Revolution from Above*

In October, 1917, the Bolsheviks seized power in Russia and sought to blaze that humane path out of backwardness that had eluded the social democrats before World War I. They failed. They—or more precisely, their executioners—did, indeed, carry out a brutal modernization; however, it led not to the classless society, but to an anti-socialist "socialism" which became the prototype for a system that now rules one third of the globe.

So the Communist claim to be socialist must be challenged in the same spirit that prompted Marx to refuse the bourgeoisie the right to appropriate ideals like liberty, justice and equality for its own class purposes. In making a similar analysis of the contradictions between word and deed under Communism—of the real ends that the noble phrases rationalize—issues are defined which are relevant to two of the most important movements in the world today. These matters profoundly concern those people seeking freedom within the Communist world, men and women whose courageous critique of the official rhetoric is an attempt to transform the reality it conceals. And they relate to the masses of the Third World who are so often summoned to suffer in the name of emancipation only to be subjected to the new forms of oppression that were pioneered in Russia.

And, most important of all from the special standpoint of this book, Communism corrupted the very ideal of socialism itself by equating it with a totalitarian denial of freedom. In this context, the Russian experience has been one of the profoundly conservative events of the century: it subordinated the actions of some of the most revolutionary spirits of the Western working class to Moscow and thereby weakened the movement for radical change within the advanced capitalist countries; it "proved" the conservative myth of Burke and Dostoevsky, the theory that any attempt to alter the established order of injustice would lead to a new tyranny. It is a central thesis of this chapter that the fate of the Russian Revolution does not in the least demonstrate that men must passively accept an inhuman society as if it were decreed by God. What it does show is that under the very specific conditions of economic backwardness and capitalist failure, there is a basis for an anti-socialist "socialist" society.

These conditions now characterize the situation in most of the ex-colonial nations. That is why it is preposterous to see an international conspiracy as the main reason why a third of the globe is now ruled by Communists. There are, to be sure, Communist agents and spies, but that is a mere detail compared with the economic and social reality that makes the totalitarian accumulation of capital—Communism—often seem to be the only way out of an economic backwardness fostered by capitalism. That is why Communism, even though it is totalitarian, has so often won volunteers to its banner, while capitalism, even when it is relatively democratic, usually relies upon dictators and despots. In this chapter, then, I am not simply writing about Russia but also about the emergence of a new form of class society, bureaucratic collectivism, which claims to be a model of emancipation for the majority of mankind.

In doing so, I will outline an ironic process. The Bolsheviks, those bitter, principled foes of the imperial socialists who wanted to tutor the natives in the ways of civilization, unwittingly prepared the way for just such a revolution from above, only on a scale and at a cost that no colonialist social democrat would ever have dared to suggest.

### I · LENIN

At the beginning of the twentieth century Russia was the last major nation that could have had a capitalist revolution (I do not count Mexico, which well might be an exception to this statement, among the major powers).

Russia had, as Fritz Sternberg has written, "co-ordinated in-dustrial development, a development of both heavy industry and the manufacturing industries. There was nothing of the sort in colonial countries. Their industries developed without any co-ordination and, in particular, the production of raw materials bore no relation to their own requirements but was determined solely by the trading needs of the metropolitan centres. In this period, Russia enjoyed a growing volume of trade with a num-ber of other countries, whereas colonial countries usually traded only with the country which controlled them as part of its empire, or with countries which required raw materials."

In other words, Russia had not been locked into that colonial division of labor that made indigenous capitalism impossible in almost all of the non-European world. So capitalism was on the agenda, and Lenin agreed with Stolypin, the Czar's minister and most effective anti-revolutionist, on how it might come. As Lenin put it, "the old landlord economy, bound as it is by thousands of threads to serfdom, is retained and turns slowly into a purely capitalist 'Junker' economy." Germany, in short, was the model: the feudal elements, instead of being swept away by a plebian revolution, would modernize themselves, and the society, from the top down. That, essentially, is what Stolypin was trying to do before he was assassinated by an *agent provocateur* in 1911. By allowing peasants to contract out of the communes, he hoped to create a class of landowners who would be loyal to the autocracy.

It was not just the assassin's bullet that put an end to this capitalist trend in Russia. For if some of the auguries were quite favorable to a capitalist development, others were semi-colonial in character. Russia was a backward land whose economy on the eve of World War I was probably below the levels of most South American countries today. Its industry was, to be sure, extremely concentrated and advanced, but for precisely that reason repre-sented only enclaves of modernity which did not disturb the vast reaches of the peasant society. The bourgeoisie in Russia was controlled from abroad.

It was these semi-colonial characteristics of pre-Revolutionary Russia that provided the Communists with the argument that they had found a new path for the impoverished majority of man-kind. As Varga, the famous Soviet economist, put the claim, "Russia inaugurated with its revolution a new type of national development, a way of moving to socialism which does not pass through capitalism and gives a historical example of the other colonial, and even semi-colonial, countries, not only in the Orient and Asia, but in the other continents as well."[1]

The unprecedented character of the Russian Revolution did not come as a surprise. The shrewder Marxists had anticipated it some years before the event.

Marx had glimpsed the paradoxical essence of the problem in 1867 in his introduction to the German edition of *Das Kapital.* He wrote of his native land, "we suffer, like the rest of continental West Europe, not from the development of capitalist production, but from its lack of development." This socialist complaint that capitalism had not sufficiently triumphed was based, of course, on the knowledge that its victory was a crucial precondition opening up the struggle for the just society. In the absence of such a capitalist development, "old growths, obsolete modes of production . . . outlived social and political relations" persisted. With Bismarck's revolution from above, Germany made the leap to industrialization, yet Marx's insight still applied to any backward capitalist economy. In 1894 Engels reminded the Italian socialists of what Marx had said on this count. In Italy even more than in Germany the bourgeoisie was weak and the forces of the old order were strong. And in Russia that was even truer than in Italy.

There were, to be sure, socialists who tried to impose the Western European stages of economic growth on the Russian reality. In that perspective, capitalism was on the agenda and the coming bourgeois revolution would be made by the bourgeoisie. But other Marxists understood that history was not going to repeat itself mechanistically and that the uneven development of Russian society had opened up the way for possibilities not to be found in the holy texts of Marxism. In 1888 the original manifesto of the Russian Social Democratic Workers' Party anticipated the uniqueness of the coming transformation: "The further East one goes in Europe, the weaker, meaner and more cowardly in the political sense becomes the bourgeoisie, and the greater the cultural and political tasks which fall to the lot of the proletariat."

Then, in the aftermath of the 1905 Revolution, three Marxists —Kautsky, Lenin and Trotsky—became even more specific about the unprecedented nature of the transformation that was going to take place in Russia. In the process they confronted a

problem that is basic for Asia, Africa and Latin America at this
very moment: What happens to the bourgeois revolution when
there is no bourgeoisie effective enough to carry it out? If capitalist modernization is not an alternative, is non- or anti-capitalist
modernization possible?

In 1906 Karl Kautsky, the dean of pre-war Marxism, delivered
himself of a sweeping judgment: "The age of the bourgeois revolution, i.e., the revolution whose driving force is the bourgeoisie,
is over—in Russia, too. For there the proletariat is no longer a
dependent instrument of the bourgeoisie, as was the case in the
bourgeois revolution, but an independent class with independent
goals. Where, however, the proletariat emerges in this way, the
bourgeoisie ceases to be a revolutionary class. The Russian bourgeoisie, insofar as it has independent class politics and is liberal,
hates absolutism, but hates the revolution more, and hates absolutism above all because it sees in it the basic cause of the revolution. To the degree that the bourgeoisie seeks political freedom,
it does so because it sees in it the only way it can find to put an
end to the revolution."

But, Kautsky went on, if "one cannot call this a bourgeois
revolution," neither can one immediately conclude then that
"it is a socialist revolution. In no case can it bring the proletariat
to sole power, to dictatorship. The Russian proletariat is too weak
and underdeveloped for such a role. Yet it is quite possible that
in the progress of the revolution, victory will come to the social
democratic party and the social democrats would do well to
encourage a spirit of victory in its followers since one cannot
effectively struggle if victory is precluded at the outset."

He concluded that the Russian Revolution must be thought of
"neither as a bourgeois revolution in the usual sense, not as a
socialist revolution, but as a complicated, unique process which
is situated on the borderline between bourgeois and socialist
society, demanding the end of one and preparing the coming of
the other. . . ." It was, we know with hindsight, quite prescient
of Kautsky to glimpse the coming of a revolution which was
neither bourgeois nor socialist, but what he could not possibly
grasp at that time was that it would create a completely new
kind of class society.

Lenin, who was, of course, quite familiar with Marx's and
Engels' speculation on the possibility of the European revolution
beginning in Russia, agreed with Kautsky and cited him enthusiastically (he was later to brand him a "renegade" from the

proletarian revolution). The coming upheaval, he wrote in 1908, would be a bourgeois revolution, but the bourgeoisie would not —could not—lead it. Either the landlords would transform themselves into capitalists, as the Germans had done, and take the liberals and rich peasants along with them, or else the alliance of workers and peasants would force through a radical democratic transformation, sweeping away the czarist superstructure and creating an "American" kind of agriculture with widespread farm ownership.

Trotsky was more audacious than either Kautsky or Lenin. Like them, he held that the Russian bourgeoisie was too weak and timid to play a decisive role in the revolution; like them, he recognized that the workers would, given the peculiarities of Russian development which concentrated them in great numbers at key points in the society, have an importance out of proportion to their numbers. But unlike Kautsky and Lenin, Trotsky believed that the workers would have to exercise sole power, to create their own dictatorship. The peasants, he said, could not possibly share the government with the workers for they are too dispersed and isolated to rule. And the workers, once in power, could hardly limit themselves to a bourgeois revolution "only to step aside when the democratic programme is put into operation, to leave the completed building at the disposal of the bourgeois parties and then to open an era of parliamentary politics where social democracy forms only a party of opposition. . . ." For "once master of the situation, the working class would be compelled by the very logic of its situation to organize national economy under the management of the state."

It is, of course, impossible to summarize an epochal event like the Russian Revolution in a paragraph, but something like the scenario predicted by Trotsky did come to pass. E. H. Carr notes in his history of the Revolution: Lenin in April, 1917, essentially adopted the tactic put forward by Trotsky in 1906. The Bolsheviks took complete control of state power in the name of the workers (the alliance with the Left Social Revolutionaries, a peasant party, did not last long, and in any case, it was dominated by the Bolsheviks) and established their own exclusive dictatorship.[2]

But how, then, could the Bolsheviks create a socialist society in a backward peasant country which clearly lacked the preconditions that Marx had defined for socialism?

Lenin, Trotsky and their comrades were not only aware of

Marx's position on this question, but utterly persuaded by it. On the eve of leaving his Swiss exile for Russia in 1917, Lenin wrote a farewell letter to the Swiss workers: "Russia is a peasant country, one of the most backward of European countries. Socialism *cannot* triumph there *directly* and *immediately*. But the peasant character of the country, the vast reserves in the hands of the nobility, *may*, to judge from the experience of 1905, give tremendous sweep to the bourgeois democratic revolution in Russia and *may* make our revolution the *prologue* to the world socialist revolution, a step toward it." This situation would "create the most favorable conditions for a socialist revolution and would, in a sense, start it."

But the key for Lenin in 1917—as for Trotsky in 1906—was that the world revolution would rescue the Russian Revolution from its own backwardness. His letter to the Swiss workers concluded, *"The German proletariat is the most trustworthy, the most reliable ally of the Russian and the world proletarian revolution."* For Lenin understood, as Trotsky had said earlier, that "left to its own resources the Russian working class must necessarily be crushed the moment it loses the aid of the peasants." In 1919 he bluntly said, "The real test to which our revolution is being subjected is that we, in a backward country, succeeded in capturing power before the others. Shall we be able to hold on at least until the masses in the other countries make a move?" He answered his own question: ". . . we shall soon see the birth of a World Soviet Republic."

Yet Lenin did not simply wait for the Western Europeans to revolt. He had overthrown the Kerensky government, which traced its legitimacy back to the February Revolution, and he had dissolved the Constituent Assembly, which had been elected in a free vote. To prepare for, and then to defend, these actions and to justify the dictatorship of a workers' party in an overwhelmingly peasant country he had to show that such policies were honorable and explicable in Marxist terms. However, he did not content himself with arguing that such tactics were proper in a backward Russia which was racked by civil war and threatened by foreign intervention. Instead, he universalized a strategy that had emerged out of the conditions in his own country and proposed it as the road to socialism everywhere. In the process, he laid the ideological basis for a totalitarian regime which, I suspect, he would have abominated.

Lenin's method in defending himself was bizarre: he took the most utopian and near-anarchist element in all of Marxism, the theory of the "withering away" of the state, and cited it as an excuse for his own minority dictatorship. He acted as if his policies in Russia derived from a talmudic reading of Marx and Engels, as if the secret of ruling in Moscow and Petrograd in 1917 had been discovered by Marx in the Paris of 1871. There were, I think, two reasons for this scholastic rationalization of his own power politics.

On the one hand, Lenin in this period lived in the euphoric anticipation of the European socialist revolution. That event was not only going to save Russia from its backwardness, it was also going to prove that Marx and Engels had truly been the scientists of revolution and that their perspective, which seemed to have been shattered when the Second International collapsed in 1914, was once again confirmed. It was this chiliastic mood, the Soviet economist Varga has commented, that led him to his "excessive confidence" in the writings of Marx on the Commune and Engels on the state.

But on the other hand, Vladimir Ilyich Lenin was never so mesmerized by a text that he forgot about politics. In his scholarly writings of this period, and particularly in *State and Revolution,* the Marxism he evokes is utterly one-sided and tendentious and always points to the same conclusion: that Marx would have overthrown Kerensky too. Lenin had demonstrated in his earlier writings that he was quite conscious of the ambiguities in the Marxist formula "dictatorship of the proletariat." He understood that costly, unfortunate paradox, that Marx had used "dictatorship" in this case to describe the most democratic system possible. So, for instance, in 1905 he had said that the dictatorship of the proletariat signified "defense against the counter-revolution and the actual elimination of everything that contradicted the sovereignty of the people."

Lenin also knew that Marx's comments on dictatorship right after the revolutionary defeats of 1848 had been revised. He had, as Chapter IV documented, insisted on the fact in a brilliant series of articles in 1905. But in 1917 all that was forgotten—or more precisely, deliberately pushed aside. In *State and Revolution* he now argued that "a Marxist is solely someone who extends the recognition of the class struggle to the recognition of the dictatorship of the proletariat." And by "dictatorship" he did not mean anything subtle or dialectical, but rather the armed minority rule of his own party.

Thus the texts from Marx and Engels that Lenin chose predetermined his conclusions (in fact, of course, the conclusions dictated the choice of texts). He cited writings from the period of disillusionment with democracy after 1848, from the time of the Commune and the criticisms by Marx and Engels of the obsessive legalism of the German social democrats. The crucial point these quotations were supposed to prove was that it was necessary to "smash" the bureaucratic military machine of the state. In the actual Russian circumstances that meant overthrowing Kerensky, but Lenin did not confine himself to this one instance. If Marx had once suggested that Britain and the United States might make a peaceful transition to socialism, that was no longer the case: they had become as bureaucratic and militarist as Germany.

So intent was Lenin on proving his point that he even picked isolated passages out of classic Marxist documents that on the whole contradicted him. He made much of the fact that Engels had written to Kautsky criticizing the original draft of what was to become the Erfurt Program of the German Social Democracy. In that letter, as Lenin points out, Engels had reproached the Germans for not even mentioning the demand for a democratic republic out of fear of new anti-socialist laws and for seeming to suggest that all of their aims could necessarily be fulfilled through peaceful methods.

But then Lenin omits to emphasize that in the very same letter Engels had remarked that not only Britain and the United States, but France—that very France which had drowned the Commune in blood only twenty years before—might also make such a peaceful transition. And, to move to an even more portentous irony, the quotations from Marx's account of the civil war in France in 1871 are used to make a regime of libertarian democracy—universal suffrage, immediate recall of officials, no official paid more than a worker, etc.—the precedent for the creation of a minority dictatorship in Russia.

By 1919 Lenin, who was a man of considerable candor, could no longer justify his regime in anything like the classic Marxian fashion. The dictatorship was no longer the means of defending the rights of the overwhelming majority against a counterrevolutionary minority. Now, "state power in the hands of one class, the proletariat, can and must be an instrument of winning to the side of the proletariat the non-proletarian working masses, an instrument for winning those masses away from the bourgeois and petty-bourgeois parties." For, Lenin argued, capitalism beat the masses "to a downtrodden, crushed and terrified state of existence," and gives the bourgeoisie the possibility of perpetrating "falsehood and deception to hoodwink the masses of workers and peasants, to stultify their minds."

There was a classic name in Marxist literature for this tactic of using a minority dictatorship to reeducate the majority and to clear their minds of the corruptions of capitalism: Blanquism. Indeed, in *State and Revolution* Lenin had quoted Engels' 1891 Preface to Marx's *Civil War in France* as "the last word" of Marxism on the subject of the state, but he did not note that it contained a short summary of the Marxian critique of the followers of Auguste Blanqui. By 1919 he could not have read Engels' comment with any comfort, for it defined his own position: "Brought up in the school of conspiracy, bound together by the resultant strict discipline, their point of departure is the idea that a relatively small number of decisive, well-organized men can, in a given, favorable moment, not only seize the helm of state, but through their great and ruthless energy drag the masses into the revolution and group them around their small band." Something like this tactic was implied in Lenin's determination to use the dictatorship not to express the will of the majority, but to create it.

Already in 1921–1922 Martov, a Left Internationalist Menshevik whom Lenin had sought as an ally in 1917, compared the reality of Russian life to those promises based upon the workings of the Paris Commune. He wrote, "The 'Soviet state' has not established in any instance electiveness and recall of public officials and the commanding staff. It has not suppressed the professional police. It has not assimilated the courts in direct jurisdiction by the masses. It has not done away with social hierarchy in production. It has not lessened the total subjection of the local community to the power of the state. On the contrary, in proportion to its evolution, the Soviet state shows a tendency in the opposite direction."

But is one then to conclude that Lenin was some kind of moral monster who duped the masses with a demagogic offer to create total freedom in 1917 and then used the deceitful power he had won to enslave the people? That is to miss the extraordinary pathos of the man. In 1917, as Martov among others understood, he truly and sincerely believed that the final conflict was at hand and that the creative energy of working men and women could be substituted for all the old hierarchies and administrations. But day by day the backwardness of Russia and the impossibility of socialism subverted, and eventually overpowered, his iron will. It was exactly as Marx had said it would be: the attempt to reach justice through the socialization of poverty had led to the return of the "old crap" of class society.[3]

One of the most basic reasons that this inexorable triumph of Russian poverty over Lenin's will took place was that there was no proletarian revolution in the West.

Lenin had a ready explanation for the failure of the European workers to rise up against capitalism. Europe was indeed ripe for a socialist revolt, he told a Moscow conference in 1920, but the treacherous social democrats "worked to save the bourgeoisie at the last moment." This analysis was, of course, an extension of the theory that the European socialist leaders based themselves on a labor aristocracy which was comfortable enough under capitalism and did not want any great upheaval. But Lenin was wrong; the reason that the proletariat did not seize power in Germany or France was much more profound than he imagined.

As E. H. Carr put it, "The majority of Russian workers in 1917 had nothing to lose but their chains; standing at a level of subsistence not far removed from starvation, and maddened by the meaningless sacrifices of the war, they had neither hope nor belief in existing institutions, and were desperate enough to accept with alacrity the revolutionary leadership of a small group of determined men bent on overthrowing them. The majority of the workers of Western Europe—and not merely a privileged minority as the Bolsheviks believed—had a standard of living which, poor as it may often have been, was still worth defending. At any rate they were unwilling to sacrifice it lightly in pursuit of the prospective benefits of revolution; no propaganda damaged the Bolshevik revolution in Western Europe as much as that which fastened on it the low standards of living of the Russian people and the privations of the civil war."

Antonio Gramsci gave these facts a brilliant theoretical dimension. The Russia of 1917, he said, was still in a stage of development like Europe before 1848: ". . . the state was all and the civil society was gelatinous and primordial." Topple the czarist bureaucracy and there was nothing to replace it with; there was a void. But in Western Europe, on the contrary, "in the tremors of the state one suddenly perceived the robust structure of civil society. The state was only the forward trench, behind which stand the networks of forts."

So the most crucial single justification for making a socialist revolution in a peasant country—the imminence of proletarian revolution in Western Europe—was a delusion. Lenin responded to the resulting impasse during the last years of his life in two different ways: he audaciously sponsored the revival of capitalism in Russia; and, in poignant, or perhaps tragic, moments he acknowledged the failure of his policies and desperately turned back to the dreams of peasant socialism which he had scorned during all of his life.

By 1920 Russia was in a shambles. Three years of foreign intervention and civil war had taken an enormous toll and many of the most militant and dedicated Communists had been killed. The peasants, who had followed the Bolsheviks because they promised them land and an end to the war, were suddenly refusing to deliver their surplus grain to a government that appropriated it by force. At this point, Lenin acted with characteristic boldness by proposing to end "war Communism," that egalitarian and managed response to military problems, to denationalize a part of the economy and to allow for the planned growth of a capitalist sector in the countryside.

In arguing for this *volte face,* Lenin now said that there were two preconditions for the success of a socialist revolution in a backward country: "First, if it is given timely support by one or several advanced countries. . . . The second condition is agreement between the proletariat, which is exercising the dictatorship, that is, holding state power, and the majority of the peasant population." And countering the reluctance of some of the Bolsheviks to adopt such a seemingly pro-bourgeois policy, he warned that the rising at Kronstadt in 1921 was an expression of peasant discontent which the old policies of seizing grain had caused.

The New Economic Policy did indeed revive the economy through its capitalist methods, but it was a far cry from the socialist revolution proclaimed in October, 1917. Moreover, by 1921 Lenin, who only a few years before had looked to the rapid coming of the World Soviet Republic, was saying that "it would be madness on our part to assume that help will shortly arrive from Europe in the shape of a strong proletarian revolution." So what, then, was left of the dream? A lesser man would not have dared to confront his failure, especially when it concerned the fate of nations and the very prospect of socialism itself. Lenin, however, contemplated the abyss.

The essays of 1923—*On Cooperation, Our Revolution, How We Should Reorganize the Workers' and Peasants' Inspection* and *Better Fewer, But Better*—were written during a period of his life that was as personally trying as it was politically difficult. He was sick and dying, cut off from the normal routine and isolated from the political life of the state he had created. His wife, Krupskaya, was even insulted by Stalin, and this was one more proof of the latter's insensitivity and arrogance, qualities that were to leave a bloody mark on the history of the times. Vainly, Lenin tried to struggle against the current, to begin anew. He sought an alliance with Trotsky as a way of fighting the bureaucratic and dictatorial trends that were overwhelming the Revolution. But he died before he could finish his new beginning.

The workers, Lenin said in *Better Fewer, But Better,* "would like to build a better apparatus for us [state and Soviet apparatus] but they do not know how. They cannot build one. They have not yet developed the culture required for this; and it is culture that is required." Thus the Lenin who in 1917 believed that the Soviets had found a way to involve the entire people in the administration of government. In *On Cooperation* he said of the Soviet state machinery that "we took [it] over in its entirety from the preceding epoch." And in his letter of December, 1922, he was even more specific: "In effect we took over the old machinery of state from the Tsar and the bourgeoisie. . . ." Thus the Lenin who wanted to smash the bourgeois state altogether.

Then, in a sort of dialogue with the Marxist theoreticians of the Second International in *Our Revolution,* comes an extraordinary admission: "'The development of the productive forces of Russia has not attained the level that makes socialism possible.' . . . They [the Second Internationalists] keep harping on this *incontrovertible proposition* in a thousand different keys, and think that it is the decisive criterion of our revolution." (Emphasis added.)

And in a most remarkable description of the revolution he had led—it would not have been even comprehensible to the Lenin of 1917—he says of his opponents in the Second International, "It does not occur to any of them to ask: but what about a people that found itself in a revolutionary situation such as that created during the first imperialist war? Might it not, *influenced by the hopelessness of its situation,* fling itself into a struggle that would offer it at least some chance of *securing conditions for the future development of* civilization that were somewhat unusual." (Emphasis added.)

But how, then, did Lenin propose to get out of the impasse that he had—poignantly, almost, it seems to me—defined? He gave two answers. First, in *On Cooperation* he confessed that "there has been a radical modification of our whole outlook on socialism. The radical modification is this: formerly we placed and had to place, the main emphasis on political struggle, on revolution, on the winning of political power, etc. Now the emphasis is changing and shifting to peaceful, organizational, 'cultural' work." So now, there are two main tasks: to reorganize the machinery of state and to carry out educational work among the peasants (the workers, those classic heroes of the Marxian vision, have vanished). "This cultural revolution," Lenin concludes, "would now suffice to make our country a completely socialist country. . . ."

How does this differ from the utopian socialism, and particularly the Russian populism, that Lenin had criticized all his life? His answer was that the utopians did not see the necessity for a determined struggle for power, but that once the working class wins the state, those very same ideas about cooperation and the peasantry become revolutionary. Yet for all his disclaimers, the fact is that the Lenin of 1923 had adopted views much closer to the Russian Populism of Chernyshevsky than to Marx. The workers were now seen as lacking the culture to build socialism; peasants, improving themselves through nonviolent cooperation, were to take their place.

His second answer to his dilemma was equally un-Marxist. In *Better Fewer, But Better,* he wrote, "In the last analysis, the outcome of the struggle will be determined by the fact that Russia, India, China, etc., account for the overwhelming majority of the population of the globe. And during the past few years it is this majority that has been drawn into the struggle for emancipation with extraordinary rapidity, so that in this respect there cannot be the slightest doubt what the final outcome of the world struggle will be. *In this sense*, the complete victory of socialism is fully and absolutely assured."

Yet this is no solution of the problem but an aggravation of it. For if the great barrier to socialism in Russia was the backwardness of the country it had conquered, how would that be alleviated by joining it to economies, such as the Chinese and the Indian, that were even more backward? That these three nations form a numerical majority of mankind is not crucial either. For in the Marxian analysis it is the economic and social weight of peoples, not their numbers, that is ultimately decisive. A relatively small minority of Europeans have, after all, dominated the world for some centuries precisely because of their technological —and in Lenin's sense of the term, cultural—superiority.

The issue cannot be blustered away, as in Roger Garaudy's comment that "Marx could only conceive of one model of socialism: that of a social system following immediately after a capitalism which is fully developed to the point of decadence. A half-century later, Lenin confronted a new problem: the possibility of passing directly from feudal societies (in Asia, for example) to socialism." For one thing, Lenin never really outlined such a transition, but in the last desperate years of his life, yearned for one; for another, if there is any one proposition of Marx's that has stood the test of time, it is his insight that "rights can never be higher than the economic level of society and the cultural development, which the economic level determines." It is true, however, that one must now add a second possible form of transition to socialism: not simply from capitalism to socialism, but from the anti-socialist system that calls itself socialist to a genuine socialism (this latter possibility, which, at various times, received mass support in Poland, Hungary, East Germany and Czechoslovakia, will be discussed later on).[4]

These last writings of Lenin were, as even the Russian edition of his works recognizes, the "equivalent of an outline program." For all the contradictions and ambiguities they contained, they were clearly inspired by a passion to create a socialist order even under impossible conditions. And they marked the audacious failure of the Marxian revolution in Russia, for once the Western proletariat failed to rise up, Lenin's hopes were doomed. To that question, which still confronts the Third World today—who will make the equivalent of the bourgeois revolution where there is no bourgeoisie capable of carrying it through?—Lenin had originally answered: the workers and peasants in an alliance. Then, under the force of circumstances in 1917, he adopted Trotsky's solution to the problem: the Russian workers will make the revolution in conjunction with the victorious workers of Western Europe. And finally, just before he died, Lenin veered quite close to the old Russian Populism: the peasants will, through a cultural revolution, make the good society.

None of these answers worked. None of them do today, even though each still has passionate adherents. But Joseph Stalin abandoned all the niceties and carried out a brutal revolution from above. He had found an effective substitute for the bourgeoisie: not the workers or the peasants or the European proletariat, but the Communist Party.

## II · STALIN

Joseph Stalin was the architect of a new form of class society which I shall call "bureaucratic collectivism." Under it, the state owns the means of production, and the elite Party bureaucracy owns the state.

By totalitarian means it is able to extract a surplus from the direct producers and to invest it in industrial modernization and its own class privileges. It does these things in the name of "socialism," and yet it is based on the continuing expropriation of the political power of the workers and the peasants.

Such a society, it must be emphasized, does not require Russian sponsorship. It can be run by Maoists who detest Moscow, or even by nationalists who jail Communist leaders (these variants of it will be examined in Chapter XI). It is, in other words, a structural tendency of modern life, a possibility in all of those countries forced to search for non- and anti-capitalist modes of modernization (and even in developed capitalist economies). If, in what follows, I go into some detail with regard to what happened in Russia, it is because these events were so profoundly prototypical.

The historical conditions that gave rise to Stalinism are clear enough. After Lenin's death in 1924 it became more and more obvious that the European revolution was not going to save Russia from the consequences of its backwardness. The encouragement of capitalism in the countryside also threatened to subvert the anti-capitalist principles of the regime and, in any case, did not provide sufficient funds for accumulation and industrialization. Socialism was impossible and the regime was opposed to a capitalist restoration. Where, then, could it go? Stalin's answer was "socialism in one country."

In the first edition of *The Foundations of Leninism* in 1924 Stalin had adhered to the Leninist orthodoxy: "To overthrow the bourgeoisie the efforts of one country are sufficient; that is proved by the history of our revolution. For the final victory of socialism, for the organization of socialist production, the efforts of one country, particularly of a peasant country like Russia, are insufficient; for that, the efforts of several advanced countries are required." Two years later he made a momentous amendment to his formula. Now it was possible to build socialism in one country and to achieve victory, but for final victory—"the full guarantee against attempts at intervention"—the workers had to prevail in several countries. "Socialist production" was proclaimed as a possibility in a single, poor land.

In his writings of this period Stalin could only find one quotation from Lenin—and given the Lenin cult which he had sponsored, a citation from the holy writ was now as necessary as the appeal to the authority of Marx and Engels had once been—that even seemed to justify his position. In 1915 Lenin had remarked, "Uneven development and political development is an absolute law of capitalism. Hence the victory of socialism is possible first in several, or even in one, capitalist country." There is, however, every reason to believe that this cryptic reference was not intended to apply to Russia at all. For just a year later Lenin wrote that "Socialism will be achieved by the united action of the proletarians, not of all, but of a minority of countries, those that have reached the *advanced* capitalist stage of development. . . . The undeveloped countries," he continued, "are a different matter. They embrace the whole of Eastern Europe. . . ." As Carr notes, Lenin's 1915 statement was an attempt to convince French or German workers that they did not have to wait for each other's revolutions but could seize power on their own.

Between Lenin's death in 1924 and Trotsky's defeat in 1928, "socialism in one country" meant a policy of encouraging peasant capitalism. The Trotskyist opposition was accused of being anti-peasant on the grounds that its plans for industrialization would exploit the countryside. But with his triumph over the Trotsky-ists, Stalin turned upon his old factional ally Bukharin, the theorist of socialism "at a snail's pace" who had advocated a long, gradual evolution into the new order. In that struggle between Stalin and Bukharin, Trotsky's inability to conceive of an alterna-tive to either capitalism or socialism led him to make a disastrous error.

For Trotsky, Russia could either go forward to socialism or back-ward to capitalism. And since Bukharin was the strongest defender of private peasant property in the Party, that made him the chief danger, the representative of the tendency to revert to capitalism. Therefore for all of Trotsky's bitter opposition to Stalin, he could not bring himself to form a bloc with Bukharin against him—and even envisioned joining with Stalin against Bukharin. To the day of his assassination, Trotsky remained locked in his either/or of capitalism or socialism for Russia. Meanwhile, Stalin went on to make an anti-capitalist, anti-socialist revolution. He was even almost candid about the unprecedented nature of his undertak-ing.

In 1929 Stalin began to "eliminate" the *kulaks* as a class. Later, in a history of the Bolshevik Party which he personally super-vised (and which, of course, paid great homage to his genius), he spoke of the event in this way: "This was a profound revolu-tion, a leap from an old qualitative state of society to a new quali-tative state, *equivalent in its consequences to the revolution of October, 1917.*" (Emphasis added.) This is, I believe, a quite ac-curate description but also rather indiscreet. For if the October Revolution transferred power from the bourgeoisie to the workers, what, then, was the qualitative leap of 1929? Stalin would respond that it was a giant step forward in laying the foundations of "so-cialism in one country," but I would take his Marxist language more literally: the event was, indeed, "qualitative," for it marked an important moment in the expropriation of whatever political power remained to the workers and peasants and a turning toward a new form of class society.

But then, in the very next sentence, Stalin commits still another indiscretion: "The distinguishing feature of this revolution is that it was accomplished from above, on the initiative of the state, and directly supported from below by the millions of peasants who were fighting to throw off Kulak bonds and to live in free-dom on the collective farms." Now the second part of this sen-tence—that the peasants were trying to force their way into collective farms—was, as will be seen shortly, sheer fantasy. But even more remarkable is that Stalin himself characterizes the process as being *"accomplished from above, on the initiative of the state."* For there is in Marxist literature a very precise meaning to "revolution from above": it describes how Bismarck, in the absence of a vigorous bourgeoisie, carried out the modernization and unification of Germany in a counterrevolutionary fashion which, on occasion, used demagogic measures that were called "socialist," including the nationalization of certain industries. And Lenin himself had used the phrase in just that sense.

One can only speculate now as to why Stalin used such a suggestive phrase to describe his triumph. But there is no question that it offers an illuminating, if unwitting, insight into how profoundly he had not simply revised, but utterly taken leave of Marxism. At different points in his life, as earlier chapters have noted, Marx had variously assessed the imminence of revolution and the degree to which the working class had developed a truly revolutionary consciousness. Yet at no moment in his entire life did he ever lose faith in that principle which he inscribed in the statutes of the International Workingmen's Association: "The emancipation of the working class must be conquered by the working class itself."

Lenin had, as we have seen, moved toward a Blanquist version of the dictatorship of the proletariat in which the state did not express the majority but created it. Even then, he always made it clear that this definition of the phrase was exceptional, a product of those unique—perhaps impossible—Russian conditions. But Stalin seized upon this precedent and utilized it to root out every single shred of popular sovereignty. Already in 1926 he proclaimed that the party "cannot share" its leadership with other parties, and therefore could not tolerate factions within its own ranks, since these would only reflect the differences that were denied voice outside it. This led to the truly incredible theory of self-criticism, which he spelled out in 1928: "Since our country is a country with a dictatorship of the proletariat, and since the dictatorship is directed by one party, the Communist Party, which does not, and cannot, share power with other parties, is it not clear that to make headway we ourselves must disclose and correct our errors—is it not clear that there is no one else to disclose and correct them for us?" The notion that an elite, minority dictatorship would voluntarily police itself not only flies in the face of everything Marx wrote about the brute and self-interested realities of power; it outrages the most untutored common sense as well.

So it was that when Stalin initiated his revolution from above, there was no protest and no self-criticism. Or rather, the protest and criticism took forms that were to be disastrous for the Soviet state to the present moment.

In that brutal process of collectivization and purges, at least six and a half million lives were lost, a figure that Zbigniew Brzezinski takes to be a low estimate. Robert Conquest has argued that in the period 1936 to 1938 alone there were a million executions and two million died in the camps. Conquest puts the human cost of forced collectivization at three million deaths. Moreover, the peasants, who according to Stalin's myth were fighting to gain admission to the collectives, responded in helpless outrage by destroying their farm animals. Between 1928 and 1933 the number of horses in the Soviet Union fell from 33.4 million to 14.9 million, the cattle from 70.4 million to 33.7 million, and sheep and goats from 145.9 million to 41.8 million.

This human and agricultural catastrophe was provoked by a savage war against the peasantry which had no rationale in all of Marxist literature. Engels had insisted that cooperative production on the land would develop under socialism "not by means of force, but by example and by offering social help toward this end." He—and Marx—had even considered compensating the large landowners and industrialists for their property: "Marx had—many times—expressed his view to me that we would find it cheaper to buy out the whole gang." And Lenin in the last years of his life had seen an alliance between the Communists and the peasants as one of the two preconditions of the survival of the Revolution itself.[5]

But then, Stalin was making a different revolution from the one Lenin had sought, and there was great method in the madness of his brutality. Under capitalism, the accumulation of capital, industrialization and centralization resulted from the competition of private entrepreneurs (often with generous state aid) and tended toward monopoly. In Russia, as has been seen, that bourgeois modernization process did not take place and there was no economic basis for socialism either. So the party, using its totalitarian power, was able to rig the market to its advantage, extract an enormous surplus from the workers and invest part of that gain in the privileges of the bureaucracy and part of it in the creation of an industrial society.

In the twenties in Russia, when genuine intellectual discussion was still possible within the Communist Party, E. Preobrazhensky, a leading economic theorist for the Trotskyist opposition, was candid about what he called "primitive socialist accumulation." This involved "restriction of individual demand" and it "subordinates the growth of wages to the function of accumulation, *limits the growth in the quality of social relationships* and maintains a gap between the wage level and the value of labor power." (Emphasis added.) Preobrazhensky and the Trotskyists could be this frank about the appropriation of the surplus in the Soviet Union because they did not believe it possible to build socialism—which they understood as a matter of the "quality of social relationships" and not simply as economic growth—in a single, and relatively backward, country.

Under such circumstances, it is not surprising that Stalin made a principled defense of inequality. The scripture cited for this position was Marx's *Critique of the Gotha Program*, in which the two stages of the socialist transformation were described. In the first phase of Communism, Marx had said, people would not be paid according to their needs but rather in some proportion to the quantity and quality of their work. This, he argued, was an unfortunate necessity given the fact that socialism matured within a capitalist society in which such bourgeois conceptions of rights prevailed. It was only in the higher phase that society would inscribe upon its banner "from each according to his abilities, to each according to his needs." But since both Marx and Engels believed that the length of this transition period would depend upon the degree of development of the forces of production, they shortened their estimate of it as time went on. In 1891 Engels thought it would be "short, meager but morally useful." Stalin, on the other hand, celebrated inequality with enthusiasm and projected it over an entire epoch. "Equalitarianism," he told Emil Ludwig, "has nothing in common with Marxian socialism."

But even the principle of "from each according to his ability, to each according to his work," which Stalin made a central rule of his regime, was, according to the insider's testimony of Varga, perverted. "The labor of ordinary citizens was badly paid even if they demonstrated capacities which were above the average and performed their tasks well. On the other hand, the labor of the privileged of the *nomenclatura* [a czarist term for a list of people to be given special treatment by the state, a practice that Varga says Stalin adopted] was very well paid, sometimes exorbitantly so, even if they did not show any special capacity."

The existence of such an elite suggests that one is in the presence of a class society. And indeed, there is now enough evidence to begin to generalize the Stalinist reality in terms of the Marxian definition of the "innermost secret" of a social order: how the surplus is pumped out of the direct producers. When this is done, the preposterous and utterly un-Marxist explanations of Stalin made by the Communist leaders—that he committed "mistakes," that an entire generation of bloody history is to be accounted for by a "cult of personality"—are torn to shreds.

In Russia the decision of how to divide up the surplus is made by the bureaucracy and enforced through totalitarian controls. For decades now output has increased enormously, but consumption has not risen as fast as production. Instead, there have been massive investments in heavy industry and in the privileges of the ruling class. So the unpaid portion of the working day has been growing and the living standards of the people have gone up slowly. In the precise, Marxist usage of the term, then, the Soviet Union is an exploitative society. Indeed, Friedrich Engels described a quite similar phenomenon in 1884. He was writing to August Bebel about "state socialism," i.e., Bismarck's statist capitalism. "If you want to study a model of state socialism then: *Java.* There the Dutch government has organized all of production on the basis of the old communist village community so socialistically and taken over the sale of all the products so handsomely that, outside of 100 million marks for administrators and the army, a pure profit of about 70 million a year . . ."

Under this system in Russia, the party leaders do not receive their cars, villas and foreign trips because they own stock certificates, but rather as a privilege of their political position within the bureaucratic hierarchy. These class privileges of the bureaucracy, it must be emphasized, are not simply unfair in some abstract, ethical sense. They work to determine the very shape and fabric of the society. In the late 1950s, for instance, 75 percent of the students in Moscow University were the children of officials, 20 percent of workers, 5 percent of farmers, yet the officials constituted only 20 percent of the population, workers 48 percent and farmers 31 percent.

Given this structure, totalitarianism was not the result of Stalin's malevolence but a crucial and functional element in the system.

Since the state apparatus and the new ruling class are one, the former had to be utterly pervasive. Under capitalism, a strike against an individual company is not an act of treason. To be sure, the government often intervenes in the name of "law and order" on the side of the business—a practice that was particularly vicious and widespread in early American labor history—but it does not have to regard every outbreak of the class struggle as revolutionary. But under the Soviet model, the economic and political direction are identical. If the government were to permit a strike, a genuine trade union or any kind of autonomous activity within the economy, it would be tolerating an alternate source of political power. And since political power in this system is the means of establishing economic and social power, that would amount to sanctioning revolution.

In his *Notes on Machiavelli,* Antonio Gramsci understood this point quite brilliantly, though his own attitude toward it was ambiguous. Gramsci wrote, "Totalitarian politics tend, precisely, (1) to work so that members of the given party find in this one party alone all the satisfactions which they previously found in other organizations and thus break all their ties with alien cultural organisms; (2) to destroy all other organizations and to incorporate them in a system in which the party alone is the regulator. . . . This happens," Gramsci continues, "(1) when the given party is the bearer of a new culture and it is a progressive development; (2) when the party wants to hold back another force, the bearer of a new culture, from becoming totalitarian in this way and it is an objectively reactionary, regressive development if reaction (as always) does not admit its identity and attempts to be the bearer of a new culture."

This is a remarkable statement on the part of the founder of the Italian Communist Party for it admits that the methods of Communism and fascism (and he is clearly thinking of Mussolini, not Hitler) are the same and that the two phenomena are to be distinguished only in their "objective" impact upon history. But since that "new culture" which Gramsci saw in the Soviet Union and which gave it the right to use the same methods as the fascists in the name of process never existed, his analysis is an implicit condemnation of contemporary Communist practice.

But then, this totalitarian structure is not simply a matter of economics or politics. Like all other class systems, it invades the spheres of the mind and spirit as well. In Chapter IV it was shown how the pre-World War I experience of the European social democracy with its continuous increments of electoral success gave rise to a mechanistic, Darwinist reading of Marx and Engels. Totalitarianism was even more extreme on this count. Stalin, as Iring Fetscher has pointed out, was at great pains to deny the Hegelian origins of Marxism, i.e., the subjective component in Marx's thinking, with its stress on the self-emancipation of the proletariat. Instead, he based himself upon Engels' most dubious speculations on the dialectic and turned Marxism into a universal key to all knowledge.

This ideological development served several functions. If the Party, as the living incarnation of Marxism, knew "objectively" what was good for the working class, then it could emancipate the workers without their participation or even over their violent objections. Ironically, as Fetscher notes, Stalin's anti-Hegelianism in theory gave way to a profound Hegelianism in practice: the Russian dictator represented the Idea working itself out in history independently of the will of the people. Secondly, this rewriting of Marxism helped to establish and justify Stalin's own position in the Soviet system. If the leader of the party was the most profound scientist of them all, if he most brilliantly perceived the "laws" of history according to which society was being created, then his deification was rational.

Thus, I cannot agree with the economist Charles Wilber that "there is no inherent reason why the Soviet model must be operated by a dogmatic totalitarian Communist Party. A halfway democratic socialist regime could probably supply whatever compulsion was necessary to implement the model." Now it is certainly true that one need not be a Communist to follow in Stalin's footsteps, as Chapter XI will document. But it is not true that the system can be operated democratically, and particularly not halfway democratically. Under Communism, it is precisely the totalitarian monopoly of political power that allows the bureaucracy to extract the surplus from the direct producers and use it for its own ends. If the producers were allowed to participate in those decisions, it would signal a revolutionary shift of control from the top to the bottom. For then the bureaucracy could retain its position in society only if the masses voluntarily voted to tax themselves in order to build even more steel mills and better apartments for the party hierarchy and to finance the secret police. That hope, one suspects, would be a rather thin reed for Stalin's successors to lean on.

I do not mean, however, to suggest that there is no internal resistance or dynamic possible within such a society (that was an underlying theme of Hannah Arendt's *Origins of Totalitarianism*). There have already been enormous changes within the totalitarian framework. After the period of capital accumulation, productivity in the modern sector went up, the influx of the rural masses into the cities tapered off and it became necessary to rely more upon material incentives than upon brute force. Slave laborers can dig a canal with picks and shovels but they cannot be lashed into doing scientific work.

Indeed, Stalin's monstrous success may well have created a basic contradiction for present-day Soviet society. The whip and the purge did successfully extract a considerable surplus out of the people and lay the foundations for industrialization. But modern industrial society cannot be efficiently run at gunpoint, even by a de-Stalinized guard. It needs a certain openness and access to information, in its elite sectors, at the very least. Thus Stalin's bureaucratic centralization, which had helped to carry out the bloody mobilization of a backward economy, became a fetter on further growth once a sophisticated technological structure had been built. The Soviet *mode* of the production, totalitarian bureaucratic collectivism, is thus in conflict with the *means* of production, a sophisticated technology. It is this fact that accounts for the lackluster and aimless Russian economy of the sixties—and for the demands on the part of some of the shrewder bureaucrats for a limited autonomy.

But this hardly means that the bureaucracy in Russia is going to abdicate power. Paradoxically, one can see the severe limits on reform within this system precisely in the process of de-Stalinization initiated in 1956. The dictator was criticized for his "excesses," above all, for sending police to arrest bureaucrats and party members in the middle of the night. But the Communists could not allow a genuine Marxian analysis of how their dead, and mad, leader had managed to dominate an entire nation for a generation and to build there a new form of society. That would raise fundamental and revolutionary questions about the very basis of the society. The bureaucracy, as Max Shachtman has remarked, admired Stalin in that he raised it above the masses, but hated him in that he raised himself above it. It could afford to criticize him on the second count; it had to revere him on the first.

Therefore from the very first Nikita Khrushchev carefully delimited his attack on his former comrade. Stalin, he said, played a

progressive role up to the Seventeenth Congress of the Party in
1934, i.e., the revolution from above initiated in 1929 and the consequent human destruction and exploitation were a good thing.
It was at the Seventeenth Congress that Stalin turned so brutally
against the old Bolsheviks, including many who had supported
him, and at that point his "mistakes" began. Yet even this very
modest critique turned out to be too much for the bureaucracy.
Khrushchev was overthrown in 1964 and re-Stalinization was the
order of the day.

A seemingly obscure doctrinal point illuminates these developments. In Khrushchev's 1961 Party Program Russia was said to be
entering the phase of Communism. In 1966 at the Twenty-third
Congress, it was only making the "transition to Communism." The
danger in Khrushchev's exuberant boast is obvious: if the Communist stage of society has been reached, according to the catechisms of Soviet Russia, the rule of "to each according to his
needs" is supposed to prevail. But that rule is not at all compatible
with the hard, disciplined labor the Soviet leaders exact from their
people; it contradicts Stalin's maxim of "to each according to his
work." So it was necessary to project the stage of Communism
into the vague future and to insist in the here and now on the
inequalities that are characteristic of "building socialism."

In the fall of 1970 K. S. Karol, a veteran of the Red Army and
a man of impeccable Leftist credentials, reported on the situation
in Russia fourteen years after de-Stalinization. Members of the
collective farms, he said, are not even given the internal passports
that would permit them to move freely within the country. They
work as little as possible on the common plot—in the Ukraine, according to the official statistics, only 180 days a year, in Georgia,
135—and spend the rest of their time farming their private plots.
Even though the industrial system is planned, there is little
cooperation between enterprises: of one hundred big Soviet factories, seventy-one make their own pig iron. As a measure of manpower control, the state has decreed that a worker cannot leave
a plant for three years after he is hired.

But then it is hardly necessary to depend upon travelers in the
Soviet Union for a sense of what is happening there. There is also
persuasive testimony from insiders.

In his *Testament*, as I noted earlier, Varga compared the privileges of the Soviet bureaucracy to the *nomenclatura* under the
czar. As he describes their rewards, they include "high salaries.

'envelopes' passing from hand to hand, being able to get goods which cannot be found on the regular market, private canteens, large apartments sometimes luxuriously furnished, as well as *dachas* with gardens, tennis courts, swimming pools, personal cars and chauffeurs and first-class retreats."

The Chinese Communists generalize their indictment of such privileges (I find the Chinese criticisms of the Russians, and the Russian criticism of the Chinese, quite persuasive). "The members of this privileged stratum," the editorial departments of *Red Flag* and the *People's Daily* wrote in 1964, "have converted the function of serving the masses into the privilege of dominating them. They are abusing their powers over the means of livelihood for the private benefit of their small clique. The members of this privileged stratum appropriate the fruits of the Soviet people's labour and pocket incomes that are dozens or even a hundred times those of the average Soviet worker and peasant. They not only secure high incomes in the form of salaries, high awards, high royalties and a great variety of personal subsidies, but also use their privileged position to appropriate public property by graft and bribery."

And in one of the most significant statements on this question made from within the Soviet Union, academician Andrei D. Sakharov wrote, "It is sometimes suggested in the literature that the political manifestations of Stalinism represented a sort of superstructure over the economic bases of an anti-Leninist pseudo-socialism that led to the formation in the Soviet Union of a distinct class—a bureaucratic elite. . . . I cannot deny that there is some (but not the whole) truth in such an interpretation. . . ."

Sakharov is an independent member of the Russian establishment who usually makes his criticisms from within the system. Yet even he will speculate on the possibility that Communism is a new form of class society. But there are others within the Communist world who have not simply discussed this as a possibility, but have tried to transform it in reality.[6]

In some cases, the freedom movement under Communism begins with the students and intelligentsia. In Poland in 1956 the publication *Po Prostu* was the original center of the resistance, in Hungary in 1956 the Petoffi Circle played that role, and in Czechoslovakia in 1967 and 1968 a good deal of the anti-Stalinist impetus came from journalists and writers. The reasons for this development are obvious enough: intellectual freedom is an immediate necessity—a trade-union question, as it were—for such people, and they therefore feel the impact of totalitarianism in a most direct way. However, these movements only became effective when they linked up with the working class.

In Poland and Hungary in 1956 soviets—that is, councils of workers—appeared for the first time in European history since they were destroyed in Russia by the Stalinist revolution from above. In Czechoslovakia in 1968 the factories were centers of the movement and the cooperation of the entire working class made it possible to hold a clandestine congress of the Communist Party. In East Germany in 1953 and in Poland in 1970 the uprising began first of all among the workers. And as *Le Monde* reported in 1971, the Polish events saw the proletariat move from bread and butter issues to the demand for free elections within the unions and workers' councils. (At this writing, that historic struggle is far from over.)

The emergence of soviets as a form of struggle against a Communist ruling class was almost a predictable irony. For just as in Western capitalist society people become anti-capitalist by taking the official values of democracy and equality seriously, so, too, in Communist society the governmental ideology has a subversive potential. Indeed, the Communist rhetoric is even more potent than the bourgeois democratic since it uses the language of the most revolutionary ideal ever proclaimed—the classless society— to facilitate class oppression. Therefore the moment that people take the propaganda seriously, they become possible recruits for a movement of opposition.

And Communist slanders to the contrary notwithstanding, these upheavals within Communism in East Germany, Poland, Hungary, Czechoslovakia and among the intelligentsia in the Soviet Union itself have never advocated a return to capitalism, much less the fascism with which they are sometimes charged. They have always proposed what the Czechs call "the human face of socialism." As early as 1956 Edda Werfel, the Polish philosopher, paraphrased *The Communist Manifesto:* "A spectre is abroad in Eastern Europe, the spectre of human socialism, and it terrifies not only the capitalists but the Stalinists as well."

The proponents of freedom within the Communist societies are quite aware that the very meaning of socialism is at stake. "To explain what socialism really is," wrote Karel Kosik, the Czech Marxist philosopher, "one must distinguish between real and alleged socialism." And Svetozar Stojanovic, a Yugoslav Marxist scholar, has argued that in the Soviet Union "expropriated feudal and bourgeois property became the basis of statist [*étatist*] property," and "the broad masses were transformed into an object of exploitation by a new ruling class." The crucial question, Stojanovic concluded, is not so much the choice between capitalism or socialism but between "statism and socialism."

Stojanovic's remarks are quite apropos of a brief summary of the analysis of this chapter. Bureaucratic collectivism developed in Russia for the very specific historical reasons that I have outlined. But the event also had global implications. That is quite obvious in the case of the Third World peoples who, like the Russians, want to modernize but cannot do so in the capitalist way. It may also even be relevant to the Western welfare states where an intensification of the present integration of corporate and governmental power (a trend that is treated in Chapter XII) could end up in a "liberal" bureaucratic collectivism.

So Stojanovic is quite right to say (he uses the term "statism" where I would write "bureaucratic collectivism"), "Historic experience after Marx has shown that two possibilities and tendencies are inherent in capitalism—the statist and the socialist—and not only one, as Marx supposed. The epochal dilemma, capitalism or socialism, is progressively being pushed into the background and the epochal dilemma, statism or socialism, is coming to the fore."

So Communism does indeed represent one of the historic alternatives in the present era. But ironically, this self-proclaimed Marxist society has blazed the way to the anti-socialist variant of the future. I propose to explore a few aspects of this fact in the closing pages of this chapter for a political reason. Communism is unquestionably anti-capitalist and therefore there are those on the Left in the Western countries who regard any criticism of it as playing into the hands of their own ruling class and thus a betrayal of radicalism. More often than not, these people argue that somehow the basic direction of Communist society—above all, the nationalization of the means of production—is right and that perfidious bureaucrats have only temporarily usurped popular power.

I believe that Communism could well be the model of the inhuman status quo of the twenty-first century. It is for this reason, and not because I want to accommodate myself to capitalism (which receives its due later on), that I must evaluate it so care-fully.

Since 1956 the number of people who take Soviet descriptions of Russian society at face value has been declining throughout the world. But there is a sophisticated attitude that defends Stalin's action in the name of socialist values: of course, Russia is not classless; of course, totalitarian force was used; but that was his-torically necessary. One of the most brilliant representatives of this way of thinking is Isaac Deutscher.

The Bolsheviks, Deutscher wrote, "could not achieve socialism; for that presupposed economic abundance, high popular standards of living, of education and of general civilization, the disappear-ance of striking social contrasts, the cessation of domination of man by man and a spiritual climate corresponding to this general transformation of society. But to the Marxist the nationalized economy was the essential prerequisite of socialism, the genuine foundation. It was quite conceivable that even on that foundation the edifice of socialism might not rise; but it was unthinkable without it."

Later on Deutscher summarized his position: "Yet however 'illegitimate' from the classical Marxist viewpoint, Stalin's revolu-tion from above effected a lasting and as to scale unprecedented change in property relations and ultimately in the nation's way of life." As time went on, Deutscher continued, the industrial founda-tions that Stalin laid became more advanced and therefore contra-dicted the Stalinist superstructure. "Thus, by an irony of history Stalin's epigones began the liquidation of Stalinism and thereby carried out, *malgré eux-mêmes,* part of Trotsky's political testa-ment."

This analysis, which was first formulated in its essentials by Trotsky in *The Revolution Betrayed,* is more sophisticated than the theory that the sheer fact of Soviet industrialization justifies the crimes of Stalinism. Of course, Russia is now economically ad-vanced as compared to the czarist period and socialism one day may build upon that heritage which was purchased at such a frightful human cost. But then, Japanese capitalism and South African racism have accomplished their own prodigies since World War II. The role of the socialist in Japan, South Africa and Russia—or in any nation which is advancing by cruel and ex-ploitative means—is to seek alternatives, not to celebrate produc-tion statistics. Deutscher, a man of considerable Marxist culture, was aware of this fundamental distinction. So he is saying something much more complex than the simpleminded admirers of steel mills—or of Mussolini's trains running on time—could ever imagine.

Following Trotsky, Deutscher holds that nationalized property is, in and of itself, superior to private property from a socialist point of view. Since the Soviet state is indeed a defender of such public ownership of the means of production, he therefore gives it critical support even though it is totalitarian. The sad political consequence of this attitude was that in the fifties Deutscher regarded the general strike in East Germany and the rebellions in Hungary and Poland as attempts at "bourgeois restoration" because they challenged a Communist bureaucracy which, in spite of itself, was doing the virtuous work of history. It was as if Marx had come out for the British troops and against the Indian masses.

The fundamental error in all this—and it is particularly fecund for the misunderstanding of the trends leading to the next century —is that gigantic assumption that nationalization is inherently progressive. Marx had understood as a youth that it was possible that "the bureaucracy possesses the state as its own *private property*." When that happens, he said in an anticipatory epitaph for the Communist bureaucracy, "*Authority* is therefore the principle of its knowledge, and the deification of authority is its *basic credo*." (Emphasis in the original.)

In a remarkable essay written in 1916 when he was a leader of the Left wing of the Bolshevik Party, Nikolai Bukharin updated that Marxian insight. He was analyzing German "war socialism"— the planned mobilization of the economy by the bourgeoisie in order to further its own reactionary interests. "The regulation of production by itself does not mean socialism at all," Bukharin wrote; "it exists in any sort of economy, in any slave-owning group with a natural economy."

In the first stage of capitalism, Bukharin said, the state was the instrument of the dominant class. Then other capitalist organizations develop and the state becomes one institution among many. "Finally the third stage arrives, *when the state absorbs these organizations and again becomes the only over-all organization of the dominant class, with a technical division* of labor inside it; the formerly independent organizational groupings are transformed into divisions of a gigantic state mechanism which descends with crushing force upon the obvious and internal enemy.

Thus arises the final type of the contemporary imperialist bandit state, the iron organization which with its grasping, prehensile paws seizes the living body of society."

In the twenties some of the opposition groups within the Bolshevik Party applied the theory of "state socialism"—that is, of anti-socialist "socialism"—to the Russian Revolution itself. The Workers' Truth group, for instance, charged that the Soviet state had become the instrument of a new bourgeoisie. But Christian Rakovsky, one of the oldest and most respected of the Bolsheviks, was even more prescient. He quoted Marx on how the state could become the private property of a bureaucracy and then wrote of Stalin's policies (the essay dates from 1930): "Before our eyes a great class of rulers has been taking shape and is continuing to develop. . . . The unifying factor of this unique class is that unique form of private property, governmental power." More recently, Charles Bettelheim, a French Marxist of Maoist sympathies, has written, "if the workers do not dominate the state apparatus, if it is dominated by a corps of functionaries and administrators and escapes the control and direction of the working masses, it is this corps of functionaries and administrators which effectively becomes the owner (in the sense of a relationship of production) of the means of production."

I would generalize. Where the state owns the means of production, the crucial question is, Who owns the state? The people can own the state in only one way: through the fullest and freest right to change its policies and personnel. Therefore in a nationalized economy exclusion from political power is not something unfortunate that happens in a "superstructure"; it determines the social and economic base of the system itself, it secures class power to those who "own" the state, which owns the means of production. In Russia in the first half of the twentieth century the bourgeoisie was not in fact able to modernize and the Party-state carried out that function and developed into just such a bureaucratic collectivist power. In China and other nations of the Third World there were similar developments after World War II. And in the advanced Western countries it is possible that there will be a transition not from capitalism to socialism, but from capitalism to bureaucratic collectivism.

Yet there is hope. From the East German general strike of 1953 to the Polish strikes of 1970–1971, there is abundant evidence that the quest for freedom persists among the people under Communism and that they quite rightly call the name of their dream "socialism." Those Russian intellectuals in jail, those Czech workers seeking the human face of socialism, those millions in the various freedom movements we have already seen, have understood out of the wisdom of their daily lives a fact that has eluded some of the sophisticated theorists: that Communist totalitarianism is not socialism; indeed, that it makes socialism all the more an urgent necessity.[7]

# IX

# Socialist Capitalism

AFTER WORLD WAR I socialists in Europe first faced up to the dilemmas of running capitalism, which persists to this hour.

The social democrats, as Joseph Schumpeter put it with wry accuracy, took office but not power, and there was no precedent for the anomalies that followed in any of their theories. In the early Marxian formulations of *The Communist Manifesto* the workers were to quite literally seize power by means of armed force and the change from the old order to the new would be violent, insurrectionary and quick. But when Marx and Engels abandoned much of that perspective and began to think and act in terms of a more gradual and democratic revolution, they did not work out the details of the transition period—specifically, how the socialists should act when they had only reformist power within a capitalist system they were committed to transform basically.

This problem, as Chapter VII documented, was anticipated in the debates over colonialism. But in that case, the choices, although all of them were intolerable, could at least be evaded. The Belgian socialists who had to choose among impossible options with regard to the fate of the Congo were only a minority in the parliament. They could, and did, walk out on the vote when the moment of decision came. So in this period the social democratic parties could still insist that at some apocalyptic moment in the future capitalism and socialism would confront each other in that "final conflict" of which the "Internationale" sings. In the meantime, they viewed their parliamentary activity as providing a forum for propaganda and education and as a means for defending the immediate interests of the workers, but not as an instrument for running the society. In those innocent days it seemed obvious that in a bourgeois system it was the bourgeoisie, not the socialists, who would rule.

In 1904 Guesde, the rather mechanistic Marxist who led one of the main wings of French socialism, summarized this attitude in a motion at the Congress of the Socialist International in Amsterdam. "The Party," his text read, "disclaims responsibility for political and economic circumstances based on the capitalist mode of production, and it therefore refuses to support any measure calculated to help the ruling class in power."

But after World War I it became impossible for the socialists to "disclaim responsibility." Capitalism in Europe had been so shaken by that senseless carnage—particularly in defeated Germany and Austria-Hungary—that the bourgeoisie could not rule in the old way. But the masses, as will be seen, were in no mood for a sudden, and total, revolution. The political situation had thus moved far enough to the Left to bring the socialists into office— most notably in England and Germany and a little later in France —but not far enough Left to give them decisive, system-changing power. And this is as far Left as it has gone to this day.

But if the truth be told, if the social democrats had had revolutionary power thrust upon them, they probably would not have known what to do with it. In all their pre-World War I versions of the socialist future it was precisely the moment of victory that was shrouded in vagueness. Marx and Engels had refused to draw up any blueprints of the good society out of the fear that they would produce nothing more than a professorial panacea and out of the conviction that the living movement would have to define the revolution in the course of making it. So the socialists were as uncertain about creating the far future as they were about administering the complicated, and quite bourgeois, present.

These problems have yet to be resolved. The social democrats have, to be sure, learned much since the confusions of the years just after World War I. In France under Léon Blum in the thirties and in England under Clement Attlee after World War II they pioneered in some of the most important social innovations of the century. And in the 1970s they constitute the democratic movement of the European Left. Yet, it is one thing to make capitalism more rational, more humane—and therefore more stable—as they have done, and another thing to create socialism. The ultra-

Leftists of various persuasions have a simple way out of this difficulty: they propose to make a revolution on the model of *The Communist Manifesto* and thus avoid all the bothersome details of transition. Only, the great mass of the people in the advanced countries, including the majority of the working class, will have nothing to do with such a bloody romance. So the problems faced by socialists within capitalism are likely to be on the agenda for the foreseeable future; and, if they are ever to be solved, it is necessary to become much more precise about the design of the good society in the far distance.

This chapter will deal with the dilemmas of socialist partial power as they exist here and now; Chapters XII, XIII and XIV will attempt a redefinition of the socialist vision itself. In the more immediate analysis I make no pretense of even outlining the history of European socialism from 1918 to the present. I have abstracted from most of the political intricacies of the period and passed over entire areas, like foreign policy. My focus is on the question of how socialists administer capitalism—or, more precisely, how they might run it—not in order to shore it up, but to transform it. That issue, I believe, underlies all the others.

Finally, these problems can best be summarized in terms of a paradoxical concept: socialist capitalism. On the one hand, that phrase is an accurate description of the contradictory situation in which the Left found itself administering the system it was sworn to abolish. On the other hand, it also states the new program of the European social democracy in the sixties and seventies in which a controlled and managed capitalist growth is seen as a means to socialist ends. This idea, I hope to show, is a sincere and well-meant illusion held by men who are trying to respond honestly, and even radically, to circumstances not dreamed of in the writings of Marx and Engels. The fact is that as long as capitalism is capitalism it vitiates or subverts most of the efforts of socialists. If, then, the ideal of a new society has certainly become much more complex than ever before, it still must, for very practical reasons, demand a socialist socialism.

# I

There were two periods in recent history when if a revolution of the type envisioned in *The Communist Manifesto* were possible, it should have occurred: at the end of World War I in the defeated nations and during the Great Depression of the thirties. In both cases, the status quo was in a shambles, yet in neither case did the masses respond to an insurrectionary appeal. In post-World War I Germany the men and women who had been talking of a basic socialist transformation for years did not even carry out the thorough democratization of capitalism. And in the thirties there were many social democrats who with a rigorous if mad logic were championing conservative bourgeois economics at a moment when bourgeois society was coming apart at the seams.

It was not fantasy on the part of Lenin and Trotsky to argue that the German Revolution was imminent in 1917–1918. The years of horrible warfare had embittered millions and there were anti-war strikes and demonstrations within the military. After the defeat there were various councils of workers and soldiers based on the Soviet model, the prestige of the army had been shattered and the Marxist Left was able to organize a Communist Party of half a million members in a matter of three years. So from 1917 to 1921 it was quite logical to await the "German October," the point at which the radicalized masses would tear down the old structure and begin to build the new.

October never came. Some of the reasons for its failure to take place were noted in the last chapter. As Gramsci and Carr pointed out, even in the ruins of military defeat the German working class had more of a stake in their society than the Russian masses (most of whom were, in any case, peasants), and the society itself had a much more stable infrastructure than czarist Russia. But there are those, usually on the ultra-Left, who ignore such objective factors. The revolution did not fail, they say; rather it was betrayed from within by Right-wing social democrats. I take up their charge in brief detail because for two generations now it has provided the half-truth that has allowed many radicals to ignore the complicated, and very Marxist, whole truth: that the conservatism of some of the socialist leaders was an effect as well as a cause of massive trends within capitalist society which are by no means finished.

During the First World War there were three major tendencies in the German Social Democracy. The Majority socialists, led by Friedrich Ebert and Philipp Scheidemann, backed the war effort; the Independents—with both of the antagonists in the debates on revisionism, Karl Kautsky and Eduard Bernstein, among them

—opposed the war on a radical democratic basis; and the revolutionaries, like Rosa Luxemburg and Karl Liebknecht, fought against the war on Marxist grounds and were to create the *Spartakusbund* and then the Communist Party of Germany.

When the war ended and there was an apparent revolutionary situation, Ebert and Scheidemann and the other Majority socialists saw their most urgent responsibility in the restoration of order. So they invoked the mechanical Marxist theory of stages, that rationale of so many anti-Marxist policies: first, they said, there must be democracy; then the situation will ripen for socialism. So the old imperial bureaucracy was allowed to remain in place, with the socialists only overseeing it, and the fear of Bolshevism drove the social democrats to cooperate with reactionary para-military formations. All this would seem to be the clearest proof of the thesis that it was the treason of the conservative Social Democracy that thwarted the German revolution.

And yet, there was no revolutionary outcry against this betrayal. On the contrary, at the National Congress of Councils—the German "Soviets"—in December of 1918 the followers of Ebert and Scheidemann carried the day. In the elections of January, 1919, they won 39 percent of the vote as compared to 5 percent for the Independents (the Communists boycotted). When Rosa Luxemburg, by then the leader of the German Communist Party, tried to analyze Ebert's victory at the Congress of Councils, she could only cry foul and insist that the people would repudiate the leaders who had sold them out. And just before her assassination she wrote that the real issue was "how one converts the achievements and inner ripeness of the revolution into facts and power relationships."

Rosa Luxemburg was wrong. That could be seen three years later when one of her Communist comrades, Paul Levi, wrote to Lenin. The Communist International had decided that the Germans must make a revolutionary offensive in 1921. Levi asked Lenin to intervene against this perspective, warning him that even though the Communist Party now had half a million members, the masses had not yet recovered from their post-war apathy, resignation and pro-Western orientation. An insurrection, he said, would have to be led against the proletariat; it could not be made in its name. Events proved Levi to be quite right—Communist militance in 1921 provoked a costly fiasco—but he was expelled from the party for his prescience anyway. Ironically, in 1923, when the French and Belgian occupation of the Ruhr provoked widespread protest and the preconditions for an uprising were much more in evidence, the chastened Communists were pursuing a cautious line and did not act. But then, their power was partly offset by the armed Right in the Black Reichswehr and the *Freikorps.* The moment passed and in the elections later in the year there was a significant shift of proletarian votes from both the socialists and the Communists to the Right.

In other words, there is no question that Ebert, Scheidemann and the Majority socialists acted as a brake upon the revolution and kept it not simply from socialism, but from even a thorough-going democratization of capitalism. But a Marxist cannot explain why no revolution took place simply on the basis of their alleged treason. For the question then arises as to why the masses, even in a period of military defeat and social breakdown, placed their confidence in these very men. And the answer is, as Gramsci in particular understood, that society had become so much more dense in its social relationships than in the days of *The Communist Mani-festo,* that the workers had so many more ties to it, that many of them shared Ebert's and Scheidemann's passion for "order."

But even if the Majority socialists had not been so obsessed with the preservation of order, they had no idea of how to pro-ceed to socialism in any case—and no one else on the Left did either. The Communists had their panacea of "All Power to the Soviets," but the Councils in 1918 had perversely voted for the German Kerensky, not the German Lenin. The Majority socialists were against nationalization on the grounds that the economic situation was too chaotic and that the Allied governments would respond to such an action with a blockade. The Independents were for workers' control of industry, but they never got near enough to power to test their ideas. As G. D. H. Cole summarized the situa-tion, "The German Socialists were indeed wholly unready to tackle the socialization which they had always pushed out of the discussion as something that would happen 'after the Revolution' and that needed no consideration until the Revolution had oc-curred."

There was, however, one Majority socialist who had something like a precise idea of what should be done. Rudolf Wissell wanted to create councils which, as Carl Landauer describes them, "closely resembled compulsory cartels, except that representatives of workers and consumers were supposed to participate." Landauer continues, "The strong point in Wissell's theory was the recognition that mere nationalization could not fundamentally improve the standard of living of the masses and might actually reduce it temporarily. The share of the rich in the social product is not large enough to make it possible to increase substantially the share of the underprivileged by mere redistribution. . . . Consequently, the raising of the lower stratum of society depends on the enlargement of the social product."

Wissell lost support among his comrades when he voted against the nationalization of the coal industry in the Socialization Commission set up by the Weimar Republic. But his proposal of a planned capitalism which would respond to social needs through an increase in national product was something of an anticipation of the theory of the "social market economy" which the German socialists were to adopt in 1959. He was thus a precursor of the idea of a socialist capitalism.

The Germans were not alone in their confusion. In 1924, when the first Labour government took office, the Independent Labour Party (an affiliated section of the Labour Party itself) was in favor of Ramsay MacDonald putting forth a program which would certainly be defeated—his was a minority government—but which would educate the masses and help create a genuine socialist majority. The Prime Minister, not unexpectedly, was for proving Labour's right to rule by making gradual reforms in alliance with the Liberals.

So both the German and the British social democrats had, by the mid-twenties, reluctantly accepted the role of socialist administrators of capitalism. There is not the least question that the German leaders in particular must bear a burden of historical blame for not having acted much more radically than they did. If there is no evidence that the masses were ready for an abrupt transition to a completely new order, they certainly would have rallied to a program of thoroughgoing democratization of the bureaucracy and the military. But that does not prove the ultra-Leftist contention that it was social democratic treachery that aborted the German Revolution. The fact of the matter is that every time the working class was consulted during this period— in the Congress of Councils, in the elections, in the relative membership strength of the parties appealing to socialist consciousness —they gave their support to the conservative wing of the movement. For a Marxist, such a striking fact can hardly be explained by the trickery of a few individuals. That a revolution along the lines of *The Communist Manifesto* did not take place in a ruined, defeated and demoralized Germany is persuasive testimony to the fact that history had simply not developed as the young Marx thought it would.

Capitalism had indeed turned out to be as destructive and crisis-prone as the *Manifesto* suggested, and that was one reason why the system could no longer be run capitalistically. But it had also demonstrated a greater resilience and appeal than Marx and Engels had imagined in their early analysis of it. The working class was discontented enough to rally to a socialist party, but not so discontented as to make a socialist revolution. Under these circumstances, an aggressive leadership could have moved much further to the Left than the German Majority socialists, but it still could not make the leap to a completely new society. So the post-World War I collapse of the established order only led to a socialist version of capitalism.[1]

In the mid-twenties in Germany the Majority and Independent socialists had reunited and the party attempted to put a Marxist facade on its change in tactics. In the process Rudolf Hilferding developed an extremely optimistic theory of the transition to socialism, one that owed much to a theme Engels had emphasized regularly toward the end of his life: that the trustification of capitalism and the separation of ownership and control in the corporation were halfway houses to socialism. As it became more and more obvious that ownership played no functional part in the system but was simply an irrational title to its surplus, Engels had said, the masses would reject the established order. In Hilferding's rewriting of this analysis "organized capitalism" replaced the "competitive struggle of the entrepreneurs." This planned capitalism would be relatively easy to take over: "seizing the ownership of the six biggest banks would amount to taking over the most important spheres of industry."

By 1928 this moderate policy had won the socialists some support among white-collar workers, but the victory was short-lived. Capitalism, which had not become as rational and conflict-free as the socialists thought, broke down. And now the social democrats were faced with an even more agonizing version of their basic dilemma of how to run the system socialistically. The question was no longer one of how socialists should administer capitalism, but how, or whether, they should put it back together again.

At this point, the either/or thinking that had dominated the movement before World War I reasserted itself with a vengeance. Either one must take the decisive step forward to socialism— which was still rather vaguely defined—or one must obey all of the rules of the capitalist order itself. As one of Hilferding's associates at the time, W. S. Woytinsky, summarized this attitude, "Depressions result from the anarchy of the capitalist system. Either they come to an end or they must lead to the collapse of the system." In this analysis there was no room in between capitalism and socialism for transitional reforms. That was an illusion of petty-bourgeois reformists. The choice was either capitalism or socialism. This seemingly radical and Marxist thesis was to become the justification for Adam Smithian policies.

Thus a leading socialist theorist, Fritz Naphtali, put forward arguments that would have warmed the heart of a classical economist: ". . . the crisis with all its destruction of the value of capital, with its changes and shifts of purchasing power, is a means of correction which must necessarily be accepted. Afterwards, on the basis of large-scale capital destruction, a better proportion will emerge between production and consumer's purchasing power which is the condition of a new upswing. I believe therefore that we must stick to this tenet: if we tend towards a policy of controlling the business cycle in its various forms, corrective measures may not be taken at the time of crisis but during the period of prosperity."

In England the Labour Party adopted a position similar to that of the German socialists. Philip Snowden, who had responsibility in this area, was against spending money during a depression, and in 1931 Arthur Henderson, speaking on behalf of Labour, accepted the principle of a balanced budget in a House of Commons debate. Harold Macmillan, who was then a "Left-wing" Tory advocate of national economic planning and was later to become Prime Minister, remarked sarcastically that in the early thirties the British socialists were "obedient devotees of the classical creed."

This is an oversimplification that contains an unfortunate element of truth. As leaders of a working-class movement, the socialists could hardly confine themselves to reciting the truisms— almost all of them false—of the prevailing bourgeois economics. So they embraced a contradiction. On the one hand, they stuck to classical orthodoxy on the question of a balanced budget. On the other hand, the Labor and Socialist International rightly saw that the crisis represented a "disproportion between productive capacity and consumption" and proposed public works, state expenditures to increase consumption, the forty-hour week, workers' holidays and unemployment compensation.

There was only one socialist party that really fought its way out of this contradiction: the Swedish. When they took office in 1933, they initiated the first program of consciously planned deficits in history. But most of the European socialists, like that reluctant Keynesian Franklin Roosevelt, were fiscal conservatives at heart. Ironically, in Britain the Labourite who championed Keynesian reform was Oswald Mosley, who broke with the party on the issue and then became the leader of British fascism.

As Robert Skidelsky described the Labour Party during the Depression—and the judgment would apply to almost all the European social democracies at that time—"It thought in terms of a total solution to the problem of poverty when what it was offered was the limited opportunity to cure unemployment." Fritz Tarnow, a trade-union leader in the German movement, put the same point more poignantly and dramatically at a socialist congress in 1931: "Are we sitting at the sickbed of capitalism, not only as doctors who want to cure the patient, but as prospective heirs who cannot wait for the end and would like to hasten it by administering poison? We are condemned, I think, to be doctors who seriously wish to cure, and yet we have to maintain the feeling that we are heirs who wish to receive the entire legacy of the capitalist system today rather than tomorrow. This double role, doctor and heir, is a damned difficult task."[2]

In France the dilemma of being doctor and heir so weighed upon Léon Blum, the leader of the socialists between the wars, that he boasted that for fifteen years he had done everything he could to keep his own party out of power. "The political position of socialist parties during the pre-revolutionary period," Blum wrote, "is always, in one way or another, a false position." So Blum tried to school his comrades in the difference between the "conquest" and the "exercise" of power. "Conquest" described that condition of blessedness of which socialists had been dreaming since the days of Marx: the magic day when history would leap from capitalism to socialism. "Exercise" was a way of talking about the reality that had confronted socialists ever since they became a political force: what to do in order to make capitalism more tolerable when that is the limit of one's political mandate.

Finally, in 1936, capitalist collapse and working-class militance forced Blum to accept the exercise of power. In a legislative whirl-wind—twelve laws were voted in ten days—the Popular Front established paid holidays for the workers (the French working-class vacation is, to this day, lengthier than that of their similars in the other advanced capitalist economies), the forty-hour week, the reform of the Bank of France, the extension of compulsory education from thirteen to fourteen years of age, the nationaliza-tion of war industries, social security, the organization of state markets and much more. All this was an enormous gain. André Philip, a participant and observer, writes, "Those who lived through that period will never forget the emotion of old workers going on vacation, discovering the sea and the mountains which they had never known."

But the Popular Front also established a limit. These reforms, as Philip remarked, were as far as "distributive socialism" could go. Now, it was a question of transforming the actual structure of society. Some of the French socialists simply repeated the tradi-tional belief in a sudden day of revolutionary change. As Paul Faure put it in 1934, "It is a mad chimera to seek partial and progressive realizations of socialism . . . within a capitalist system which is still maintained in order." But there were others who tried to revise the socialist doctrine to bring it into line with the new reality.

As a result of this rethinking, a concept that was to become a key to socialist programs after World War II came to the fore: economic planning. It was also an important moment in the development of the theory of socialist capitalism.

The most prominent figure in this redefinition of socialism was a Belgian, Henri de Man. His reputation is still under a cloud because, believing that Hitler had won an irreversible victory, he did not join the Resistance in his homeland. And since his theories in the thirties were designed to appeal to that same petty-bourgeois strata which helped the Nazis to power, it has been charged that his very analysis, as well as his conduct, was pro-fascist. Moreover, in France a socialist leader who had similar ideas, Marcel Déat, did actually go over to the extreme Right. So Carl Landauer has denounced De Man's *Plan du Travail* as "at least semi-fascist." I agree more with G. D. H. Cole: the proposal was a "major contribution" to socialist thinking however one judges its author.

As De Man described his *Plan*, ". . . in place of the class struggle between capitalists and workers, a common front of all the productive strata against the power of parasitic money." In this way, the socialists would be able to reach out beyond the working class and even to attract that desperate petty bourgeoisie which had finally backed Hitler. There would be more abundant money, cheaper credit and state regulation—but not nationalization. All this would be a mixed economy with private and public sectors coexisting side by side.

Whatever De Man's personal politics, his ideas were prophetic, anticipating the social democratic practice after World War II. They pointed toward a program of socialist capitalism: that the Left would plan, and orient the uses of, capitalist economic growth. They did indeed offer a way out of the sterile counterposition of Karl Marx and Adam Smith, with no space for innovation in between them. But they did not, as we shall see, solve the basic socialist dilemma. They only raised it to the level of a principle.

That is why Adolf Sturmthal's epitaph for the thirties—"Labor was strong enough seriously to interfere with the smooth working of the existing institutions of society, but it was neither sufficiently strong nor sufficiently constructive to rebuild society"—still applies in the seventies. For it is true on the one hand that, as Ralph Miliband, a Left critic of the social democracy, admits, "it is no doubt mistaken to suggest a picture of popular revolutionary fervor as the basis of support for left wing parties." But, on the other hand, even though the theory and practice of socialist capitalism thus emerged as an honest response to a tortuous history, and even though it was a tremendous advance over vague theorizing about the withering away of the state, it is by no means adequate to the demands of the times. The socialist experience with the nationalization of industry is a case in point.[3]

# II

In the period immediately after World War II what most people consider the essential socialist proposal—the nationalization of private industry—was carried out on a wide scale in Western Europe. In the long run the most dramatic beneficiary was capitalism.

These nationalizations were sometimes instituted by socialists, as under the Labour Government in England, or carried out by nonsocialists, like De Gaulle, who responded to mass pressure. The fact that a significant section of the Continental bourgeoisie had collaborated with, or in the cases of Germany and Italy joined, the fascists had weakened the hold of capitalist ideology upon the people. In the Resistance movements and the armies there was a pervasive feeling that a return to the miseries of the thirties could not be allowed.

In Britain coal, gas, electricity, railways, air transport and the Bank of England had been taken over by 1948 (steel was nationalized, denationalized and renationalized later on). In France the nationalizations paralleled those in England and added insurance and a large part of commercial banking. In Austria coal, steel and the banks were statified, and in Italy the ENI, a giant state enterprise in the fuel and power sector, was established in 1953. Then there were the nationalizations of collaborationist or fascist enterprises: Renault and Gnome-Rhône in France, Volkswagen in Germany, major chemical, vehicle- and machine-building and electrical-engineering units in Austria, and the IRI (Institute for Industrial Recovery), which accounts for between 10 and 15 percent of industrial output in Italy.

The paradox that these extensive structural changes in the economy actually would aid capitalism had been foreseen by socialists for at least half a century. More to the point of this chapter, this experience also reveals a central flaw in the notion of socialist capitalism. As long as the system is dominated by private corporations and wealth, that fact will tend in the long run to make all collectivist measures discriminate in favor of the status quo. So there is yet another dilemma for the social democrats: if state property within a capitalist system is run on a social rather than a profit-making calculus, it will usually subsidize the private sector; if state property operates according to the profit calculus, it then behaves like, and often in concert with, the capitalists.

The German socialists, as Chapter IV documented, had long ago understood that nationalization was not *per se* socialist. "When the contemporary state nationalizes certain industries and functions," Kautsky had written in his popularization of the Erfurt Program of the German Social Democracy in the 1890s, "it does so not in order to limit capitalist exploitation but to expand and strengthen it. . . ." Nationalization, as Kautsky and Engels and the other theorists of the Bismarckian period were forced to realize, could easily be an instrument of capitalist policy.

Moreover, the pre-World War I socialists were acutely aware of the danger that state property would become the basis of a new form of tyranny and exploitation. Jaurès put the fear eloquently: "Delivering men to the state, conferring upon the government the effective direction of the nation's work, giving it the right to direct all the functions of labor, would be to give a few men a power compared to which that of the Asiatic despots is nothing, since their power stops at the surface of the society and does not regulate economic life."

It was in this mood that the French socialists voted for a resolution in 1910 which said, "It is not by a single stroke nor even by the force of the majority that we shall bring the new order into being. The morning after the insurrection, the capitalist order will still exist, and the proletariat, seemingly victorious, will be impotent to organize its own victory if it is not already prepared to take charge of it by the development of institutions of every kind, of unions and cooperatives, and if it has not gradually begun, through them, an apprenticeship in social control."

Indeed, it was in 1894 that Jaurès made a proposal which was to be typical of the serious socialist's image of social property. In his outline of a plan to nationalize the mines he provided for a central council with one third of the members elected by the workers (including the engineers), one third from workers' and peasants' unions in other areas of the economy, and one third named by the Government. For him, and for almost all the social democratic thinkers, the forms of nationalization were even more important than the fact of it, for they would determine who would actually control the "state" property.

The Austrians, who had developed an extremely sophisticated school of Marxism, had the same attitude as Jaurès. "Who shall administer the socialized industry?" Otto Bauer asked. "The state? Not at all! If the state rules over all the factories, then it would become much too powerful as against the people and their representatives. Such an increase in the power of the regime would be dangerous for democracy. And at the same time the state would badly administer the socialized industry. No one administers industries as badly as the state. Therefore we social democrats have never demanded the statification, but rather the socialization, of industry."

So after World War I the British Miners' Union called for nationalization of their industry under an administration of a council with one half of the members elected by the men in the pits and the other half named by the Government. The Independent socialists, as was seen in the last section, urged workers' control rather than state ownership in their proposals for nationalization in Germany. And the Geneva Conference of European Socialists in 1920 came out for the administration of national property by institutions completely independent of the political organs that would control it, and provided for worker and consumer membership on the governing boards of industry.

Strangely enough, it was the Fabians, certainly the most gradualist and seemingly the most democratic of the socialists, who were most statist. Sidney Webb viewed every extension of governmental power—including the licensing of dancing rooms and dogs—as a step toward the revolution. Of the individualists, he wrote, "Such is the irresistible sweep of social tendencies that in their every act they worked to bring about the very Socialism they despised. . . ." Thus, as elitists who looked for a "permeation" of socialism from the top of society down to the bottom, they did not share the concern of Jaurès and the other socialists for a democratization of the work place itself.

"Here in London," Engels wrote in a bitter letter to Sorge in 1893, "the Fabians are a band of pushers who are smart enough to understand the inevitability of a social transformation but find it impossible to trust the work of this change to the raw workers and so are accustomed to place themselves in the lead: anguish before revolution is their basic principle. . . ." But even so, when Webb came to write the famous "Clause Four" of the Labour Party principles—it was printed on the back of the membership cards and became, as shall be seen shortly, a matter of great debate in the late fifties—he specified that the nationalized industry should be operated under "the best obtainable system of popular administration and control of each industry and service."

So the socialist conception of nationalized property was, and is, more complicated than many socialists, and most nonsocialists, realize. And after World War II socialists in a number of countries tried to design the public property which they introduced so that it was not simply a state-owned mimicry of the private corporation. In Germany the social democrats championed the principle of "co-determination." Under this system, there is worker representation on the board of directors in certain basic industries. The results have been somewhat ambiguous, but even a critic of the idea like Ralf Dahrendorf has to admit that it is enthusiastically supported by the workers themselves. In 1970 the socialists made the extension of co-determination a major electoral plank in the political campaign, but the narrowness of their victory and the fact that they had to form a coalition with the Free Democrats made that pledge difficult, if not impossible, to fulfill.

But it is in France where the profound difficulties of carrying out a genuinely socialist nationalization within a capitalist economy are most evident. As André Philip describes what happened, "One dreamed right after the Liberation [when the Nazis were driven out in 1944–1945] that we would build the nationalized industries as autonomous enterprises whose direction would be tripartite: controlled by the representatives of the state, of the workers and of the consumers. In fact, worker representation has been progressively reduced; individuals have been introduced into the direction on the grounds of 'technical competence'; the consumers, far from representing the users, have defended special interests which, wanting to buy the goods or services of the nationalized industry cheaply, ended up by imposing a financial deficit upon it."

The problem is, as Philip clearly recognized, that it is extremely difficult, perhaps impossible, to create an island of socialist cooperation within a sea of capitalism. In the France of the fifties and sixties, as I showed in *The Accidental Century*, the workers were not able to effectively occupy the seats legally provided for them on the state planning bodies. The corporations would send members of their well-paid technical staffs who were able to make profitable use of the official—and publicly subsidized—data on economic trends. The trade unionists simply did not have the trained manpower to compete with the businessmen in this process. As a result, planning in the "common good" was biased profoundly in favor of the wealthiest and most powerful forces in the society.

In England in 1945 when Labour came into office, it did not simply provide social insurance coverage from "womb to tomb" and create the welfare state (that phrase dates only from 1947). It nationalized, as has been seen, a significant portion of British industry. One immediate result was to rescue some of the most inefficient capitalists in the society by socializing their losses. That was true for both the railroads and the coal mines. And even though the compensation stock paid only a bit over 3 percent, compared to 4 percent for ordinary shares in the period, there was no great redistribution of wealth but rather a transfer of private funds from areas of capitalist failure into more remunerative investments.

More recently, when the Wilson Government renationalized steel in the 1960s, it not only paid £450 million in compensation, but far from seeking a "popular administration" of the industry, left many of the previous managers in control of the public enterprise. After the war when the Attlee Government had first nationalized steel, it became a major Tory project to denationalize it. But by the sixties business understood that the state can undertake investments and rationalizations that are beyond the power of private enterprise. The London *Economist* reported the attitude of steel executives in January, 1970: "The British Steel Corporation would like Labour to start rationalizing the industry before the elections—and the Tories not to de-nationalize it afterward."

Indeed, in the twenties and thirties sophisticated Conservatives like Harold Macmillan were enthusiastically in favor of the nationalization of losing industries (much as the American railroads in the seventies are seeking to socialize their deficits in passenger service but to retain their profits from freight hauling). In 1945 the Westminster Conservative Association republished Macmillan's earlier analysis to prove that Attlee's socialist program had been stolen from the Conservatives.

But nationalization did not simply serve the negative function of socializing the losses of capitalist incompetence. It also operated as a subsidy to the private sector. As Douglas Jay, a British socialist theorist, has observed, "State monopolies in Britain, and indeed many other countries, tend . . . not to appropriate capital gains, but to *destroy* them as a result of undercharging for the product." In part, this is because the businessmen who share in the direction of the public property are, as André Philip described the situation in France, able to impose uneconomic decisions on those enterprises which maximize gains in the private sector. In part, it is because socialists believed that a nationalized industry should be more responsible, more socially conscious and less greedy than a capitalist firm.

It would seem simple enough to avoid this problem by having the public enterprise charge market prices. In September, 1968, a *Fortune* article on "Creeping Capitalism in Government Corporations" gleefully reported that such was the European trend. Nationalized industries, it said, are emphasizing "profitability as a yardstick, and efficiency as a guide for the allocation of resources." If this is true, what is the *socialist* argument for nationalizing an enterprise if it is then going to behave as capitalistically as possible?

Part of the problem, which is obscured by emotional reactions to the very word itself, is that many of the arguments in favor of nationalization have nothing to do with socialism. It has been argued that public utilities should be socially owned because of the essential services they provide; that monopolies should be taken over so that they cannot exact high profits in return for an inefficient allocation of resources; that basic industries crucial to the entire economy should be run by the government; and so on. In 1971 the Tory Prime Minister of England, a champion of rather fundamentalist bourgeois economics, was forced to propose the semi-nationalization of Rolls-Royce when that venerable British firm went bankrupt. Such an act of statification obviously need not be in the least socialist.

So in the post-World War II experience with nationalization one sees what happens to public ownership within a basically capitalist context: it functions more as the servant of the rich than of the poor. In redeeming their pledges of social property, the socialists unwittingly turned out to be among the best doctors that capitalism could find. They modernized, rationalized and helped plan capitalist economies. In the process they succeeded in their immediate goal of providing an infinitely more decent and humane life for the great mass of people. But public property seemed destined either to subsidize, or to imitate, private property, and that was not what socialists had intended at all. For socialist capitalism was, and is, a variant of capitalism: more human and infinitely preferable to the sweatshop version of the system, but capitalism nevertheless.[4]

## III

It was in the late fifties and early sixties that the European socialists faced up to the contradictions of their experience. In a series of programmatic revisions in Britain, Germany, Sweden, Austria and other countries, there was an attempt to bring theory into some minimal relationship with practice.

Basically, as my analysis will indicate in this chapter and in Chapter XII, the revisions went too far: they made socialism indistinguishable from intelligent American liberalism, a program for the humanization, but not the transformation, of capitalism. That modest goal is something very much worth fighting for, and those commentators who saw no difference between Labour and the Tories in the 1970 British elections were made to look rather silly when the Tories celebrated their victory by an attack upon social services. But valuable as the social democratic reforms are, they do not add up to a vision of a new society. And it is from the point of view that such a vision is still relevant—or rather, more relevant than ever—that I evaluate the new definitions of socialism.

I am not saying that the "Left" critics of the social democratic revisions were right. On the contrary. The "Left" in these debates generally represented a conservative and traditional sentimentality which wanted to pretend that all the unprecedented shocks and surprises of the past half-century had not happened. The "Right"—for instance, Anthony Crosland in England—was much more radical, for it was willing to face difficult and unpleasant facts that did not square with received doctrine.

Thus, Wolfgang Abendroth, one of the leading opponents of the German socialist revisions of the Godesberg Program of 1959, argued, "In a time in which 80 percent of the economically active population are workers [*Arbeitnehmer*], the Social Democrats no longer proclaim themselves a workers' party but a people's party." But that is to ignore the crucially important political distinctions among the various strata of people who work for someone else— between blue-collar workers and white-collar, the poor and the highly educated, etc.—and to maintain a rather simplified Marxist orthodoxy (for Marx became quite aware of the growing importance of the intermediate strata, as his *Theories of Surplus Value* show) by a sleight of hand. The German social democrats in the early sixties received 87 percent of their votes from the working class fairly narrowly defined. In order to achieve a majority, they obviously had to appeal to groups that would respond to the rhetoric of the "people's party."

In France André Gorz, a Left socialist who scornfully rejects the Harold Wilson-Willy Brandt politics as a form of neo-capital-

ism that helps the big bourgeoisie against the less efficient capitalists, was quite candid about the limitations of his revolutionary
perspective in May, 1968. He wrote, "The transition to socialism
suddenly became a question of immediate actuality; but there
was no organized force capable of making precise the nature of
the transitional society, its distribution of power, institutions, economic, cultural and international policy, etc. Capitalism suddenly
revealed that one could go beyond it, but no one knew how to
make the leap." And in England the *May Day Manifesto* of the
Left critics of the Labour Party made a number of trenchant
points (and some vague and inaccurate ones as well), but could
only conclude its scathing analysis with a call for a "break and
development in consciousness. . . ." For intellectuals, that is a
possible, perhaps a necessary, program; for a government or a
mass party, it is clearly not.

In short, everything that has gone before in this book demonstrates that the definition of socialism must be revised, yet the
traditional Left has been conservative and romantic rather than
precise. My quarrel with the European social democrats is not
that they were impious to abandon obsolete formulas, but that
the way in which they did so was wrong. In what remains of this
chapter I will outline their new program of socialist capitalism
and make some preliminary criticisms of it. In Chapter XII I will
try to suggest an alternative to it.

The new social democratic definition of socialism is based on
an analysis of economic trends that sees private property as much
less important than it was in the period of the rise of the socialist
movement.

Given the separation of ownership and control, Anthony Crosland asserted in the fifties, the modern businessman is no longer
interested in maximizing profit in order to get high personal income or consumption. He is much more sensitive to popular attitudes and certainly doesn't want an economic crisis. Moreover,
the changes in income distribution have now altered the context
in which the profit motive functions. "Now it is quite true," Crosland wrote, "that production for profit, conducted within a framework of very unequal incomes, must give a distribution of resources highly distasteful to socialists, because it takes no account
of needs, however urgent, but only of monetary demand. It is
further true that the means chosen (state ownership) could in
principle fulfill the objective of a different and more equitable
distribution of resources.

"But," Crosland continued, "the objective can be achieved by other means and has been largely so achieved today. The statement that production for profit gives a bad distribution of resources (caviar for the rich before milk for the poor) is only a shorthand. What is meant is that production is undertaken for profit; that the distribution of incomes determines what is profitable; and that if this is very unequal, then the wants of the rich will be met before the wants of the poor. But if purchasing power is distributed more equally, it becomes more profitable to produce necessities and less profitable to produce luxuries. Today the redistribution of incomes, and the rise in working-class purchasing power, have banished the worst effects of production for profit by calling forth a quite different pattern of output."

In this analysis, if there is economic growth and increasing income equality, the socialist goals will be fulfilled without requiring widespread, and questionable, tinkering with the very mechanism of the economy. But high savings for investment can only be achieved through high profits. So, "The problem of profit is thus the central economic dilemma facing contemporary social democracy." The problem is resolved by combining high profits with low-profit incomes, i.e., by seeing to it that there are ample funds which working entrepreneurs can utilize for internal investment, but discouraging dividends to passive rentiers at the same time. "Post-war experience," Crosland concluded in the early sixties, "demonstrates conclusively that governments now have sufficient weapons to enforce their will (provided they have one) on private industry."

In France in 1969 Jean-Jacques Servan-Schreiber put much of this theory in summary form: ". . . the fundamental truth of our epoch is that social justice is not only a moral objective but the condition of industrial growth. If that is what it means to be socialist, we should be socialist. But if, according to the dogmas and catechisms, proceeding toward the abolition of competition, authoritarian planification and the collectivist society are socialist, then we are not."

The key to the new definition of socialism, then, is economic growth. With ownership no longer decisive in the private sector and sophisticated private managers in control, the socialist party will stimulate economic growth. Its tax policies and other measures will favor incomes derived from work and penalize mere rentiers and thus the market economy will be made to respond to social priorities. As befits the party that is the lineal descendant

of Karl Marx, the German social democrats made the most ranging, and explicit, statement of this point of view in their new
Basic Program adopted at a Special Party Congress in November,
1959.

"The aim of social democratic economic policy," the program
proclaims, "is ever-increasing prosperity and a just division of the
fruits of the people's economy, a life in freedom without demeaning dependence and without exploitation." This aim is endangered
by the concentration of economic power in capitalist society in
which huge organizations dispose of millions and command tens
of thousands of workers. But the objection to this trend is one that
could be made by an anti-monopoly Adam Smithian: "Where the
big enterprises predominate, there is no free competition." Moreover, "through cartels and combines, the big enterprises still more
increase their power and the corporate leaders win an influence
over the state and politics which is compatible with democratic
principles. They usurp the state power. Economic power becomes
political power."

At this point in the traditional socialist program there would
have been a demand for the widespread socialization of such
enterprises. The Godesberg Program, however, offers a different
approach to the struggle against concentrated economic power.
"Private property in the means of production has a right and title
to be defended so long as it does not hinder the creation of a just
social order. Efficient middle and small enterprises should be
strengthened so that they can stand the competition with the big
enterprises." Private property, particularly where it is competitive,
is to be the rule, social property the exception.

Another way to encourage competition, the program holds, is
through public corporations which can influence prices and innovation. "Public property [literally, common property, *gemein-
eigentum*] is a legitimate means of public control which no modern
state can surrender. It serves the preservation of freedom against
the superpower of huge economic units. In the economy, the
decision-making power has more and more been taken over by
managers serving anonymous interests. Thus private ownership
of the means of production has largely lost its decision-making
power. The central problem today is economic power. Where
other means guarantee a sound system of economic power relationships, public property is useful and necessary."

So the German social democrats had defined a new situation.

The worker, their new program said, was no longer the "defense-less proletarian without rights who must drive himself through a sixteen-hour day in order to get a starvation wage." Through struggle, the working class had achieved certain basic guarantees and had improved the lot of the entire society and therefore "the Social Democratic Party has ceased to be a party of the working class and has become a party of the people."

In the floor debate Heinrich Deist defended the proposed program and on some points was even more specific in his revisions than the document itself. The right of free initiative, he emphasized, must be at least as great in the public as in the private enterprise. Public property therefore must be free from daily interference on the part of the authorities. It was precisely this kind of assertion which was to lead John Kenneth Galbraith to argue in *The New Industrial State* that socialism, in the sense of the political control of the enterprise, had become technologically impossible. In a nationalized industry, Galbraith said, parliamentary responsibility had to be excluded if the enterprise were to be able to "act responsibly and promptly on decisions requiring specialized information." If Galbraith is right—and he certainly has identified a trend, but not, I think, a necessity (the point will be taken up in greater detail in Chapter XII)—then this would be the technical explanation of why the socialists failed to live up to their pre-World War II promises of a real democratization of industry.

Deist also made much of the dangers of concentration of power in state hands. He quoted Hilferding on this count but, as has been seen, he could have cited Jaurès, Bauer or many other leading socialist thinkers. But he took this insight further than they had. He now endorsed the basically conservative thesis that "there is a relationship between the room for freedom in the economy and the freedom of the entire society." It is true, he said, that private managers can exercise political power—but no less true that public managers can have the same effect.

Clearly the program, and Deist's interpretation of it, placed an unprecedented socialist emphasis on the virtues of the free market. Where Engels had seen capitalist planning and trustification as harbingers of socialism which were to be applauded, Deist now pictured them as intolerable deviations from the competitive model which the socialist party would use all of its power to restore. In the years that followed the adoption of the Godesberg

Program—which saw the social democrats enter into the "Great Coalition" with the Christian democrats and then win the Chancellorship under Willy Brandt—the practical conclusions drawn from it were more and more Keynesian in character. In 1959 the Left wing had opposed the adoption of the Godesberg Program in the name of traditional socialist values. At the SPD Congress in 1970 it based its critique of the party leadership in part on their failure to fulfill the promises made at Godesberg.

As *Der Spiegel* commented right after the SPD Congress in 1970 about one of the most prominent and politically popular members of the Brandt Cabinet, "A year and a half after the formation of the Great Coalition, 47 percent of the West Germans thought that the Minister for Economics, Karl Schiller, was a member of the Christian Democrats. Only when the SPD Executive allowed Schiller to say before television and newsreel cameras, 'We Social Democrats' did the citizens realize that the professor was a comrade."[5]

In late 1970, the Young Socialists—the organization of members of the SPD under thirty-five years of age, nicknamed the Jusos —posed a number of questions about the evolution of the German social democracy. At their Congress in Bremen in December, 1970, they came out for "reforms which would change the system" (*"an einer systemuberwindenden Perspective"*) which included demands for a vast expansion of free social services in health, transportation, and education, for planned social investment and co-determination in industry as a step toward new, and communal, forms of property. The party leadership replied that "we Social Democrats strive for a step-by-step (*'schrittweise'*) change in social structure."

At first it seemed that this debate put the generations on a collision course. Karl Schiller responded to the Jusos by emphasizing his belief in "entrepreneurial initiative" and stressing the more conservative aspects of the Godesberg Program, and a poll showed that two thirds of the Germans were hostile to the radical demands. The Burgermeister of Munich, Hans-Jochen Vogel, angered because the Jusos had with some success become a factional force in the party itself, announced that he would not be a candidate for re-election. But in the late spring at a Juso conference on municipal politics, the remarkable development was the degree to which Vogel and the young theorists agreed. Vogel, for instance, was sympathetic to the demand for free medical and edu-

cational services. At this writing, the debate within the German
social democracy is continuing.

So one must ask, did the Godesberg Program, and the similar
rewritings of the definitions of socialism in Western Europe, mean
the end of the socialist dream? Has the vision of mankind leaping
from the Kingdom of Necessity into the Kingdom of Freedom
culminated in the pragmatic contradiction of socialist capitalism?

In part, these revisions were absolutely necessary. It would
have been senseless after the half-century of experience with
nationalization simply to repeat that public ownership was the
sovereign remedy for all social ills. The old Marxian pretense in
which the party was a secular church, with a *weltanschauung*
and interior world of its own, had similarly become obsolete.
Therefore it made good sense to formally disavow any desire to
have a party position on religious or philosophical matters (that
had long since been dropped in practice, but the enemies of the
social democrats still try to depict them as revolutionary godless
Bolsheviks). And the narrow notion of a class party was well
forgotten. Once he got over the simplifications of *The Communist
Manifesto*, Marx himself never believed that society was polarizing into two, and only two, classes, and he and every serious
socialist tactician who came after him were aware of the need
to reach out beyond the proletariat.

And the post-war changes in European economic structure
made it particularly imperative that the broadness of the social
democracy be emphasized. In Britain, for instance, the proportion
of white-collar workers in the economy is increasing three times
as fast as between 1911 and 1931, and a third faster than the
1931–1951 rate. Therefore the socialist parties, if they wanted to
win a majority, had to emphasize their concern and appeal to
these new and growing strata.

But even though much of this modernization of doctrine is
overdue, it went too far. The Godesberg Program and the theory
of the "social market economy" do not go beyond American liberalism. They stay well within the bounds of capitalist society
and, as so often has happened in the past, show how socialists
can be much too optimistic about capitalism.

First of all, the redistribution of income within capitalist society
is not taking place at all, or at least not in the way that the revisionist social democrats suggest. In England—and to be fair
to Crosland, much of the statistical work for these assertions was

published after his major contribution to the debate—economists like Thomas Balogh and Richard Titmus have documented the persistence of severe income inequality. In that country, and in almost every nation in Europe (including Sweden, where the facts were given wide publicity by Olof Palme's Social Democratic government in 1970), there is a poverty which persists despite the general post-war prosperity.

More to the point, Balogh and Titmus and others have pointed out that a good part of this intractable poverty has been caused by the dislocations of economic growth. There are, Titmus has said, a welfare state and a dis-welfare state, and the former is often only an inadequate attempt at "partial compensation for social costs and social insecurity which are the products of a rapidly changing industrial-urban society." In the 1970 British elections even intellectuals who supported Labour had to admit that poverty had far from vanished. Moreover, the private market, even when it operates within a context established by a socialist government, has a powerful and inherent tendency to maximize profits without regard to public consequences. That means, as Chapter XII will detail, that much more social investment and planning than are dreamed of in these social democratic programs will be required just to reach their modest goals.

But perhaps most important of all is the basic assumption of the new European socialism that the state can relatively easily impose its socialist will upon the private sector. In fact, capital fights back; it does not meekly accept the programming of social democratic ministers. That was apparent enough in 1936, when in the month between the election that assured him the leadership of the nation and Léon Blum's actual taking of office, $4 billion in gold francs went abroad. For, as the Godesberg Program notes, but does not adequately stress, economic power is political power, and as long as the basic relationships of the private economy are left intact, they provide a base for the subversion of the democratic will.

Harold Wilson's experience in the sixties is an excellent case in point. In 1963 Wilson did what Hugh Gaitskell had failed to do: he won his party to a new orientation. As an old Bevanite, he had support on the Labour Left; as a shrewd tactician, he avoided any head-on confrontations over socialist doctrine; and he redefined socialism more dramatically than any of the revisionists. The socialists, he said, would modernize Britain, expand the economy through planning and give social direction to the technological revolution. "If there had never been a case for socialism before," Wilson told a cheering Labour conference, "automation would have created it."

Wilson became Prime Minister in 1964 and in the elections of 1965 won a substantial majority. Planning was placed under George Brown, which meant that it had a powerful advocate in the Cabinet. Yet, the whole scheme did not really survive the first plan, which, in any case, was never put into effect. Instead of carefully managed expansion, the Government alternately encouraged affluence and austerity in a "stop-go" pattern not unlike that of the Tories. And after three years of defending the pound tenaciously, Wilson devalued in order to get out of the straitjacket which, seemingly, he himself had insisted upon wearing. Why?

Wilson "defended" the pound, and followed a number of other policies, because bankers in Britain and elsewhere made it quite clear that they would only supply money if the Government promised not to engage in social experiments. When, for instance, increased pensions were announced in 1964, the immediate reaction of the financial community was to sell £10 million on the world market. The governor of the nationalized Bank of England attacked Wilson, his democratically chosen superior, and demanded conservative policies, including a wage freeze. When the Tories returned to power in 1970, they made the governor an ambassador.

As Titmus described the situation, ". . . to many of our creditors and currency colleagues in West Germany, France and the United States, the 'Welfare State' is equated with national irresponsibility and decadence. These opinions, moreover, do not differ markedly from those expressed in public statements on welfare during the past fifteen years by bankers, insurance directors, financiers and others in the City of London." So great was this pressure during the first eighteen months of Wilson's Administration that Andrew Schonfield, an extremely shrewd observer of the British economy, concluded that the Government's insistence on an incomes policy was "a declamatory device to impress foreign bankers."

There was a radical way to get out of the sterling impasse. The Government could, as James Dickens of the Labour Left proposed, have nationalized the privately held dollar securities of British citizens. The owners would have been compensated in pounds and the nation would have had enough dollars to put its

currency on a firm non-speculative basis. But, as George Lichtheim noted at the time, Britain depends on foreign banking for
its livelihood and the international reprisals against such a cavalier
attitude toward private property would have been swift. On such
a question, foreign and native bankers and businessmen have more
votes than British citizens.

But the financiers were not the only problem. The industrialists
also attended to their private priorities rather than to the common
good. As Michael Shanks, who was Co-ordinator of Industrial
Policy in the early Wilson years, put it, "By and large exports are
very unprofitable compared to home sales even in today's not
exactly buoyant market. The result is that, despite every induce-
ment, a large proportion of firms are not exporting at all and in
too many others, exporting is regarded as a chore."

However, the most devastating effect of private power on public
policy is not to be found in Labour's failures but in its successes.
When an economy expands, there is, as Wilson himself aptly noted
in 1960, a "law of increasing returns to the rich." In the absence
of rather drastic countermeasures, the benefits of a governmentally planned prosperity will be distributed according to the
existing inequities in the society, i.e., the rich will get the most,
the poor the least. And, as John Hughes of Ruskin College, Oxford,
computed the figures in 1968, income from property increased
more than earnings in the Wilson years.

So the socialist program of giving political direction to an economy still privately controlled—whether by owners or managers
does not really matter—was hamstrung by the ability of wealth
to limit, and even veto, public policy. It is, after all, not only in
America that regulatory agencies become the creatures of those
they are supposed to regulate. In bad times a socialist government
will have to pay a ransom to get the good will of the corporations;
in good times the boom its policies induce will tend to favor its
enemies more than its constituents. And that will be the case until
there are more basic structural changes in capitalism than have
been proposed in the various revised socialist programs.

But if socialist capitalism as proposed by the European social
democrats is thus inadequate to the times, that does not in the
least mean that these parties are irrelevant.

By and large the socialist parties of Europe have been from the
end of the First World War to the present the leaven in their
various societies. Their accomplishments in the creation of the

welfare state—for instance in that incredible victory described by André Philip where it took a near-revolution to win the effective right of a worker to see the ocean—are of the first magnitude. So even if the worst fears expressed in this book—that the socialist vision has been abandoned—were to be confirmed, these parties would still command my loyalty. But, in fact, the fate of socialism is by no means settled. With the issue still in doubt, it is an unpardonable sectarianism to say, as Daniel Singer does in his *Prelude to Revolution,* that "social democracy no longer has any connection with socialism." For if there is any hope for the renewal of the socialist ideal advocated in the later chapters of this book, in Europe it is located in the mass socialist parties, which did not as we have just seen, embrace the contradictions of socialist capitalism out of choice. And if a new and real alternative were to appear on the Left—not some vague rehearsal of Marxian pieties about ending alienation, but a program starting where the masses are now and making it possible for them to move forward—the social democrats of the Continent and England are the ones who will have to put it into effect.[6]

# X

## The Substitute Proletariats

AFTER WORLD WAR II "socialisms" appeared everywhere. There were Chinese, Cuban, Arab, Israeli, African, Indian, Yugoslavian, Chilean and other "socialisms," each claiming to represent a unique point of departure for the future and often denouncing all the rest as frauds or even fascism in disguise.

Yet however different, and even violently hostile, these various systems, almost all of them (the Israelis are a special case) have one thing in common: they have collectivized a poverty qualitatively more profound than that found in the Russia of 1917. The classic path of capitalist industrialization, in which enterprises within a market economy play the decisive role and the state aids and subsidizes them, is no longer possible in such countries. But then, neither is that socialism envisioned by Marx, for it can only be built by an educated working class on the basis of a modern technology, and both these preconditions are absent in most of Asia, Africa and Latin America.

In the Third World, then, one confronts a revolutionary development so unprecedented that there is not a hint of it in the writings of Karl Marx.* There is, of course, an obvious relationship

---

* I use the term "Third World" to describe the developing societies of Asia, Africa and Latin America. But I do not for a moment hold that there is a natural

to the Russian development described in Chapter VII. In each of these "socialisms," as in the Soviet Union, the state is substituted for the bourgeoisie as an agency of modernization. But the differences are very real. Since the Third World begins at even lower economic levels than the Russia of 1917, the contradictions inherent in the socialization of poverty are even more acute there than in the first Communist state.

These "socialisms" are also distinguished by another crucial characteristic: they are in search of a new proletariat. The Russian Revolution was begun by a working-class rebellion, and even though Stalin was to expropriate every vestige of workers' power, it continued to speak in the name of the proletariat even after it became bureaucratic collectivist. But in the Third World such a pretense is much more difficult to maintain. So peasants, the urban poor, military officers and educated elites have at different times been assigned the role Marx had designated for the organized working people.

The emergence of these substitute proletariats is of the most profound significance. Marx did not nominate the workers as agents of the socialist revolution out of sentimentality. They were, he said, becoming the majority of society and therefore stood to gain by the most thoroughgoing democratization; they were concentrated in large numbers and forced by the conditions of their daily life to organize for economic self-defense and thus to learn how to act collectively; they were disciplined and schooled in the ways of that modern technology that made socialism possible.

---

solidarity among some "nonwhite," or non-European and non-American, majority. There are antagonisms within the Third World which are quite murderous, as the civil wars in Nigeria and the Sudan or the various struggles between China, India and Pakistan demonstrate. Moreover, there are profound economic differences among these countries. Latin America, for instance, has a real purchasing power which is twice as great as all the other developing areas and four times that of India and Pakistan. ("The Alliance for Progress and Peaceful Revolution" by Paul N. Rosenstein-Rodan, in *Latin American Radicalism*, Irving Louis Horowitz, Josue de Castro and John Gerassi, eds. New York, Vintage Books, 1969, p. 53.) John Kenneth Galbraith has quite usefully distinguished three types of economic underdevelopment: the Sub-Saharan, in which a minimum cultural base for modernization is lacking; the Latin American, in which social structure inhibits change; and the South Asian, in which population growth is a crucial problem. (*Economics, Peace and Laughter*. Boston, Houghton Mifflin, 1971, pp. 228ff.) The element they all have in common, and which provides the objective basis for grouping them together for the purpose of an analysis that also must take into account the differences between them, is that they are all seeking ways to industrialize in a period in which the "bourgeois revolution" is no longer a possibility.

Above all, Marx argued that the socialization of the means of production, which was in the common interest of mankind, was in the self-interest of the propertyless wage earner. The working class was thus the first, and last, class whose egotism was objectively idealistic.

Marx was both right and wrong. His ultimate revolutionary hopes for the Western proletariat have certainly been disappointed; yet he was prophetic when he saw in the ragged, degraded factory hands of the mid-nineteenth century a new and progressive force for social change. But what is important here is that his thesis described empirical links between the conditions of life of the proletariat and the political role he thought it would play. I propose to make a similar analysis of the substitute proletariats of the Third World, the peasants and the urban poor in particular. It will show why they cannot build a socialist society, or as Che Guevara and the Cubans hoped, create new and selfless men. In the process I hope to go beyond an idealization of the dispossessed and to explore the precise possibilties of resistance that a normally cruel history affords them.

In saying this I do not for a moment want to denigrate the agony of people, often threatened by starvation, trying to claw their way forward to the material possibility of minimal decency. Their plight is in large measure the result of an international division of labor imposed upon them by the capitalist West and it deserves the compassion—and active political solidarity—of any concerned person. But one should not therefore respond as some on the Left did to the heroic struggle of the Algerians against French colonialism. They not only sided with the national liberation movement against the French, but uncritically accepted its claim to be the carrier of a new, and socialist, order as well. Victory produced a bureaucratic and Islamic dictatorship, not the good society. Similarly, in the case of Vietnam, people in the American peace movement who quite rightly fought their own Government's disastrous intervention wrongly took everything the Vietcong and North Vietnamese said at face value. They ignored, for instance, the fact that Ho Chi Minh had by his own admission carried out a bloody collectivization in the North over the dead bodies of some tens of thousands of "his" peasants.

It is precisely because these peoples of the Third World are striving for a genuine emancipation under conditions that must thwart their efforts that it is necessary to separate out and analyze the ideological elements in these "socialisms." There will be a future in which their dreams become possible, and the tactics of the present must not be allowed to corrupt it in advance. It is, in short, in the name of socialism in the Third World that I write this critique of its "socialisms."

# I

For most of the countries of Asia, Africa and Latin America, capitalist modernization is now impossible.

It has been the hope of American planners in the post-war period that there is a progressive capitalist alternative to Communist industrialization. John Kenneth Galbraith put this aspiration in the language of the democratic Left: "The revolution that is required here, we should remind ourselves, is less the Russian Revolution than the French Revolution." It was this proposition that was the central justification for the Alliance for Progress in its early, idealistic period. It is, I think, wrong.

That bourgeois—or "French"—revolution which Galbraith seeks cannot possibly take place in most of the Third World. Under special circumstances, as in Iran, it is conceivable that oil revenues can be used to sponsor industrialization coupled with land reform, but even that produces a highly statified—in this case, monarchical—variant of capitalism. In general, however, there are massive historic reasons that preclude a capitalist development with or without American aid (more precisely, as Chapter XII will show, American trade and aid policy has been a barrier to modernization in the poor lands).

But then, couldn't these countries settle for a slow rate of growth? Raul Prebisch of the United Nations' Conference on Trade and Development (UNCTAD) posed and dealt with that question at a New Delhi meeting. He asked, "Could they not be content with a relatively moderate pace, like that of the industrial centres during their historic development?" And answered, "The historic experience of these countries can never be repeated, either as concerns the pace of development or in any other respect. Perhaps it would be possible to repeat it if we could revert to the production techniques of a century ago, if we could prevent news of the new forms or private consumption and social well-being from spreading continuously—a development which is the natural outcome of communication techniques—and if we could turn back the clock and erase the progress which the masses of the people have achieved in their political and social development."

What Prebisch was describing is one of the cruelest facts of contemporary life: that the preconditions for modernization are becoming progressively more and more expensive. Russia in 1913 was probably below the level of development of most South American countries today, yet the prospects for industrialization there were much more propitious. The necessary investments in technology have become much more massive since 1913; political movements are more demanding; and, above all, there is a highly developed global division of labor which is hostile to the industrialization of poor lands. When the Western European countries, the United States, Australia and Japan emerged as capitalist powers, the world was not already dominated by another group of even stronger nations. Capital, Barbara Ward has estimated, is sixty times more costly to the developing countries of the twentieth century than it was to the new capitalisms of the nineteenth.

Gunnar Myrdal reports that in Southeast Asia, "instead of a rising demand for exports aiding the early stages of industrialization as in most Western countries, exports must be pushed by systematic government action." Indeed, the subordinate position of these nations on the world market accounts for much of their economic structure and partly explains the absence of a strong, indigenous bourgeoisie. For, as we have seen in Chapter VI, to the degree that the original capitalist powers invested in the colonies and semi-colonies, they created enclaves of modernity. Therefore the local capitalist was more often than not a collaborator with foreign money rather than an innovating entrepreneur on his own.

Russia had undergone the beginnings of a capitalist development prior to the October Revolution in 1917. Its industry was, to be sure, heavily under the influence of foreign capital and had some of the characteristics of an enclave, yet it was not basically subordinated to some metropolitan economy as in the case of the colonies and semi-colonies. In this setting the scarce entrepreneurial talents could be united in very large industrial units, as Alexander Gershenkron has documented. Russia had, in short, arrived quite late on the capitalist scene, yet it still might have developed in the authoritarian, German-Japanese variant of that mode. It was located midway between Oriental despotism and Western capitalism.

But in the Third World nations that became formally independent after World War II, or as with the Latin Republics, began to search for economic independence at that point, the circumstances were not so positive. Not only were the material economic preconditions of modernization lacking: the cultural and spiritual prerequisites were missing too. For in an influential tradition descending from Max Weber, "it has been argued that these countries not only lack the economic prerequisites for growth but that many of them preserve values which foster behavior antithetical to the systematic accumulation of capital."

For example, the Latin emphasis on family loyalty keeps many South American companies from hiring talented outsiders, and pre-capitalist traditions in that area orient businessmen toward quick profits and withdrawal from commerce altogether rather than toward reinvestment and long-range industrial planning. These attitudes are not, of course, individual psychic peculiarities but are grounded in the economic structure, particularly in its backward sectors: the material and the spiritual conditions act and react with each other. As Gunnar Myrdal described this interworking, "Some of the characteristics commonly ascribed to South Asians—their bent to contemplation and their appreciation of leisure, etc., sometimes on a more intellectualized level reflected in religious doctrine, philosophy or belief in specific 'values' of a country or of all Asia—may, in fact, be due to deficiencies in nutrition and health."

The experience of Israel is particularly revealing in this context. The land the original Zionists settled was poor, yet within several generations they and their descendants have created a modern, democratic and socially oriented society. One of the main reasons for this accomplishment—apart from the devotion and idealism of the movement itself—was that Israel was, in a sense, the last country created by Europe. Like the United States, Canada, Australia and New Zealand, it began with a crucial resource: a modern population which had already been schooled in industrial rationality. This suggests that of the two Marxian preconditions for socialism—a productive economy and a conscious working class—the latter may well be the more important. It is precisely these modern attitudes that are lacking in every other country of the Third World.

From this perspective, one understands how unique was the process described in *Das Kapital*. For, as Marx realized but never was able to develop at great length, the majority of mankind was not evolving toward the preconditions for capitalism. Now that same majority wants not capitalism, which is impossible in any case, but an even higher form of society. And the brute question first raised in the Russian Revolution is posed even more forcefully: What social force will play the role fulfilled by the entrepreneur in the West?

On the rhetorical surface the answer of Third World "socialism" to this question is preposterous. The peasants or the urban poor, it is said, can simultaneously be substituted for both the bourgeoisie and the proletariat. This means that the same class must exploit itself by working harder for less in order to provide surplus for investment (a surplus that the bourgeoisie once extracted) and at the same time abolish exploitation (the proletarian role). Such a contradiction could not be resolved in Russia, where the workers were supposed to be enthusiastically increasing the unpaid portion of their labor time, and it is even more ridiculous to think that peasants or the lumpenproletariat of the cities, lacking the cohesion and discipline that daily life imposes on the working class, have organized their own totalitarian subjugation as a means to freedom.

Actually, the peasants and the urban poor are substitute proletariats only in the heaven of theory. In reality, the party-state, which is a new ruling class, substitutes itself for the proletariat, the bourgeoisie and everyone else.[1]

## II

Peasants were the mass basis of the Chinese Revolution—but it was not a peasant revolution for which they fought and died. Rather, they were the unwitting agents of a revolution from above which made them its victims.

The stage was set by the failure of capitalism.

The most dramatic proof of capitalist ineptitude in China was the fact that a Communist eventually rallied some businessmen to his banner. For all his twists and turns, Mao had generally followed the line he put forward in 1940: China is going through a "bourgeois democratic revolution in a semi-colonial country" which would be "protracted." Therefore he had regularly attempted to win over elements in the bourgeoisie. Just before the

Communist seizure of power Chiang's weakness was so glaring that a leading business weekly in Hong Kong reported, "The remaining foreigners in Shanghai are looking for an improvement when the Communist-appointed administration will assume control; as it has been for the last three and a half years, life appeared to many as intolerable in chaotic Shanghai."

So Chiang's efforts to build a modern capitalist state in China were in such a shambles by 1949 that businessmen, both foreign and native, turned to the Communists, who were emphasizing the gradualist aspects of their "new democratic" program. There had been, to be sure, some Nationalist progress between the destruction of urban Communism in 1928 and the Japanese invasion in 1937. But when the Japanese came, Chiang was driven out of the cities and separated from whatever liberal and dynamic elements were to be found in the bourgeois camp. His party, the Kuomintang, had always been an uneasy alliance between industrialists and agrarian conservatives, and the war tipped the balance in favor of the latter and ruled out the capitalist path to modernity. Just before the Communist victory Nationalist mismanagement of the economy was so spectacular that prices had risen 11,600 percent as compared to 1936–1937. Under the circumstances, it is not surprising that some businessmen preferred Communist order to capitalist anarchy.

But what force did the victorious Communists represent?

The Maoists themselves would reply that they were a proletarian party playing the leading role in a multiclass democratic movement of workers, peasants, the urban petty bourgeoisie and the national bourgeoisie (and sometimes they would even add "the enlightened gentry"). In fact, the Communists were a new ruling class and, for a number of reasons, this can be seen more clearly in China than in any other bureaucratic collectivist country.

One of the profound differences between the Chinese and Russian revolutions is that the former emerged out of a genuine working-class insurrection whose conquests then had to be destroyed to make way for the power of the new class while in the latter the party established itself as a decisive force, independent of all the classes in the nation, before it took control. In part, this was because the Chinese Communists had listened to Stalin. In the 1920s the Russian leader had given them the catastrophic advice that they should trust the revolutionary bona fides of Chiang, a policy that led to the near-extermination of the party by its supposed allies. From that time until the late 1940s, as Benjamin Schwartz has shown, the party lost all systematic contact with the urban workers.

Thus when Mao designated the proletariat as "the basic *motive force* of the Chinese Revolution" (emphasis added), he was speaking metaphorically, since most of the working class did not participate in the movement at all. What the "proletariat" means in this context is the Communist Party substituting itself for the workers. But when Mao at the same time acknowledged that the peasantry is "*the main force* in the Chinese Revolution," he was being more objective. The problem is, as Engels had understood long ago, that it is not necessarily the class that does most of the dying that determines the class content of a revolution. "In all of the three great bourgeois revolutions [England, France and Germany]," he wrote, "the peasantry provided the army with striking power and the peasants were the class that after the victory was won most surely was ruined by the economic consequences of this triumph." In China the peasants died, just as they had under Cromwell, to raise a new class above them..

Indeed, traditional Marxism had always argued that the peasantry was, by virtue of its conditions of life, incapable of truly independent action on its own behalf. "The peasants with small plots," Marx wrote in *The Eighteenth Brumaire*, "constitute an enormous mass whose members live in the same situation but without entering into a variety of relationships with one another. *Their mode of production isolates them from one another rather than bringing them together in reciprocal relations. . . .* Their field production, the plot, does not allow any division of labor, any application of science, and thus provides no variety of development, no differentiation of talent, no richness of social relationships. . . . So the great mass of the French nation is formed by the simple addition of similar quantities, like potatoes make up a potato sack. . . . The peasants are therefore incapable of defending their class interests in their own name, either in a parliament or in a constituent assembly."

It was precisely because Lenin and Trotsky remained faithful to this Marxist insight that they believed that the workers would have to play a decisive role in the Russian Revolution even through they were a minority and the peasants a majority. Even so, they agreed with Karl Kautsky that the position of the peasant had changed somewhat since Marx's day. As the villages became part of the world market, their isolation was shattered; and as the peasants were drafted, they were brought into contact with city life and ideas. This last point was particularly prophetic, for it was the presence of so many peasants in uniform that made them a major force in the Russian events of 1917.

But as the euphoria of the October Revolution began to abate and the Communists realized that they were not going to be quickly saved from their backwardness by the victory of the German workers, they began a profound revision of Marxist theory which pointed toward Mao's adaptation. At the Second Congress of the Communist International in 1920, a manifesto proclaimed, "What we now mean by the word 'mass,' is not what we used to mean by it a few years ago. *That which was the mass* in the epoch of parliamentarianism and trade unionism has become the elite in our days. Millions and tens of millions who have lived up to now outside of all politics are in the process of transforming themselves into a revolutionary mass." "The pariahs," the International said, "are rising."

And a few years later an almost despairing Lenin was, as we have seen, to take solace in the fact that the non-Europeans constituted a majority in the world and thus guaranteed a victory to socialism. Yet the Russians still insisted—in theory—on the primacy of the working class in the transition to a new order. (In fact, the workers were being deprived of all the rights they had won in the Revolution.) In the early 1920s a Tatar Communist leader was too blunt about what was really happening. Sultan-Galiev proposed "the establishment of the dictatorship of the colonies and semi-colonies" over the industrial metropolis and the creation of a Colonial International. Stalin, whose protégé he was, had him purged for being so candid about the real import of Lenin's last theories. This was probably the first time that Lin Piao's thesis of the countryside of the world conquering the cities of the world was stated in Marxist language, and the Russians labeled it heresy.

So Mao was making a departure from Stalinist, as well as Marxist, theory when he openly turned toward the peasants after the urban Communists had drowned in their own blood in 1927. Yet—and the point is crucial—he did not thereby make himself into a peasant leader. As Harold Isaacs brilliantly summarized the Communist experience on the road to power, "During the decade following 1927, the Communist Party had become a party of de-urbanized intellectuals and peasant leaders whose main strength lay in the military force which they created and with which they ultimately won power. Apart from its broadly agrarian character and pre-occupation, this party and this military force had no consistent class base through the years . . . it shifted from one section of the peasantry to another, now seeking the support of the lower strata, now of the upper strata, at times adapting itself without difficulty even to the landlords. It came as a force from the outside, bringing its program with it."

Mao's troops were indeed peasant, but his program and cadre were not. And this is nowhere more clear than in the way the Chinese Communists vacilated, as it suited their own purposes, on life-and-death issues for the peasantry. In 1928, for instance, Mao was leading movements against the "landlords, the landed gentry and the bourgeoisie," but in 1935 the national bourgeoisie was welcomed into the anti-Japanese struggle. In 1937 he proclaimed that the "confiscation of the land of the landlords shall be discontinued," but by 1939 (the period of the Hitler-Stalin pact when the Communists of the world were turning sharply "Left") he was saying that "the landlords, as a class, are a target and not a motive force of the revolution." Then, after the Germans invaded Russia, Mao reminded the party that "the whole set of measures taken during the Agrarian Revolution are inapplicable under present circumstances." A leader who was genuinely rooted in, and expressing the aspirations of, the peasant masses would hardly shift his position at the behest of Moscow in this way. But a Mao could. His final tactic, the one that carried him to power, was to minimize his hostility to the rural wealthy. "As to the rich peasants," he wrote in the very important programmatic statement of 1945, *On Coalition Government*, "we have encouraged them to develop production."

Thus the Chinese Communists were not a party of workers, or even of peasants, even though at various times they led significant elements of both those groups. They had been forced out of an organic relationship with any of the classes of the society, which is why they themselves can be seen so clearly as an embryonic class. They reentered the cities, in Isaac's phrase, as "a force from the outside." As Trotsky understood in a brilliant anticipation of the Chinese reality, "The absence of a strong revolutionary party and of mass organizations of the proletariat renders control over the commanding stratum impossible. The commanders and the commissars appear in the guise of absolute masters of the situation and upon occupying the cities will be apt to look down from above upon the workers."[2]

Mao's myth represents him as a leader responding to spontaneous currents of feeling among the masses. Yet before his victory he clearly manipulated his peasant followers, now befriending landlords, now fighting them. And after the conquest of power, the particularly deracinated government he led was capable of the most abrupt changes in line because it did not feel itself limited by the organizations of the people. On occasion, the millions saw a crack in the monolithic state, or after being pushed too far and too fast were able to force a retreat upon the revolutionaries-from-above. But they never won the right to decide their own destiny. It is this reality that makes of the history of the Communists in government such a dizzying succession of zigs and zags.

In the first period of Mao's rule, from 1949 to 1955, it seemed that he was going to redeem his old promise of "the land to the tiller." There was a wide distribution of plots to the peasants. In 1952 less than 1.5 percent of the peasant households were in cooperatives, and the official target was to raise this number to 20 percent by the end of 1957. In February of 1953 the Central Committee of the Party proclaimed, "On the basis of present economic conditions, the individual economic system of the peasants will necessarily continue to exist and expand for a long time to come. It is even necessary to permit the continued development of the economic system of the wealthy peasant. Moreover the Common Program states that the peasant's ownership of land will be safeguarded wherever the agrarian reform is carried on."

But the voluntary collectivization the Chinese Communists hoped for simply did not materialize (and in the years to follow, the Chinese peasants were to act much like their Russian counterparts, trying to get private plots, farm animals and the like). Then in 1954 flood damage reduced the harvest and in 1954–1955 the peasants hoarded their short supplies. (There had been tentative moves toward collectivization in 1953 and 1954.) This was apparently a major motive for the sudden turn into cooperatives in a matter of months. (It should be obvious that under such circumstances the term "cooperative" has little to do with the ideal of people voluntarily and enthusiastically working together.) In July, 1955, 14.2 percent of the peasants were in co-ops; in May, 1966, the figure was 91.2 percent.

The political control of the peasantry was not the only reason for this sudden new departure in policy. As Mao himself emphasized in his speech on collectivization on July 31, 1955, "socialist industrialization cannot be separated from the development of agricultural cooperatives, cannot be undertaken by itself. For one thing, everyone knows that in our country the production of marketable grain and of raw materials for industry is at present at a very low level while the country's needs in this respect are increasing every year." In other words, Mao was collectivizing for much the same reason that Stalin had: the better to extract a surplus from the peasantry which could be devoted to industrialization.

This admission runs counter to an extremely simplified theory that has been popular on the pro-Communist wing of the American Left. As Paul Baran put it, ". . . contrary to the commonly held view that receives a great deal of emphasis in Western writing on under-developed countries, the principal obstacle is *not* shortage of capital. What is short is what we have termed *actual* economic surplus invested in the expansion of productive facilities. The *potential* economic surplus that could be made available for such investment is large in all of them." For Baran, the old ruling class had either wasted the surplus in luxuries, or else had not even tapped the full sources of the nation's wealth. A determined socialist government, then, can find sufficient funds for industrialization by squeezing the living standards, "primarily, if not solely [of] the ruling class whose excess consumption, squandering of resources, and capital flight, had to be 'sacrificed' to economic development."

But Mao's speech indicates, if in veiled language, that Baran's optimistic theories do not apply, at least in China, and that the peasants are going to be a primary source of the surplus which will then be used for modernization. Indeed, the Chinese leader even admitted that there was considerable opposition to his policy within the party, which anticipated a massive flight of peasants from the countryside to the city in response to the collectivization decreed from on high.

It was in this setting of reaction to considerable peasant discontent within his own country that Mao dealt with the revelations about Stalin at the Twentieth Party Congress of the Russian Communists and the uprising that took place shortly afterward in Poland and Hungary. His first tactic, announced in February, 1957, was liberal: a "hundred flowers" were to bloom and criticism of the regime was to be legitimated. But so many people vigorously availed themselves of this moment of freedom that within three months Mao turned upon the "Rightists" who had revealed themselves in China. It was no longer allowed for people to say, as two faculty members had at the Teacher's Training College at Shenyang during the "Hundred Flowers" period, that "the Communist Party having set itself up as a privileged class, we find worthless Communists in all the important posts." Mao amended his February 27, 1957, address with the proviso that free speech could only be exercised if it united the nationalities, was beneficial to socialist transformation, helped consolidate democratic centralism, strengthened the leadership of the Communist Party and was beneficial to "international socialist solidarity." Free speech, in short, was permitted if it agreed on every count with the line of the regime.

It was this sharp turn to the "Left"—that is, to a more vigorous totalitarian policy—that led to the creation of huge peasant communes in 1958. As Roger Garaudy wrote (when he was still a member of the Central Committee of the Communist Party of France), "five hundred million were called to fundamentally change their mode of existence within several weeks but without the intervention of any new technical means. Already in 1955 Mao had criticized those who thought it necessary to have tractors and modern tools so that a system of agricultural cooperatives would correspond to objective reality."

The Russian Communists had always been careful—with the exception of Khrushchev's ideological indiscretion in 1960, which was soon corrected—to specify that they were still building socialism, for if they said that they were actually entering the higher stage of Communism, then their official writ proclaimed that the state should start withering away and people should be paid according to their needs rather than according to the amount of work they did. But in the euphoria of August, 1958, the Central Committee of the Chinese Communist Party proclaimed that their land, which was much more backward than Russia and subject to a population pressure as well, was in sight of the promised day: "the realization of Communism in our country is not an event which belongs in the distant future. We must work to use the form of the popular communes as a means of exploring a concrete passage to Communism."

Within one short year the Central Committee admitted that

this was fantasy. The statistics demonstrating the enormous achievements of the communes had been exaggerated; the vast investment of manpower in the harvest had been made in such a way as to be wasteful. And later on, in 1962, the Central Committee admitted that the commune policies—and the Great Leap's experimentation with backyard iron furnaces—had provoked mass discontent.

What led Mao to make such a spectacular miscalculation? It was, once again, his character as a revolutionary-from-above. Shortly before the commune adventure he had made an extraordinarily candid speech on April 15, 1958: "Apart from their other characteristics, the outstanding thing about China's 600 million people is that they are 'poor and blank.' This may seem a bad thing but in reality it is a good thing. Poverty gives rise to the desire for change, the desire for action and the desire for revolution. On a blank sheet of paper free from any marks, the freshest and most beautiful characters can be written, the freshest and most beautiful pictures can be painted." The communes and the Great Leap were an attempt on the part of the leader to write beautiful characters on the blankness of his people. A sharper contradiction of the Marxian ideal of the self-emancipation of the working class is hard to imagine.

It turned out that Mao's elitist estimation of the character of the Chinese people was wrong. At the Lushan meeting of the Communist Party Central Committee in mid-1959, he was attacked sharply by Defense Minister P'eng Teh-huai and in effect demoted from the active day-to-day leadership of the party. The critique made of Mao from within his party was particularly revealing in terms of the peasantry. For in trying to cope with the setbacks his policy had visited upon the economy, the technocrats made concessions to the peasants who, in turn, seemed to have the very same aspirations as the Russian (or any other kind of) peasants: to farm their own plot.

This point must be stressed, for it subverts the notion of the peasantry as a substitute proletariat. Prior to Stalin it had been axiomatic among Marxists that the peasant was a petty bourgeois who wanted nothing more than his own private piece of land, however small it might be. Then the Russian dictator terrorized millions of peasants into collective farms at the unconscionable human and economic cost that has already been described. Now Mao came along and asserted that the Chinese peasants were an even more remarkable exception to the Marxist rule than the Russian peasants were once supposed to be. They were, it was said, fighting to surrender their private plots to the collectivity. But when that fantasy led to the same loss of production it had provoked in Russia, the ruling class was forced to act in terms of reality: they appealed to that immemorial peasant psychology, so deeply rooted in the conditions of life, which Mao had tried to ignore. Thus, in a study lyrically favorable to Mao, Joan Robinson describes how the encouragement of private household trade and an increase in consumer goods was the antidote to the Great Leap forward.*[3]

But Mao did not take all this backsliding passively, and in 1966 succeeded in launching the "Cultural Revolution." Here again, there is a sudden, and astounding, turn, explicable only if one understands the degree to which the warring factions of Chinese Communism stand above the people they theoretically represent. The revolution was directed, as the Central Committee resolution of August, 1966, put it, against those who "after having infiltrated themselves into the Party, achieved leading posts but followed the capitalist way." This vast "proletarian" upheaval had as its "courageous pioneers"—schoolboys.

At times this led to bizarre events. In Shanghai in December, 1966, and January, 1967, the Maoists bitterly attacked the official party leadership for seeking "to sap the will of the workers through material incentives." But in the course of stirring up the rank and file, Mao's wife discovered that they went out on strike not against those seeking to reintroduce capitalism, but precisely for higher wages. The proletariat was, in short, following the "evil road of economism." Then on January 8, 1967, students were used as strikebreakers to open up the port of Shanghai. "It seems difficult to admit," Roger Garaudy has remarked, "that the utilization of students as strikebreakers is a means of 'taking over the leadership in order to return it to the proletarian revolutionaries.'"

It was after this debacle that the People's Liberation Army was called in to take over the Cultural Revolution. This was the

---

* Mrs. Robinson, as Chapter V made clear, is a brilliant economic theorist. It is therefore quite sad that, on the basis of what seems to have been casual contact, she presumes to report Maoist myth as fact. But then, the line changed after her book was finished and she had to include a postscript taking account of the fact that Mao and his comrades had turned from spontaneity to discipline without consulting the people or even their admirers, like herself.

process that brought Lin Piao to the fore as Mao's successor. It also led to that remarkable change in the official personality of the regime's symbolic arch-rival, Liu Shao-ch'i. In the heyday of the Cultural Revolution the President of the People's Republic of China was accused of being the main "capitalist roader" in the society and the Red Guards were called upon to challenge him and all of his treacherous (Communist) friends for their Rightism. But when that movement became too economically costly, Liu was charged with the Left deviation of anarchism. In March of 1968 a Chinese Communist press statement denounced "China's Khrushchev [Liu]" because he said "with ulterior motives: 'Do as the masses want' and 'mainly depend on the spontaneity of the mass movement.'" But that, of course, was what Mao had been saying only shortly before. One way of interpreting this dramatic *volte face* would be to see it as a change of heart. Another, and much more accurate, interpretation would understand that the masses in the Cultural Revolution had been allowed freedom only insofar as it suited Mao, and that once his purposes had been served or their cost had proved too high, he simply turned off the people's "spontaneity." When that was done, the hapless Liu was simply shifted from "Right" to "Left" deviationism.

But how does this reading square with Mao's onslaught against the bureaucracy? To answer this question one must return to the complexities of ideology in the Marxian sense of the word: as a *sincerely held* false consciousness of reality. Mao most certainly does not say to himself, "I am a revolutionary from above, a bureaucratic collectivist who uses the vocabulary of Marx and Engels to legitimate the rule of a Communist elite over the great mass of workers and peasants." For it is a crucial aspect of any subtle theory of historic action—particularly one deriving from Marx—to see that Marx can truly believe in what he is doing and yet achieve purposes he does not intend.

Thus the development of a privileged bureaucracy is an objective inevitability given Mao's policy of extracting a surplus from workers and peasants and investing it in industrialization. The people do not surrender their surpluses voluntarily, and the Chinese peasants have acted like peasants everywhere in trying to maximize their private plot of land; and investments are not made, as in the case of bourgeois modernization, according to the "automatic" calculus of the market. Under such circumstances, to attempt to fulfill Mao's plans will not, and cannot, lead to social-

ism, but it will certainly produce totalitarianism (since all associations that might make a claim on scarce resources must be
interdicted) and a technocratic stratum (since the revolution takes
place "from above").

These are bitter truths which Mao resists. So in the name of
the utopian elements in his ideology, he organizes a new revolution from above (the Cultural Revolution hardly occurred spon-
taneously and wound up with the army in command) in order to
fight the evil trends he sees in the original revolution from above.
But eventually reality overwhelms even the most relentless of
wills, and in the "New Trend" trials and executions of 1970, Mao
was forced to repress the very disrespect for authority he himself
had promoted. That was when Liu underwent the remarkable
transformation from "capitalist roading" to anarchism.

So in the exercise of power, as in the struggle to win it, Mao
acted above the heads of the people. The peasantry was not a
substitute proletariat in the sense of being predisposed toward
collectivism: its yearnings were classically petty bourgeois. Neither was it a proletariat like the Polish, Hungarian and Czechoslovakian workers, a force capable of organized resistance to a
totalitarian regime. Rather, like the Russian peasantry in the
thirties, it responded by fighting for private plots and cutting back
on production when the pressure from above became intolerable.
So there were fits and starts in the policy of the Communists because, except when they occasionally had to give in to mass opposition, the intra-party debates took place in a political vacuum
undisturbed by workers or peasants.

"Mao's Thought," then, is indeed an original accomplishment,
but not in the terms in which he defined it. It was the adaptation
of anti-socialist "socialism" to a society even poorer and less
proletarian than Russia.[4]

## III

There is another class that has been nominated by some theorists
as a substitute proletariat in the socialist revolution: the urban
poor.

The poor, it must be remembered, are not at all equivalent to
the working class. The workers are usually subjected to the discipline of modern methods of production and have a natural

tendency, arising out of their conditions of labor, to organize themselves into collective associations. The poor are unemployed or underemployed, and when they find a job usually do so in the most backward sectors of industry. Their miseries are therefore both greater and more amorphous that those of the workers. And this is particularly true of the new class which is being formed in the cities of the Third World.

In the nineteenth century most European cities developed along with the capitalist system (Italy, where fairly big urban centers predated capitalism, was an exception). As a result, the peasants who were forced off the land found work—miserable, inhuman and incredibly exploitative work, but work nevertheless—waiting for them. In those vicious times, as Barbara Ward has pointed out, cholera acted as a murderous equilibrating force which kept a balance between available employment and the size of the working population. But in the period after World War II, in Africa, Asia and Latin America masses flooded into the cities where their labor was not needed. One reason for this has already been noted: the enclaves of modern industrial technology in developing countries are capital-intensive and simply do not require the huge working class that tended the machines in the nineteenth century in Europe and the United States.

So a new class emerged in the *bidonvilles* and *favellas* of the Third World. It was urban and impoverished, but not a part of the working class. And in the United States itself the vast migration of blacks from the rural South into the cities was somewhat similar. Marx, as Chapter III related, had identified a similar stratum long ago, calling it the lumpenproletariat. It had even more profound grievances against the established order than the workers, yet it lacked any principle of organization and genuine solidarity. It was, therefore, susceptible to manipulation by charismatic demagogues and inclined toward violence.

There was, as we have seen, one major theorist who was diametrically opposed to Marx on this count: Mikhail Bakunin.

"What predominates in Italy," Bakunin wrote in *Statehood and Anarchy*, is that "lumpenproletariat of which Marx and Engels, and with them the entire German socialist-democratic school, speak with such profound and unmatched contempt. It is only with this proletariat, and not with the bourgeoisified layer of the working masses, that there resides the spirit and force of the future social revolution." Historically, Marx's perspective was vindicated, for the peasants of Southern and Eastern Europe did not make the libertarian revolution of which Bakunin dreamed, but the workers did effect democratic changes in the bourgeois order.

The new lumpenproletariat of the Third World is not, of course, composed of the Bohemians and other social types Marx found in nineteenth-century Paris. Yet its position in society is strikingly similar to those earlier lumpenproletarians: urban, but not working class, and poor to the point of reckless desperation. And so a number of theorists—Frantz Fanon, Herbert Marcuse, Eldridge Cleaver—emerged who based their strategy on just this class. They are modern Bakuninists, even though they sometimes speak in Marxian terms. And they are as wrong as their unacknowledged master.

It may well be that this stratum will indeed play a historic role which Marx could not have imagined—but it will not be a socialist role. In Algeria the urban poor were a factor in the defeat of the French. And it could be in Brazil, and other Latin nations, that Glaucio Ary Dillon Soares is right to say that "the future main political conflicts will not derive from the opposition between the interests of the owners of the means of production and the proletariat; rather the main sources of political conflict would be the conflicting interests of the growing middle class and the growing unemployed and underemployed sectors of the working class."

Still, even though such a class can let loose an elemental force in the society, it cannot be the basis for a socialist structure. For, like the peasantry, it lacks the cohesion, the organization and tradition that are required if a class is to dominate a modern nation. Algeria is a case in point. After the revolution it did not become the Fanonist utopia "where the branch meeting and the committee meeting are liturgical acts." Instead, as one of Fanon's admirers, Peter Worsley, admits, there is "Boumedienne's Islamic, chauvinistic, authoritarian, military regime." There has been a tremendous proliferation of bureaucracy so that, as Samir Amin, the Egyptian economist and expert on the Third World, wrote of the entire *Maghreb* (Algeria, Tunisia and Morocco), "Compared with 1955, the number of executives and civil servants (who earn relatively high salaries) had multiplied six times by 1965, whereas the number of manual and white-collar workers and artisans had only risen by 30 percent."

Amin then made this extraordinary deduction from the facts: "From this it may be unhesitatingly concluded that the departure of the Europeans has so far been to the exclusive benefit of the former group [executives and civil servants]. The direct consequence of independence and the subsequent European exodus has been the establishment of new and relatively privileged classes; for the broad mass of the population, neither the level of employment nor real income per head had improved; indeed quite the reverse. Thus Muslim society today exhibits much greater class distinctions than in 1955 when the choicest positions were all occupied by Europeans."

I wish that Fanon's romantic predictions had come true. I sympathize with those opponents of French colonialism—particularly those in France itself who courageously risked much in the struggle—who were swept up in the enthusiasm of the moment and misunderstood the actual direction of the revolution. But the Left can no longer indulge in such fantasies when so many facts are in. And unfortunately many of the same doomed hopes are now being projected, for similar reasons, for Southeast Asia.

The peasants and the urban poor are not a substitute for the proletariat; the economy of a backward nation does not provide the material basis for socialism. The best and most enthusiastic will in the world cannot transcend these cruel limitations, as the Cubans learned when they tried to create a "new man" where the conditions for him did not exist. Socialist faith, as the next section will show, is not a substitute for the proletariat.[5]

# IV

In the classic texts Marx and Engels had always assumed that socialism was only possible where there was such abundance that invidious competition and self-seeking were not necessary. Where there is poverty, they wrote in The German Ideology, there is a struggle for necessities and consequently the "old crap" of class society. They attacked the "religion" of an associate who had said, "We don't have anything to do any more with taking care of our shabby selves, we belong to mankind." Marx and Engels thundered, "With this infamous, loathsome servility with regard to a 'Mankind' separated and differentiated from the 'self,' which is a metaphysical and even a religious fiction, with this extreme 'shabby' and slavish humiliation, this religion ends like all the others. Such a doctrine, which preaches the pleasures of fawning and self-sacrifice, is perfect for courageous *monks,* but not for energetic men in an epoch of struggle."

But the "socialisms" of the Third World, lacking the material preconditions for a just society, regularly appealed to just such a monastic self-denial. That, certainly, was the tone of the Maoist exhortation, and in Cuba it became, as will be seen in a moment, a source of economic disaster for the regime of Fidel Castro. One consequence was that even such sympathetic commentators on socialist theory as Wassily Leontiev and Robert Heilbroner concluded that socialism had not yet solved the problem of motivation. They did not realize that this question is impossible of resolution under the impoverished conditions in which it has been posed in countries like China or Russia of the twenties and thirties. (Socialism is, however, quite possible in the Russia of the seventies if the totalitarian state were to be democratized from below.)

In Cuba this problem can be seen quite clearly. The example is particularly compelling since it can be completely documented by the reports of sympathizers, and even members, of the regime, including Castro himself.

In all of the countries of bureaucratic collectivism there is a tendency to emphasize nonmaterial incentives. Stalin had his Stakhanovites whose furious pace of work made them official heroes of the society. China had its Cultural Revolution in which the mobilization of the enthusiasm of the masses was supposed to permit the nation not only to skip the capitalist stage and proceed directly to the building of socialism, but also to enter the promised land of Communism in fairly short order. In Cuba a number of factors made the emphasis on voluntarism particularly strong. The Fidelistas had themselves accomplished the impossible—overthrowing a dictator on the basis of a nucleus of youthful revolutionaries. They were culturally Latin, undogmatic and genuinely popular with the people.

The most passionate exponent of the theme of revolutionary will was Che Guevara. He asked, "How can we produce the transition to socialism in a country colonized by imperialism, without any development of its basic industries, in a situation of monopoly production and dependent on a single market?" And answered, "Within the great framework of the worldwide capitalist system, struggling against socialism, one of its weak links can be broken. In this particular case we mean Cuba. Taking advantage of unusual historical circumstances and *following the skillful leadership of their vanguard, the revolutionary forces take over at a particular moment.* Then, assuming that the necessary objective conditions already exist for the socialization of labor, they skip stages, *declare* the socialist nature of the revolution and begin to build socialism." (Emphasis added.) And in another context he wrote, "We maintain that in a relatively short time the development of conscience does more for the development of production than most incentives do."

But in Guevara's letter to his family, written before the fateful last period of his life, he rightly identified himself as a Don Quixote: "Once again I feel Rosinante's bony ribs beneath my legs. Again I begin my journey carrying my shield." Such idealism is enormously appealing (I spent an evening with Guevara once, and for all my political disagreements with him could not help but be attracted by his charismatic grace), but it can lead to debacles in a modern society.

The year 1970 was supposed to mark a triumph for the revolution. As Edward Boorstein, an economist and Fidelista, wrote in late 1966 or early 1967, "But by the end of this decade, the full benefits of socialism will begin to show themselves in Cuba. . . . Increased output of milk and meat, chickens and eggs, pork and other agricultural products will have produced a big improvement in diet. The output of shoes and clothing will be greatly increased. With a large expansion of the cement and construction industries, the building of houses will be under way on a grand scale." Yet on July 26, 1970, Fidel told 150,000 people in Havana that the economy was in a deep crisis. *The Economist* of London reported that the milk supply was down 25 percent, cement production down 23 percent and that some of the workers in the fields were without shoes. Why?

René Dumont, the French agricultural expert who served as Castro's personal advisor on a number of occasions, answers that the mobilization enthusiasm without careful planning leads either to waste or to the militarization of the entire society. Already in 1963, he reports, the harvest was down by 25 percent but the amount of work days invested in it had increased: "If unemployment thus disappeared, it was not to the profit of production." Moreover, during such harvests the volunteers, who are hardly productive at all, retain their urban salaries, which are higher than those of farm workers. In 1970 *The Economist* reported that there were shoeless cane cutters because too many workers from the shoe factories were in the fields!

One solution to these problems has been the militarization of work. For by a cruel irony, a society that sought to base itself on voluntarism has become more and more like an army. But, Dumont reports, the agricultural brigades are no more efficient than the volunteers. Their conception of work is based on a kind of guerrilla romanticism, but the "storming" of an economic problem can have a profoundly counterproductive effect, e.g., when soil and vegetation is burned along with trees when a field is being cleared with brutal dispatch.

Even more disturbing from the point of view of the professed values of Castro's Cuba is Dumont's comment, "If the military society that we observed at the Isle of Youth and in the Column of the Centenary of Camaguey prefigures Communism, as I was told, then this Communism is perilously close to an army." The result approaches "Stalinism with a human face." The regime, Dumont says, has no right to demand great sacrifices of the people if it does not allow them to participate in the decisions—and if, in the old Hispano-American tradition, it relies upon a *caudillo* capable of grievous economic errors.

Not long after Dumont's book was published there was a kind of official corroboration of his theory of the militarization of Cuban life. In March, 1971, Castro's government passed a law aimed at 400,000 "parasites" in the country. It provided penalties ranging from six months to two years of forced labor in "rehabilitation centers" for those convicted of vagrancy, malingering or habitual absenteeism from work or school. Once again, in the absence of the preconditions of genuine voluntary cooperation, the pretense of "socialist man" can only be maintained through drastic compulsion. It was in this period of the further Stalinization of Cuba that European intellectuals who had staunchly defended Castro for years attacked his treatment of the poet Huberto Padilla. After Fidel jailed him, Padilla, a maverick poet, recanted in a self-criticism reminiscent of Russia in the thirties.

Two other recent observers of the Cuban scene—both devoted to Fidel and his revolution—confirm Dumont's judgment. The late Leo Huberman and Paul Sweezy told of finding widespread discontent and economic shortages (housing, far from being plentiful, as Boorstein suggested, is not keeping pace with population growth). And, they note, "Power is concentrated in the Communist Party, within the Party in the Central Committee, and within the Central Committee in the Maximum Leader." So "Cuba's governing system is clearly one of bureaucratic rule." Since Huberman and Sweezy still believed in a rather simplified theory of historic stages, they could see only two alternatives for Castro's Cuba: either forward to socialism or backward to capitalism. They did not understand that the very society they described—one that is bureaucratic and collectivist—is capable of enduring for a considerable period of time, viz., in Russia, for more than half a century.

But perhaps the most candid critique from within the Fidelista camp came from K. S. Karol. Karol visited Cuba a number of times in the sixties and engaged in long and probing conversations with Fidel himself. In describing the argument over material and nonmaterial incentives, he writes, "Neither Che nor his opponents had come to grips with the problem of political power in, and the political organization of, all those societies where centralized or reformist experiments in planning and economic management were taking place. The 'classics,' which both sides so assiduously quoted, had never equated socialism with mere economic efficiency, i.e., with economic control by a small group deciding, in the name of the people, on the best way of organizing work and leisure. One can look in vain to Marx for this concept of permanently delegated political and economic authority."

In a conversation with Fidel, Karol raised some of these basic questions. "The people," Castro said, "wanted a revolution because they hoped for higher wages, more consumer goods, abundance for all immediately, and so on." But the economic level of the country would not permit such gains. Karol then asked one of the most fateful questions of the twentieth century: "How, with whom, and for whose sake must revolutionaries run a socialist self-management?" Karol paraphrased Fidel's answer: "The revolutionary leadership, he said, must fulfill two parallel tasks: it must create a material basis for socialism and it must foster the political consciousness of the masses."

At this point, Karol became diplomatic. A Pole who had been educated in the Soviet Union and fought in the Red Army during World War II, his mind turned to Russian analogies, but "there was nothing Fidel liked less than comparisons between the Russia of yesterday and the Cuba of today. He would certainly blow up at me if I told him that his thesis bore a suspicious resemblance to Soviet theory at the time of the great industrialization campaign. In the U.S.S.R., too, they had said: Let us first create the material foundations and build up a socialist mentality; the rest will follow by itself. . . . The Cuban leaders failed to appreciate that the U.S.S.R., too, had once had a revolutionary vanguard, composed of devoted and dynamic men who were not simply tools of the Stalinist terror. . . . If, despite all that, the U.S.S.R. has failed to become a proletarian democracy, it is doubtless because the economic effort of a vanguard commanded from on high cannot inspire a whole country, let alone lead it forward to socialism."

In Yugoslavia, on the other hand, there was an attempt to involve the people in decision-making, but once again, the context of poverty prevailed over the schemes for self-administration. The regime remained a one-party state (and even the Yugoslavian theorist Svetozar Stojanovic, who is particularly sensitive to the dangers of "statism," defended this policy), but it decreed that there would be plant and communal councils. Yet, given the economic and cultural level of the society, the workers were not prepared to take part in long-range planning and used their voice to speak on only the most immediate of issues. There was "participation without the power to decide." And when the regime opened up a private sector, there was a tremendous growth of competition, a drive for individual rather than cooperative enrichment. In each case, one cannot demand more nobility from the people than the conditions of their life permit. When there is scarcity, that fact is more important than the finest of constitutions or the most benevolent of authoritarianisms.

In the Yugoslavian case (and in the Third World generally) these problems are aggravated by the animus of the capitalist world market against both economic development and social justice. In his study of workers' control, "Daniel Chauvey" (the name is a pseudonym) defined this aspect of the situation quite brilliantly: ". . . in a nation as poor as Yugoslavia the idea of 'socialism in a single country' has even less sense than elsewhere. It is necessary, no matter what the cost, to export the nation's goods on the world market in return for those imports which are indispensable to the survival and political independence of the country. But Yugoslavia cannot plan to sell at a loss forever in order to pay for its imports and it does not possess enough gold mines to make up for the permanent deficit of its balance of payments.

"It was necessary," Chauvey continues, "to orient the economy in such a way as to give priority to the production of those products which could be competitively exported. The Yugoslavian leaders thus found themselves faced with a new problem. It was not enough to free the enterprise from all paralysing state controls, to give up the rigid plans worked out by governmental specialists. One does not direct an enterprise whose objective is to succeed on a capitalist market as if it were a question of responding to the priority needs of a society which have been democratically determined by the society itself. It was urgently necessary, then, to create a new social-professional category capable of conducting the Yugoslavian enterprises to victory on the capitalist market."

In other words, the problem of underdevelopment is not something which is defined once and for all. The world capitalist market is working night and day to impose its disciplines, its needs, its priorities upon the poor countries and to make it even more difficult for them to listen to their own people. Without the presence of a single soldier Western capitalism thus makes itself a senior, and often dominant, advisor to the Yugoslavian government.

The problem is that the issue of incentives—and of socialism itself—has thus been posed in countries lacking a material basis for their democratic—and socialist—resolution. In saying this, my purpose is not to denigrate the idea of nonmaterial incentives. On the contrary, it is to defend them. Romantic dictatorships may pretend that impoverished people are aching to volunteer for sacrifices and to forget their own individual needs, but that is not so. And if such governments persist in their own myths, they will have to introduce some form of nonmarket compulsion and "socialism" comes to resemble a barracks. Moreover, as Cuba's experience demonstrates—and the Great Leap of the Chinese Communists as well—these voluntary abnegations decreed from on high lead to the most wasteful extravagance.

A poor country, as René Dumont observed in one of his books on Africa, cannot afford a "socialistic rhetoric" (un verbalisme socialisant) which keeps it from identifying actual problems. And which, I would add, corrupts the future for those countries that are—or, like developing countries, will be—economically ripe for the generous motivations of an authentic socialism.[6]

# V

So neither peasants nor the urban poor nor sheer will power can substitute for the proletariat in the socialist revolution. But anti-Communists, or non-Communists, can take the place of the Communist Party in the bureaucratic revolution. Indeed, one of the most revealing commentaries on what has happened in Russia and China is that something quite similar to it has been carried out by army officers in countries like Egypt, the Sudan and Peru. As Communism came to resemble a barracks, there were colonels and generals who suddenly discovered that they were not Rightists but "socialists."

The Egyptians are a case in point. When Nasser and the young army officers in Egypt originally seized power in 1952, they were pro-capitalist, their land reform program favored the better-off peasants, and the National Union, the regime's political party, was directly dominated by the Misr Bank and the National Bank of Egypt. In 1959, when the Iraqi revolution seemed heading toward Communism, Nasser was outraged: "The Communists had their plan to dominate Syria; but, upon failure, found consolation in the revolution of Iraq. The Communists emigrated to Baghdad in order to turn Iraq into a Communist state from which Communism will spread to the rest of the Arab countries, thereby creating a Communist fertile crescent."

Then in 1960 the very same Nasser nationalized the banks, and heavy and medium industry were statified in 1961. So in 1962 the National Union was turned from a creature of the banks into the Arab Socialist Union. And in the wake of the Six Day War, Nasser told his countrymen that the Russians were their best friend, supplying arms in the struggle against imperialism but never trying "to dictate conditions to us or to ask anything of us." The Government had moved from Right to Left in theory, without changing its personnel.

Such developments created problems for the Russian theorists. What, precisely, was the character of the regimes in Egypt, Syria, Ghana (under Nkrumah), Indonesia (under Sukarno), Algeria and other Third World nations which proclaimed themselves "socialist" but which were not Communist—and sometimes jailed Communists? By 1964 some of the more daring Communist ideologues were inventing a new historic category: "If the conditions for proletarian leadership have not yet matured, the historic mission of breaking with capitalism can be carried out by elements close to the working class. Nature does not suffer a vacuum." These elements were the young officers, the students and the lower ranks of the bureaucracy.

All of this was, needless to say, infuriating to the Arab Communists, particularly those languishing in jail under governments officially labeled as "progressive" by Moscow. Some of them, like the Syrian Khalid Bakdash, were blunt in their criticism of the Russians. Arab socialism, he said, is "a mere conglomeration of scientific and utopian socialism, petty bourgeois ideas, narrow nationalism, religious prejudices and subjective idealism." But it was the Sudanese Communists who suffered these ironies most cruelly. They had helped the officers around General Gafar El Nemiery into power. Then, however, the military decided that it was "socialist" and, to the consternation of the Communists, nationalized industry and thus robbed the party of its most distinctive slogan. Not long after, Nemiery jailed the leading Communists and began to negotiate, with Russian backing, for a federation with the Egyptians and Libyans. While the Russians encouraged this policy, their followers in the Sudan attacked it on the grounds that it was simply bringing bureaucratic state regimes together. Thus the Soviets saw Arab socialism as part of the wave of the future and the Arab Communists saw it as reactionary. So it was that the Russians signed a treaty with Sadat in 1971 right after the Egyptian president had purged the pro-Communists from his cabinet, and in the Sudan in the summer of 1971, Nemiery, the beneficiary of so much Russian aid, proceeded to hunt and kill his one-time Communist allies.

Communists could not possibly solve the theoretical problem of "Arab socialism" (or of Third World "socialism" in general) because the answer would be much too embarrassing. As long as socialism is defined as a movement of self-emancipation of the people that uses democracy to make the economic system as classless as possible, it has little or nothing in common with the military mentality. But once "socialism" connotes a system of totalitarian discipline, class privileges and the extraction of economic surpluses in order to expand the power of the state, there is no reason why a patriotic officer should not embrace it. For now socialism is the idealization of the barracks.

There are, to be sure, differences between the nationalist versions of "socialism" and Communism. The nationalists, as Richard Lowenthal has pointed out, do not necessarily nationalize all industry, but rather concentrate on foreign capital; and lacking an ideology of any substance, they are more prone to corruption. *Le Monde* commented in a survey of African development, "The constant reference of some chiefs of state to socialism does not do a very good job of concealing the absence of ideology in their regimes. . . . Under the pretext of collectivization the imposing bureaucratic machine was built [in Mali] and, as in many of the neighboring states, an administrative bourgeoisie actually governed to the profit of its caste interests." René Dumont, in a similar analysis of Nasserism, talks of the "state bourgeoisie" in Egypt. And Ghana under Nkrumah is a classic example of "socialism" becoming the private property of an elite leadership.

Finally, the most recent, and fascinating, cases of military "socialism" are to be found in Latin America. In both Peru and Bolivia officers have followed this course. In the latter country there was even an extraordinary symbolism: the general who led the successful hunt for Che Guevara is the one who tried to carry out this "Leftist" program and who freed Guevara's associate, Régis Debray, from jail. Indeed, Victor Alba reports that young Latin officers study Che—and Mao and Giap—but avoid Marx. They are concerned with the guerrilla and Third World aspects of "socialism," i.e., those elements in it that can be adapted to the armed forces, but not with the basic vision of a classless society.

In Chile, one is much closer to the classic Marxian model. The mass base of President Allende's power in that country is the working class that was organized in the Communist and Socialist parties—but, significantly, that provided him with only a minority victory over his two rivals in the election of 1970. Allende, in contrast to the Spartan collectivism of China and Cuba, has tried to stimulate economic expansion by expanding the consumption of the people. Yet he is perilously dependent upon the world economy, there has been a strike of capital within his country, and the totalitarians and insurrectionists within his own ruling coalition could pressure him to move in an anti-democratic direction. It is much too early to attempt even a preliminary assessment of this phenomenon, but it does seem to be somewhat atypical in Latin America because of Chile's level of economic development and democratic consciousness.

So there are non-Communist versions of that bureaucratic collectivism pioneered by the Russian Communists. And the fact that military officers have played such an important role in these regimes should not come as a surprise. For as "socialism" was militarized by the Communists, it became a convenient ideology for any modernizing authoritarian and it even began to speak to some of the prejudices of the traditional military. Generals and colonels could substitute themselves for the bourgeoisie and the proletariat just as well as Communists.[7]

## VI

Finally, this critique of totalitarian and authoritarian "socialism" in the Third World should not be taken to imply that there is a simple democratic alternative to it. India, which has tried to modernize in freedom, shows that a democratic socialist elite faces many of the problems that bedevil the Communists. Its efforts have produced all the contradictions of that socialist capitalism discovered by the European social democrats, but within a context of excruciating poverty.

Fortunately, the extraordinary scholarship of Gunnar Myrdal—the three volumes of *Asian Drama: An Inquiry into the Poverty of Nations* and the policy-oriented summary *The Challenge of World Poverty*—provides an overview of this complex experience by one of the most distinguished social democratic intellectuals of the century. In basing this brief glance at the Indian model on his work, I will purposely quote him somewhat out of context. In this section I will concentrate primarily on the problems of democratic collectivization in the Third World, citing Myrdal's negative analysis. In Chapter XII I will turn to the solutions.

The crucial problem in India is more complicated than Myrdal once thought and is depressingly similar to the one described by Marx more than a hundred years ago. Originally, Myrdal believed that the economic effects of democracy were the great difficulty in such a country. In his *Economic Theory of Underdeveloped Regions* (published in 1957), he had quoted Aneurin Bevan, the leader of the British Labour Left, approvingly: "It is highly doubtful whether the achievements of the Industrial Revolution would have been permitted if the franchise had been universal." So in the Third World, he argued, free institutions might menace the accumulation of an investment surplus by diverting funds to immediate consumption. But in his later work Myrdal came to believe that, in India at least, there is no "revolution of rising expectations" which might try to use democracy in order to press the claims of the masses.

In this later mood he wrote, "Because of the narrow social base of the elite and the absence of any pressure from the masses, the leaders were under no compulsion to govern vigorously and disinterestedly." Nehru and Gandhi had assumed, somewhat like Bevan, that if there were universal suffrage, the people would not permit a minority to monopolize the nation's wealth. That was not the case, for the majority of the Indian people remained apathetic, hostile to planning and development and satisfied with their static society. That vast immobilism of Indian life, which Marx thought British imperialism would destroy, resisted even the achievement of national independence.

So it was that the attempt to create "socialism" took place within a context still dominated by many of the traditions of the Indian past. Land was either divided into small plots or else held by absentee landlords and labor was still considered to be a demeaning pursuit. "Socialism," Myrdal reports, "is merely a vague term for the modernization ideology with an inherent stress on equality as a primary planning objective." Indeed, when the Congress Party in 1955 declared itself in favor of a "socialist pattern of society," newspapers owned and operated by big business criticized it for its lack of definiteness.

But then, business in India has little reason to be dissatisfied with the "socialist" measures that have been taken so far. Myrdal writes, ". . . the investment and pricing policies pursued by public enterprises are usually such that, by holding down prices, they swell the profits of the private sector. Thus, when put into practice, the vaguely socialist notion that public enterprise must render services at low prices in fact boosts considerably the returns on private capital. Instead of being used to supplement government revenue and help to mop up purchasing power, the public sector functions to inflate private profit." In other words, the contradictions of socialist capitalism are at work in India as well as Europe, only in the former case they afflict a people menaced by starvation.

This problem, however, is not confined to the industrial sector, for the existence of widespread inequality has meant that all the public expenditures for community democracy and local services have tended to strengthen the position of the upper strata in the villages. They are the ones who are best able to take advantage of a government program and therefore they benefit disproportionately from funds that are theoretically spent for the public good. Thus all the schemes for proceeding slowly into the modern world by emphasizing the values of the traditional institutions fail because these institutions are both anti-modern and anti-egalitarian.

This trend, Myrdal suggests in *The Challenge of World Poverty*, can be seem most dramatically in the "green revolution" which is taking place through the introduction of new strains of grain developed through research financed by Western foundations. To many in the United States this development was to be India's salvation from hunger; Myrdal believes it may even increase starvation. Given the passivity of the masses and the patterns of absentee ownership and sharecropping, the overwhelming majority of the people will not be able to use the new seeds. However, the entrepreneurial minority in the countryside will be able to take advantage of them. If they are then able to use the available state aid for labor-saving investments, the whole process will increase the size of farms and destroy the employment of many who eke out an existence as agricultural laborers today. As a result, a vast increase in India's capacity to produce food might well, because of the social and economic setting in which it takes place, lead to the immiserization of millions of people, to hunger and even to starvation.

Here, then, is the other side of the coin from the totalitarian and authoritarian "socialisms" of the Third World. In the countries where there is a coercive forced march toward the future, the people are brutalized, enormous sacrifices are forced and the lack of any real popular participation makes spectacular waste and/or corruption possible. But in a country like India, where the government supports democratic freedoms, the masses are dormant and the state does not take the tough measures that are necessary—and which would disturb the elite class from which the planners themselves come.

It is possible that the breakup of the old Congress Party—which was quite literally socialist capitalist in character, uniting industrialists and Marxists—will offer some new hope. Certainly the huge mandate given Indira Gandhi in 1971 might be a sign of an awakening among the people. But even if that is the case, the attempt to create a democratic socialist society under conditions of poverty will hardly be easy. For if the millions have indeed stirred, then it is possible, as Bevan and the earlier Myrdal thought, that they will use their freedom to maximize immediate consumption and retard those investments which, in the long run, offer them the only way out of their misery.

I wish it were not necessary to write in such a gloomy mode. I would infinitely prefer it if everything in this chapter were false. It is hardly a joyous labor for a socialist to carefully detail the tenacity of injustice and the difficulty of overcoming it. And when the writer is a citizen of the relatively affluent West describing how Third World peoples must endure yet more misery, even under the best of circumstances, the task is even more onerous. I wish that Mao's fantasies, and Fanon's and Che's and Mahatma Gandhi's, were true. But they are not, and it would be patronizing —and chauvinist—to pretend otherwise.

There is no force on earth that can simultaneously substitute itself for the bourgeoisie and the proletariat, increasing the surplus taken from the people and emancipating them at the same time. A new ruling class incarnated in the party-state can indeed take the place of the bourgeoisie, but it does so by turning against the proletariat, the peasantry and everyone else. There are, to be sure, alternatives that lie in between capitalist and bureaucratic collectivist accumulation and offer more of a hope than either capitalism or Communism. They will be discussed in Chapter XII. But for now, the truth is sad. Peasants, the urban poor, military officers and even democratic socialist elites cannot force their way into the promised land by following Stalin or Gandhi or anyone else. The facts are inhumane, but recognizing them is the prerequisite for an effective humanism. For only then can one act to repeal these ancient, but man-made, injustices.[8]

# XI

## The Invisible Mass Movement

THERE IS A SOCIAL DEMOCRACY in the United States, but most scholars have not noticed it. It is our invisible mass movement.

America, as Chapter VI documented, was indeed an exceptional capitalist society. Its utopian tradition was deeper than that of any European country, which made the practical work of transforming the existing order all the more difficult. Its workers were split along national lines, and that inhibited the development of a unified class consciousness. Its standard of living in the first three decades of this century was not as princely as some historians suggest, yet in comparison with the Eastern European conditions the later immigrants had left, it was high. These are among the reasons why a great socialist movement did not spring to life in the New World.

But America was not as exceptional as is often thought. The triumph of capitalism in this country provoked more bitter class violence than in Europe and forced workers into unions and unions into politics. To the degree that the nation was more affluent and egalitarian than the Old World, these factors often acted as an incitement to rebellion, since labor did not know its "place." At the same time, the unevenness of prosperity and the primitiveness of industrial legislation, which lagged far behind Europe, provided more straightforward reasons for militancy.

By the early 1920s the elements in American working-class life that were similar to those in Europe had driven the trade unionists far away from the laissez-faire "voluntarism" of Samuel Gompers. In 1924 labor backed the independent candidacy of La Follette and even made a formal alliance with the Socialist Party in the process. But the failure of that campaign, and the general paralysis of the American Federation of Labor during the rest of the decade, seemed to put an end to this social democratic impulse. In the conventional interpretation, when the workers turned massively to Franklin Roosevelt in 1932, that sealed the fate of American social- ism and proved the utterly exceptional character of this country's history.

In fact, the turn to Roosevelt during the Depression marked the beginning of the appearance of a mass social democratic movement in the United States.

I say "social democratic" rather than "socialist" for a number of reasons. The most obvious is that American unions are formally pro-capitalist and ambiguously anti-socialist (the ambiguity will be detailed later in this chapter). There is, however, a historical warrant for calling such a movement social democratic when it is not socialist. For Marx and Engels, the social democrats, as contrasted to the socialists, were first of all the radical democrats in the French and German revolutions of 1848. The term disap- peared from the vocabulary of the Left in 1850 and then reap- peared in the 1860s to describe the followers of Lassalle. For this reason Marx and Engels did not like to use it. It often applied, Engels reminisced in 1893, to people who "in no way inscribed on their banner that society should completely take over the means of production."

But then, "social democrat" came to be synonymous with "socialist," and Engels accepted the fact: "The names of living political parties are never completely satisfactory; parties develop; names remain the same." I do not now propose to go back to his 1893 distinction between "socialist" and "social democrat" as an act of piety, but rather because it helps to define a complex reality. There is in the United States today a class political movement of workers which seeks to democratize many of the specific economic powers of capital but does not denounce capitalism itself. It champions, to use the language of the First International, the political economy of the working class—but not socialism. And its impact upon the society is roughly analogous to that of the social democratic parties of Europe. That is why I call it the American social democracy.

In understanding this strange development it is first necessary to see why the Socialist Party of Eugene Victor Debs did not become the institutional expression of the social democratic impulse in American life. Then the beginnings of the social democracy in the twenties and thirties will be described. And finally, the formalization of this trend will be analyzed, as well as the reasons why almost all American intellectuals failed to notice the momentous event. A new political party appeared, but with an old and nonpolitical name, and they did not look beneath the label. The result was, and is, an invisible mass movement.

# I

In the traditional reading of American history the Socialist Party, which was dramatically successful between its foundation in 1901 and its electoral high point in 1912, vanished somewhere around 1920 without really leaving a trace. If one looks simply at the institution, there is some plausibility to that view, for the party never became a serious electoral force after the Debsian era. But if one examines the historic forces involved in the rise of Debsian socialism, it becomes obvious that they did not suddenly disappear but rather took on new forms.

In 1912 the party had 118,000 members spread out over every section of the United States. The *Appeal to Reason,* a socialist weekly published in Girard, Kansas, had a circulation of 761,747, and there were 323 English and foreign-language socialist newspapers whose total circulation was probably more than two million. In 1912 Debs received 6 percent of the Presidential vote and there were 1,200 socialist office-holders in 340 cities, 79 mayors in 24 states among them. Historians then argue that in a certain year—1912, when the Left wing was expelled, and 1919, when the Communist split occurred, are two of the favored dates—this formidable movement went into a quick and irreversible decline. There was, to be sure, the imposing figure of Norman Thomas, who dominated the party from the late twenties until his death in 1968, but the organization itself never even approximated the strength and influence it had won in the days of Debs.

Some, like Daniel Bell, say that the socialists were "too much a Marxist party," that it was "*in* the world in that it proposed specific reforms of society; but it was not *of* society, in that it re-

fused to accept responsibility for the actions of government itself." Others, like Ira Kipnis, hold the exact contrary: "The
Socialist Party had been organized to combat the institutions,
practices and values of monopoly capitalism. Instead it had been
corrupted by them. Like other movements sworn to change the
American economy, it had proved too willing to settle for a few
favors and promises from the dreaded enemy."

On the whole, Bell has the better of the argument: it was the
sectarianism of American socialism, not its expediency, that
vitiated so much of its organizational effort. But this fact is not
to be explained as a simple subjective failure of the socialists themselves or even as a uniquely American phenomenon, as Bell suggests. The problem of proposing reforms but not accepting
governmental responsibility plagued the socialist movement all
over the world prior to World War I, as Chapter IX showed. And
the individual psychologies of the American socialists were, in
considerable measure, a historic product.

The isolation of the German-American socialists and their obsession with doctrine had helped establish a sectarian tradition;
so had the native American utopianism, with its periodic call for
total withdrawal from the evil society. The heterogeneity of the
working class had prevented the American Federation of Labor
from reaching out beyond the aristocracy of labor, and that, in
turn, had caused an overreaction on the American Left. Gompers
and his associates were assigned exclusive blame for a situation
which was, in some measure, a result of objective conditions. It
was then assumed that an act of radical will could overcome the
difficulties America posed to its trade-union and socialist movements. As a result, many of the most militant socialists divorced
themselves from the AFL and thus forfeited the chance to win
it to their point of view.

Debs, who was an early sympathizer of the Industrial Workers
of the World (the IWW, or "Wobblies") but later became dis-
enchanted with them, expressed a common attitude: working in
the AFL was as "wasteful of time as to spray a cesspool with attar
of roses." The Wobblies did have brief successes in organizing
the Western metal miners, migrant farmers and lumberjacks, and
they led in some historic Eastern strikes, like Lawrence. Yet their
tactics were only capable of reaching out to workers on the move.
They refused to negotiate a contract, to check off dues, to maintain a strike fund—or even to have a sick and death benefits program, which, they believed, would dim the ardor of the class

struggle. Above all, they could never decide whether they were a union or a revolutionary party, and therefore did not succeed in being either.

Up until 1912 the Wobblies had support in the "impossibilist" wing of the party and their leader, "Big Bill" Haywood, was elected to the National Executive. But then, when the party came out against sabotage and effectively drove out the ultra-Leftists, that did not put an end to the sectarianism of the movement. When America entered World War I the Oklahoma socialists—who had achieved the highest-percentage socialist vote of any state in the nation—armed themselves in the Green Corn Rebellion in order to overthrow the militarist government.

And yet, even with all of these eccentricities, the Debsian socialists did reach out to masses of people. There were the Jewish workers in the needle trades in New York; a near labor party under socialist auspices in Pennsylvania where James Hudson Maurer, a leading party member, was the president of the State Federation of Labor; a significant socialist tendency in Chicago's union movement which played a major role in the campaign for a labor party in the early twenties; in Milwaukee under Victor Berger the party and the AFL were united; in Oklahoma, Kansas, Arkansas, Texas and Missouri the socialists spoke for agrarian radicalism; in the Rocky Mountains and on the Coast there were miners, loggers and middle-class reformers around the party.

All these different groupings—skilled workers, industrial workers, middle-class reformists, agrarian radicals—felt that liberalism was not enough, that it was necessary to restructure society as a whole. Did that growing socialist sentiment cease to exist in 1912 when the party moved against its Left wing, or in 1917 when it opposed the war, or in 1919 when the Communists split? In his study *The Decline of Socialism in America* James Weinstein provides the beginning of the answer: up until 1924 socialist convictions continued to affect the United States, but largely outside the Socialist Party. That, I will argue, is a trend that has continued to this very day.

One reason why so many scholars have overlooked our invisible mass movement is that they have identified the fate of social democracy in America with the organizational structure of the Socialist Party. In the process they have, unwittingly for the most part, adopted the prejudices of the socialist Left wing and failed to see how the movement in this country followed the English, not the German, pattern.

The Debsians, like most socialists around the world in that period, had looked to the German Social Democracy as their inspiration. They rejected the idea of a labor party, which they regarded as inexcusably reformist, and argued that the American workers would steadily increase in class consciousness and make the party a contender for political power under its own banner. It, and not the conservative, craft-dominated AFL, would be the central organization of the working class. In those days when A. M. Simons wrote to William English Walling and suggested the "English policy" of working toward a new party which would be based on the unions, Walling was outraged. If the Socialist Party merged with the AFL, he said, they would together *only* be able to elect twenty or thirty Congressmen. Therefore the party must refuse such a policy and grow among "'brainworkers,' farmers and unorganized labor." Then, having become a power in its own right, it might discuss merger or common work with the AFL. In retrospect, Walling's attitude seems incredibly sectarian, yet it must be remembered that the socialists had built their membership from 10,000 to 118,000 in eleven years and that the AFL only reached a minority of the labor force. Walling was quite wrong, but he was not preposterous.

After World War I, when there were so many labor party stirrings around the nation, most socialists, of both the Right and Left wings, were opposed to that perspective. And even when the Socialist Party affiliated with the Conference on Progressive Political Action in 1922 and supported La Follette in 1924, the ranks were uneasy and wanted recognition as a specifically socialist faction of the new movement. Their intransigence did not prevail in American life, but it did win over the American historians. They, like the Debsians, assume that the criterion of socialist success in this country is established by the German model, in which the party grows with its own name and program. They therefore have not recognized the belated fulfillment of the "English policy" in the emergence of a de facto social democratic party based upon the unions and operating within the Democratic Party.

So the exceptional conditions of American life and the sectarianism to which they gave rise overwhelmed the Socialist Party but not the social democracy.[1]

## II

It was in the 1920s that a historic change took place in America: the majority became urban. Paradoxically, the first effect of this change was to be conservative, yet ultimately the shift was an important factor in the rise of the American social democracy during the Great Depression.

After the First World War immigration was drastically reduced. At the same time, the American farmer, who had been moving to the city for decades, left the land in greater and greater numbers. During the ten years from 1920 to 1929, 19,436,000 made the trek, and in every year except 1920 and 1921 more than two million people came from the countryside to the metropolis. As Irving Bernstein assesses the effect of this great internal migration, "This large labor supply, inured to the low level of farm income, relieved an upward pressure on wage rates that might have occurred. Workers drawn from a rural background were accustomed to intermittency and so did not insist on regularity of employment. Although they adapted readily to machinery, they were without skills in the industrial sense. The fact that the price of skilled labor was high and of unskilled low induced management to substitute machines for craftsmen. The displaced farmers . . . brought with them . . . the conservative outlook and individualistic accent of the rural mind."

This was one of the main reasons why the labor movement, in contrast to the normal pattern, declined during the relative prosperity of the twenties. The high levels of employment had brought men and women into the working class who, given their agricultural background, were suspicious of union organization. It was only when the economic and political upheavals of the thirties took place that they were galvanized into motion along with their foreign-born fellow workers. But there was a very important intimation of the changes that were to come: the Al Smith campaign of 1928.

When the twenties began, the Democratic Party was predominantly Anglo-Saxon, Protestant and rural. But during that decade the city masses, the immigrants and the ex-farmers became restive, and the party acquired a new constituency. In 1928 that faction triumphed by nominating Smith for President. Their man lost badly but the emergence of a new political alignment had been signaled: in many of the big cities of the nation the Democratic vote had doubled. So under seeming conditions of "normalcy" in the twenties, momentous transformations had been taking place but, more often than not, had been ignored. The working class had become Americanized and proletarianized; the cities were turning into a political force.

Then came the Depression. Despite all the boasting of American business during the twenties about how well the worker was being paid, wages lagged behind productivity. In classic Marxian fashion, the capitalist genius for production was on a collision course with the capitalist limits on consumption. In 1929 the crash took place.

The immediate impact of the catastrophe in the labor movement was not radical. When various unions responded to it by demanding in 1930 that the AFL abandon its voluntarist opposition to state-supported unemployment insurance, Matthew Woll, one of Gompers' spiritual heirs, fought bitterly against the move. It took an internal struggle which lasted for two years before the Federation finally endorsed the proposal in November, 1932. Even then, there were still some powerful leaders, like William L. Hutcheson of the Teamsters, who were opposed to a minimum wage. It is quite likely that Senator Hugo Black refrained from putting a minimum-wage clause in his thirty-hour-week bill out of fear of union opposition.

For a brief moment it seemed that the disastrous collapse of American capitalism would revive the Socialist Party. In the campaign of 1932 Norman Thomas received almost a million votes and in November of that year 1,600 locals had been chartered. In 1934 the party had almost 21,000 members on its rolls, the highest total since the Communist split in 1919, but less than a fifth of the top Debsian enrollment. And yet, even though the free enterprise system was coming apart at the seams and a quarter of the labor force was walking the streets, the thirties saw the effective collapse of the Socialist Party as an electoral alternative.

The Socialists, to be sure, contributed to their own downfall. The Detroit Convention of 1934 saw a heated debate over whether the party would require an absolute majority before taking power or whether, when power was in the streets, it would seize it though only a powerful, massive minority. It was this quarrel over a hypothetical situation—which was an exercise in fantasy—that led to a split in 1936. In that year the pro-Roosevelt socialists

quit, the membership dropped to 6,500 and never rose above
that level in the rest of the decade. But it was not just the sectarianism of the socialists that thwarted them at the moment of capitalist
collapse, it was also the reformism of Franklin Roosevelt.

For history was following a devious version of the "English
policy." And just as the English working class woke from a thirty
years' sleep (the phrase is Engels') in the 1890s when the New
Unionism brought unskilled workers into the ranks, so the emergence of the Congress of Industrial Organizations (CIO) was a
decisive turning point in the United States. In a way, John L.
Lewis, the leader of the industrial union drive, is a perfect symbol
of the change that had taken place. For even though Lewis had
run against Gompers for the presidency of the Federation in
1921, he was anything but a radical. In the twenties he had
fought the Leftists in his Mine Workers union with all the resources at his command, including violence and the accusation
that his opponents were Communists. And he held to the voluntarist philosophy so deeply that he backed Herbert Hoover in
1932.

Lewis' mind was changed by events. Starting with the simple
and fundamental trade-union desire to organize more workers,
he had fought to get a pro-labor provision included in the National Industrial Relations Act, the law that established the NRA.
In Section 7(a), Congress did give formal approval to union
rights, but in most cases employers ignored that part of the
legislation. Lewis, however, aggressively used 7(a) as a potent
organizing weapon. As a leaflet of the Kentucky Federation of
Labor put it, "the United States Government has said LABOR
MUST ORGANIZE. . . . Forget about injunctions, yellow dog
contracts, black lists and the fear of dismissal. The employers
cannot and will not go to the Government for privileges if it can
be shown that they have denied the right of organization to their
employees. ALL WORKERS ARE FULLY PROTECTED IF
THEY DESIRE TO JOIN A UNION."

In fact, the workers did not have such guarantees. But Lewis,
by persuading them that they did and identifying the moral
authority of the President of the United States with his campaign,
turned the empty Congressional promise into a reality. In the
process there were bitter strikes and company guards gunned
down union men, but the membership quadrupled in one year.
This success was stunning, so much so that it was to split the
labor movement.

As Arthur Schlesinger, Jr., summarizes the moment in his brilliant history of the Roosevelt years, "Most old-line AF of L leaders . . . could hardly get over the fact that the depression had driven them to the point of accepting such statist ideas as unemployment insurance and the NRA: the conception of the government as a partner in an organizing drive was too much. Moreover, where Lewis, as the head of an industrial union, thought instinctively in terms of a single drive for each great industry, most of the Federation, committed to the craft idea, thought of organization, not by industry, but by skill."

The internal struggle lasted until October, 1935, when Lewis —now, significantly, in the company of his former rebel opponent in the Mine Workers, John Brophy—launched the CIO. In a matter of four years the dreams of the Wobblies and socialists were fulfilled and that vast mass of unskilled and semi-skilled workers finally entered the American labor movement.

The political impact of this working-class insurgency was profound. In 1932 Franklin Roosevelt had not even bothered to make a major labor speech and there was no sign that the workers had made a distinctive contribution to his victory. In the spring of 1934 when Senator Robert Wagner introduced his bill to provide a Federal structure for collective bargaining, the White House had been suspicious of the proposal. It was only when the NRA was declared unconstitutional that FDR began a belated campaign for the Wagner Act. Thus even if Roosevelt's first term had been indecisive, it ended with his moving toward the organized workers.

So it was that in April, 1936, Lewis, Sidney Hillman and George L. Berry announced the formation of Labor's Non-Partisan League. It was at this point that David Dubinsky of the Garment Workers and Emil Reive of the Hosiery Workers resigned from the Socialist Party to join in the campaign for Roosevelt, an act rich in symbolism. For the moment that the unions politicalized themselves, the idea of the independent electoral growth of the Socialist Party on the model of the German Social Democracy lost whatever residual relevance it had. Labor, it was then clear, would move Left only in terms of the "English policy." And that is precisely what began to happen in 1936 when, with business contributions to Roosevelt falling off, the unions contributed three quarters of a million dollars toward his reelection and became an independent political force in American life.

Among historians, Richard Hofstadter has been one of the few who understood this momentous event: "The demands of a large and powerful labor movement, coupled with the institutions of the unemployed, gave the New Deal *a social democratic tinge that had never before been present in American reform movements.*" (Emphasis added.) In 1936 it was only a "tinge"; in a generation it was to be much more than that.

But there is one group of contemporary theorists who regard Hofstadter's view—and mine—as quite wrong. Significantly, they speak as the Leftist critics of American historiography. William Appleman Williams, the dean of this school, holds that the New Deal "represented an operating consensus among the most astute members of the national corporation class and the reformers (or corporation socialists)." And James Weinstein argues that the Roosevelt Administration was the ideological heir of the National Civic Federation, that united front of Samuel Gompers and sophisticated businessmen.

The motivation of these attacks on the New Deal in the thirties relates, I believe, to the politics of the late sixties and early seventies. The white, middle-class and young Left in America in these years became bitterly anti-liberal. Some Leftist historians then projected this attitude back into history and thus became sensitive only to what was conservative and timid in liberalism. There is no question that the shrewder corporate interests— represented, say, by a financier like Bernard Baruch or, for that matter, by that most brilliant of anti-socialists, John Maynard Keynes—conceded reforms in order to stave off more radical transformations. But from the point of view of American workers, a decisive turn had been made and *the basic relationship of political forces had been altered.* Moreover, the very conditions of life at the point of production had been changed.[2]

Significantly, the one American organization appealing to radical sentiment that treated the New Deal coalition as incipiently social democratic, the Communist Party, was the only successful group on the Left in this period. While the Socialist Party, which counterposed itself as an alternative to Roosevelt, was losing members, the Communists, during their "Popular Front" period in the thirties, were making impressive gains. It is certainly true that in this the American Communists were the beneficiaries of a historic accident: the exigencies of Russian foreign policy which determined all Communist policy in this country required them, from 1935 to 1939 and again during World War II, to turn toward Roosevelt. Ironically, their political subservience to a foreign power helped them relate to their own country with much greater skill and subtlety than the socialists.

The original Communist movement of 1919 had been based on two distinct elements: a great many foreign-born radicals from Russia and Eastern Europe, who had been recruited because of the Russian Revolution; and a smaller grouping of native-born Leftists from the Socialist Party. The young party was immediately beset by intense factional struggles and by a great deal of ultra-revolutionism.

In 1923 the Comintern in Moscow forced the American Communists to take a more sane, less apocalyptic attitude. Yet even though the substance of the policy dictated from afar was quite rational, a fateful precedent had been set: that decisions about the United States were to be made in Russia. As Theodore Draper has written, "something crucially important did happen to this movement in its infancy. It was transformed from a new expression of American radicalism to the American appendage of Russian revolutionary power. Nothing else so important ever happened to it again."

At the Seventh Congress of the Communist International in 1935 Moscow ordered a change in line. Since the late twenties Communists around the world had been ultra-militant, attacking the social democrats as "social fascists." In Germany this policy contributed to the rise of Hitler; in the United States it led Communists to launch a physical attack against a socialist meeting in solidarity with the anti-fascist Austrian workers. In 1935, however, the Russians decided that alliances with the Western capitalist democracies were necessary to protect them against Hitler. A Franco-Russian pact was thus signed that year, and Communists were told to make a rapprochement with the very liberals and socialists who had so recently been described as disguised fascists.

It was this change in the International Communist line that oriented the American Communists toward the New Deal. Once they received their orders, they carried them out with imagination and devotion. The Communists, their leader Earl Browder said, did not share "any of the illusions about the efficacy of Roosevelt's policies to fundamentally solve the political and economic problems of the country." But, in the very next breath, "the Communist Party recognizes unqualifiedly that in this battle the forces of reaction, fascism and war are concentrated more and more in the camp opposing Roosevelt's plan, while the forces of popular democracy, and first of all the labor movement, are rallied in its support. In such a line-up there is but one possible place for the Communists, on the side of democracy."

It was tragic that this line was imposed by Moscow and carried out by people who, for the most part, sincerely believed that they were struggling for socialism rather than, as was the case, acting as the pawns of Russian foreign policy. Later, when some of those involved were to realize how they had been deceived, they were to become bitter, and for many Americans the Communists were proof that all radicalism was alien to this country and conspiratorial. But in the thirties the Communist line decreed in Moscow for reasons of Russian self-interest worked better in the United States than the socialist policy, which had been democratically determined.

One socialist, Arthur McDowell, put the situation accurately in 1938. He wrote, "The extreme opportunistic swing of the CP to support Roosevelt in 1936 enabled the Communists to operate in the CIO with greater freedom than the Socialists who stubbornly adhered to their principles of independent labor political action in face of the labor stampede to Roosevelt." McDowell was certainly right about the opportunism of the Communists, though it was related to Russian, not American, considerations. But he, and many of his fellow socialists, did not ask themselves why labor was "stampeding" to FDR. They insisted on the traditional model of the Socialist Party as an electoral alternative and thus missed participating in the most important political development in the history of the American working class.

Norman Thomas realized what was happening to the party. In 1938, having witnessed the steady decline that followed upon the upsurge in 1932, Thomas argued that the party should stop running candidates and take part in the larger political movements of the day. His policy was not accepted, and with the war issue becoming more and more central to American life, it became difficult, and finally impossible, for a principled anti-warrior to seek a rapprochement with Roosevelt. Had the party followed Thomas' lead in 1938, it might have been able to maintain some kind of serious base in the unions. But it did not, and socialists like Walter Reuther, when confronted with the choice between the party's political tactic and that of the labor movement itself, unhesitatingly chose the latter. The tragedy was that the two were counterposed.

On the other hand, by 1939 "the Communist Party had become an important, if not yet a major force in American political life . . . [it] had taken some major steps toward becoming a 'mass organization.' . . . It was now a powerful force in the CIO, the youth movement, the intellectual world and in a few large cities." So the one Leftist success after Debs occurred when the Communists were obliged by Moscow to recognize the social democratic aspects of the New Deal.

The thirties, however, were only a first step toward the American social democracy. Labor had entered into politics with a distinctive program and had organized on a class basis. But it had not yet given this new reality an institutional form. That was to take place during World War II, and then in the fifties and sixties.[3]

## III

The New Deal itself had been incomplete and ambiguous. When, in Roosevelt's phrase, Doctor Win-the-War took over from Doctor New Deal, the crucial problem of the Depression, unemployment, was not solved. There were still millions out of work in 1939 and full employment came only with the vast growth of the war industries. Indeed, Keynes himself wondered if any peacetime government was prepared to intervene as massively as his theories required. In this context, Arthur M. Schlesinger, Jr.'s analysis of FDR is much too positive. "Rejecting the platonic distinction between 'capitalism' and 'socialism,'" Schlesinger writes of Roosevelt, "he led the way toward a new society which took elements from each and rendered both obsolescent." In fact, it was precisely this pragmatism, and particularly the refusal to apply Keynesian principles in any systematic fashion, that led the President to reduce his social programs in late 1936 and early 1937 and to thereby trigger a new recession. Roosevelt was clearly to be preferred to his Republican opponents, many of whom were still mumbling laissez-faire incantations in the midst of a capitalist collapse. But his brilliant, charismatic leadership hardly achieved the synthesis that Schlesinger describes. Moreover, as Chapter XII demonstrates in some detail, the American economy remained quite capitalist—and problematic—long after Roosevelt reformed it.

It was only after World War II that the liberal-labor forces developed a more comprehensive approach to the society (there had been a pro-planning wing of the New Deal in the early days, led by men like Tugwell and Berle, but they had lost out by 1935). Roosevelt had given impetus to this development in the campaign of 1944 when he advocated a legally guaranteed right to work (an idea which probably began with the French socialist Louis Blanc in the 1840s). But a conservative Congress had taken that excellent idea and reduced it to the generalities and pious wishes of the Employment Act of 1946, a statute so broad that Eisenhower was to use it to rationalize deflationary policies that led to chronic unemployment and recession.

It was not until the Administration of John F. Kennedy that the government employed Keynesian state intervention in a carefully planned way. Significantly, there was a debate over how this was to be done. Kennedy, with a hostile Congress and a razor-thin Presidential mandate, opted for a tax cut. Within his official family, John Kenneth Galbraith was one of the few who spoke up for social spending as a better stimulus. Outside the White House, the labor movement and economists friendly to it, like Leon Keyserling, championed this social Keynesianism. The goal of the Roosevelt Administration had been to use Federal power as a means of restoring the health of the private economy. Now the unions, and some of their intellectual and civil-rights allies, were profoundly modifying this formula by insisting that state intervention also reorder the basic economic priorities of the society and favor the social rather than the free-enterprise sector.

It was as a result of these experiences that the AFL-CIO in 1963 initiated a programatic redefinition that had much more in common with the defeated socialist proposals of 1894 than with the voluntarism of Gompers. The 1963 Convention voted that "experience has shown that we cannot rely upon the blind forces of the marketplace for full employment, full production and effective use of our resources to meet our urgent national needs. Other advanced, free and democratic nations have found that they can achieve their economic and social objectives only through a rational national economic planning process involving the democratic participation of all segments of their populations together with government. We urge the creation in the United

States of a National Planning Agency, which through similar democratic mechanisms will evaluate our resources and our needs and establish priorities in the application of resources to the meeting of needs."

At the 1965 Convention the Federation again called for a national planning agency and endorsed a 50 percent increase in Social Security, a massive program to rebuild the cities, a national health-care program, a peacetime "GI Bill" and a resources conservation policy. In 1967 George Meany told the delegates, "Increasingly the problems of our members—which they share with everyone else—are not so much the problems of the work place itself, but problems of environment and problems of living and raising a family in today's complex, crowded urbanized and suburbanized society." In a sense, this was turning Gompers upside-down: instead of concentrating exclusively on collective bargaining and being suspicious of all government action, the AFL-CIO was now making overall economic planning central to its concerns.

The United Automobile Workers under the leadership of Walter Reuther participated, of course, in these AFL-CIO decisions. Reuther, as a former socialist, was the most consciously ideological of all the top trade-union leaders. In 1970, after the UAW had broken with the Federation and formed the Alliance for Labor Action with the Teamsters and other unions, it passed one of the most radical resolutions ever adopted by a labor convention. "Actions taken by corporate managements," it said, "self-perpetuating or chosen by and responsible to a few large stockholders, can have more impact on the lives of Americans than decisions by democratically elected government officials responsible to the people as a whole. Such awesome power cannot be permitted to be exercised without effective means to assure that it will be used responsibly. The 'corporate conscience,' it should by now be evident, does not provide the needed safeguards."

The union went on to champion reforms that included a new law setting official, and enforceable, standards of corporate responsibility and a requirement that all corporations with annual sales of $250 million or more create independent review bodies "which would be given free access to all corporate files, which would have the responsibility of recommending to the corporation's board of directors changes in practices injurious to the public interest and the duty to report to the public when such recommendations were rejected." These proposals, and the analysis that preceded them, were at least as Left as the practical policies of the European social democrats.

Given his personal background, people expected such politics from Reuther. So in a sense, the fact that George Meany and the AFL-CIO itself moved in this direction was even more significant, for it signaled the liquidation of Gompers' voluntarism by his own heirs. And Meany as well as Reuther was responsible for the political commitment that made national health insurance a serious issue in the 1970s.

The unions were doing much more than just passing resolutions. During these years they were building a political apparatus which is a party in everything but name.

In 1943 the CIO had taken the first step to permanently institutionalize its political efforts with the establishment of the Political Action Committee. That was in keeping with the activist and political origins of industrial unionism. But it was perhaps even more significant, given the venerable tradition that was being shattered, that the AFL founded Labor's League for Political Education in 1947. It had been prompted by the conservative Congress elected in 1946 and the Taft-Hartley Law, which it wrote. Initially, then, the Federation was simply trying to protect itself, but once this institution was created, it took on a life of its own. Then, with the merger of the AFL and the CIO in 1955 and the establishment of the Committee on Political Education, labor's political involvement became even broader and more systematic.

Throughout the Kennedy and Johnson administrations in the sixties the union political organizations and lobbies were the strongest single force for progressive social legislation in Washington. In terms of actual political pressure on issues like poverty, racism and Social Security, the labor contingent did infinitely more than the middle-class intellectuals and churchmen who so often dismissed the unions with contempt (the reasons for this will be examined shortly). Then, in the elections of 1968, special circumstances revealed the extent to which the unionists had become a political party in their own right.

The Democratic Party was split that year, with the middle-class reformers and minorities mainly backing the primary campaigns of Robert Kennedy and Eugene McCarthy, and the AFL-CIO joining the regular Democrats in defending President Johnson and then Vice President Humphrey. Humphrey was nominated in

Chicago by a coalition that included the pro-Johnson Southern-
ers, like Governor Connally of Texas, the machine pols, like Mayor
Daley of Chicago, and the unions. But almost as soon as he became the candidate, the Daley and Connally forces deserted him.

As a result, the unions were the decisive element in the Humphrey campaign in a way that had not been true in the Kennedy
and Johnson races of 1960 and 1964. Theodore White, who had
all but ignored labor in his accounts of those earlier elections,
wrote in awed terms of what that labor support meant. The AFL-
CIO registered 4.6 million voters, printed 55 million leaflets and
pamphlets in Washington and another 60 million in the localities.
It supplied 72,225 canvassers, and on election day, 94,457 volunteers. And these figures, it must be remembered, do not take into
account the very substantial contributions of unions like the Auto
Workers that were outside of the Federation. Humphrey, nominated under the very worst of conditions, just missed becoming
President.

One might try to explain this phenomenon in traditional—non-
class—American terms by saying that the unions were simply
acting as an interest group. However, interest groups do not
identify with a single party but try to put pressure on both the
Republicans and Democrats (they often have a prominent vice
president belonging to each of the major parties). They emphasize
their specific demands, not their long-term support. But labor had
clearly made an on-going, class-based political commitment and
constituted a tendency—a labor party of sorts—within the Democratic Party.

The way in which this development transcended the interest-
group approach can be seen clearly in some of the back-room
politicking over the reapportionment of the state legislatures.
Everett McKinley Dirksen, the Republican leader in the Senate,
was very anxious to repeal the Supreme Court's one-man/one-vote
ruling as applied to the state houses. So he offered to go along with
the unions in promoting their most self-interested goal, the repeal
of the Federal authorization for state "right to work" laws, if
labor would moderate its support for reapportionment. If the
unions had been acting as an interest group, they would have
snapped up Dirksen's offer, since it would have guaranteed passage of a law that was explicitly in their favor. But they chose to
maximize a much more long-term perspective and to stick to their
support for reapportionment.

Labor's orientation toward playing a role in the center of

American politics, where one-man/one-vote was so important, had prevailed over narrow organizational concerns. The unions, in short, had created a social democratic party, with its own apparatus and program, within the Democratic Party. But how, then, can it be explained that this mass movement has remained invisible for so many intellectuals?

Part of the answer is semantic. The unions changed their philosophy and their actions, but kept most of the old labels. Yet, as soon as one probes a bit, it becomes evident that the laborites were using, in Leon Samson's perceptive insight, socialist definitions of capitalism. When George Meany reaffirmed his faith in the traditional values, he asserted that "the distinguishing feature of the American system is its emphasis on people, on free institutions and the opportunity for betterment." A good many observers heard only the ritual salute to the old order and did not even realize that it was being used to justify significant democratic structural changes in the status quo.

An exchange in 1959 between Meany and Congressman Alger of Texas should help to underscore this point. Alger had just congratulated Meany on his anti-Communism and then said, "The only thing that troubles me deeply is this—when I analyze the legislative program of the AFL . . . I cannot determine in my thinking the difference between your program and what is honest-to-goodness socialism." In part of his reply Meany commented, "I still do not know what socialism is, despite the things that I have read. But if socialism means that under a democratic system, this republican form of government that we have, there are people who desire to secure for the great mass of the people, the workers, the wage earners, the farmers, and others, a better share of whatever wealth the economy produces, and that by providing that better share we provide a broad base of purchasing power to keep the economy moving forward—if that is socialism, then I guess I am a Socialist and have been a Socialist all my life. I do not figure that, but if that is what socialism means, that is the sort of thing I am interested in."

Meany's definition of socialism, it will be noted, more or less coincides with that of the revisionist social democrats described in Chapter IX. That, as I explained there, is too limited a program for the creation of a new society. But what is relevant here is that the president of the AFL-CIO has the same general outlook as the European social democracy. He speaks in American accents and his nation's history does not require him, or even allow him, to present himself as an anti-capitalist. The political content of his remarks, however, is quite analogous to that of mainstream European socialists. Too many scholars in the United States have heard only the rhetoric of the present labor movement—which is formally, even ritualistically, pro-capitalist—and have not bothered to examine either its programs or its political organization.

Secondly, the emergence of the American social democracy was not dramatic, and that guaranteed that many intellectuals, with a theatrical taste for history and politics, would overlook it. The institutionalization of the political impulse of the thirties even seemed to some a retreat. A party, with a staff and day-to-day tasks, is a much less exhilarating affair than a march of the unemployed and the hungry. But a party is also more effective in actually changing the balance of power within a society.

Thirdly, the formalization of the social democratic trend in American labor took place in the 1960s. And it was during that decade that the unions supported the war in Vietnam, while the middle-class liberals and radicals were, for the most part, passionately opposed to it. The estrangement over the war was deep and emotional on both sides, and one of its by-products was that academics and journalists were much less able to see the profound change in labor's social programs and political organization. In a similar vein, people rightly sympathetic with the demands of blacks for decent jobs confused a fairly small minority of old-line locals in the building trades with the entire labor movement and did not even know that the industrial unions, which are the dominant form of labor organization in America, had done more to raise minority living standards than any other institution in the country.

So, in the words of one of the few writers who noticed the historic fact, "in their support of the Democrats as a mass, pro-welfare state party, American trade unions have forged a political coalition with important—although hardly complete—structural and behavioural similarities to the Socialist Party–trade union alliances of Western Europe." In a unique, devious way, with all the wrong symbols and phrases to bewilder people, American capitalism drove working people into unions, then into political struggle, and finally to the organization of an independent, class-based political movement with a ranging program for the democratization of the economy and the society.

That is the American social democracy, our invisible mass movement.[4]

# XII

## Beyond the Welfare State

AFTER ALL THE FALSE STARTS, failed plans and outright betrayals, is there any meaning left to socialism?

The basic socialist indictment of capitalism is more true today than it was in the nineteenth century. The corporations have progressively "socialized" the economy, basing production on science and the most intricate web of human cooperation. Yet, for all the changes in capitalist attitudes, decision-making and appropriation have remained private even when they are exercised by corporate managers rather than owners. And so, as Marx and the early socialists predicted, the contradiction between unprecedented social productivity and the private institutions that direct it has become more and more intolerable, and made us progressively fearful of our own ingenuity. We purchase progress at the expense of the poor, the minorities, the old; we are even more threatened by our affluence than by our poverty.

The socialist solution remains utterly relevant: the social means of production must be socialized and made subject to democratic control. The crisis of socialism, then, does not concern what to do about the epoch, but rather what to do about tomorrow morning. The problems of transition, of applying the analysis of the century to a specific moment in time, have proved to be infinitely more complex than socialists ever imagined. Marx was vague on this count, and for good reasons: his age suffered from a surfeit of overly explicit useless panaceas. But now that the movement he inspired has become a major factor in world politics, now that late-twentieth-century man is too little visionary rather than too much, the details of the dream have become crucial.

The welfare state, Communist totalitarianism and the world market must all be basically transformed. These chapters will concentrate on the fundamental changes necessary within advanced capitalism—using America's admittedly ramshackle welfare state as the prime example—and in the Third World. Under Communism, as the previous analysis should have made abundantly clear, democratization of economic power is also most urgent, since the irrational, private priorities of the bureaucratic class are imposed on the society by means of a totalitarian plan. But I do not make that case central to my discussion because of limitations of space and knowledge—and, above all, because there is a socialist freedom movement in existence in the Communist countries, which even now is elaborating its new definitions of socialism despite the secret police. One day it will tell us, in practice as well as in theory, what socialism means in those lands.

I will begin with an eye on the middle distance and proceed toward the far future. We must be specific about the year 2000 and what socialism could mean at that point; but the concrete reforms must be animated by nothing less than a vision of the potential of the twenty-first century.

# I

There are three basic reasons why the reform of the welfare state will not solve our most urgent problems: the class structure of capitalist society vitiates, or subverts, almost every such effort toward social justice; private corporate power cannot tolerate the comprehensive and democratic planning we desperately need; and even if these first two obstacles to providing every citizen with a decent house, income and job were overcome, the system still has an inherent tendency to make affluence self-destructive.

In thus documenting the limits of the welfare state it might seem that I am contemptuous of past reforms and present liberals who do not share my conviction that there must be fundamental, structural change. Nothing could be further from the truth. The welfare state was an enormous advance over the cruelty and indifference to human suffering that characterized early capitalism. It was achieved through great sacrifice—sometimes of life itself —on the part of "ordinary" people, who, even though they had usually been denied an adequate education, tutored the wealthy in some of the fundamentals of social decency. And to the extent that there is a mass "Left wing" in the United States, it is composed of precisely those groups—trade unionists, minorities, middle-class idealists—who fought these great battles and are determined to resist any reactionary attempt to undo their accomplishments.

This point is not simply a matter of keeping the historical record straight; it has profound political implications for the future. It is important that socialists demonstrate the inherent inability of the welfare state, based on a capitalist economy and social structure, to deal with problems that demand anti-capitalist allocations of resources. But this does not mean, as some young Leftists in recent times have thought, that the welfare state is then to be dismissed as a fraud that prevents the people from coming to truly radical conclusions. For if millions of Americans do become socialists, they will do so because in the course of struggling to make that welfare state respond to their immediate needs, they will have discovered that they must go far beyond it. If those people who are now socialist arrogantly dismiss these battles as irrelevant, they will play no role when masses of their fellow citizens do turn Left.

Socialists, then, must be in the forefront of every fight to defend, and extend, the welfare state even as they criticize its inability to solve fundamental problems and propose alternatives to it. In this context, the following analysis of the severe limits capitalism imposes on the welfare state is not designed to prove that liberals of the mass Left are foolish and deluded, but rather that their liberal values can only really be completely achieved on the basis of a socialist program.

First of all, the welfare state, for all the value of its institutions, tends to provide benefits in inverse relationship to human needs. And not—the point is crucial—because of a conspiracy by the affluent, but as a "natural" consequence of a society divided into unequal social classes.

It is possible to offset this inherent tendency within capitalist society to distribute public benefits according to the inequalities of private wealth, but only if there are vigorous radical reforms.

What is more, any movement that attempts to carry out such reforms will be going against the grain of the system itself. This has not kept socialists from participating in every one of these struggles, nor will it in the future. But if the gains are to be permanent, if they are not to be reversed when a period of innovation is followed by a swing back to capitalist normality, then there must be basic, structural changes. Instead of episodic victories within an anti-social environment, there must be a concerted effort to create a new environment.

One way to put this is to say, with André Gorz, a leading theorist of European Left socialism, that there must be structural reforms. These are incremental in character, yet they have a revolutionary import since they involve actual shifts in the make-up and institutions of power itself. Thus, I will propose to vastly increase the proportion of resources allocated by democratic decision-making and to redistribute income so as to change the relationship between, and reality of, social classes. It is extremely important to transcend the sterile old debate of reform versus revolution in this way. Yet I think Gorz errs in a number of important points with regard to his own excellent idea. He cannot quite rid himself of that old Jacobin—or more exactly, Babouvist—notion that there will be a "day" of revolution when all the reforms culminate and history turns a corner. Given the complexity of modern society, this is not going to take place.

More to the point politically, Gorz dismisses almost all social democrats (and the French and Italian Communists as well) as agents of neo-capitalism. If it is indeed true that the objective results of their innovation have led, over the vigorous protests of most capitalists, to a more stable capitalism as well as to higher living standards, it is wrong to see this as intentional. It is just one more unanticipated consequence of the difficulty of making a transition between social orders. And the social democrats, leaders as well as followers, are precisely the ones who are going to first challenge the profound limitations which even the most sophisticated capitalism places on reform.

The class divisions of welfare capitalism, which are the root cause of this problem within neo-capitalism, are not, it must be stressed at the outset, simply unfair in some abstract sense. Were that the case, a sophisticated conservative argument might be persuasive: since to some extent the growth of the economy benefits everyone, even those who are worst off, there is no point in endangering these gains on behalf of some ultimate egalitarianism. What really concerns the poor, this theory continues, is not the rise or fall of their *relative* share of affluence but the steady increase in their absolute standard of living. Actually, inequality does not merely mean that there are sharply unequal proportions of goods distributed among the various social sectors of the population. It signifies a socio-economic process, at once dynamic and destructive, which determines that public and private resources shall be spent in an increasingly anti-social way and thereby threatens the well-being of the entire society.

Housing is an excellent case in point. The Government, even under liberal administrations, has been much more solicitous about the comfort of the rich than the shelter of the poor. This policy is not only morally outrageous, it has had disastrous social consequences as well. Yet it must be emphasized that in thereby investing billions in the creation of public problems, Washington did not act maliciously but only followed—unconsciously, automatically, "naturally"—the priorities that are structured into America's class divisions. Thus:

in 1962 the value of a single tax deduction to the 20 percent of Americans with the highest incomes was worth twice as much as all the monies spent on public housing for the one fifth who were poorest; and this figure does not even take into account Government support of below-market rates of interest to build suburbia;

in 1969, the *Wall Street Journal* reported, the $2.5 billion for urban freeways was a far greater subsidy to car owners who daily fled the central city than was the $175 million provided for mass transit to city dwellers; and Richard Nixon's 1970 budget continued this perverse allocation of resources by providing public transportation with only 6 percent of the funds assigned to highways;

and, as the National Commission on Civil Disorders (the "Riot Commission" of 1968) computed the figures, during roughly the same thirty-year period, the Government helped to construct over ten million housing units for home builders, i.e., for the middle class and the rich, but provided only 650,000 units of low-cost housing for the poor.

But it would be a mistake to think that Washington discriminates only against the poor. For, as a White House Conference told President Johnson in 1966, *the entire lower half of the American population is excluded from the market for new housing,* a market that could not exist without massive Federal support. This point needs special emphasis, if only because many people, with the best of intentions, concluded from the rediscovery of poverty in America in the sixties that the bulk of the nation was affluent while only a minority were poor. But the statistics, far from describing a simple division between the rich and the poverty-stricken, show that we have in this country a *majority*, composed of the poor, the near-poor, more than half the workers and the lower middle class, which does not even have a "moderate standard of living" as defined by the Government itself.

So when Washington used its powers to improve conditions for a wealthy elite, the poor suffered most because they had the most urgent claim on the funds thus squandered on the upper class, but a majority of the people, including tens of millions who were not poor, were also deprived of benefits that should have rightfully been theirs. Worse, in carrying out these discriminatory policies, the Federal programs did positive harm to those most in need. As an American Presidential Commission recently reported, ". . . over the last decades, Government action, through urban renewal, highway programs, demolitions on public housing sites, code enforcement, and other programs, has destroyed more housing for the poor than government at all levels has built for them." But then, this is a familiar injustice: "Fifty years ago," wrote Alvin Schorr in 1968, "a British Royal Commission for inquiry into the Housing of the Working Classes observed, with dismay, that poor people rarely benefited when land was cleared and model houses erected."

In the America of the seventies these fantastically skewed priorities have momentous social consequences. For Washington has, in effect, been aggravating the very social problems to which it would then point with alarm. By financing the flight of the middle class from the metropolis and helping industry locate in the suburbs, the central city was allowed to rot—with Federal encouragement. As a result, such related evils as violence, bitter old age, intensified racism and the decay of the traditional centers of culture all grew worse. A study commissioned by the Government itself and chaired by Milton Eisenhower gave the darkest view of these trends. The National Commission on the Causes and Prevention of Violence said that "lacking effective public action," the centers of the great American cities would be safe only in the daytime when crowds gave the individual security and that they would be dangerous and empty at night. The big downtown apartment buildings would become "fortified cells for upper-middle and high-income populations living at prime locations in the city." The ghettos would become "places of terror with widespread crime, perhaps entirely out of police control during nighttime hours." And the suburbs would be ringed by freeways patroled by lightly armored cars.[1]

So the Government's discriminatory social policies have done much more than exacerbate inequality; they have helped to promote a fantastic anti-design for living. How, then, can we explain why sincere and dedicated men—as those who presided over these disastrous programs usually were*—would lavish public funds to thus aggravate social problems? The answer is to be found in the class character of American society and the commercial logic which both derives from it and pervades governmental decisions.

The 1969 report of the Council of Economic Advisors provides candid documentation of this pattern. "Investing in new housing for low income families—particularly in big cities—," the Council said, "is usually a losing proposition. Indeed the *most profitable investment* is often one that demolishes homes of low-income families to make room for business and higher income families." (Emphasis added.) Now, it is obvious that the criterion of profitability to which the Council refers is private, since, as the gloomy projections of the Violence Commission demonstrate, the social cost of the present system is bankrupting the society. Yet this private calculus is precisely the one the Government follows. As the Urban Problems Commission put it, ". . . renewal was and is too often looked upon as a federally financed gimmick to provide relatively cheap land for a miscellany of profitable or prestigious enterprises."

---

* From the Housing Act of 1949 until the present, liberal democrats in the White House and the Congress tried to channel resources into the housing of the poor. But under Truman, Kennedy and Johnson, they were unable to overcome the conservative coalition of Southern Democrats and Republicans on Capitol Hill. Under Eisenhower, the Republicans in both the executive and legislative branches refused to carry out the stated aims of the 1949 law even though it had been co-authored by one of their own conservative leaders, Senator Robert A. Taft. In November of 1964 there was a liberal Congressional majority and a President with a far-ranging reform program. But before any major innovations could be funded, the war in Vietnam was escalated in the spring of 1965 and caused a general retreat from all social investments. As a result, the bold rhetoric of the Model Cities Program eventually became a facade for a pathetically ineffective and conventional effort.

For in a society based on class inequality and suffused with commercial values, it just doesn't "make sense" to waste resources on social uses or beauty or anything that cannot be quantified in dollars and cents. Our legislators, drawn almost exclusively from the middle and upper classes, cannot bring themselves to forget those principles, which are sacred to the private economy. To them it seems logical to invest the Federal dōllar in those undertakings that run the lowest risk and will show the highest and most immediate return.

Housing is only one example of how the welfare state observes the priorities of maldistributed wealth even when it attempts to serve the common good. Other cases in point can be found in literally every department of government. The American welfare system in the sixties reached only a third of the poor and provided them, on a national average, with one half of what they needed. Meanwhile, in 1969 the richest one sixth among the farmers (individuals and corporations) received two thirds of the agricultural subsidies, or about $2.5 billion. Given the relation of social classes in the fields, America's commitment to promote "agriculture" is also a commitment to help the rich at the expense of the poor. And if one considers the various deductions in the tax codes as an indirect form of government expense—by not collecting money from an individual, Washington increases his income as surely as if it sent him a check—they total up to $50 billion, with the bulk of that sum going to oil men, home builders, stock-market speculators and others at the top of the economic pyramid.

The railroads are another example of how Washington follows private criteria even in making public decisions. By 1970 inept management and unplanned Federal subsidies to competitors, like $80 billion for the highways, had brought the industry to the verge of bankruptcy. Business and government then proposed a classic neo-capitalist solution: the losses would be socialized (passengers), the profits would remain private (freight). But when the Government did intervene through Amtrak, it determined the routes it would subsidize on the basis of a profit-and-loss calculus and deprived a good number of citizens of service on the grounds that they were not worth the trouble. What was required was a national transportation policy in which the planners would dispose of profits as well as of losses and could treat the problem in a systematic fashion, taking environmental costs into account in the process. That, however, would have placed the common good above various corporate interests; it demanded encroachment on private rights and the primacy of usefulness rather than of profitability.

But it is in education that the effect of systematic inequality is most damaging. America is becoming a "knowledge economy" in which higher and higher educational credentials are required (sometimes unnecessarily) in order to get a good job. This is one of the most important areas of socialized effort in the society since, through either public schools or aid to private education, the state supplies the modern economy, in Galbraith's phrase, with "its decisive factor of production, which is trained manpower." But even though public spending for education in the sixties increased at a faster rate than the Gross National Product, those Americans in the most desperate straits were not reached.

In the sixties a rather optimistic study of social mobility in the United States found that there is an "oversupply" of youth at the bottom of the economic structure; the 1969 Manpower Report of the President said that the unprecedented recent boom had clearly revealed that "economic expansion alone was insufficient to employ many people who had been bypassed in the general advance because of inexperience, lack of skills and cultural deprivation." Now, it is bad enough that such a group should exist, but what is truly intolerable is the extent to which social class structure denies it effective access to tax-supported education and works to make deprivation both self-perpetuating and hereditary.

For if, as Christopher Jencks and David Riesman document in *The Academic Revolution,* society is divided into blue- and white-collar groups, high school seniors from a white-collar background are four times as likely to have academic scores in the top rather than the bottom 10 percent, while blue-collar students are twice as likely to be at the bottom rather than at the top. One way of coping with such depressing statistics is to argue that they reflect the "middle-class bias" of the tests used to evaluate students. There have been demands to do away with IQ tests and standard grading, to assign each racial and ethnic group a quota of admissions in state-supported colleges (the top 10 percent of Negroes, Puerto Ricans, Mexican-Americans and other minorities would have places reserved for them, so there would be competition within these communities but not among them or with the nonethnics).

To those who charge that the tests are unfair to the poor, Riesman and Jencks cogently reply, "Life is unfair to the poor.

Tests are merely the results. Urban middle-class life in general and professional work in particular seem to nourish potential academic skills and interests in parents, while lower-class life does the opposite." The conclusions they come to are actually much more radical than those offered by people who simply denounce educational racism—or even propose separate but inferior college faculties for the children of the poor and the minorities. Riesman and Jencks write, "So long as the distribution of power and privilege remains radically unequal, so long as some children are raised by adults at the bottom while others are raised by adults at the top, the children will more often than not turn out unequal. . . . We suspect that these differences account for more of the class variation in college chances than all other differences combined."

Jencks and Riesman then go ahead to raise a basic psychological point. Suppose that by an act of political will the schools could be transformed so as to favor the minorities while the fundamental social inequalities were left intact. That, they hold, "could be a formula for misery. A mobile, fluid society in which men move up and down is simultaneously a competitive, insecure and invidious society. . . . What America needs," they conclude, "is not more mobility but more equality. So long as American life is premised on dramatic inequalities of wealth and power, *no* system for allocating social roles will be very satisfactory."

So in education, housing, agriculture, welfare and every other area of social life it is necessary to attack the systematic concentration of economic power in order to achieve serious reform. The fulfillment of liberal values, in short, requires structural changes in our class relationships, changes that transcend the capitalist limits of today's welfare state. And, to turn now to the second major reason why American society on its current basis cannot deal with its crises, there must also be national economic and social planning on a scale that our present institutional arrangements will not tolerate.[2]

There is no question but that the seventies will see planning in the United States. The really crucial questions are: What kind of planning? Planning for whom? The problems of welfare capitalist society are becoming so obvious and overwhelming that conservatives and even reactionaries have understood the need for state intervention—if only to maintain as much of the old order as possible.

In 1969 Spiro Agnew wrote an enthusiastic introduction to the report of the National Committee on Urban Growth Policy which concluded that the nation should spend public funds to build ten new cities for one million people each and ten new towns for 100,000 citizens each. But if it was surprising to find a conservative Republican Vice President endorsing such an idea, it was even more remarkable that Richard Nixon proceeded to attack it from "the Left." In his Population Message of July, 1969, Mr. Nixon noted that the number of Americans was going to increase to 300 million by the year 2000 and that this growth would be predominantly urban. "Are our cities prepared for such an influx? The chaotic history of urban growth suggests they are not and that many problems will be severely aggravated by a dramatic increase in numbers."

Nixon then turned to the "radical" proposal for new towns and cities which Agnew had approved. He criticized its inadequacy because "the total number of people who would be accommodated if even this bold plan were implemented is *only* twenty million—a *mere* one fifth of the expected thirty-year increase. If we were to accommodate the full 100 million persons in new communities we would have to build a new city of 250,000 persons each month from now to the end of the century." (Emphasis added.) Then, in rephrasing what would once have been regarded as the classic Marxian critique of capitalism, the Republican President defined the fundamental problem: "Perhaps the most dangerous element in the present situation is that so few people are examining the questions from the viewpoint of the whole society."

Mr. Nixon is the representative of precisely those special interests, concentrated in the Republican Party, that were able to enlist a good part of the welfare state in behalf of their private purposes. And although he uses a patch or two of Marxist-sounding rhetoric, he could hardly afford to acknowledge the basis of Marx's insight: that an economy dominated by self-seeking units is, precisely because of that fact, incapable of seeking the common good of the "whole society." So when Mr. Nixon talks in this way, there is no real question of innovations that would threaten the power and privilege of his most important supporters. But he, and other conservatives, are sophisticated enough to understand that the "chaotic" growth of modern society is no longer tolerable and that, in order to hold back the future, a modicum of planning and discipline must be imposed on the corporations.

This realization has penetrated to all of the advanced societies in the West so that Andrew Schonfield can point out that planning is "the most characteristic expression of the new capitalism."

Marx and Engels, as also some of their more perceptive followers, had understood that capitalism might try to regulate the "anarchy of production" but they felt that this attempt would only be a brief moment of transition before the advent of socialism. But what we must now confront is an entire historical period in which it is of the capitalist essence to plan. In the absence of a vigorous mass movement capable of democratizing this trend toward collectivism—in the absence, in other words, of a socialist alternative—planning will be conservative, manipulative and in the service of social and economic privilege. That is why it is so important to define the limits of neo-capitalist planning and to contrast it sharply with the socialist proposals in the same area.

The first distinction between capitalist and socialist planning has to do with money. Meeting the social problems just described will require an investment of billions of public dollars. In 1967 Senator Abraham Ribicoff noted that the various existing programs don't even reach people with incomes of $8,000 a year. In December, 1969, three years of inflation later, *Fortune* reported that "the shortage of acceptable shelter that has been afflicting the poor and the black is reaching to the white middle class and even to quite affluent families." And in mid-1970, George Romney, the Secretary of Housing and Urban Development, estimated that 80 percent of U.S. families could not afford the average cost of a new house. To deal with a crisis of this magnitude will clearly require a shift of massive resources from the private to the public sector, since the market is not even reaching a majority of the people. But while Mr. Nixon criticizes the new towns and cities proposal as being inadequate, it is obvious that he and his conservative colleagues are not about to propose such a basic revision in the uses of the national wealth. They are, after all, principled pinch-pennies with regard to Federal spending, i.e., they sincerely believe that the common good is maximized by keeping the allocation of resources as private as possible. Given this basic, and capitalist, limit to their thinking, any planning measures they urge are going to be inadequately funded.

It is significant, for example, that in all the Nixon Administration's talk about new cities and towns one of the key conclusions of the Urban Growth Policy report is ignored: "the development of new communities by solely private means will occur in those rare circumstances where the dynamics of growth in particular areas will afford a timely and reasonable return on private invest- ment." The infrastructure for a metropolis of one million is, of course, extremely costly, and even though such undertakings have paid for themselves in Europe, the time period before there is any return is quite long. And yet in February of 1970 when Maurice Stans, Nixon's Secretary of Commerce, made the most authoritative and detailed Administration statement on the new- city proposal, he only advocated some tax and other government subsidies to the private sector. But if, Stans and Nixon himself have insisted, it will need a new city of 250,000 every month be- tween 1970 and 2000 just to house the increase in population, their timid program is already doomed to failure. In February of 1970, David Rockefeller, president of the Chase Manhattan Bank, defined the kind of measures which would be necessary just to cover the "start-up" costs of a modest federal effort: $10 billion in Federal support and the systematic use of eminent domain by a quasi-public corporation.

A second basic distinction between capitalist and socialist planning has to do with comprehensiveness.

When President Eisenhower proposed in May, 1968, that there be new, integrated communities with jobs, schools and parks and high-speed transportation links to the old cities, he was unwit- tingly committing himself to radical innovation. Assembling an integrated population and providing its members with decent work, education and transportation is not something to be ac- complished by Adam Smith's "invisible hand." It requires long- range projections and a conscious coordination of Government policies. It could not be done, to take but one crucial example, if land were left to private speculation. For in order to assemble the huge areas needed for such extensive projects at a remotely reasonable cost, the public authority would have to use its power of eminent domain and establish land banks. So conserva- tives may be forced to recognize the magnitude of the urban crisis but they cannot solve it within their own economic cal- culus. What Eisenhower, Nixon and Stans really were talking about in their advocacy of new cities is a version of the old schemes to provide Federal subsidies to private interests, which are then supposed to fulfill a social purpose. But even supposing that such a tactic could provide the necessary billions in money (it cannot), the housing industry hardly has the resources, the overview or the legal right to engage in national, regional and metropolitan planning.

And yet, if it is easy enough to demonstrate that planning within a capitalist context is, at best, utterly and necessarily inadequate, this does not mean that socialist planning is without problems. These problems have to be faced candidly.

The principle of socialist planning is clear: the people rather than the corporations with Government subsidies should decide priorities. In practice, it is not that simple. Is it true, as John Kenneth Galbraith optimistically assumed in *The Affluent Society,* that the masses have basically decent values which are perverted by the manipulators who dominate the communications system? Galbraith contends that the fundamental reason why so many people regard the public sector as a place of compulsion and the private market as an area of free choice is that they have been programmed to do so by the media. If that is so, then the radical reform of the advertising industry would allow the electorate to get the truth and to vote for that social spending which is in its objective and long-term interest.

A more ominous possibility has been suggested by two Labour members of Parliament on the basis of the experience of the Wilson Government in England. After 1965, David Marquand wrote, social expenditures under the socialists went up—but the voters did not like it. "In a democracy," he argued, "Socialist Governments can only succeed if the absolute total of private consumption continues to rise while its share of the national income is falling." David Fletcher was even more pessimistic: "Gone, in fact, is the delusion that we Socialists represent the 'real' interests of the People, and that the People would see it if only they were not blinkered by the 'capitalist press.' . . . Aspirations that once had to be expressed in social terms (that is, in the organized demand for more schools, more welfare and more public control of other people's lucrative activities) are now personal or family ambitions (that is, an individual's desire for a good job, an enhanced status, a good education for Johnny) as a passport to a good job and a bigger car to carry the family farther."

These gloomy conclusions are obviously based on the bitter experience of men who wish they were not true. Yet I suspect that they overstate the case. For it will become more and more obvious in the rest of this century that the greatest threat to living standards in the advanced countries is, indeed, social in character, i.e., it comes from the congestion, pollution and ecological mayhem resulting from an unplanned technological revolution. Nevertheless, Marquand's point introduces an important caveat for any movement attempting democratic planning, and his rule of thumb—that the absolute total of private consumption rises while its share of the national income falls because more resources are allocated to social purposes—is a good one.

Socialist planning, in short, is not a total panacea; neither, for that matter, is democracy. The people are quite capable of making the wrong decision after having been given all the facts. But the only possibility of making a humane choice is if the institutions of democratic planning relentlessly encroach on the private sector in such areas of decisive importance as housing, transportation and education. Neo-capitalist planning with its commercial priorities is inherently limited and unable to solve the crises it recognizes. With socialist planning that is massive, comprehensive and democratic, there is at least the possibility that man will be able to master the environment he himself has created.[3]

The third major reason why capitalist society must be basically transformed is this: Let us assume that the system proves to be much more ingenious than the preceding analysis suggests. Suppose it constructs a welfare state that really does respond to the needs of the poor and that, without fundamental changes in structure, it manages to accommodate itself to democratic planning. Even then—and I admit this possibility for the purpose of argument only—even then, it would be necessary to go beyond capitalism to socialism. For if this society somehow found a way to deal with poverty, racism, inequality and unmet social needs, it would still be incapable of dealing with its own prosperity.

This problem is not a consequence of wrong-headed choices on the part of muddled executives; it is a trend within the system and cannot be corrected without sweeping changes. The economic theory of "external economies" and "external diseconomies" helps to explain why.

An external economy occurs when an act of consumption creates a collective good, e.g., when the decision of a high school student to remain in school raises his skill level and makes him a more productive worker rather than a candidate for welfare.

External economies usually derive from public investments in schools, hospitals and the like. External diseconomies are a result of an opposite phenomenon: acts of consumption that create a collective evil, e.g., the air pollution visited upon society by a private automobile. These are particularly associated with giant industries and, as one moderate economist put it, "seem to be far more prevalent than external economies."

So the fundamental tendencies of late capitalist economies toward bigness and concentration will produce goods whose social costs often exceed their social benefits. This, it must be emphasized, is an inherent pattern in a society where huge investments are privately made. To offset this trend, such decisions would have to be made with major consideration of the social costs—a kind of calculus (as will be seen shortly) that is at odds with the very character of the capitalist economy. There follows an extraordinary paradox: the richer capitalism becomes, the more self-destructive it is. (This is a sort of economic analogue to Freud's psychological insight that the more sophisticated society becomes, the more repressive it is, since instinctual energy must be disciplined in order to make large-scale organization possible.)

In traditional Marxist theory economic crisis was the result of overproduction within a society of systematically limited consumption. Many contemporary economists now argue that the cyclical breakdown of capitalism, which turned relative abundance into immediate want, has been mastered. That, as will be seen shortly, is much too optimistic an analysis, since the contradictions of capitalism bedevil Keynesians as well as anti-Keynesian conservatives. But even if we do assume for a moment that the cyclical crisis of capitalism is under control, it has been succeeded by an even more bizarre problem: that affluence itself is becoming increasingly counterproductive.

So—to cite one striking example—as the seventies began, the President of the United States told the nation in his Message on the Environment, "Based on present trends it is quite possible that by 1980 the increase in the sheer number of cars in densely populated areas will begin outrunning the technological limits of our capacity to reduce pollution from the internal combustion engine." One would think that such an apocalyptic presentiment would have been the prelude to decisive action. Yet only one week before he thus warned that the society was destroying the very air it breathes, Nixon proposed a budget in which mass transportation (which would cut down "the sheer number of cars" as well as serve a number of other social purposes) received 6 percent of the money assigned to building highways, i.e., to making sure that the sheer number of cars would indeed increase.

But the automobile is only one case in point. As Jerome C. Pickard of the Urban Land Institute has commented, "the concentrated character of future urban regional development will place a great strain on regional resources: on water supply, air and the land itself. The pollutants generated in such large scale urban and industrial concentration may threaten a large segment of the environment inhabited by a majority of the United States population."

By the seventies the menacing consequences of uncontrolled and maldistributed affluence had become so obvious that even the thoughtful business press had begun to doubt whether the market could on its own maximize welfare. One of Marx's fundamental theories was thus being vindicated in a way he himself would never have imagined. The forces of production, Marx held, come into contradiction with the mode of capitalist production, i.e., the revolutionary technology cannot be contained within the social and economic system. In Marx's view, the evidence of this clash was to be found in depressions. Today, however, it is precisely because capitalism has moderated the tendency toward periodic crises that it throws up a new form of the Marxian contradiction. For private decision-making is no longer capable of regulating a technology whose social consequences become more and more destructive.

Lyndon Johnson stated the problem well enough in his 1967 message on "Protecting Our National Heritage," but, like his successor, he could not bring himself to urge the radical measures that are necessary to deal with it. "We must realize," Johnson said, "that in dealing with fuels for motor vehicles we are dealing with matters of enormous importance to every section of the nation and to many economic units. America's technology and natural resources development are intimately involved in any program that effects fuels and their uses." And then Mr. Johnson proceeded to the wish that corporate polluters would realize that "out of personal interest, as out of public duty, industry has a stake in making the air fit to breathe."

The day that Mr. Johnson made that statement, the president of Ford Motor Company attacked the dangers of government overregulation, and the *Wall Street Journal* observed that business was mobilizing to fight Johnson's modest reforms. When he signed the Air Quality Act of 1967, President Johnson pretended that he had been given "new power to stop pollution before it chokes our children and strangles our elderly—before it drives us indoors or into the hospital." The *Wall Street Journal* was more realistic: "This was a major victory for such industrial groups as the coal producers, who vigorously opposed toughening Federal standards."

In his 1970 Message on the Environment, Richard Nixon confirmed that the *Wall Street Journal* had been right and Johnson wrong. There were, he said, "insufficient Federal enforcement powers" to fight air pollution. But Nixon could not, of course, hint at why this was so: that the corporations, which had become conscience-stricken about pollution at the precise moment there was a public outcry and the possibility of punitive legislation, had themselves subverted previous efforts to clean up the atmosphere. For the President the crisis was only an "inadvertance." And even though Mr. Nixon's anti-pollution proposals were much less bold than his generalities, the *Wall Street Journal* editorially cautioned him about too sweeping an attack on the internal combustion engine. That, it said, might lead to "severe disruption of many of the nation's largest industries."

There, in the example of the automobile, is the essence of the problem: it is foolish to think that giant industries will voluntarily desist from the profitable spoliation of the environment; and it is impossible for a government committed to maximizing the autonomy of those corporations to take the drastic action that is required.

In the not so distant past such a conflict between corporate interest and common good was thought of as exceptional. As Gardner Ackley, a leading New Economist of the sixties, put it concisely a few years ago, "If one were to examine all of the thousands of decisions made daily by the managers of the modern corporation, I think he would be struck by the relatively small number in which significant questions of conflict between public and private interests arise." A year later Karl Kaysen, another distinguished liberal economist, challenged Ackley's faith in devastating fashion.

Kaysen wrote, "The inter-related set of questions involving urban renewal, urban planning and transportation planning raises
questions that go right to the heart of the usual value assumptions
of the economist. The whole field is dominated by the existence of
externalities, i.e., it is clear that there is no simple meaningful
sense in which the range of decisions can be left to market forces.
It is further clear that our past methods for dealing with the
major externalities are increasingly inadequate, if they ever were
adequate. Zoning by a fragmented set of competing jurisdictions,
highway planning uncoordinated with land-use planning or
without comprehensive urban-suburban transportation planning
simply fail to meet the issues. What alternate decision-mechan-
isms are available?

"The natural bias of economists," Kaysen continued, "is toward
believing that consumers 'ought' to get what they want in some
ethical sense of the word. Economists accordingly tend to resist,
as a matter of fundamental principle, changes in decision-making
processes that substitute planner's choices for consumer's choices.
Yet in the face of what consumer's choices are leading to, some
such substitution appears inevitable. At the very least, planners
will determine, much more narrowly than present processes do,
the range of alternatives from which consumers may choose. The
key question becomes, 'By what political mechanism are planner's
choices reviewed and controlled?' "

This is a remarkable admission. Yet as much as I agree with
Kaysen's perspective on the future, I think he is too easy on the
capitalist past. He contrasts the market choices, which supposedly
pampered the consumer, with planner's choices, which are said
to be more restrictive. Yet a great many of the consumer's desires
are in fact engineered, and even when that is not the case, his
freedom is circumscribed by the possibilities open to him. Many
people in the middle class "freely chose" single-unit suburban
homes because decent, reasonably priced housing in the city was
not available. The citizen faced with shoddy public transportation
or the private automobile was hardly exercising an exhilarating
discretion when he chose the latter. In other words, planning
could and should broaden the range of choice for the majority.

Nor was this consciousness of the inadequacy of the classic
capitalist model confined to economists. In September, 1969, the
Yankelovich polling organization surveyed a representative sample
of the chief executives of the five hundred largest corporations

and fifty largest banks. It concluded that there was a "coming conflict in business discipline" because of the contradiction between social need and private investment. "We predict," the article in *Fortune* said, "that nothing that has happened since the 1930s will inject more confusion, sow more dissension and conflict and threaten more chaos than the effect of these pressures [for meeting social needs] as they mount in the early years of the 1970s."

Finally, if neo-capitalism has ameliorated the more traditional forms of economic crisis, it has far from solved them. And here again, the private priorities of the corporation invade governmental policy.

When John F. Kennedy was elected President in 1960, the debate among his economic advisors had as much to do with the class struggle as it did with academic theory. The economists from the AFL-CIO and individuals like John Kenneth Galbraith and Leon Keyserling wanted Kennedy to adopt a social variant of Keynesianism and to eliminate the unemployment he inherited from Eisenhower by expanding consumption and making investments in public projects. Other advisors wanted a much more cautious—and business-oriented—policy. In 1962 there was a 7 percent tax credit for business investment and accelerated depreciation allowances for plant and equipment. These amounted to a multibillion-dollar increase in the cash flow of the giant corporations. These measures were then followed by a tax cut which, since it sought to increase private consumption spending and was based on the inequities of the tax code, assigned the largest benefits to the richest people.

This tactic, as I demonstrated in *Toward a Democratic Left,* promotes the values of Adam Smith with the techniques of John Maynard Keynes. It is the "natural" way for a capitalist society to fight crisis. For Kennedy could only have followed his more socially-oriented advisors if he had had a massive majority in the Congress to offset the political-economic power of the corporations. Under normal conditions, it was, and will be, the wisdom of capitalist reform to favor business in order to win its support. Thus, the full power of the Federal Government will be used to exacerbate the disparities of income in the society.

But then, such a policy also reproduces and intensifies the contradictions of the capitalist structure itself. As Nat Goldfinger, the director of research for the AFL-CIO, has pointed out, the tax credit and accelerated depreciation allowance had the effect of setting off a capital-goods boom. And that, of course, was the point of Richard Nixon's similar policy measures in 1971. However, by stimulating the economy in such a way, Washington is using its considerable power to maximize productivity but not the power to consume. In the short run, the capital-goods boom will generate employment and buying power, as the experience of the sixties shows. But in the absence of vigorous measures to raise the effective demand of the millions, these policies also lay the basis for a crisis of "overproduction" in which productivity outstrips consumption. By concentrating so many resources in the capital-goods sector, they also have an inflationary impact. Hence the simultaneous inflation-recession of the late sixties and early seventies was at least partly caused by Federal action.

And finally on this count, that state of equilibrium so dear to the classical economists still evades the Keynesians. For, as Chapter V suggested, when employment is high enough to approach a socially desirable level, unit labor costs for industry go up, profits go down and there are tendencies toward recession. And when unemployment is high enough to lower labor costs, there is an intolerable waste of human beings. But under a policy of structural reform, where working men and women would be shifted into extremely valuable social pursuits that would increase their productivity even as they provided needed goods and services in education, health care, environmental protection and the like, it would be possible to have full employment and price stability. That, however, would mean going beyond the basic principles of the capitalist use of human beings, for it would assign more and more workers to the "nonprofit" sector. Nonprofitable, that is, from the point of view of business, but enormously profitable for society.

So contemporary capitalism is not only heir to many of the traditional evils of the system, even if sometimes in ameliorated ways, it also cannot deal adequately, no matter how sophisticated it has become with either poverty or affluence. Left to itself, the system creates a welfare state that provides some benefits for all, yet favors the rich and discriminates against the desperate; it generates problems, like those of the urban environment, that demand comprehensive planning; and even when it functions to produce the highest standard of living the world has known, the social consequences of that achievement are so appalling as to vitiate much of it.

We socialists support every struggle for the partial and liberal reform of this inadequate structure. Yet we insist—and I believe that the previous analysis has documented the point—that the fundamental solution of these problems requires measures that go beyond the limits of the capitalist economy.[4]

## II

Neo-capitalism, for all its sophistication, cannot make desperately needed social investments, plan comprehensively and massively or cope with either poverty or affluence. Socialism can. This section will seek to explain how.

In the process, I will use a dangerous distinction. One begins with the specific problems that have just been identified and seeks a solution to them which, while structurally altering the capitalist society, will take place within some of the limitations that society imposes on political action. Then it is possible to define an ultimate vision of socialism based on the very un-capitalist assumption that the basic material needs of the people have been satisfied and that productivity has grown to such an extent that man can free himself from the psychology and eco-nomics of scarcity. That theme will be the subject of Chapter XIV.

In distinguishing between the immediate transition to socialism and the final goal, I am using a necessary, but quite risky, idea. Marx had insisted that the new society would be conceived within the womb of the old and therefore would be born with the heritage of the past as well as the hopes of the future. It was only when men had learned to live cooperatively through a long ex-perience and when abundance was an economic fact that the old bourgeois limits could be transcended and society inscribe on its banner "From each according to his ability, to each according to his needs." But this theory of the two stages of socialism was used by Joseph Stalin to justify murder and totalitarianism. For when-ever the injustices and oppressions of Soviet society were attacked, Stalin could reply that this was, after all, only the first and im-perfect phase of the transition to the millennium. Yet long after Stalin died, and more than half a century after the Bolshevik Revolution, the "temporary" institutions of anti-freedom are still basic to that society.

In other words, if it is indeed impossible to take a single giant stride into utopia, one still cannot, as Stalin taught, arrive at a society of community and brotherhood by way of gradual terror and coercion. So if the changes in capitalist structure that are proposed in what follows are only transitional, they must also move in the direction of the ultimate vision of socialism. They cannot, as under Communism, be antithetical to it.

First of all—and this is urgent practical politics within the present confines of capitalism as well as a step toward socialism —investment must be socialized.

There are, as has just been seen, huge decisive areas of economic life in which private capital will not invest because there is no prospect of sufficient profitability (or, what amounts to the same thing, where anti-social allocations are more profitable than social allocations would be). This is true of the fundamental determinants of the urban environment, like housing and transportation. Therefore the society must shift resources from the privately profitable sector of the economy to the socially necessary. This is a decision that only the Government has the power to make and which must be taken as a result of a democratic process. And it can only be accomplished on a national scale and within the framework of planning.

This does not mean that the housing design or the exact mix of public and private transport will be settled by a ukase issued in Washington. A qualitative increase in the rate of social spending can be channeled through the most diverse kinds of organizations: through departments of national, regional and local government, public corporations, cooperatives, private nonprofit institutions, neighborhood associations and so on. But a progressive income tax nationally administered is the only source of funds for such a gigantic appropriation, and the various regional and local choices —where to build a new city, for instance—have to be integrated into a national plan.

John Strachey, the late British socialist theorist, thought that such a process of transforming "the social form taken by accumulation into a consciously set-aside fund" was the "essence of the transition to socialism." That is, as will be seen, an overly optimistic assessment of this development, since more than investment must be socialized. Yet it does emphasize the fact that Federal planning and Congressional appropriation could be one way of directing production for use rather than for profit.

In areas like housing and transportation this program obviously requires much more than simply spending money. For even conservatives have come to realize that government programs have to be coordinated: the Nixon Administration talks of a national urban policy. And the National Commission on Urban Problems ( chaired by an outstanding liberal economist, and former Senator, Paul Douglas) recommended that "the President and his Economic Advisors, the Federal Reserve Board, the Treasury Department and other major agencies of government be required to state what effect any major change in economic policy (e.g., interest rate changes, tax reductions or increases, balance of payments proposals) would have on the successful building of the number of housing units set by the President in his annual housing construction goal message."

But all of these suggestions, the liberal as well as the conservative, assume the continuation of the present structure of the housing "industry"—if such a modern word can be used to describe such a backward sector. Yet the Government will fail in its commitments unless it creates a new industry. New cities cannot be built by a myriad of private developers, each making his own decisions about a small parcel of real estate. And the present procedure of clearing areas that are already urban and then turning them over to profit-seekers has already had the disastrous effect of subtracting from the housing supply, increasing the rent on existing, inadequate dwellings, and in general making life more miserable for the poor and minorities. So there must be a social land bank, a new technology, an industry created to modern scale and national and regional plans. And that will take more ingenuity than just writing a Federal check.

This one case could be duplicated in every other area of social need and it points up the second socialist proposal for changing our institutional structure: that decisive investments must be democratically planned as well as financially socialized.

There should be an Office of the Future in the White House. Each year the President should make a Report on the Future— with projections ranging five, ten or even twenty years ahead— which would be submitted to a Joint Congressional Committee where it would be debated, amended and then presented to the entire Congress for decision. This process should establish the broad priorities of the society and annually monitor the result of past efforts. It would be, for instance, the proper forum for establishing the broad concept of regional planning; but it would not engage in the actual planning of individual projects.

At this point, a candid admission is in order. The changes outlined in the previous paragraph could be welcomed by social engineers and technocrats determined to impose their values on the people. They could be used by sophisticated corporate leaders to make the status quo more rational and stable. And they might create an entrenched bureaucracy with a self-interest of its own. The critics of socialism who cite such dangers ignore, or conceal, the fact that they are the consequence of the complexity of *all forms* of modern technological society and that socialism is the only movement that seeks to make a structural and democratic challenge to the trend. But even more important, it must be understood that there is no institutional reform that, in and of itself, can guarantee genuine popular participation in this process. Only a vibrant movement of the people can do that. That is why socialists do not foresee an ultimate stage of human existence in which all questions are answered and all conflicts resolved. Even in the very best of societies the democratic majority must be on the alert.

There is, however, one important area where planning is made more simple because of tendencies within the economy itself. The dominant trend of this century is to move economic activity away from primary pursuits, like agriculture, and even away from industry, into areas like service and education. This is one of the reasons why college expenditures have increased faster than the GNP since 1950 and that schoolteaching has been one of the fastest-growing professions.

A great many of the areas thereby expanded have been traditionally public or private nonprofit: schools, hospitals, social services and the like. A 1970 analysis in *Fortune* has even suggested that it is impossible for the nation to achieve its health goals unless there is an even greater increase in the employment of paraprofessionals. When there was a renewal of social consciousness in the sixties, the corporations began to move into these new markets and designed various human-care programs according to the logic of profit. Yet education, health and personal problems are obviously antagonistic to commercialism, for these are spheres in which one should never stint in order to cut costs and increase the return. The only humane criterion is that of need, and these growth "industries" are therefore natural candidates for social investment.[5]

But even if society would thus socialize more and more investment, consciously planning the allocation of resources for cities, transportation and human care, that in itself would not change the prevailing order. For the control of the means of production and of wealth is not simply economic power; it is political power as well. So if private ownership of huge corporations were to co-exist over a long period of time with planned social investments, the corporate rich, be they managers or owners, would come to dominate the new, supposedly democratic institutions. That is one of the main reasons why socialists cannot abandon their insistence upon social ownership.

It might seem quixotic to raise such a point just as the socialist parties of Europe have abandoned it. The Continental social democrats, as Chapter IX documented, have almost all adopted the idea of a "social market economy" in which the state controls, but does not own, the crucial means of production. Given this decision on the part of the mass democratic socialist movements, is it not mere nostalgia, or worse, dogmatism, to bring up this discredited panacea of the Left?

Paradoxically, I will base my case for social ownership on the same economic trend—the separation of ownership and control under contemporary capitalism—that was cited by many socialists in the sixties as a reason for giving up the traditional position on the nationalization of industry. Moreover, I think there is a strategy for achieving social ownership that does not involve a sudden, apocalyptic leap from private to public property (which is, in any case, impossible under democratic conditions), but rather employs structural reforms.

First, there is the trend toward the separation of ownership and control and its bearing on social ownership.

For the Continental socialists who revised their basic programs in the late fifties and early sixties, this development made the classic case for nationalization irrelevant. Now that rational, plan-oriented managers have taken over from individualistic capitalists, they argued, it is no longer necessary to change the title to property. For the socialists in control of the government will follow full-employment policies which will yield a growing fund for social spending and, in any case, the corporate executives will see that it is to their interest to observe the broad priorities established by the state.

I would argue that this very same trend separating ownership and control increasingly demonstrates the functionless character of the legal title to property and suggests a very practical, un-apocalyptic method of doing away with it.

Marx, as I noted earlier, had understood that the joint stock company—the first institutional expression of the separation of ownership from control—contained an anti-capitalist premise insofar as it made economic functions independent of capital itself. That, he felt, was one more sign of the transition to socialism. The Fabians, with their penchant for basing the socialist case on neo-classical economics, emphasized this development. A third of the English corporations, Sidney Webb wrote in the original *Fabian Essays*, are joint stock companies "whose stockholders could be expropriated by the community with no more dislocation of the industries carried on by them than is caused by the daily purchase of shares on the Stock Exchange."

In the 1920s John Maynard Keynes, a principled anti-socialist, was describing the self-socializing tendencies of capitalism as the "euthanasia of the rentiers." More recently, John Kenneth Galbraith has suggested that the "functionless stockholder" is becoming an anachronism, and A. A. Berle, a pioneer in the empirical studies of the ownership-control pattern, echoed Sidney Webb: "Transition from private collectivism to state collectivism is the easiest thing in the world where [as in the case under the corporate system] collectivism is already well organized for production." And Robin Marris, in his critique of the contemporary corporation, has pointed out that "once the classic idealization of capitalism is thus destroyed [when, that is, it is seen that the managers are not working 'for' the stockholders], there is no *economic* case for its superiority over socialism."

It was a distinguished conservative, however, who most clearly drew the socialist conclusions from this economic tendency. Frederick A. Hayek wrote, "So long as the management is supposed to serve the interests of the stockholders it is reasonable to leave the control of its actions to the stockholders. But if the management is supposed to serve wider public interest, it becomes a logical consequence of this conception that the appointed representatives of the public interests should control the management."

There are two reasons why I believe that Hayek's straightforward proposal of socialization is to be preferred to the European socialist notion of the state programming a market economy with social goals. First, as we have seen, the recent experience of the Continental social democrats confirms the tendency of the corporations to try to dominate, rather than obey, the government that is supposed to be controlling them. And second, it is now

possible to have a relatively painless transition to social ownership if socialists will only learn how to encourage the "euthanasia
of the rentiers." The Swedish social democrats have an ingenious
contribution to make in this area. They propose to socialize the
functions of property while leaving the title to it temporarily
undisturbed. In this way, socialization will be part of historic
process rather than a sudden and drastic leap into the future.

We tend to reify private property into something indivisible so
that one either owns or does not own. But in the case of the
means of production (and they, not personal property, are what
concern socialists), one can think of private property as conferring
a series of functional, and divisible, rights. In the classic theory of
laissez-faire, ownership allowed a man to utilize existing fixed
capital resources; to determine investment policy; to deploy the
labor force; to set wage levels; to distribute profits; to retain
profits; and so on. This model has, of course, already been modi-
fied, i.e., wage levels are fixed through collective bargaining agreements overseen, and encouraged, by the state; tax policies can
provide incentives for internal financing or for distributing profits;
etc. What is required now is a much more profound, and conscious, socialization of more of the functions of property. Taking
property as, in A. A. Berle's phrase, a "packet of permissions,"
what is proposed is not a sudden, wholesale takeover by the state
but a process progressively abolishing all these private permissions
and substituting democratic decisions for them.

For example, private investment decisions must be socialized.
The right to locate, or relocate, a plant in a given area can no
longer be conceded to be a private matter. For in order to engage
in regional planning and to aid in the construction of new cities
and towns, the geography of employment has to be publicly determined. A strict system of licensing the permission to build a factory could work toward this end. The Attlee Government initiated
some measures of this type, and various Italian governments have
tried to use such techniques to promote the development of the
south. There were even reports in 1970 that the Nixon Administration would have a similar policy for the location of power plants.

Technology has to be monitored too. The decision to build a
supersonic transport has so many consequences (noise, air traffic
congestion, airport construction) that even if it were not a
Government-subsidized project, the public interest should be asserted. There is a need, as a National Academy of Science panel

pointed out, for "technological forecasting." One cannot trust these matters, as the *Wall Street Journal* put it in a telling anti-capitalist phrase, to the "mindless market."

The National Academy panel made another important point about technological forecasting: that it must be carried out by an independent agency and not by an interested bureaucracy. For "the Bureau of Public Roads has hardly been noted for its devotion to the natural beauty of the countryside." More generally, as has been seen, it is quite possible for a publicly-owned enterprise to behave in the same aggressive, self-interested way as a private corporation. Here again, the crucial issue is not so much the legal form of ownership as the kind of economic calculus it follows.

Profit is still another function of property that must be subjected to social control. In 1967 the Council of Economic Advisors—hardly an anti-capitalist agency—noted that Government direction of the economy had smoothed out the cycle of boom and bust and therefore removed a great deal of the risk in the marketplace. Under such conditions, it argued, business should be prepared to take a lower rate of return. But in point of fact, American corporations chafed under the voluntary controls of the Kennedy and Johnson administrations, even though their profits rose by 78.7 percent between 1960 and 1970 and their cash flow (profits plus depreciation) was up by 85 percent in the same period. When Richard Nixon came into office, he abandoned all efforts to persuade industry and labor to obey guidelines in price and wage policy. Whereupon, the London *Economist* reported, the steel industry increased its prices in twelve months by 7 percent—as contrasted to a 6 percent rise in the previous ten years. And in 1971 a major price increase by Bethlehem Steel finally forced even the conservative Mr. Nixon to proclaim a contrary public interest.

So government cannot leave profit policy up to the good conscience of the corporation, but it can use an array of techniques to socialize this important area of economic life: selective price and wage controls in an inflationary period; a requirement that big companies open up their books and justify any increase in prices before an independent board; the use of vigorous tax policy (more on this shortly). But however it is done, the fundamental purpose of this reform is clear enough. The society cannot afford to leave to private decision how the prices of basic goods are to be set—or how the huge annual increments in wealth are to be distributed.

There are other structural changes that could socialize some of the functions of property. The voting rights of all speculative, short-term shareholders could be abolished (which would make it clear that many of the transactions on the stock market are nothing but a socially approved form of gambling—and an enormous waste of resources and energy in a parasitic operation without real economic function). Or it has been proposed that the Government give itself the right to act as if it were the majority stockholder in all major industries, but without taking legal title. In this scheme, the corporation would be left to its own devices as long as it conformed to the national plan and did not irresponsibly impose social costs upon the country. But when its private egotism led to anti-social behavior, the Government would intervene the same way major shareholders do when confronted with poor management. The state would not assume permanent control, but only see to it that the direction of corporate policy was changed so as to observe the proper social priorities. The consumerist movement which emerged under the leadership of Ralph Nader in the late sixties and early seventies moved—and is moving—in precisely this direction and has received mass support in the process.

In France in 1970 the Radical Party at the urging of Jean-Jacques Servan-Schreiber adopted a policy "to abolish the hereditary transmission of property in the means of production." In effect, Servan-Schreiber advocated a confiscatory tax on the stock holdings of very wealthy individuals. There have been debates on how effective the measures proposed would be, yet the principle is both clear and excellent. A quite similar idea was proposed by Douglas Jay of the British Labour Party who urged that a government investment bank be made the recipient of the stock paid as death duty and also of the savings of the workers.

Taken individually, none of these changes would basically transform the power relations of the capitalist society. But if they were part of a comprehensive policy which sought to progressively limit the rights of property in the means of production, they could encourage and direct the euthanasia of the rentiers. The gradualism of this strategy is derived not from any abstract principle, but from the actual experience of socialist governments over half a century—as well as from a sense of what might be acceptable to the American people. In the United States (in all of the advanced capitalist countries, for that matter) there is neither political support nor administrative feasibility for the sudden decisive nationalization of an entire economy. In any case, a socialist movement could take the opportunity such a process would afford to promote as much diversity and variety as possible within the forms of social property.[6]

For the question of exactly how ownership is to be socialized is another area of confusion in the socialist tradition. It is quite clear that vague metaphors—the state will "seize" or "take over" the means of production—provide no guide for political action in a complex technological economy.

The nineteenth-century socialists, as earlier chapters documented, were deeply confused about the status of ownership in the society they sought. There was one tradition, with origins in Saint-Simon, that emphasized state action, planning and socialized investment; there was another, represented by Fourier and Proudhon, that envisioned communes and free associations carrying on production; and Marx, to complicate matters, borrowed from both lines of thought. As time went on, it became clear that the very complexity of a modern economy required that social property function within a context controlled by the state. But this, as Chapter IX showed, does not mean that socialists equate social property with enterprises run by the central government. There is a quite successful model in the United States for what a public corporation can accomplish: the Tennessee Valley Authority. It is, like a private corporation, able to accumulate capital for future investment out of present income, yet it is under the broad supervision of the Federal Government in Washington (and under constant attack by the private power industry which cannot tolerate this demonstration of how a governmentally chartered enterprise can be more efficient, and produce cheaper power, than the private sector). Moreover, in 1969 the TVA proposed to innovate in an important area of social need by coming forth with plans for an integrated new town and pointing out how its comprehensive structure made it much easier for it to plan, and finance, such a project than a private developer.

This initiative touches upon one of the most important aspects of corporate organization. As Robin Marris has noted, "the most fundamental difference between business firms and government departments lies in the former's capacity for autonomous growth."

Indeed, one can argue, as Marris has, that the essence of the most sophisticated stage of corporate capitalism is not the famous separation of ownership and control but the fact that an organization is financially independent, i.e., that it can use retained profits to fund growth and is therefore not subject to the constraints of the money market.

This point became a political issue in England in 1971. The Heath government, much more traditionalist and Tory than the Conservatives had been under Harold Macmillan, moved to force the nationalized coal industry out of all operations not directly related to the mines. For the Coal Board, under the chairmanship of Alf Robens, had innovated and undertaken projects on its own, like chemicals and gas explorations. From a neo-capitalist point of view, that was intolerable, for it meant a public enterprise was moving into areas where private corporations could profit. And, as have been seen, conservatives are primarily willing to socialize losses. So Heath moved to limit the Coal Board and Robens resigned. Sir John Eden, the conservative Minister of Industry, was frank about the rationale for the move: "By and large the public sector should be concerned primarily with those activities which cannot sensibly be done by the private sector." "Sensibly" means profitably.

If the conservatives had carefully sought a way to discredit public ownership, they could not have come up with a better plan. The national enterprises are to be confined to the sectors that capitalism has so fouled up that they are no longer profitable, like coal in England and passenger rail service in the United States. Once given this thankless job, social property is then hobbled with restrictions that do not apply to the private sector. Such enterprises will then be doubtless attacked by conservatives as a burden, unprofitable and unimaginative, i.e., for being all the things the conservatives had made them.

This is clearly intolerable. Socialists are not in business to socialize the mistakes of capitalists but to create a new social order. Therefore they must insist upon the rights of public property in profitable areas and demand that the managements of social enterprises have at least as much of a right to innovate as private decision-makers. In other words, in giant industries, the TVA type of public corporation rather than the Post Office should serve as a model. There are, to be sure, obvious risks to this approach. It is precisely the autonomy of a socially-owned enterprise like the

Port of New York Authority, its independence from democratic control, that has allowed it to use its resources for creative anti-social purposes like increasing pollution. This point is central in John Kenneth Galbraith's critique of socialism in *The New Industrial State*. In the last century, according to Galbraith, firms were run by entrepreneurs, and the state, or the collective of workers, could take over from them without too much trouble. Now, however, there is the corporation with its intricate "technostructure" of scientists and administrators. If the socialist state tries to exercise too close a control over such an organization, it almost guarantees waste and incompetence; but if it grants the socialized industry the right to independent action, the latter will probably follow its own purposes rather than those of the national plan. "The technical complexity and planning and associated scale of operation," Galbraith concludes, "that took power from the capitalist entrepreneur and lodged it with the technostructure, removed it also from the reach of socialist control."

Galbraith correctly notes that this was one of the problems that caused the socialists in Europe to retreat from the commitment to public property after World War II. But then, ironically —for he writes as an American liberal who is critical of a socialist dogma—he takes an ambiguous position somewhere to the Left of many of the revisionist social democrats. "It is impossible that there is, in fact, more to the case for the autonomous public corporation than the modern socialist now sees. The problem of the technostructure . . . is whether it can be accommodated to social goals or whether society will have to be accommodated instead to its needs. *The nature of the legal ownership has an undoubted bearing on the amenability of the technostructure to social goals.*" (Emphasis added.) The ambiguity in Galbraith's position is that he never really follows up this insight except in fairly vague reference to the gradual withering away of the "functionless stockholder."

I propose to be more specific. Granting that Galbraith has identified a serious problem—the Scylla represented by the Post Office, the Charybdis represented by the Port Authority—it is impossible for society to carry out liberal reform, to plan and to allocate social costs properly, unless it asserts a decisive interest over the huge corporations. That means that there will indeed be an ever-present danger of inefficiency, dullness, poor service and all the rest. But that risk is to be infinitely preferred to the one incurred by leaving the corporate structure in its present, irresponsible form. There are, in short, no "perfect" solutions to these enormous problems, and any intelligent person can foresee difficulties in any proposal. Nevertheless, the public corporation with both the right to internal financing and the responsibility to democratically elected representatives of the people is, with all the problems admitted, a right step in the best direction.

Moreover, there are many instances where cooperative and neighborhood forms of ownership are relevant. The problems that have just been discussed arise primarily in the giant decisive enterprises that are so large-scale and basic to national planning that the state must assert a major interest in them. But there are a great many less complicated economic functions which can be carried out by—to use the phrase Marx borrowed from the Proudhonist tradition—the "associated producers." In the United States, for instance, the New Deal promoted rural electrification by providing relatively cheap credit to local cooperatives, and in this way electricity was brought to the rural areas (the notion of central-state financial aid to such small units is one that can be found throughout nineteenth-century socialism: in Proudhon, Louis Blanc, Lassalle and the Belgian socialists among others).

In this context, the idea of functional socialization is not simply a political necessity; it is also an opportunity for innovation. In the old apocalyptic proposals for the sudden and decisive nationalization of all basic industry there was little room for promoting diversity and a variety of institutional forms. But in proceeding to socialize the specific functions of property over a period of time there is much more of a chance for originality and imagination.

With the rise of pollution as an issue, the Government has been pushed into monitoring the levels of mercury in food and into banning the use of cyclamates and other additives. There is even evidence in the United States, for all its explicit anti-socialism, that a campaign that would thus assert public control over the corporation might be politically popular. As I noted earlier, Ralph Nader and his colleagues have organized extremely effective campaigns to limit the sovereign power of the big companies and forced safety reforms in the automobile industry. In the Nader campaign to gain public representation on the General Motors board there has been a growing realization, among the young in particular, that "private" choices with public consequences must be socialized. Indeed, it seems to me that Nader, who is a reformer acting empirically, has in many ways raised more radical questions, and possibilities, than the European social democrats. His lead should be carefully followed.[7]

There is still another avenue of socialist action, and it, like the Nader campaign, may also be quite popular. The vigorous use of tax policy as a means of achieving a more egalitarian society is relevant to the immediate neo-capitalist present.

To a considerable extent, the Left has ignored the enormous potential of tax reform in forwarding the transition to a decent society. If, as Chapter IX demonstrated, there is a tendency under capitalism for reforms, and even structural changes like nationalization, to benefit the wealthy rather than the poor, then taxes provide a most important corrective. It is not simply a question of seeing to it that the wealth generated by the intervention of the state serves the society on a democratic basis, but also of the possibility of transforming the very organization of inequality itself.

In most cases the discussion of maldistribution focuses upon income, for that is an area of abundant government statistics. But if one begins instead by examining the shares of *wealth*—"the sum total of equity in a home or business, liquid assets, investment assets, the value of automobiles owned, and miscellaneous assets, such as assets held in trust, loans to individuals, oil royalties, etc." —the disproportions are even more shocking. One quarter of the consumer units in the United States have no wealth at all (or "negative" wealth, i.e., more debt than assets); 61 percent of the consumer units own 7 percent of the wealth while a little over 2 percent of the total have 43 percent. Indeed a majority of the wealth in the United States—57 percent, to be exact—is held by just a bit over 6 percent of the consumer units. It is this permanent structure of inequality which underlies, and is reinforced by, the annual inequities in income.

Thus, there has been no significant change in the distribution of income since 1944. Moreover, the effective rate of taxation on the rich and the upper middle class (the top 15 percent of the society as measured by incomes) declined in the years between 1952 and 1967. Many of the taxes in this country—for Social Security and Unemployment Insurance, to take Federal examples, and on consumption in the case of state levies—are regressive. All of these tax rates are based on reported rather than actual income and do not take into account the command over resources in expense accounts, pensions and other perquisites which are rampant in the upper reaches of the economy. The same trends can be observed in England despite the achievements of the Attlee and Wilson governments.

So the American and other advanced capitalist tax systems are a labyrinth designed to favor the wealthy who can afford lawyers and accountants. "Income," as defined by the Internal Revenue Service in the United States, is not income at all: it excludes a good portion of capital gains, worth $7 billion a year; it does not tax the rent a middle-class family saves by owning a house, an item worth $8 billion a year; it exempts various state and local bonds; and so on. In this setting, the simple equitable act of making income equal income for purposes of tax computation would be a major contribution to social justice.

But even such a modest reform is intolerable on the basis of the capitalist ideology. In the summer of 1969 when the Congress considered—and promptly forgot—the idea of limiting some of the privileges of stock speculators by changing the favored status of capital gains somewhat, the *Wall Street Journal* responded in an angry editorial. By requiring these people to pay a little more in the direction of a fair share, the Government would "punish the nation's most productive citizens." And this disincentive to the stockholder could actually lead to a decrease in economic activity and Federal revenues: "Obviously enough the tax reformer's chief aim is not more money for Uncle Sam but more 'justice' as among individual taxpayers."

Among the many problems with this analysis is the fact that it is based on an obsolete model of capitalist society. If the stock market had as its prime function bringing together risk capitalists and industrial innovators, it is indeed possible that an increase in justice would lower the rate of return on such money and slow down economic change. But in reality, American corporations more and more accumulate their own investment funds internally or else turn to institutional investors. In 1964, for instance, after paying taxes and dividends the corporations retained $59 billion to finance their future plans. And a good many of the people in the Market, far from being the "nation's most productive citizens," are functionless parasites. As Joan Robinson put it, "The shareholders and rentiers, indeed, make a great negative contribution to industry, for much of the best talent of every generation is engaged, one way or another, in the lucrative business of swapping securities around amongst them and so is kept from constructive activities. The notion that the Stock Exchange, with all its ancillary apparatus, is the most efficacious means of supplying finance to industry, compared with other available methods, is a fig leaf which it wears to preserve its self respect."

Effective inheritance taxes would be another important source of social funds and an opportunity for working toward greater equality. In the United States they are quite low—or quite avoidable, which amounts to the same thing. In classic capitalist theory a man must be able to leave his fortune to his children if he is to have an incentive to work hard all his life. That motive could be easily protected by providing for relatively low death duties on the first transfer from father to son, which would encourage the father, and very high rates on the second transfer, from son to grandson, which would give the son a reason to strive as hard as his father. This is something like that ingenious Saint-Simonian notion of abolishing inheritance over three generations and counting on the greed of the first generation to make it indifferent to what happens to its grandchildren.

In all these reforms, in short, the point would not be to penalize hard work or actual risk-taking but to severely limit, and eventually eliminate, the tribute society pays to passive wealth or to stock gamblers. For as the process of accumulation becomes much more social with industry generating its own investment funds or getting them from institutions, it becomes absurd to pay generations of functionless coupon-clippers on the grounds that their distant ancestors made a signal contribution to the society. So it is property income that would be the target, and it is easy enough to distinguish between it and the reward for present accomplishment. One would also seek to get the enormous increase in land values which take place without any effort on the part of the owner. This was $25 billion a year in the United States between 1956 and 1966.

Moreover, of all the reforms proposed here, the use of taxes as a means of increasing justice and equality should be the most politically promising, for it attacks the wealth of a functionless minority and would provide benefits for a huge majority. If all the artful outlived rationales for favoring the rich can be shown to be what they are, masses would support their abolition.

So there are three main areas of transitional programs moving in the direction of a socialist democratization of economic power: the socialization of investment; the progressive socialization of the functions of corporate property, and then that of property itself; the employment of tax policy as an instrument for social justice. Each one of these structural reforms corresponds to a need in the society which can be documented in the official reports, and more to the political point, several of them could become quite popular with the majority of the people.

There is, then, still very much meaning to the idea of socialism as it relates to the middle distance. After examining how we must go beyond the world market as well as the welfare state, i.e., socialism's relevance to the Third World, I will turn to the far future. For if socialists no longer imagine an existing society of total perfection, they must hold fast to a vision of a new order which can animate all the approximations of it.[8]

# XIII

## *Beyond the World Market*

OF ALL THE LAWS of history enunciated by Marx, one of the most brutal unfortunately proved to be true: that the socialization of poverty will lead not to classless and more humane relationships among people, but to new forms of poverty and class rule, new modes of the struggle for necessities. That has been borne out in Russia, China, Cuba, Egypt and every other country that has sought salvation through the collectivization of want. There were, to be sure, sincere and dedicated idealists involved in each case. They were either overwhelmed or corrupted by conditions beyond their control. The best of them went into opposition, the worst into domination.

Socialist rhetoric has a very real role to play under these circumstances where socialism itself is impossible. It fulfills precisely those functions Marx assigned to religion: it articulates the deepest aspirations of the people in such a way as to take their minds off present misery by concentrating on future beatitude. In thus acting as an ideology—as a functional false consciousness—it can facilitate totalitarian accumulation and the creation of a new class society, as under Communism, or elitist corruption as in some of the African "socialisms."

So a bitter truth is the beginning of socialist wisdom with regard to the Third World: that in vast areas of the globe the technical and human preconditions for socialism do not exist. This does not mean that socialists have nothing to say to the majority of mankind. In the long run, it is only through the frank recognition of this fact that the socialist ideal will survive until these nations finally do succeed in their economic development. And in the short run, socialists in both the Third World and the advanced countries have a distinctive contribution to make. They cannot provide a magic and painless transition from backwardness to modernity, but they can show how that transformation can be carried out as humanely and democratically as possible, and at least orient it in the direction of socialism.

So I am not suggesting apocalypse but probing a confused, difficult process in which honesty is, among other things, the best policy. But before the specifics can be detailed, a major objection which derives from a rich socialist tradition has to be confronted. Short of a revolutionary transformation, it is said, the advanced capitalist nations must behave malevolently toward the Third World for they are economically fated to be imperialist. Therefore a perspective such as the one presented in this book— that the transition to a new society will be longer and infinitely more complex than the founders of modern socialism thought— rules out any decency in the foreseeable future which will not be completely socialist.

Here again, the slogans must be rejected and the complexities recognized. If the hungry people of this globe must wait until there are successful revolutions in Europe and North America that abruptly and decisively reverse all the old social relationships, they might well wait forever. Or if they must make their own revolutions in a world dominated by conservative superpowers (Communist as well as capitalist) which continue to subvert their efforts, they will either fail or be driven to such extremes of totalitarian force that it will amount to the same thing.

These intolerable alternatives are not fated. If one looks up from the historic inexorabilities, one can see possibilities for relatively humane change in the Third World. This chapter will define them by first countering the quietist "radical" theories that nothing good can be done short of socialist revolution, and then by outlining just a few of the concrete steps that might be taken within both the advanced and the developing economies. It will propose difficult new departures, not miracles.

The basic socialist insight underlying this analysis can be put simply enough, even if the details are often difficult to describe.

The capitalist world market is fundamentally hostile to the modernization of the poor countries and works to keep them in the same relative position of inferiority to which they were forcibly assigned in the nineteenth century. There is, therefore, an urgent need for world economic planning which would consciously allocate resources on the basis of international usefulness rather than the profit of advanced capitalisms. And within the developing nations themselves it is also necessary to go beyond market criteria which intensify rather than solve their problems.

Capitalism, in short, is an irrelevance for the majority of mankind, or worse, a means of perpetuating ancient wrongs and economic backwardness. Communism is perhaps relevant, but certainly totalitarian. But there is the possibility that socialists, in the Third World as well as the affluent economies, can carry out structural reforms that will begin to transform the international system of economic injustice itself.

# I

There has never been any question among socialists whether the capitalist powers in fact exploit Africa, Asia and Latin America. Of course they have, and still do. The only issue, and it is quite relevant in the contemporary debate over economic development, is whether this wrongdoing is a matter of life and death for them.

As early as 1848 Engels had observed that it was expanding trade on the world market that permitted Britain to keep pace with the rising productivity of its manufacture and thereby avoid a crisis of overproduction. And in the third volume of *Das Kapital* Marx made capitalism's global drive so important—and his analysis is often ignored—that it is worth quoting him at length. He wrote that "there is no doubt that in the sixteenth and seventeenth centuries the great revolutions which took place in trade, along with the geographic discoveries, rapidly increased the development of merchant capital, and constituted a crucial moment in furthering the transition from the feudal to the capitalist mode of production. The sudden expansion of the world market, the multiplication of the circulating commodities, the competition among the European nations to get hold of the products of Asia and the treasures of America, the colonial system, all contributed tremendously to the destruction of the feudal fetter of production.

In its first phase, the modern mode of production only developed in those places where the preconditions for it had evolved within the feudal system. . . . In contrast, when in the sixteenth and part of the seventeenth century the sudden expansion of trade and the creation of a new world market had a decisive influence on the decline of the old and the rise of the new capitalist mode of production, that took place on the basis of the already created capitalist mode of production. *The world market itself was the basis of the mode of production.*

"On the one hand," Marx continued, "the imminent necessity to produce on an ever-increasing scale forced a ceaseless expansion of the world market and thus trade did not revolutionize industry but industry trade. So predominance in trade is now linked to the greater or lesser preponderance of the conditions for big industry. One compares, e.g., England and Holland. The history of the decline of the merchant preeminence of Holland is the history of the subordination of trade to industrial capital." (Emphasis added.)

All of this has a modern, almost a Leninist, ring to it. The capitalist drive on the world market arises out of the inner necessity of a mode of production that must constantly expand itself. Indeed, in this perspective, the very rise of the system itself and the victory over feudalism was linked with the conquest of markets and spheres of influence in the non-European world. But this process, Marx and Engels always thought, must eventually reach its limits and the moment would signal nothing less than the end of capitalism.

In his 1848 analysis Engels wrote that "notwithstanding California and Australia, notwithstanding the immense and unprecedented emigration, there must ever, without any particular accident, in due time arrive *a moment when the extension of markets is unable to keep pace with the extension of British manufacture,* and this disproportion must bring about a new crisis with the certainty it has done in the past." But this prediction did not work out. Thus at the end of his life Engels was forced to recognize that the business cycle of boom and bust within the capitalist economy seemed to be slowing down and becoming more moderate. With characteristic optimism he saw this trend as the precursor of an even greater crisis than ever before; he argued that capitalism's drive for global hegemony had only postponed its downfall.

"The colossal expansion of the means of commerce," Engels wrote, "—ocean-going steamships, railroads, the electric telegraph, the Suez Canal—has for the first time really created a world market. The previous monopoly position of England in industry has been broken by a number of competing lands; the *investment of surplus European capital in all parts of the world has become infinitely greater* and opened up entire new areas so that the system is much more broadly diversified and can overcome local overspeculation more easily. Through all these developments, all the old crisis drives . . . have been greatly weakened, or done away with. Moreover, competition yields in the domestic market before cartels and trusts, and is limited on the external market by protective tariffs with which all the great powers, except England, surround themselves."

And then Engels, having so candidly described how his expectations were unfulfilled and capitalism had proved to be so much more resilient than he and Marx had thought, moves to his dialectical conclusion: "But these protective tariffs are only armaments for the final, general campaign which will decide the domination of the world market. So each element that works against the repetition of the old crises conceals within itself the seeds of a much more widespread and powerful crisis in the future."

In other words, Lenin's extraordinarily influential study *Imperialism* was not a unique insight on his part or even, as is widely thought, a steal from the Liberal economist Hobson. It was grounded in Marx's own analysis, and particularly in Engels' later comment upon it, and had been spelled out in considerable, though contradictory, detail by Karl Kautsky and Rosa Luxemburg. But where Lenin staked out his own special ground was in his insistence that imperialism was the only possible policy for capitalism; indeed, that it constituted its final, and inevitable, stage. He was filled with contempt for Kautsky's notion that the giant capitalist powers could somehow agree to a peaceful "ultra-imperialist" exploitation of the world that would avoid war. The bourgeoisie, Kautsky had said, might internationalize itself under the slogan "Capitalists of the world, unite!" That, Lenin answered, was pernicious nonsense.

The details of that debate are best left to specialists in the history of Marxism, but its central point is quite contemporary. For if there are alternatives to imperialism that are at least possible under capitalism, then socialists can, in carrying out their arduous transformation of the system, pursue policies that are relevant to the Third World even though the old order has not yet been utterly revolutionized. The reason that this is indeed the case has little to do with Kautsky's analysis—the Left at the end of the twentieth century is hardly going to champion "ultra-imperialism" as an alternative to war—but it does build on his basic intuition: that imperialism is *a* policy of capitalism, not *the* policy.[1]

In Lenin's famous definition there were five major determinants of the imperialist inevitability in the last phase of capitalism: "The concentration of production and capital developed to such a high stage that it has created monopolies which play a decisive role in economic life; the merging of bank capital with industrial capital, and the creation, on the basis of this 'finance capital,' of a 'financial oligarchy'; the export of capital, which has become extremely important, as distinguished from the export of commodities; the formation of international capitalist monopolies which share the world among themselves; the territorial division of the whole world among the greatest capitalist powers is completed."

A key to this insatiable capitalist drive for global expansion is the fact that "an enormous 'superabundance of capital' has accumulated in the advanced countries." These funds, Lenin argues, cannot be used to raise the consumption of the masses, and that is why they must be sent overseas. For—and this is a crucial point—"surplus capital will never be utilized for the purpose of raising the standard of living of the masses in a given capitalist country, for this would mean a decline in profits for the capitalists. . . ."

In fact, as I pointed out at considerable length in *Toward a Democratic Left*, Western capitalism, through no fault of its own, escaped this Leninist impasse. It was indeed true, as Lenin said, that economic rivalries were one of the main factors leading to the First World War. But what he did not notice was that the entire working class and not just a labor aristocracy benefited from the process. As Fritz Sternberg has demonstrated, real wages were up between 1850 and 1914 in all industrial countries; in France and Great Britain they almost doubled during that period. In and of itself this does not refute Lenin's analysis, since profits, and the surplus, were rising at the same time. But it does point to a crucial change which Lenin did not anticipate: the enormous growth in the consumption of the masses *within* the advanced nations and the consequent expansion of the internal and intra-advanced capitalist market.

That rising living standard was, to put it quite mildly, precarious until after the Second World War. Indeed, the Great Depression of the thirties was caused in part by precisely the kind of factors Lenin had described. Income inequality, as John Kenneth Galbraith has demonstrated, was a major cause of the crash in 1929 since output per worker went up by 43 percent during the decade, while wages were stable. Thus "the economy was dependent on a high level of investment or a high level of luxury consumer spending or both. The rich cannot buy great quantities of bread."

But after World War II capitalism did change. In large measure this was the result of the political activity of the democratic Left —of socialists in Europe and liberal-laborites in the United States —who effectively championed countercyclical economic policies and an extension of the welfare state. This, as Chapter XII documented, did not bring about justice, for the shares of wealth were still maldistributed and poverty persisted for a sizable minority of the people. But even so, there was a basis for new markets— and new outlets for capital—within the advanced capitalist system. The state, even under conservative governments, had committed itself to maintaining purchasing power at a certain minimal level and that was undreamed of in the Leninist philosophy.

This was the point of departure for the major development on the world market after World War II: the decline in the importance of the Third World and the growth in intracapitalist investments. This pattern, it must be stressed, was not new, but now it intensified. As far back as 1913 Henryk Grossman pointed out in his famous study of capitalist economic crisis, 52.2 percent of Germany's foreign trade went to Western Europe and only 5.4 percent to Asia. "The three small, but highly developed, capitalist lands," Grossman wrote, "the Netherlands, Belgium and Switzerland, with a total population of only about 20 million consume as much [of Germany's goods] as such Asian states as British India, China, the Dutch Indies, Persia, Turkey, Palestine, etc." The same, he commented, held true for the English.

But then after World War II intracapitalist investment in affluence became even more lucrative than the previous "normal" exploitation of colonial poverty. Between 1950 and 1966 the share of the developing world in international trade declined from 31.2 to 19.1 percent; if the oil industry is excluded, the drop is from 24.4 to 14 percent.

The historic viciousness involved in this process should be emphasized. The Third World was made dependent upon its exports because the advanced capitalist powers in the nineteenth century could make profitable use of them and were able to enforce their own world division of labor. But then, when it became possible to make more money through investing in luxury rather than by speculating on hunger, Europe and the United States turned their backs upon the peoples they had used so brutally, developed import substitutes, traded among themselves and condemned their former suppliers to backwardness.

A French Marxist has caught the unconscionable irony in this. The copper and tin of the Third World, A. Emmanuel writes, "are no more primary than the coal which was only yesterday one of the principal exports of England; sugar is almost as 'manufactured' as soap or margarine and is certainly more 'manufactured' than Scotch whiskey or the great wines of France. . . . But the prices of the one group go up, and of the other, down, and the only characteristic that is common to the prices is that they are respectively those of rich and those of poor countries."

In the late sixties and early seventies there seemed to be a countertrend, a shift back toward investment in the Third World. To the extent that it took place, it was one more example of advanced capitalism manipulating poor countries in order to maximize the profits of the rich. Multinational corporations began to set up plants in places like Singapore, Taiwan, Mexico and Korea, where labor is much cheaper than in Europe and the United States. They then used these installations as bases for exports, sometimes to the affluent market itself. In this way they are able to flee the relatively high wages which the workers have won in the metropolitan centers.

Once again, these investments are made according to the same principles that guided the imperial expansion of the nineteenth and early twentieth centuries: to fit the convenience and increase the profits of the already rich nations. Thus, the industries chosen to get capital in such undertakings must be labor-intensive and not depend on economies of scale, i.e., must be backward in comparison with the plants that are built in the home country. The emphasis is on textiles, clothing, furniture and other wood products, lathes and other simple machine tools. This can indeed promote the Gross National Product of a developing nation—as it has rather dramatically in Taiwan and South Korea—but it misshapes the economy and makes it the adjunct of a foreign power rather than an entity moving toward autonomous self-induced growth. And although it may well have beneficial side effects, the process is one more example of the exploitation of poverty.

In other words, in every period of Western capitalist involvement with the Third World the overriding consideration has been the wealth of the advanced nation, not the health of the poverty-stricken. First, the colonial lands were assigned the role of producers of raw materials and agricultural products; after World War II (or even somewhat earlier), when that no longer suited the needs of the big powers, their exports were allowed to languish; and in the late sixties and early seventies, when investment in cheap labor in Asia and Latin America was seen as a way of escaping union wages back home, the corporations seemed again prepared to export some capital, not to help with economic development, but in many cases to distort it by subordinating the needs of impoverished people to those of the rich.

So the details can be debated but the main trend is clear: in the post-World War II period Western capitalism has been less and less dependent upon the poor countries than before. There is, however, one major exception to this generalization: oil.

Of all the major commodities in international trade, the one with the greatest gap between the average cost of production and price is crude oil. This is not a quirk of nature but the result of a carefully designed international system which works to make the prices artificially high. More to the point, petroleum investments account for 42.2 percent of U.S. funds in the developing countries and generate 71 percent of the profits from those areas. If one looks at American capital abroad, but excludes oil, then the money in the Third World is only one sixth of foreign investment, and the profits only one seventh. In other words, oil is an extremely important, and quite imperial, element in the American economy, but if its political power can be overcome, then the dollars that have been sent to Asia, Africa or Latin America are not in the least a matter of life or death for the society. The advanced capitalisms, then, are not as crucially dependent on neo-colonial investment as the classic Leninist analysis would suggest. This, to be sure, is true not because the rich nations became conscience-stricken, but only because they found more profit in other areas.[2]

There have been some recent attempts to defend Lenin's interpretation against these facts, but they are just not convincing. Harry Magdoff, for instance, argues that Lenin had taken note of the capitalist interest in investing in the metropolitan powers and therefore that the new trends are not a departure from his basic analysis. Ernest Mandel, the leading theorist of the Trotskyist Fourth International, takes a similar tack. He admits that "capital is no longer, or even primarily, flowing toward the colonial or semi-colonial 'underdeveloped' countries" but holds that the fact that the "major part of American capital exports has been invested in other imperialist countries" does not contradict the classic Marxian analysis. It is certainly true that Lenin noted that imperial nations coveted each other's industrial areas. But three of the five major characteristics of imperialism as he defined it are concerned with getting control over investments and raw materials in the colonial world and that was clearly his central point.

In the orthodox Marxist view every one of the advanced countries would tend to produce a surplus of capital and therefore one of them could not solve its internal problems by investing in another of them for it would be torn by the very same contradictions. That was why Lenin could argue that the big capitalist powers had to expand into the colonial world. And once one admits, as Mandel and Magdoff do, that this is no longer the dominant trend, then the Leninist analysis falls and it is no longer bourgeois sentimentality to suggest that a capitalist system under the political control of democratic socialists could behave with a modicum of decency within the international economy. For it is no longer fated to do evil.

Even more surprising than the Magdoff-Mandel approach is Gabriel Kolko's use of the "domino theory," a standard rationale for the American intervention in Vietnam, to back up Lenin. "The accuracy of the 'domino' theory," Kolko writes, "with its projection of the eventual loss of whole regions to American direction and access, explains the direct continuity between the larger United States global strategy and Vietnam." But how, then, explain the fact that the loss of the most classic of all imperialist regions—the 700 million people in the Chinese market—has had little effect upon American prosperity? As Varga, the Soviet economist, pointed out toward the end of his life, the failure of the standard Leninist scenario in that regard is rather striking.

Or there is Gunnar Myrdal's grim, but quite accurate, comment: ". . . if the whole of the Indian subcontinent . . . should sink into the ocean tomorrow, this would cause only minor disturbances to the curves of international trade."

This point cannot be glossed over on the grounds that though American dependence upon the Third World is no longer massive, it remains strategic, i.e., that this nation must have access to certain crucial raw materials. For even as Kolko makes this point with regard to bauxite, he is forced to recognize that "in recent years technical innovations have increased the utility of domestic ores." For the fact of the matter is that if the American economy were really threatened with regard to some crucial raw material, it would quickly develop a substitute for it.

Thus Lenin's theory of the essential and inevitable role of imperialism in Asia, Africa and Latin America no longer holds. The Third World is less important to the advanced capitalist powers than at any time in their history; and their prosperity is much more dependent on the maintenance of high mass consumption within their own borders—and within the other wealthy countries—than upon the exploitation of the world's hungry.[3]

## II

But if capitalism, and particularly a capitalism being transformed by structural reform, is not inevitably fated to global wrongdoing, that does not mean that it has become benign. On the contrary. Subordinating the needs of the ex-colonial masses to the priorities of big corporations may not be absolutely essential for the developed countries, but it is certainly profitable and convenient, the "natural" course of action for a society that reveres the market mechanism. So if it is not necessary to revolutionize these economies totally in order to permit them to foster economic development, there must be a most determined political struggle that will work basic, and socialist-tending, changes in them.

Specific proposals toward this goal will be made in a moment. But first it is necessary to understand how capitalism since World War II has, for all its generosity and concern, acted to perpetuate poverty and economic backwardness in the Third World. By doing this one gets a better idea of precisely which systematic injustices must be dismantled by a positive program. One also begins to deprive Americans of their excessive international innocence. Because this nation has only rarely been colonialist, i.e., sent troops in to control foreigners, the man on the street is usually blissfully unaware of the degree to which it has been imperialist, i.e., used economic power to dominate other countries. Indeed, our aid and trade policies, which the average citizen probably thinks have been much too altruistically devoted to serving Asia, Africa and Latin America, have actually been money-makers.*

Even when it was sincerely trying to be decent in its provisions for foreign aid, the United States Government was—sometimes unwittingly, but not always—shoring up the capitalist system and guaranteeing the profits of rich corporations. The Marshall Plan and other funds for Europe were outright grants; the monies for the hungry lands have increasingly been loans. The aid was assigned according to military and political priorities rather than on the basis of economic need, so that the principal beneficiaries were Chiang's Taiwan, South Korea and Vietnam. Until the Chinese invasion of 1962, India, the largest democratic country in the world, received a pittance compared to various anti-Communist dictators. Moreover, much of the money provided by Washington was "tied"—the recipient nation was obliged to spend it in the American market, even if the goods it needed were more expensive there—and thus was more of a subsidy to American business than genuine aid to the people of the Third World.

In almost every case it was also an explicit aim of American aid to promote a favorable atmosphere for private American investment. Sometimes this was blatant; India was threatened with a cutoff of aid because it would not agree to terms proposed by American oil corporations setting up a fertilizer industry; in Peru (before the generals took over, and perhaps as an incitement to that coup) the funds for a domestic peace corps were actually held up because it would not be sufficiently pliable in oil negotiations.

American trade was organized on a similar anti-developmental basis. In the official theory, the optimum use of the globe's re-

---

* In what follows I will summarize an analysis that was documented in *Toward a Democratic Left* and then explore some of the more recent evidence to show that it remains very much in force.

sources would be achieved if all equal nations did business with one another without any restrictions. So the United States, the most powerful economy in the history of mankind, demanded reciprocity from countries struggling to cope with starvation and backwardness. When the American corporations did go into those lands, they tended to create enclaves of modernity, or else to exploit cheap labor. In either case, their activity was usually inimical to balanced economic development. Through the repatriation of profits—or, where that was legally difficult, through bookkeeping tricks in which the parent company in the United States charged inflated prices to its overseas subsidiaries—the companies took enormous sums out of these areas.

But the American Government did not passively enjoy the economic trends which reward the rich nations and penalize the poor; it encouraged these evils. Thus tariffs in the United States (as in most industrial countries) discriminate against processed materials, i.e., provide disincentives for industrialization, through high tariffs, and low-tariff incentives for those countries which will passively accept their role as a raw materials producer. Before the "Kennedy Round" of tariff negotiations, officials, including President Kennedy himself, expressed the fear that these talks would only serve to create a "rich man's club." That is what happened, for almost all the proposals of the poor countries were either turned down or ignored.

Most of these barriers to development erected by the advanced capitalist powers—and by the fat Communists, too, for as Che Guevara pointed out bitterly, they charge their allies world market prices for their help—are unknown to the average citizen. They involve the intricacies of a global market mechanism that prices the sweat of poor people cheap and the work of sophisticated machines dear, or else complicated international agreements comprehensible mainly to experts. All the man in the street knows is that his government is giving money away to foreigners and that the recipients are ungrateful. Indeed, his resentment is one of the reasons why capital outflows to the poor countries from the advanced capitalist powers declined during the sixties (it fell, for instance, from .87 percent of GNP in 1965 to .72 percent in 1966).

Yet the sophisticated reality is that both aid and trade are money-makers and have the effect of shifting funds from the hungry to the affluent. In June of 1969 Gabriel Valdes, the Foreign

Minister of Chile and spokesman for a Latin-American conference on development, told Richard Nixon, "The present interests of development policy in Latin America are not identical with those of the United States. These interests are even progressively becoming contradictory. Popular belief thinks that our continent gets real financial aid. The reality of the figures shows the contrary. We can say that Latin America contributes more to the financing of the United States and the other industrial countries. *. . . The sums of money taken out of our countries are much larger than the sums invested."* (Emphasis added.)

Mr. Nixon responded to this plea by emphasizing the role of American private investment in Latin America, i.e., by proposing to intensify those policies that had led to the evil defined by Valdes. It was, one diplomat said, "a dialogue of the deaf."

As Charles K. Wilber computed some of the figures, between 1950 and 1964 United States investments of all kinds in the developing countries was a little more than $6 billion. During the same period the outflow of income from the developing countries to the United States amounted to $21.5 billion—a deficit of $15.3 billion. Meanwhile, the developed economies were treated much better. During the same period they took in $14.3 billion in investment and sent out on $11.5 billion in return, thus showing a positive balance of $2.7 billion. And this pattern is typical of the entire post-war period in both aid and trade: money was sent to the rich, tribute was extracted from the poor.

Two recent cases in point—copper and coffee—illuminate the brutal power relationships that stand just behind these statistics.

In the summer of 1969 Kenneth Kaunda of Zambia announced that he was going to nationalize his country's copper industry. At first there was something of a panic reaction in the advanced nations, and *The New York Times* reported that it was "a prevalent opinion among copper industry analysts" that Kaunda's move would drive the technicians out of Zambia. But the *Times* reported, there were those who felt that the technicians would stay "if the price were right." Within a very short time Kaunda had to respond to the threats of a boycott. In August, 1969, he told Congressman Ogden Reid that the nationalization would be carried out with "fairness and equity."

As the *Times* reported, "Mr. Reid said Mr. Kaunda had also left him with a clear impression of his wish to maintain an investment climate in Zambia. The President had also said that he intended to conduct both the negotiations and the subsequent operations on the basis of sound business principles." In cash terms that meant that Kaunda was retreating from his original position that the owners would be compensated on the basis of the "book value" of their investment. Now, he told Reid, they would receive payment for the "true value" of their holdings.

Under these circumstances nationalization would profit the private owners. As *The Economist* put it, "The shrewdest businessmen in that part of the world have argued for some time that a 49% share in a business whose success is underwritten by government participation may be more valuable than 100% of a concern exposed to all the political winds that blow."

In the course of these events no foreign troops were dispatched to Zambia and the country's sovereignty remained completely intact. Yet the realities of the economic market were more powerful in limiting Kaunda's scope of action than an expeditionary force. His small nation was, in effect, less sovereign within its own borders than the copper companies and their allies. Had he proceeded on a radical, anti-capitalist basis, he would have learned that his mines were all but worthless, just as Mossadegh found out that Iranian oil lost its value the moment he challenged the Anglo-Iranian oil company in the early fifties.

Coffee is as instructive an example as copper. After oil it is the second most valuable commodity in world trade: forty-two underdeveloped countries generate $2.3 billion of coffee business which directly involves twenty million people in bringing in the crop. In the sixties an International Coffee Agreement was set up to stabilize prices—in theory, to help the developing nations involved—but over a seven-year period it pegged prices far below those of the preceding seven years. When the Agreement came up for renewal, American interests became quite aggressive. Brazil had, with American help, set up instant coffee plants. As long as the product was sold only to Brazilians, and Americans received a portion of the profit for their troubles, that was fine. But when Brazil entered the American market with a cheap instant coffee it was a completely different matter.

In order to appease the American firms Brazil announced that it would impose a thirteen-cent tax on its own instant coffee exports, i.e., a developing nation would voluntarily make one of its major products less competitive so as to guarantee the returns of corporations in an affluent country. But that was not enough—

the American firms held out for a seventeen-cent tax. And they threatened to opt out of the International Coffee Agreement if the Brazilians refused to go along with their proposal.

Here again, sovereignty was left undisturbed—the repressive Brazilian government had, after all, been taken over from Leftists, to the delight of Washington—even as it was subverted.

And in August, 1971, when Richard Nixon unilaterally subverted the international monetary system, he imposed an extra tariff on manufactured goods without any reference to what that policy would cost the Third World. The outcry from Japan, France, Germany and the other big powers was also confined to indignation over what America's new protectionism would mean to the advanced and relatively affluent economies. But, as the Latin American countries in the UN regional economic grouping told the world, the real victims of the Nixon approach would be the poor of the world. Once again, all the rhetoric about a commitment to economic development to the contrary notwithstanding, Europe and America had acted as a rich man's club.

So the exploitation of the ex-colonial world is a declining component of advanced capitalist prosperity and not, as in the Leninist analysis, an absolute necessity, yet there are powerful forces that profit from it. Therefore a socialist political movement could reverse these trends without first revolutionizing the very basis of society, but only through effecting the most profound structural changes.[4]

## III

In order to aid in economic development the advanced countries must reject the priorities of the world market that have guided their aid and trade policies. Socialists in these countries, therefore, must take the lead in attacking and fundamentally modifying the global calculus of profit that now misallocates international resources.

Here again, it would be much more exhilarating to propose to do away with the capitalist system, nationally and internationally, and proceed to constitute the Parliament of Man. That, to put it mildly, is not on the political agenda in the West, and even if it were, the details of that grand vision are even more vague than the principles the Left has had so much difficulty in applying within capitalist society. So if socialists content themselves with incantations of a coming world apocalypse, that is a way of turning one's back on the hungry.

What is minimally required and politically possible is a re-structuring of the world market itself. Such a reform would be the international equivalent to the New Deal or the changes wrought by the British Labour Party after World War II. The international economy, like domestic America and Britain in the thirties, is under the rule of laissez-faire. Now there must be a welfare world instead.

In order to advance in that direction it is necessary to confront, and basically modify, one of the contradictions of capitalism. As a producer, the businessman buys labor power and it is therefore very much in his interest to keep wages down, to destroy unions, to limit or oppose taxes and government spending, and so on. As a seller, however, the very same businessman wants as large a market as possible. If he pays low wages himself, he still wishes, so to speak, that other businessmen will be lavish with their employees so that they will be able to buy his product. Historically, business's unquestioned dominance of Western capitalism was based on cutting costs and keeping wages low. It was the labor and socialist movements in Europe and the liberals in the United States who finally demonstrated, in theory and in practice, that high mass consumption was in the interests of the rich as well as the poor. The conservatives were, to be sure, only partly convinced: their Keynesianism is reactionary and seeks to stimulate the economy by providing tax windfalls to wealthy individuals and corporations rather than by social spending. Yet everyone but the neanderthals now understands the connection between full employment and general prosperity within an advanced economy.

On the world market, however, most theory and all practice are still in the grip of assumptions that have been discredited within the sophisticated neo-capitalisms. In vigorously using aid and trade policy to keep the Third World underdeveloped, Western capitalism only sees the poor countries under the guise of cost and competition. There are, to be sure, occasional executives or business journalists who glimpse the advantages *for the advanced countries* of global economic development. Thus Sanford Rose writes in *Fortune*, "If the developed countries let in more labor-intensive agricultural and industrial products from the underdeveloped world, they will be able to shift part of their work force into higher technology industries. Such a shift can only lead to higher average productivity and augmented income levels of the developed countries."

Rose's point has the virtue of understanding that tariff protection for low-wage backward sectors of the economy is bad for the metropolitan powers as well as for the ex-colonies. Yet even he still assumes that Asia, Africa and Latin America will primarily supply "backward" goods. In fact, the modernization of the Third World is in the interests of the entire world, even the capitalists. But the latter are, by virtue of an institutional defect in their vision, incapable of seeing how social justice would promote their own selfishness. The Left must tutor them on this point once again, all the while seeking new ways to limit the tribute paid to profit within the welfare world as well as in the welfare state.

But if capital, then, is not going to push for the industrialization of the world, what about labor? The answer to this question is not an easy one. It is quite possible to write a scenario in which the organized workers join with business in order to perpetuate the privileges of the affluent economies in the global division of labor. And it is also quite possible that those same workers, acting out of a much more sophisticated and humane self-interest, will fight for the structural reform of the international market.

The bleaker prospect is more easily put. As A. Emmanuel wrote in a French Marxist study of the problem, "it is not the conservatism of the leaders that has reined in the revolutionary *élan* of the masses, as one believes in the Marxist-Leninist camp; it is the slow but constant growing awareness of the masses that they belong to privileged, exploiting nations that constrained their leaders to revise their ideology so as not to lose their clientele." That, of course, is a key element in all the Maoist and Third World versions of Marxism.

In the United States in 1970 and 1971 it might have seemed that the trade unions were following that prediction. The AFL-CIO, long a major political force for free trade, took a protectionist position on a number of crucial questions in those years. And yet, if one examines the reasons for that move, it is possible to see the basis of a much more positive attitude, one which does not retreat from free trade but actually seeks to go beyond it. As a district president of the International Union of Electrical

Workers (IUE) explained labor's change of mind, it had been occasioned by the recent trend of American business to export jobs to Taiwan, Hong Kong, Mexico and other low-wage areas. These corporations—and they include giants like IBM and RCA —had once been protectionist, i.e., for protecting their profits against foreign profiteers. But now that the internationalization of the corporation permitted them to take advantage of sweatshop conditions, they suddenly declared themselves free traders.

One labor response to this situation is protectionism; another would be to internationalize the struggle against capital. That did not happen according to the Marxian prediction in the early stages of capitalism. But, as the IUE official's article makes clear, it could conceivably become a necessity in the epoch of the global corporation. Here again, the analogy to the New Deal is apropos. For decades the American Federation of Labor was an organization of the skilled elite, hardly touching the lives of the immigrant masses. But then, in the 1930s, John L. Lewis of the United Mine Workers became the dynamic leader in a great campaign to unionize the unorganized industrial workers. Lewis, as Chapter XI showed, did not begin as a radical, had opposed the rebel forces within his own union and had voted for Herbert Hoover in 1932. However, his practical desire to protect his own membership in the coal industry forced him to take on the steel corporations that were in effective control of the mines; and a campaign to unionize steel could only be effective as part of a national battle to bring all the industrial workers into the labor movement.

Today, if the various labor movements of the advanced capitalist economies are seen as an elite, then those masses in the Third World might be analogous to the industrial workers in the United States. And it would then be as necessary for the Electrical Workers in the American Northwest to concern themselves about wages and working conditions in Taiwan and Mexico as it was for Lewis to turn from coal to steel, to the mass of the unorganized. The unions could fight to ban imports from countries that sweat their workers—or they could try to raise the wages of the world and, through planning, shift manpower in the metropolitan centers into socially useful jobs.[5]

This last scenario might seem far-fetched. Yet at the 1969 Congress of the Socialist International in England, almost all of the delegates agreed that it was necessary to move in just this way toward a welfare world. The men and women at the Con-

gress were not dreamers, but the leaders of successful and powerful political movements rooted in the working class of their various
countries. Moreover, the discussion was candid. Jan Tinbergen,
who delivered a report to the Congress and was to become the
first laureate of the new Nobel Prize in economics, remarked
somewhat sadly that "there is not much left of that common
internationalism we socialists once had." But then he added,
"in questions of economic development we can have that spirit
once again."

Within a year there was a fairly vivid, practical demonstration
of what the point raised at Eastbourne might mean. During a
fight between British auto workers and the Ford company's
operation in that country, the leaders of the International Metal
Workers Federation met with Prime Minister Edward Heath. So
it was that Leonard Woodcock, the president of the American
United Automobile Workers, joined with Hugh Scanlon of the
British engineering unions and Jack Jones of the transport workers.
This international delegation was trying to counter a Ford threat
to move his factory out of England if wages went up. At a conference of the International Metal Workers Secretariat of the
International Confederation of Free Trade Unions (ICFTU)
shortly before the encounter with Heath, Victor Feather, the
general secretary of Britain's Trades Union Congress, had declared
that if governments did not control the giant multinational companies, the companies will soon control them.

*The Economist,* Britain's sophisticated, pro-business weekly,
summarized these trends in 1971: "The development of international union strength," it said, "should now probably be a steady
process. In some ways, the multinational companies will be their
own worst enemies. Just as the international consumer is encouraged to identify with products from specific multinationals, so
are workers increasingly identifying themselves as, say, 'Ford'
workers, irrespective of what national subsidiary of Ford they
work in. Thus increasingly the demand for parity of work conditions and reward between the international branches of the same
multinational will become a spontaneous one." If this assessment
turns out to be accurate, then the multinational corporation may
make an enormous contribution to the internationalist consciousness of the workers of the world.

So it is possible within a society transitional between capitalism
and socialism to make structural reforms that could enormously

benefit the Third World—and possible that socialist mass movements could make such programs practical and political. In outlining a few of them, it is, of course, impossible to be detailed
or precise. The Third World itself is an extraordinarily heterog-
enous collection of nations, some of them still trying to overcome
tribalism, others on the verge of modernity. But even within
these limits one can evoke the kinds of changes within the affluent economies which socialists might achieve in order to reach
out to the majority of mankind.

First of all, there must be a profound change in tariff policies.
The present, and outrageous, reality was described by the Pearson Commission of the World Bank: after the Kennedy Round,
the tariffs on the manufactured goods of the developing nations
were greater than those charged against the developed ones.
Such a situation makes a mockery of the pretense of the major
capitalist powers that they are interested in the economic well-
being of the people of Asia, Africa and Latin America. But even
more to the point, this kind of discrimination against the impoverished countries is unnecessary, for the number of jobs that
would be affected if textiles and other products of the Third
World gained free entry to the advanced capitalist market is
relatively small. If the 1965 rate of textile imports from developing areas were tripled, there are responsible economists who argue
that only 11,400 jobs would be displaced in the United States.

Even assuming that this estimate is wildly optimistic, the way
to deal with the problem is not to continue our present policy
of subsidizing a low-wage American industry through protectionist tariffs and thereby depriving the developing countries of a
chance to get dollars in one of the few areas where they are competitive. In this context, a United States policy to shift the
workers endangered by such imports would not simply make
sense in terms of the country's manpower needs, it would be a
component of a democratic foreign policy as well.

A cessation of evil-doing in tariff policy is not enough. There
must be positive measures, too. The governments of the advanced
nations should discourage substitutes for crucial Third World
products like coffee, tea and cocoa, and they should favor commodities like rubber and jute which are threatened by competition from synthetics. And with crops that can be grown in
both the rich and poor lands, like beet sugar, the latter should
be given the opportunity to supply the market. In all of these cases

where agricultural goods are involved, the problems are even fewer than in the case of textiles. For in Europe and the United States there have been public programs for controlling farm output for some time. What is required is to orient these efforts, in part at least, toward encouraging economic development in the ex-colonies. The machinery is already there.

In line with these steps the big powers should also adopt the very modest suggestion made by the Groups of 77 in the Charter of Algiers: that the advanced economies give a share to imports in the increment of their consumption. This does not demand restitution for past wrongs; it does not even require the expenditure of any great amount of money. It only calls for planning a role for the developing nations as affluence increases. In this way, the growing wealth of the developed nations can be used to decrease the gap between the rich and poor of the globe. The recent trends, of course, all point to an unconscionable increase in that disparity.

Another crucial area for innovation is research.

The developing countries are all in desperate need of the kind of research that will apply scientific knowledge to their problems. Yet none of them have the kind of educational and corporate infrastructure that can turn out this kind of applied science. The "green revolution" is an example of how the advanced nations can make an enormous contribution by a relatively small expenditure of funds. One need not fall into that "technological euphoria" which sees such a research advance as a miraculous solution for all ills. As Chapter X pointed out in summarizing Gunnar Myrdal's critique of this notion, there must be basic political and economic changes if these new seeds are truly to benefit all the people of the hungry countries. But having emphasized this fact, there is no doubt that the agricultural discoveries financed by the Ford and Rockefeller foundations can be part of an extremely important advance in the food production of nations faced with the specter of starvation.

There is another avenue of research that has an extremely great potential: population control. In the period 1960–1967, the Third World increased its Gross Domestic Product by 4.6 percent, a growth figure that compares quite favorably with European and American rates at comparable moments in their development. But because of the pressure of population, the per capita increase was only 2 percent (2.2 percent in Asia, 1.5 percent in Africa and 1.8 percent in Latin America). If science in the advanced countries could find some way for effective mass birth control in a developing nation—and the Pearson Commission argues that many, many leads have not even been investigated—that could make a major contribution to ending global poverty.

But a caveat is in order here, one which enormously, but necessarily, complicates the research task. If the contraceptive techniques that are discovered in the course of such an undertaking are only for use in the developing countries, they will encounter nationalistic resistance. For it might then seem that the wealthy economies were promoting a cheap way out of the problem of world poverty: by attacking the right of nonwhites to decide on how to limit their families. But if the population controls were of such a nature that they can be applied in advanced as well as in developing countries, there would be no impression of imposing a policy. Instead, the rich lands would simply be sharing scientific knowledge they themselves use.

Finally, in terms of orienting world trade toward economic development one must confront that institution, the multinational corporation, head-on.

In a projection made by the National Industrial Conference Board, American corporations will have 25 percent of the "free world" Gross National Product of $1 trillion by 1975 if present trends continue. And Sanford Rose writes of the global companies: "The extent of their involvement is such that, to some degree, these companies now regard the world rather than the nation state as their natural and logical operating area. . . . Carrying multi-nationalism to the logical extreme, a corporation will concentrate its production in the area where costs are lowest, and build up its sales where the market is most lucrative."

Actually, one does not have to speculate about the future power of such entities. In 1967 the corporate product of General Motors was worth $20.2 billion, which made it the eighteenth largest industrial power in the world, ranking just behind the Netherlands, but ahead of Argentina and Belgium. The Ford Motor Company was twenty-third in the world standings, Standard Oil of New Jersey was twenty-fourth, Royal Dutch Shell thirty-second, General Electric thirty-fourth.

It is not just the size of these businesses that is so awesome; it is the fact that their multinational character allows them to evade the control of various governments. When, for example, the Rumanians wanted to buy a paper mill on credit from an American firm, the transaction was against the law in the United States. So the company simply had the matter handled by its English subsidiary. Or, in those developing nations with foreign exchange difficulties that forbid profits being used for dividends beyond a certain limit, "a multi-national corporation could simply 'take out' its dividends by raising prices on intra-corporate sales proportionately."

These problems, as one might imagine, have already been examined from a sophisticated corporate point of view. George W. Ball, a leading member of the economic and political establishments in the United States, has proposed an International Companies Law to be administered by a supranational body which would place "limitations, for example, on the restrictions that a nation state might be permitted on companies established under its sanction." From Ball's point of view, the problem is to get more freedom for the corporations. Similarly, Jean-Jacques Servan-Schreiber's call for the Europeanization of business is designed to maximize corporate priorities—in this case, to get industrial units big enough to compete with American companies.

But there could be an International Companies Law written from a standpoint quite different from Ball's: to bring the multi-national corporations under control. Rather than limiting what the various impoverished nations could do in order to contain the giant enterprises from the advanced economies, it would make it impossible for the corporations to siphon out cash through pricing policies, or to invest only in areas of high profitability without any regard for social consequences. It could, through taxing or licensing the global giants, provide a source of revenue for international economic planning. Plainly the details of such a world statute are well beyond the limits of this book; but the idea of it is not.

Indeed, this issue may well open up an entire new chapter in socialist theory and practice. In the nineteenth century the Left saw capital as nationalist and the workers as internationalist. In the late twentieth century the terms have been reversed somewhat: capital is international, workers are often fiercely nationalist. But, as has been seen, if the labor movements of the advanced countries are to deal with this situation, they will have to become internationalist once again, out of the necessities of daily struggle.

And so, as time goes on, the socialist plank of nationalization must give way to the idea of internationalization. If, as is quite possible, supranational institutions emerge out of the drive for European unification, the socialists of the Old World will unquestionably form a Continental caucus (as they do in the Parliament of Europe). Their program will seek to subject the Europe-wide institutions to democratic control, and to establish common, and high, standards of wages in the social services. That, however, is only a first step, for eventually there must be international planning, international democratization, and at that point the socialists will either recover their original internationalism or else become irrelevant.[6]

## IV

What is required, then, is world and regional economic planning.

The international corporations have been engaged in just such global calculations for some time now. There is no reason that the techniques that have been employed in the private sector in the service of profit cannot be used in a world public sector. The economists at the United Nations have already done work on an econometric model, and that could well provide a point of departure for a qualitative increase in multilateral foreign aid which is distributed not according to the priorities of diplomats and the military, but on the basis of need and the ability to use funds.

For, as I documented in *Toward a Democratic Left,* one of the reasons that American economic aid programs have not been much more effective is that fostering development in the Third World has been their last purpose. At the very height of the Marshall Plan the United States contributed more than 2 percent of its GNP for the reconstruction of capitalism in Europe and even went so far as to plan trade discrimination against its own corporations, i.e., it would not let American oil companies follow policies inimical to European development. If this country could even approximate that singleness of purpose with regard to Asia, Africa and Latin America, the destiny of the planet would be different.

Basically, it is not racism that makes American policy-makers differentiate so sharply between Europe and the predominantly nonwhite Third World. There were cultural, religious and political ties to the Old World, but even more to the point, the investment in the reconstruction of European capitalism paid off handsomely. In saying this I do not for a moment want to stoop to the vulgar theory that the United States acted out of a shrewd desire to earn a few more dollars. The anti-Communism of the liberals in that period was unquestionably genuine and related to a concern for democracy, not for private property (reactionary anti-Communism is another, and cruder, matter). But when this complexity of motivation is granted, it still is true that this country found it "natural" to put European capitalism back together, and that it is, among other things, angered by the socialist rhetoric of so many of the new states, and by their (from a capitalist point of view) cavalier attitude toward corporate property.

When the American aid effort turned to the Third World, the commitment was phrased in the idealistic language of Harry Truman's Point Four, but the reality was that reactionary anti-Communists got most of the money and that the investment decisions were made from the point of view of political and military strategy. Similarly, Soviet aid followed the same course and was even channeled to Middle Eastern governments that kept Communists in jail when that served the purposes of *Realpolitik*. The French concentrated their efforts on former colonies which were integrated into the metropolitan economy and remained a source of profit after independence as well as before. And the British promoted their own sterling zone for similar reasons.

This is why the internationalization of aid is so crucial: to remove these funds from the domain of the political-military tacticians and make them an instrument of planned world development.

This does not mean, as Richard Nixon proposed in 1970, that new international organizations should be set up which are subject to the control of the big powers. In the World Bank and the International Monetary Fund, for instance, voting rights are weighted on the basis of how much each country subscribes, and the developing nations only have a 35 percent voice. This, one suspects, is the basis of the Bank's decision in 1956–1957 that a $600 million loan to India would be conditioned upon a reduction of the public sector. The World Bank also has a policy of discouraging oil investments on the part of recipient countries on the ground that this area should be left to the major oil companies. And Thomas Balogh, economic advisor to the Wilson Labour Government in the sixties, rightly commented that the

"International Monetary Fund fulfills the role of the colonial administration of enforcing the rules of the game" in its international transactions.

At the 1970 meeting of the World Bank in Copenhagen the poor countries were quite explicit about the way in which that institution followed big-power commercial priorities. Loans, they said, were strictly supervised and evaluated on a profit criterion, but money for broad developmental programs was not available. And, the representative of the Third World pointed out, their foreign debt had increased to $55 billion and the service charges on it were growing twice as fast as their export earnings. At the Lima meeting of the Inter-American Development Bank in May, 1971, the charges were even more political. President Juan Velasco of Peru pointed out—with support from Chile, Bolivia, Ecuador, and Uruguay—that after his country's dispute with the International Petroleum Company and its guardian, the United States of America, Peru had been cold-shouldered by the World Bank.

But even when such obvious political interests are not involved, it is of the very nature of the banker's approach to economic development that he favor conservative economic policies which will minimize his risk rather than encourage social innovation. "Loan officials," Jerome Levinson and Juan de Onis write of the Alliance for Progress, "have consistently required that countries seeking financial assistance undertake monetary stabilization programs; they have not required programs of social reform."

All of this is not to suggest that the agents of international capital at the World Bank, the Monetary Fund, or in the Alliance are fiendishly conniving to foster special interests in the guise of aiding economic development (although that most vulgar Marxist scenario does sometimes apply). These institutions, and the men who run them, are often committed to a sophisticated and sincere intervention on behalf of the hungry. The problem is not that they are dishonest, but that they operate on a capitalist calculus even when they try to be charitable. Such a way of reckoning is inimical to the struggles of the Third World and so there must be global economic planning with a new system of values.

Indeed in April of 1971, Richard M. Nixon offered a persuasive program of exactly what should not be done. By inverting it, so to speak, the Left can make good use of the President's conservative perspective. Mr. Nixon wants a United States International

Development Institute which, as the White House summarized the program, would set conditions upon the recipient country, concentrate on a few key areas, be managed by a board "composed of individuals from both government and the private sector," and be managed "on a businesslike basis." It would "carry out its projects largely through private institutions and contractors. . . ." It is difficult to say whether the politics of the Nixon scheme, whose interventionism would be a target for every nationalist, Left, Right, and Center, in the Third World, is more foolish than its economics, which rely on a business calculus which is the problem, not the solution, for the ex-colonies.

What is actually needed is international planning and spending administered on an economic and social calculus.

The United Nations has done brilliant work in economic research in this area, particularly through its various regional commissions. It would not be too expensive or difficult to concentrate enormous scientific resources in that effort and to use its structure for the kind of research-and-development emphasis outlined previously. But once the economic models are set up, once there are clearer indications of how monies must be used for development, there must be a major transfer of funds from the rich to the poor nations.

The recent trends have been in the wrong direction. An America which made an average contribution of .89 percent of its GNP through the Marshall Plan, and once reached a rate of 2 percent of GNP, in 1968 was spending only .38 percent of GNP on foreign aid. And that figure is somewhat inflated, since it includes a food program that is only tangentially related to economic development (and is directly related to American farm politics). Moreover, aid in the United States is subject to annual appropriations and is thus quite uncertain.

An immediate socialist program within the advanced nations would seek to reverse these trends and to institutionalize long-term, automatic, multinational aid. One way of doing this would be to get all developed countries to commit themselves to devote 1 percent of their GNP, in the form of private and public capital, to Third World development. The Pearson Commission of the World Bank specified that 70 percent of that amount should be in the form of government aid, and only 30 percent in private monies. A more radical approach—and a better one—is the idea that the advanced economies pass a tax on themselves which would be used to fund international development on a regular, and multilateral, basis. In Rosenstein-Rodan's version of the idea, it would function as a progressive "income tax" on the national incomes of the advanced countries. The UN's Committee for Development Planning has come up with another variant of this idea: a development aid tax which is charged only against the specifically "affluent" goods in the big economies (cars, refrigerators, TV sets, etc.).

The details are, in a sense, quite unimportant. What is crucial— and central to the socialist commitment to a welfare world—is that there must be a regular source of funds, not raised through annual political battles and spent by the military and the diplomats, that will supply the material basis for implementing indicative world planning and supplementing it by foreign aid. Just as the socialist battle within the advanced countries is to limit the power of private wealth by placing more and more resources at the disposal of democratically determined public priorities, the same struggle must now take place on a world scale.[7]

## V

Even if socialists and their allies were to win the advanced nations to the most sweeping reforms of trade and aid policy, that would not end the agony of the Third World. The developing countries desperately need capital from without, for, as Gunnar Myrdal has noted, even the money available from the World Bank, which is supported by government guarantees, effectively has an interest rate more than double that paid by the developed nations in their early stages. But they also require enormous political, social and economic changes from within if they are to be able to utilize these resources and their own domestic potential.

At this point a crucial issue is posed: Can this developmental process be carried out with a minimum of coercion and a maximum of consent so as to make economic growth move in the direction of democracy and eventually of socialism itself?

Zbigniew Brzezinski was a member of the State Department Policy Planning Agency and an advisor to Hubert Humphrey in the 1968 Presidential campaign. As such he was associated with

political leaders who were officially optimistic about the possibilities of freedom in the ex-colonial lands. Yet he writes, ". . . it
is difficult to conceive how democratic institutions (derived
largely from Western experience but typical only of the more
stable and wealthy Western nations) will endure in a country like
India—or how they will develop elsewhere."

That, I believe, is too sweeping a judgment, even though it
does contain elements of a hard truth. In saying this, I am not
suggesting that the details of Western democracy—the parliamentary system as in Europe, the tripartite division of powers as in
the United States—can, or should, be exported to Asia, Africa
and Latin America. As Gunnar Myrdal remarks, "it is not possible
to predict the type of government any single underdeveloped
country will have five years from now." What is being asserted
is that the totalitarian denial of rights is not a necessary precondition—or even a goad—to economic development, that it might
be possible to find paths to modernity which recognize the freedom of the individual to nonviolently affect the policies and
personnel of his society.

In developing this theme it would be preposterous to think
that a few pages of analysis could suggest policies that would
solve the problems of the entire, and most heterogeneous, Third
World. There is no one strategy that applies in Chad, Venezuela
and India. But there are common problems that bedevil all these
lands and it is thus possible to give, in broadest outline, a hint of
how they might be dealt with short of totalitarianism.

The basic task can be defined simply enough; it is the question of how to accomplish it that has led to profound, and often
murderous, differences. The developing nations must extract a
surplus from their economy (and from foreign aid) not to be
consumed, but invested. However, all the existing institutions and
arrangements inherited from the age of direct Western dominance
are designed to thwart that undertaking. They channel the
surplus not to productive use, but to the profits of the metropolitan
powers and the luxuries of the indigenous elite.

When a country in this position challenges foreign control over
its resources, it is met by stern resistance on the world market
and can be forced to back down, as the examples of copper and
coffee showed. But even if, following the assumption of this section, that policy could be reversed in the advanced lands, there
is still the problem of systematic domestic misuse of the poor na-

tion's wealth. This is not confined to the obvious and outrageous expenditures of native feudalists allied with Western imperialism. It might include, in India, the small uneconomic plots of land owned by individual peasants unable to scratch out anything but a mere subsistence, or the absentee ownership of the soil by dedicated civil servants.

In order to challenge these entrenched patterns there must be a determined, effective central government. That is the first, and perhaps most crucial, aspect of a socialist development policy.

The developing states, including some that call themselves socialist, tend to be either "soft" or totalitarian. In the former case, there are deficiencies in legislation and particularly in law observance and enforcement, corruption, the collusion of officials and powerful interests. In the latter, there is a terroristic accumulation of capital. The point is to find a governmental form between these extremes: one which is forceful, but not dedicated to the destruction of all opposition and dissent. By far and large, American policy has frustrated this effort throughout the entire post-World War II period.

The United States, even in its most generous moments, as in the early days of the Alliance for Progress, has stood for a free-enterprise solution to the problems of development. And yet, as Celso Furtado wrote of Latin America, "development cannot be the simple result of forces acting within the market. Only a conscious deliberate policy of the central organs of government can really lead to such development. . . . Since the present ruling classes don't understand this problem and obstinately maintain the status quo, those in Latin America who fight effectively for development play, whether they know it or not, a revolutionary role." This insight challenges the sincere liberal wisdom of the Kennedy Alliance and it is totally counterposed to the American insistence on the dominance of the private sector in the countries that are to receive its aid.

Ironically, a country that is often cited as one of the very best examples of the effectiveness of American aid proves this "un-American" point. On Taiwan in 1970 investments in state enterprises were 70 percent of private investments and the government runs a number of large, and profitable, businesses. Indeed, the four largest companies on the island—China Petroleum, Taiwan Power, Taiwan Sugar and Taiwan Fertilizer—are nationalized. This trend toward public ownership on Taiwan became particularly marked in the late sixties and was justified by officials as "just a matter of practical requirements." For the fact of the matter is that there is neither sufficient capital nor capitalists in such a country to facilitate modernization and the state must act in their place. This is true even when the government is controlled by an aging dictator like Chiang, who professes to be a champion of free enterprise.

But if there is a strong government, that does not make industrialization an easy matter. There are Marxists who have suggested a much too optimistic reading of this problem, implying that there is a preexisting economic surplus sufficient to finance modernization which only has to be mobilized by a determined revolutionary force. For instance, Ernest Mandel, the Belgian Trotskyist, quite rightly points to the luxury consumption of the old ruling class as a potential source of development funds. But he then goes on to argue that the vast unemployment and underemployment of human beings can be rather quickly turned into an asset by the planners.

This notion is based on the assumption, roughly true in the West, that those not in the labor market, or marginal to it, are like those who are in it. But in a country like India, as Myrdal has pointed out, the unemployed and underemployed suffer from malnutrition, they are deeply inculcated with anti-developmental attitudes and they cannot be quickly shifted into productive work. For that to happen there has to be a profound change in both their material and cultural situations. Since this point is one of the most important ones made in Myrdal's monumental study of South Asia—and since it is basic to the strategy being proposed here—it is worth examining in some detail.

Projecting their Western experiences on the map of the Third World, many economists in the advanced countries have argued that economic growth can only proceed by way of greater inequality. Consumption, which is a cost to the society, must be limited so that investment can be maximized. Myrdal argues that the truth is quite the contrary. The only way to create the material basis for awakening the millions from their cultural sleep, to make them capable of creating a modern society, is to provide them with more, not less. And the cost of doing this should not be computed as an expenditure, but as an interest-yielding investment in which the payoff is increased productivity.

This, of course, is directly counterposed to the Communist

model in either the Russian or Chinese variants. In both of these societies the totalitarian state substitutes itself for the bourgeoisie and uses its enormous coercive powers to extract the surplus from the people and invest it in those projects favored by the bureaucratic class. This approach "worked" in Russia, i.e., it did induce development, but at an unconscionable human cost and with the by-product of creating a new form of class society. But beyond these two profoundly negative aspects of this model, it is not at all certain that this strategy will pay off in the Third World. These nations start at levels far behind those of the Russians, with a population pressure never faced by Stalin, and with people who need the kind of consumption incentives that Myrdal described. It must be emphasized again that the lack of popular participation in China (or in Cuba) has been a factor making for enormous economic waste, and that even twenty years of totalitarianism under Mao has not succeeded in curbing the appetite of the Chinese peasant for his own individual plot of land.

In other words, the brutal *Realpolitik* of totalitarian economics in which consumption and genuine freedom are seen as inhibiting development may well be a utopian terrorism. In countries starting at levels well below that of Russia in 1917 an increase in social discipline is necessary, but so is greater equality and greater genuine participation of the people. The latter cannot be turned on and off from on high, as in the case of the various "spontaneous" movements sponsored by Mao, for the masses are quite capable of distinguishing the fraudulent from the real in this area. That, among other things, is why the Chinese peasants have apparently used every moment of "socialist" upheaval in their society in order to extend their own private ownership.

But supposing that there must be more equality, consumption and participation in the course of development, not less, how are they going to be financed? In most countries of the Third World the answer will have to be found in the agricultural sector. Industry is, of course, the key to modernization, but in the majority of these nations the rural population is still overwhelmingly dominant. In India, for instance, industrial progress between 1950 and 1967 has been quite rapid: while GNP went up by 1–1.5 percent a year and exports by 2 percent, the production of industry was climbing at a rate of 7 percent. This, however, means that the productivity of the modern sector is on the rise, i.e., that the advance not only does not create new jobs but might even be a source of unemployment. Therefore, as Myrdal and Prebisch among others have insisted, there must be a great effort to create a labor-intensive agricultural sector.

Myrdal's proposal as to how this should be done is fascinating in two particular aspects. First of all, it is a non-Marxist's scheme which comes fairly close to the perspective Lenin had for Russia before 1905; and secondly, in it a social democrat concludes that controlled capitalism is the answer in the next phase of Third World development. Myrdal wants to encourage the growth of commercial agriculture: to promote a class of progressive, innovating farm owners, and more wage work in the field. In order to blunt the social consequences of such a structural shift he is also for providing a small plot for the members of the landless underclass—as private, not village-shared, property. But the essence of his plan is the destruction of all the feudal (or despotic) encumbrances on the soil by governmental encouragement of commerce in the fields.

Consequently, this social democratic scholar writes that he is in favor of a "deliberate political choice" to promote "capitalist farming by allowing and encouraging the progressive entrepreneurs among the group of peasant landlords and privileged tenants to reap the full rewards of their strivings." This is something like Lenin's vision, described in Chapter VIII, of a "revolutionary dictatorship of the proletariat and peasantry" in Russia sweeping away feudalism in the most radical manner and installing a Left-wing capitalism in its place.

The difference is that in Myrdal's plan the government could well be social democratic and would utilize the increase in tax revenues that would result from the increased agricultural productivity for industrial development and the campaign for greater equality. In other areas, like Latin America, Myrdal believes that a more traditional land reform—dividing up the big farms of absentee owners into equal plots—would encourage growth. But the crucial, and compelling, point that he makes is that seemingly socialistic measures, like government support for cooperatives or village community control of economic functions, bolster inequality so long as the traditional economic and social relations are allowed to stand. A genuine development policy must, above all, overturn those inherited structures. Then it can turn to the question of exactly how agriculture modernization is to be accomplished in an empirical, unideological way.

In 1971 a study of poverty in India prepared by the Indian School of Political Economy advocated policies similar to those urged by Myrdal. It opposed a land reform that would vastly proliferate the number of small, and non-viable, plots and accepted the desirability of increasing the number of profitable farms. It also proposed guaranteed employment at a minimum wage for those who are willing to work and computed the cost of such a program at $450 million. The money, the report said, could be raised by a 15 percent cut in the consumer expenditure of the richest 5 percent and a 7.5 percent drop in the spending of the next 5 percent. Such an approach would obviously entail political difficulties but it is neither impossible nor does it require totalitarianism.

In this very brief survey, then, the most important conclusion is that an alternative to both capitalist and totalitarian modernization is not only necessary, but perhaps even possible. The capitalist road to the Third World future leads backward, for it reproduces and strengthens the very economic relationships that are the cause of underdevelopment. The Communist road, outside of Russia, may well be impractical as well as unconscionably terroristic, for poverty-stricken societies may not have the energy to respond even to coercion. So it is quite possible that socialist values, like equality and democratic participation, have a special relevance in Asia, Africa and Latin America. Contrary to what so many in the West have thought for so long, a radical concern for the individual may be an economic imperative in these areas of the world.

## VI

Socialism, then, has no miraculous scheme for the Third World; but it may have relevant proposals.

There is no way that these impoverished lands can quickly and easily leap the centuries into modernity. There is a socialist analysis of neo-colonialism that shows how, even though the Leninist model no longer applies, the economic power of the advanced nations is used, wittingly and unwittingly, to perpetuate the bondage of the majority of the peoples of the world. And there is a socialist description of the various "socialisms" of the Third World, the Communist and non-Communist, which sees them building new forms of class society in the process of a bureaucratic and totalitarian accumulation of capital.

There is a socialist program for the advanced nations that is clear and precise: to transform trade and aid policy so as to make it an instrument of, rather than a barrier to, economic development. There is a socialist approach for the developing countries themselves, but it is less explicit because it is confronting utterly new problems and must have a major component of experimentalism and empiricism. However, it does see that the central state must play a decisive role in attacking outmoded institutions and channeling an economic surplus into modernization. Unlike Communism, it seeks to do these things by stressing greater equality, more consumption, genuine participation. The "productionist" ideology of Maoism in which all institutions—party, trade unions, cooperatives, etc.—function to make people work harder and consume less may well be counterproductive as well as elitist and totalitarian.

Finally, those questions first posed by Western socialism in the 1890s have not yet been answered. There are possibilities, new departures, opportunities, but that is all. Ultimately the answer waits upon the creation of a world of equality.[8]

# XIV

## *Socialism*

FINALLY, THERE IS THE VISION of socialism itself.

This is not an immediate program, constrained by what is politically possible, or even the projection of a middle distance in which structural changes might take place. It is the idea of an utterly new society in which some of the fundamental limitations of human existence have been transcended. Its most basic premise is that man's battle with nature has been completely won and there is therefore more than enough of material goods for everyone. As a result of this unprecedented change in the environment, a psychic mutation takes place: invidious competition is no longer programmed into life by the necessity of a struggle for scarce resources; cooperation, fraternity and equality become natural. In such a world man's social productivity will reach such heights that compulsory work will no longer be necessary. And as more and more things are provided free, money, that universal equivalent by means of which necessities are rationed, will disappear.

That, in very brief outline, is what socialism ultimately is. It will never come to pass in its ideal form, yet it is important to detail the dream in order to better design each approximation of it.

There is a good reason for thus beginning the evocation of the far future *sotto voce*, by insisting upon the finite character of

socialism. It was first pointed out by that great anti-socialist
Feodor Dostoevsky, and it has gained in relevance since. Messianic socialism, Dostoevsky argued, that pretense of a total
earthly salvation analogous to the Christian redemption, would
lead to totalitarianism. For man, he said, cannot be completely
refashioned, and those who claim to do so will, in the name of
nonviolence and brotherhood, be driven to force and dictatorship
in their attempt at the impossible. Dostoevsky did not understand
his own prejudices when he made this analysis—he equated
peasant, czarist and Orthodox Russia with human nature—but
the alarm he sounded was quite real.

So it is important to insist upon the limitations of socialism
as a prelude to describing how it seeks to break through so many
of our present limits. It proposes a solution not to all human ills,
but only to those based on the economic, social and political
conditions of life. It may well be, in contrast to what Marx
thought, that once man stops dying from famines and poverty and
starts to die only from death, there will be a resurgence of the
religious spirit, not an end to it. "Under Communism," Sidney
Hook once wrote, "man ceases to suffer as an animal and suffers as
a human. He therefore moves from the plane of the pitiful to
the plane of the tragic."

To grant that socialism is not the final beatitude should not
paralyze the imagination. For instance, I think that Stanley
Moore overreacted in his legitimate hostility to the demands of
some of the youthful Leftists in America for "*Gemeinschaft* Now!"
"It is not enough," he wrote, "for the proletarian revolution to
abolish the division of labor between wage workers and capitalists.
Why does Marx suggest in the *German Ideology* that communism
eliminate *all* division of labor?" But there are present tendencies,
and certainly a future socialist potential, toward redefining work
just as radically as Marx suggested.

In what follows, then, there will be a dialectical tension. On
the one hand, I want to avoid that absolutist view of socialism
that makes it so transcendent that true believers are driven to a
totalitarian rage in the effort to create a perfect order; on the
other hand, I want to suggest the truly unprecedented possibilities
for human change that exist today. For now society should move
toward the abolition of both work and money, even if it never
reaches this ideal. In making this vision specific, I will first analyze
the two most serious challenges to it: that global abundance is im-

possible; that there is no class of men, or group of classes, impelled
to seek such basic transformations of the social structure. I find
these objections quite substantial, and even disturbing, but not
persuasive. So after having dealt with them, I will restate a
socialist ideal which is profoundly relevant to the twenty-first
century.[1]

# I

From its very beginnings the socialist movement had based its
vision on the idea that technology could create enough for everyone if only it could be freed from its capitalist limitations. But in
the late 1960s and early 1970s the new concern with the environment and ecology has led some quite serious—and humane—men
to doubt this fundamental premise.

In 1818 Robert Owen was already speculating that "New
scientific power will soon render human labour of little avail in
the creation of wealth." Marx, as Chapter V discussed in detail,
made the potential boundlessness of social productivity the central
theme of his masterpiece, *Das Kapital*, and the foundation of his
socialist convictions. Strangely enough, John Maynard Keynes,
a principled anti-socialist, shared in this basic assumption. "For
the Western world," he said in 1931, "already has the techniques,
if we would create an organization to use them, of reducing the
Economic Problem, which now absorbs our moral and material
energies, to a position of secondary importance. Thus the author
of these essays, for all his croakings, still believes that the day
is not far off when the Economic Problem will take the back seat
where it belongs and that the arena of the heart and head will
be occupied, or reoccupied, by our real problems—the problems
of life and human relations, of creation and behaviour and
religion."

There were, even before the ecological preoccupations of the
late sixties, those who questioned this theory from within the
socialist camp. Anthony Crosland wrote in *The Future of Socialism* that a "saturation point where further growth would be
superfluous" is "never likely to be fulfilled." But the recent and
most powerful arguments have come from men like Kenneth
Boulding and Robert Heilbroner. Part of their case has even
been adopted by Richard Nixon.

The change that is now taking place, Boulding holds, is not

from poverty to abundance, but from the "open society . . . with an 'input' of material from mines and ores and fossil fuels, and with pollutable reservoirs as recipients of 'outputs'—to a closed society in which there are no longer any mines or pollutable reservoirs and in which, therefore, all materials have to be recycled. This is what I have called the 'space ship earth.' " In his message to Congress on the environment in 1970 President Nixon subscribed to a version of Boulding's thesis: "As we look toward the long-range future—to 1980, 2000 and beyond—recycling of materials will become increasingly necessary not only for waste disposal but also to conserve resources."

Robert Heilbroner, a very thoughtful and sympathetic critic of socialist ideas, has understood how this analysis of limited resources subverts the old dream of the Left and many other aspirations as well. On the Third World, for instance, he writes: ". . . the underdeveloped countries can *never* hope to achieve parity with the developed countries. Given our present and prospective technology, there are simply not enough resources to permit a 'Western' rate of industrial exploitation to be expanded to a population of four billion—much less eight billion—persons." And a little later Heilbroner remarks, "Socialists must also come to terms with the abandonment of the goal of industrial superabundance on which their vision of a transformed society rests. The stationary equilibrium imposed by the constraints of ecology requires at the very least a reformulation of the kind of economic society toward which socialism sets its course."

In that last comment Heilbroner is not sufficiently rigorous. For if abundance is not possible, then neither is socialism, and there is no reformulation that can evade that fact. In a society of scarcity, socialists have always and rightly argued, there will be an inevitable competition among the people for those limited resources. The very experience of daily life will therefore prepare the way for competitiveness or for a draconian system of rationing, but not for fraternity and classlessness. And, as this book has documented in so many instances, that rather harsh insight has been completely corroborated by the events of the past century and a half.

In a spaceship society socialist values would indeed be quite relevant in trying to work out the fairest way to share the available resources, but the socialist emancipation of the personality would not be possible. It might even seem to superficial observers that such an order would be forced to become more socialist:

it would, for instance, obviously have to engage in widespread planning, in political decisions as to how to make investments, and so on. Only, the socialist soul, the socialist essence, would not be there.

I am not, however, convinced by Boulding's and Heilbroner's projection of what the facts will be. Three important trends, each of which can be speeded up through political struggle, could contradict their pessimism: technological innovation, population control and a change in consumption attitudes.

In the early seventies there was a discussion of the possibility that the earth would reach an "energy ceiling." The production of energy results in heat. If its increase continues in the United States at the current rate, by the year 2070 the temperature of the earth will have risen by the equivalent of one seventh of the power of the sun's rays. Such an eventuality would have intolerable consequences, e.g., it would lead to the flooding of the coastal cities. In that case, the basic concept urged by Heilbroner and Boulding would clearly be persuasive.

And yet, all of these figures make the essentially conservative assumption that our power-generating technology will remain what it is today. If before the advent of the internal-combustion machine, one had made a similar assumption—that animal power would continue to do the hard work—one would have predicted that the United States would not be able to sustain its present population. Those multitudes of horses and mules would require so much land for pasture and so much fodder for food that there would be no room for people or cities. But the motor intervened, and the whole situation changed drastically. So it is necessary to take into account the possible, and dramatic, changes that technical innovation can bring.

There are, for instance, four quite imaginable possibilities in the field of power production alone. The Atomic Energy Commission believes that a breeder-reactor system could solve many of these problems. And the potential of tidal, solar and geothermal (from the depths of the earth) power have hardly been tapped. It would be an obvious socialist policy to give a high priority to the exploration of such new resources. And in terms of the long-range difficulties raised by Heilbroner, it is certainly conceivable that technological advances will allow the creation of that abundance which is essential to socialism.

In a prose poem published in 1971, Buckminster Fuller focused upon one of these alternative sources of energy. The tides in

Maine's Bay of Fundy, Fuller said, could provide "more economically harvestable,/Foot-pounds of energy daily/ Than ever
will be needed by all humanity." And he concluded: "I pray
you will make your stand/ Swiftly and unambiguously clear/
As being against any further incursions/ Of petroleum into
Maine/ Or of pipelines in Alaska./ I pray that you will con-
currently/ Initiate resumption of Passamaquoddy/ Together with
initiation of a plurality/ Of such Fundy tidal energy convertors/
With combined capacities/ Sufficient for celestial-energy sup-
port/ Of all human life aboard our Planet/ To be maintained
successfully/ Until Earth-based humanity/ Has successfully mi-
grated/ Into larger cosmic neighborhood functioning."

Moreover, there are the unimagined possibilities in Fuller's
"cosmic neighborhood." One of the reasons that I did not join in
the general Leftist condemnation of the American lunar program
relates to this point. There is no way of knowing what we will
discover in space—not only about resources, but about ourselves.
It is wrong to demand an immediate and obvious payoff for such
undertakings, for they are an exercise, on interstellar scale, in
serendipity. Their very existence means that the limits imagined
by Boulding and Heilbroner are not to be taken as fixed and
immutable.[2]

It would be wrong, however, merely to assert a socialist trust
in the benign potential of technology. For one thing, every
technical advance poses political problems, as the example of
the "green revolution" so clearly demonstrates. If, for example,
some kind of mineral wealth or energy source is discovered in
space, to whom will it belong? To nations or individuals, to
capitalists or Communists? Secondly, there are other workable
policies that can avoid a new and sophisticated form of scarcity.

Population is an obvious case in point. It is already quite clear
that a limitation on the birth rate is essential in the Third World,
which is why the last chapter gave a major emphasis to research
in this area. But beyond that immediate and palpable necessity,
which is a question of life and death for masses in the ex-colonies,
this issue has to be posed in terms of the questions raised by
Heilbroner. Even assuming unexpected technological innovation
and corresponding political and social changes, one cannot foresee
a socialism capable of meeting the needs of a world which increases its numbers by the billions in the course of a single generation.

Therefore the limitation of population is not simply a socialist response to underdevelopment, but a basic principle for the humane creation of the far future. This should be done, of course, on a voluntary basis, and there is reason to hope that such an approach will work. Demography is anything but an exact science, but there are significant indications that an educated populace will respond to rational persuasion on this count, particularly if birth-control research makes the individual decision even easier, and more safe, than it is currently.

Finally, there is the possibility of a massive change in attitude with regard to consumption. In Heilbroner's projections, he assumes an "American" standard of living when calculating the limitations on the world's resources. But in a socialist system, much of the waste, reduplication and pseudo-needs that are so important to capitalism would no longer be necessary, simply because the economy would be more socially rational. But there is an even deeper change that can be hoped for—and promoted.

The consumption needs of people are not eternal but, once the necessities of life are taken care of, historical and social. Adam Smith, Marx remarked, regarded lawyers, priests, state officials and soldiers as living parasitically upon production and he therefore proposed to keep their cost to a minimum. But, Marx continued, as capitalism grew more prosperous, the bourgeois lost his puritanical, abstemious attitudes and became positively feudal in the support he provided for servants and other retainers. At the same time, there was, Marx noted, an increase in unproductive work—advertising, credit, insurance—within the capitalist system itself.

It was this phenomenon that both Max Weber and Thorstein Veblen studied when they wrote of how the children of successful capitalists often turned their backs on money-making as a vulgar occupation. More recently, in the United States and Western Europe some of the children of the growing middle class have turned their backs on the commercial society in an even more radical fashion, experimenting with communal forms of living (this point will be examined at length in the next section). If these changes can be observed within capitalism, it seems quite probable that a socialist society, which would be seeking to end invidious competition altogether, might well be one in which people freely and voluntarily choose less opulent and gadget-ridden lives.

So the suggestion that scarcity, not abundance, will be the

outcome of our technological genius is a disturbing one, but far from compelling. If Heilbroner and Boulding are indeed right, then there will be a place in the spaceship society for socialist values—democratic planning, fairness in rationing, and so forth—but not for socialism. The possibility of a truly new social order of brotherhood demands as a material precondition that there be enough for everyone. Paradoxically, it is only such an unprecedented plenty which could make greed totally nonfunctional. But there are immediate and positive programs that can make abundance a real possibility: through technological innovation, population limitation and a change in consumer tastes it is still possible to work toward a world so collectively wealthy that it can provide a decent life for every man, woman and child on the planet.[3]

## II

A second challenge to the socialist vision is even more serious. It is said that there is no longer any group concerned with creating the good society.

It was a central insight of Marx that the working class was compelled by the conditions of its existence to struggle for socialism. Socialism, he said, was no longer a hope or a dream or an intellectual's plan; it had become a mighty tendency within social reality itself. In his early formulations of this perspective, like *The Communist Manifesto*, Marx wrongly thought that the bourgeois order was rapidly "simplifying" its class structure and thus counterposing an enormous working class against a tiny bourgeoisie. But as time went on, Marx himself realized that he had erred.

There is, he wrote in the *Theories of Surplus Value*, "a constant increase in the middle class which stands between the workmen on one side and the capitalist and landlord on the other, which becomes larger and larger and is fed from revenues that weigh as a burden on the working people beneath them and increase the social security and might of the upper ten thousand." However, Marx was never able to make all the changes in his theory this discovery obviously required. But in the great debates at the turn of the century his heirs all recognized that the class structure was not evolving according to the happy scheme of the *Manifesto*.

So, for instance, Kautsky wrote in 1895 of a "new, much more numerous and ever-increasing middle stratum which is developing . . . even as the entire middle class is in decline as a result of the fall in small business." The state functionaries and professionals, Kautsky said, essentially took on the point of view of the bourgeoisie. But the intelligentsia, a class based on "the privilege of education," was another matter. It was becoming more and more like the working class and one day would discover "its proletarian heart."

That turned out to be too simple and optimistic an analysis, for when the middle class was indeed proletarianized in Germany in the late twenties and early thirties, significant sections of it turned toward the Nazis to save them from the workers. Thus by the end of World War II the most distinctive single doctrine of Marxian socialism, the theory that social development was inexorably creating a revolutionary class, was no longer tenable. It was at that moment that a profound ideological crisis developed within all wings of the socialist movement.

The German social democrats who basically revised their program at Bad Godesberg in 1959 would be universally considered on the Right of the socialist movement; Herbert Marcuse, who had such influence on the new radical generation in America and Europe during the 1960s, would be placed on the Left. Yet so profound is the socialist crisis that Marcuse and the social democrats talk about the very same reality. The Godesberg Program noted that "the defenseless proletarian without rights who used to drive himself through a sixteen-hour day to get a starvation wage has won the eight-hour day, job security, protection against unemployment, sickness, chronic illness and provisions for retirement." And Marcuse writes, " 'the people,' previously the ferment of social change, have 'moved up' to become the ferment of social cohesion." The social democrats and Marcuse, of course, draw quite different conclusions from their common analysis: the former, as we have seen, abandoned the idea of a "class" political party and appealed to all Germans; the latter seeks a new proletariat from among the poor and the excluded, shifting his allegiance from the Marxian proletarians to the Bakuninist lumpenproletarians.

My perspective differs from both the Godesberg Program and Marcuse (though in the dispute between them my sympathies and political support are clearly with the social democrats). There is no question that the classic Marxist theory has been subverted, in part at least because of the social gains that Marx inspired the workers to win. But even in the richest nation on the earth, the United States, the "old" working class still has a basic, and vested, interest in the democratization of power. Moreover, there is a "new" working class coming into being on the basis of advanced technology which could rejuvenate the socialist movement. And there is yet another stratum, extremely hard to define precisely, which is also a potential ally for social change.

In analyzing these three forces which could converge in the fight for a socialist society, I am not suggesting that their victory is historically necessary. After all the unpredicted changes and defeats of the last century a socialist would be foolish to try to revive the consolations of iron laws of history which have been bent into unrecognizable shapes. But there is a possibility of creating the bloc I am about to describe, and whether it becomes reality depends, in some measure, on whether socialists are persuaded to recognize it.[4]

First, there is the "old" working class of blue-collar labor.

In the late fifties and early sixties a group of intellectuals—Raymond Aron and Daniel Bell prominent among them—declared an "end of ideology." They argued that the militant antagonisms of capital and labor were ended, or largely muted, and that social change had become a question of how experts would divide up an ever-increasing Gross National Product. In *The Accidental Century*, which was published in 1965, I challenged this thesis and contended that revolutionary changes taking place in technology and economic structure could well radicalize masses of people again.

I believe that the second half of the sixties bore out my analysis more than that of the end-of-ideologists. In every advanced nation there was unprecedented student and youth unrest, and in the United States there were also explosions of black anger and a new militancy among Spanish-speaking Americans. But more to the point of this section, in France, Italy, Germany and Spain the working class engaged in the most determined struggles since the 1930s. In the United States labor's battles were not as dramatic as in Europe, yet there was a series of major strikes in which the rank-and-file refused the contracts negotiated by their leaders as too moderate. This hardly accords with the widespread theory that the American working class is totally integrated into the system and, in any case, disappearing because of technology.

What many, many observers failed to understand was that if the percentage of blue-collar workers is declining, the absolute numbers are on the increase, and that if their living conditions are much better than they once were, they are by no means adequate. In 1965, 37 percent of the Americans in the labor market were craftsmen, foremen, operatives and laborers. As the Department of Labor projected the 1980 figures in 1970, manufacturing, transportation, construction and mining would employ more than thirty-three million, and government (state and local) and the service industries, both of which have a growing proportion of trade unionists, would account for about thirty-five million.

So the working class is by no means "disappearing" as some academics have thought. And even as scholars were explaining how the proletariat had ceased to be a historical actor, there were tens of millions of workers who faced many of the old problems of working-class life. For, as the Bureau of Labor Statistics computed the figures, in late 1966 it took about $9,200 to support an urban family of four in the United States at a "moderate standard of living" (the definition allowed, for example, the purchase of a new suit and a two-year-old used car every four years). With the rampant inflation of the late sixties, it is clear that this figure would have to be revised to somewhat more than $11,000 for 1970.

To achieve that 1966 level required a weekly paycheck of $177. The average for industrial workers was actually $114. Indeed, a majority of the American people lacked the resources of this "moderate" budget. In addition to the poor, there were tens of millions of working Americans who, if not hungry, had to struggle and scrape to make ends meet. And many of these citizens were concentrated in factory jobs that were physically grueling. So the "old" issues of wages and working conditions were still very much a factor in the experience of the majority of people. And in Europe, where per capita wealth is inferior to the United States, these trends are even more pronounced.

Though working-class discontent in America did not take the turbulent, near-revolutionary forms that it did in France and Italy in 1968 and 1969, it was still a powerful political force. In the elections of 1968 the supposedly decrepit trade unions were, as we have seen, clearly the most important single element in the coalition that, despite the most difficult odds, almost elected Humphrey President. In the 1970 Congressional elections a similar effort frustrated Nixon's plans to make big Republican gains.

Moreover, the political potential of social classes cannot be determined by a simple head count. There are nations in which the overwhelming majority is peasant and yet the society is run from the cities. For peasants are dispersed, parochial and pre-modern. They can flare into a *jacquerie* or even provide the troops for a Mao or a Ho Chi Minh. But the decisive technology of the contemporary economy is industrial, and the center of power is therefore urban. Workers, on the other hand, are concentrated in very large numbers, subjected to a common discipline in the work process, and forced, in the defense of their most immediate interests, to build collective institutions. They therefore have a cohesion, a social weight, in excess of their numbers.

I stress this aspect of working-class life since the affluent, col-lege-educated and issue-oriented people who must coalesce with the unionists so often ignore it. The new constituency that is emerging as a result of mass higher education is, as I will docu-ment in a moment, extremely important. But it does not have a solidarity imposed upon it by the very conditions of life and work, as the labor movement does. Therefore even if the percent-age of blue-collar workers is declining, and that of "professional, technical and kindred workers" is on the increase, it is the work-ing people with their own stable institutions who must be the decisive component of a socialist majority.

Paradoxically, affluence may provoke the workers to political struggle as much as poverty did. Marx had recognized the possi-bility that capitalist success would make labor rebel in 1849. "The rapid growth of productive capital," he wrote, "brings about an equally rapid growth of wealth, luxury, social wants, social em-ployments. Thus, although the enjoyments of the worker have risen, the social satisfactions they give him fall in comparison with the increased enjoyments of the capitalists, which are in-accessible to the worker, and in comparison with the state of de-velopment of society in general. Our desires and pleasures spring from society; we measure them, therefore, by society. . . ."

Something like that mood of rising enjoyments and declining satisfactions among the workers was reported by a number of observers in the United States in the early seventies. In his first

State of the Union message Richard Nixon himself remarked that "never has a nation seemed to have had more and enjoyed it less." And in a report to Nixon, Assistant Secretary of Labor Jerome M. Rossow told of the discontents of blue-collar affluence: the workers can't send their children to college—which is now becoming as essential as a high-school education was a generation ago—without great financial strain; their jobs have lost status; and they feel threatened by the militancy of the blacks. In 1971 some of these emotions even caused the striking New York City police to imitate the confrontation tactics of the New Leftists whom they abominate.

In England one can be even more precise about prosperity and the labor movement because of an excellent empirical and theoretical study, *The Affluent Worker in the Class Structure*. The well-paid workers, it reported, had not become bourgeois: "A factory worker can double his living standards and still remain a man who sells his labour to an employer in return for wages; he can work at a control panel rather than on an assembly line without changing his subordinate position in the organization of production; he can live in his own house in a 'middle-class' estate or suburb and still remain little involved in the white-collar social world."

But if this English study does not bear out the theory that the affluent workers have become middle class—they are still overwhelmingly for the Labour Party, for instance—it does raise a disturbing question. The old labor solidarity, it reports, has disappeared from much of daily life and even from the plant floor. The workers' new prosperity has made the home and private consumption the focus of their activity, and the formal and informal class institutions, like clubs and pubs, have gone into decline. They remain collectivist, for the conditions of their lives force them into unions and concerted political action. But, the English investigators concluded, their collectivism tends to be "instrumental"—not a way of life or a cell of the new society, but simply a technique for protecting fairly narrow economic interests.

Certainly something like this has happened in America. The *élan*, the marching and singing that accompanied the rise of the CIO, has largely disappeared. So has much of the intense political life that characterized the unions in those days. The movement has remained dedicated to better wages and working conditions and to political action, but the sense of brotherhood seems to have departed. If this were the only trend, then the unions could become parochial interest groups, reverting to the traditions of the AFL before World War I. And however much they might do for their members in that case, it would be absurd to think that they have a place in the fight to create a new social order.

Australia might be a precedent. Labor there became political as far back as the turn of the century and has had its own party for just as long. And yet, although the Australian Labour Party (and its largely Roman Catholic and bitterly anti-Communist offshoot, the Democratic Labour Party) is class-based and dedicated to a full-employment program, it has never declared itself for a socialist reorganization of society. In America, too, laborism could be a vehicle of such an "instrumental collectivism," maximizing a limited self-interest rather than any larger vision.

I think that objective conditions are not favorable to this privatization of both the working class and its institutions. For increasingly the social component of the standard of living is more and more important. Clean air, good schools, vibrant neighborhoods, public safety and a sense of identity cannot be purchased at the supermarket. Indeed, as Chapter XII demonstrated, if the priorities of the market prevail within the society, these crucial goods are going to deteriorate further. Therefore, whether the workers like it or not, they will be forced to public action in order to fulfill their private desires.

A 1971 study by the University of Michigan Research Center indicates that the workers themselves may well be conscious of this situation. Through depth interviews with a national cross-section of workers the Michigan scholars discovered that the prime concern of the sample was fringe benefits—medical insurance, sick leave, and retirement programs. Next came health and safety hazards and transportation problems, then unpleasant physical conditions on the job and inconvenient or excessive hours. Low pay rated sixth among nineteen complaints. What is revealing about these attitudes is that the first five complaints can be dealt with only through collective, and in most cases governmental, action. The classically "private" drive for more income was subordinated to these other, much more social, values.

In a remarkable revision—perhaps rejection is a more precise word—of his own "end of ideology" thesis written in 1971, Daniel Bell described a major trend: "It seems clear to me that, today, we in America are moving away from a society based on a private-enterprise market system toward one in which the most important economic decisions will be made at the political level, in terms of consciously-defined 'goals' and 'priorities.' " In August, 1971, Richard Nixon dramatically corroborated Bell's belated realization of the deep-lying collectivist trends of the age. Turning his back on the *laissez-faire* economics which had guided the first two years of his Presidency, Nixon declared a wage-price freeze and proposed $9 billion of encouragement for the corporations, $2.5 billion for the consumer and an IOU for the income floor he had urged for the poor.

Predictably the AFL-CIO responded indignantly to the priorities contained in the Nixon policy. Its executive council said: "Instead of extending the helping hand of the Federal government to the poor, the unemployed, the financially strapped states and cities and to the inflation-plagued consumer, the President decided to further enrich big corporations and banks. . . . Mr. Nixon's program is based on the infamous 'trickle down' theory. It would give huge sums of money belonging to the people of the United States to big corporations. He would do this at the expense of the poor, the state and local governments and their employees and wage and salary earners."

The radical aspect of this confrontation is that it concerns the very maldistribution of wealth within the system itself. The AFL-CIO is here challenging that most basic trend of neo-capitalist society whereby the state acts to reinforce inequality even as it claims to promote the common good. And if, as Bell rightly argues, basic decisions of the future are going to be made politically, then there is reason to hope that the trade unions will confront not simply questions of wages and hours, but basic issues of social and economic structure as well.

In his reflections on the socialist future after the defeat of the Wilson Government in which he was a minister, Anthony Crosland writes that the only alternative to periodic bouts of inflation and recession is an incomes policy. Indeed, Crosland urges the Labour Party to make just such an approach a central plank in its program for the seventies. President Nixon's adoption of a reactionary incomes policy in 1971 is proof that this trend exists on the Right as well as the Left. And the AFL-CIO's insistence that non-wage income, like profits, rents and dividends, be controlled could well be the portent of a basic new direction in labor politics, one which will see the unions, acting out of considerations of practical self-interest, become the political champions of increasing equality in American society as a whole.

So the "old" working class has not disappeared and neither has its very immediate interest in the democratization of economic power. It is clearly going to be the largest and most decisive element in any liberal coalition in the immediate future; it has a potential to play a most important role in a socialist coalition of the future.[5]

Then there is the "new" working class.

As neo-capitalism plans and rationalizes more and more, it produces an increasingly large stratum of engineers, technicians and highly skilled workers. In those Department of Labor projections for 1980, for instance, the occupation with the greatest growth during the seventies is that of "professional and technical workers," which will increase by 50 percent, while operatives (assemblers, truck drivers, bus drivers) will grow by only 10 percent. As a result, in 1980 it is estimated that there will be slightly more professionals than operatives (15.5 million as compared to 15.4 million). The former will be middle class in their educational attainments and life-style, but their conditions of work and the problems of unemployment will confront them with problems long familiar to the working class. (The English study of the affluent workers also noted this tendency toward "proletarianization" in that country.)

In the discussions in the socialist movement before World War I Kautsky, as we have seen, put considerable emphasis on the possibility that the intelligentsia would become more proletarian. But it was Thorstein Veblen who was really the first to make this insight more precise and to apply it, in effect, to the professional and technical workers. Veblen wrote of a "corps of technological production specialists, into whose keeping the due functioning of the industrial system has now drifted by force of circumstances. . . ." And then, in a passage anticipating the discovery of new social types by John Kenneth Galbraith, Daniel Bell and others, Veblen wrote, "These expert men, technologists, engineers, or whatever name may best suit them, make up the indispensable General Staff of the industrial system; and without their immediate guidance and connection the industrial system will not work."

Veblen thought that the engineers were becoming both class-conscious and anti-commercial, and that they would be able to run the society of the future. That hardly turned out to be true. For this analysis—and Bell's and Galbraith's—forgets that so long as the technologists are acting within capitalist institutions, however fine their personal values may be they will be overwhelmed by the structures they serve. But they do indeed provide an extremely important new political constituency and even a source for trade unionism.

In France, this possibility was highlighted during the tumultuous events of May, 1968. As Serge Mallet and Alain Touraine have reported, the most militant trade unionists in the great strike wave were not the coal miners, a classic source of proletarian intransigence, but the workers in electronics, chemicals, communications and education. Moreover, these highly educated workers made demands having to do with the democratization of the work place itself. They were simply not willing to accept the hierarchies inherited from the industrial capitalism of the nineteenth century.

The union federation in France that has been most successful among this "new" working class is the Democratic Federation of Labor (CFDT), formerly the Catholic labor movement (as the Christian Federation, CFTC). In 1952, when Eugène Descamps cited Blum and Jaurès at a CFTC meeting, he was called to order by Gaston Tessier who said, "Here one does not talk of socialism." By 1970 Descamps was the secretary general of the Federation and it had officially declared itself in favor of a socialist society. This is not to suggest that there is some automatic tendency toward socialism in this new stratum of industrial society. The English study of the affluent workers, for instance, did not discover such a trend. But the development does at least open up new possibilities for socialists, as the French case shows.

Even in the United States one can observe some of these very same tendencies. One of the fastest growing unions in the sixties was the American Federation of Teachers. If, as is possible, it were to merge with the National Educational Association (which, despite its claim to professionalism, has acted more and more like a union), the combined organization would be the second largest union in America (only the Teamsters would have more members). And there were similar trends toward collective bargaining among priests, nuns, nurses, professional athletes and other non-blue-collar categories.

John Kenneth Galbraith described another aspect of this development in *The New Industrial State*. The corporation has become so huge and makes its multimillion-dollar investments over such long periods of time that a corps of industrial planners has now become necessary. This marks, Galbraith suggests, a major new source of power, since society always pays a particular deference to its most scarce resource. Once that was land, then it was capital, now it is organized intelligence. And Daniel Bell has said that the "new men" in the emergent order are "the scientists, the mathematicians, the economists and the engineers of the new complex technology. The leadership of the new society will rest, not with the businessmen or corporations as we have known them . . . but with the research corporation, the industrial laboratories, the experimental stations and the universities." Both of these descriptions are too Veblenesque, too optimistic about the power and humane values of technicians. But they do provide insights into an important, and new, social reality.

So the evolution of capitalist society is bringing forth a new working-class stratum with a considerable socialist potential. It is middle class in its education and income, but often subjected to a production discipline like that of the workers. It is disposed by its intellectual formation to long-range planning and it has no great vested interest in private corporate property (for all the publicity about the widespread stock ownership in America, the overwhelming majority of stockholders rely on their job, not their holdings, for the bulk of their income; for them, speculation is an avocation, and as the bear market of 1969 and 1970 showed, often a dangerous one). So long as it remains encapsulated within neo-capitalist institutions, this stratum cannot act on its own, contrary to what Veblen, Galbraith and Bell think. But when it creates its own groups—unions, political clubs, even professional associations—it can affect the society and conceivably move it in a socialist direction.

It would be wrong to become euphoric about this change in class structure, for it has its ambiguities. In Sweden in 1971 civil servants went out on strike. These educated workers in the public sector were disturbed about the egalitarian policies of Premier Olof Palme's government and felt, the German socialist correspondent in Stockholm reported, that it was wrong to reduce the differentials between the educated and the uneducated worker. So it is possible that this new skilled stratum could engage in a conservative status politics designed to maintain the traditional capitalist inequities. But there is hope even in this setback, for

Palme did win his party to undertake a redistribution of income and wealth in the society in favor of the poor and the disadvantaged. In time it may well turn out that the Swedish social democrats, the first movement in the world to engage in planned deficit financing as a way of promoting full employment, may have once again played the role of pioneering innovators.[6]

The third possible component of a new socialist majority is the most difficult to define. It is made up primarily of young people with college educations (or in college) who are not technologists or professionals.

In a *Fortune* survey in 1968 which showed 40 percent of college youth to be fundamentally dissatisfied with the values of American society, the majority of this group—*Fortune* dubbed them the "forerunners"—were students in the arts and humanities. The vocational choice that attracted the largest single group among them (39 percent) was teaching. That would, of course, make them part of the "professional" category as defined by the statisticians in Washington. But it would certainly not qualify them as part of Galbraith's "technostructure" (since most of them are oriented toward primary- or secondary-school teaching and would never participate in either the research institutions or the corporations).

These nontechnicians are the most visible representatives of the "generation gap" that has been so widely discussed in Europe and America. They incarnate not merely a new definition of the meaning of age, but the consequences of changes in class structure as well.

Adolescence, as Kenneth Kenniston points out, was an invention of industrial society. Before the rise of urban industrialism children entered adult society as soon as they were physically able (and in the early days of capitalism, even before then). But with the growth of wealth and the middle class, the children of the well-off were granted a "moratorium" (to use Erik Erikson's idea) in their teens during which they were not quite children nor adults. Now, as society has grown even more affluent, it has created still another period of human life, one that "intervenes between adolescence and adulthood."

This new phase, Kenniston argues, has been the basis of New Left currents in the advanced nations in the sixties. For the radicals, Kenniston discovered, are overwhelmingly the children of the middle, and even upper-middle, class; they come from liberal homes; and their bitterness about the existing order is partly a result of having been given the leisure time and educational opportunity to take a "disinterested" critical view of it. But their anti-establishmentarianism may also reflect a certain self-interest, as Bruno Bettelheim has suggested. For many of these young people understand that they, together with their liberal education, are obsolete in a technological economy. Trained as "gentlemen" in an age that needs technicians, they become, in Walter Lippmann's phrase, "derelicts from progress."

Yet it would be quite wrong to think that the vast increase in the collegiate population is primarily a middle- or upper-middle-class phenomenon. In October, 1969, there were 7.4 million students enrolled in higher education—and 61 percent of the whites and 71 percent of the blacks came from homes whose head had not attended college. To be sure, the class bias of the American system was still very much at work—66 percent of the children from families with incomes of $15,000 a year and over were receiving advanced education compared to only 16.4 percent of those from income backgrounds of $3,000 a year or less. And yet, the students from families with less than $15,000 a year were twice as numerous as those whose parents made more than that figure. Thus it is clear that we are dealing with a massive structural mutation in the society as a whole which touches every class, and a good portion of the *Fortune* "forerunners" must have come from working-class and lower-middle-class homes. Their better-off classmates can express their convictions more visibly and dramatically, but they do not tell the whole story.

This new development is going to have enormous political ramifications. In 1910, when he was attacking Max Adler's theory that intellectuals have a natural penchant for socialism, Leon Trotsky conceded that students did represent a special case and defined their position in terms that now apply to millions in the advanced economies: "The student, in contrast both to the young worker and his own father, fulfills no social function, does not feel direct dependence on capital or the state, is not bound by any responsibilities and—at least objectively, if not subjectively—is free in his judgement of right and wrong. At this period everything within him is fermenting, his class prejudices are as formless as his ideological interests, questions of conscience matter very strongly to him, his mind is opening for the first time to great scientific generalizations, the extraordinary is almost a psychological need for him. If collectivism is at all capable of mastering his mind now is the moment, and it will indeed do it through the

nobly scientific character of its basis and the comprehensive
cultural content of its aims, not as a prosaic 'knife and fork'
question."

A mass constituency with at least some of these characteristics
is now being produced in American society. And ironically, one
of the main reasons that capitalism has thus subsidized so many
potential subversives is that it was trying to evade a most pressing
problem: automation. When that issue was first urgently posed in
the sixties there were some writers—myself included—who responded to the phenomenon with an excessive literal-mindedness
and lack of imagination. We assumed that it would have the
obvious effect of producing chronic, and even mass, unemployment. We did not realize the various disguises this trend could
adopt. One of them was the war in Vietnam, which carried out
a policy many of us had proposed—the direct governmental
creation of 1,700,000 jobs—but in a tragic, murderous fashion.
Another disguise was this protracted postponement of entry into
the labor market on the part of the liberally educated children of
the affluent.

For those who were actually preparing for and wanted careers
in the "knowledge economy," this delay was functional. But for
others, who sought enlightenment or who were simply after the
"credential" of a college degree, the experience was bewildering.
They were saved from unemployment, true. But they also found
themselves in new mass institutions of higher learning which
could give them no convincing reason as to why they were there.
So they rebelled in a thousand ways against the irrationality of
their life. And in the recession of 1970–1971, they discovered how
precarious their position was when the unplanned expansion of
higher education and an unplanned labor market worked to create
collegiate, and even doctoral, unemployment.

In France after the turbulence of May, 1968, the authorities
adopted a version of the foregoing analysis and acted upon it. *Le
Monde* reported in 1969, "The students in the various faculties
are also upset for another reason: the uncertainty of the job
market. Almost half the liberal arts graduates no longer find posts
in teaching and are not prepared for any other activity. The
situation is rapidly going to be just as upsetting for graduates in
economics, natural science and even physics, for they cannot all
find a place in teaching or research." And, in another one of those
paradoxical results of the May, 1968, student uprising, the techno-

crats are responding to this situation by opening up a new school to teach management techniques and introducing the study of technology in the science faculties so that the students will be prepared to work in industry.

But another response, coming from some of the young themselves, is to drop out of the work-oriented society altogether. This is, of course, an option taken by a relatively tiny minority, yet there is a remarkable resonance to the hippie style among those who have not disaffiliated completely yet share the dissatisfactions of those who have. Theodore Roszak argues that this phenomenon is so serious that it marks the appearance of a "counterculture" and a radical departure from the mainstream assumptions of the West since the Scientific Revolution of the seventeenth century. It integrates Oriental mysticism, psychedelic drugs and communitarian impulses; it is profoundly hostile to technological rationality.

In its extreme form the political logic of this attitude leads to a dangerous utopianism in the worst sense of that word. Roszak asks, ". . . how ready are the workers to disband whole sectors of the industrial apparatus where this proves necessary in order to achieve ends other than efficient productivity and high consumption? How willing are they to set aside technocratic priorities in favor of a new simplicity of life, a decelerating social pace, a vital leisure?" And this vision culminates in the proclamation of "a new heaven and a new earth so vast, so marvelous that the inordinate claims of technical expertise must of necessity withdraw in the presence of such splendor to a subordinate and marginal status in the lives of men."

I take this view seriously even though it expresses the attitude of only a small number of young people on the disaffiliated margin of the new educated stratum. For portions of this ideology—and for that matter, hippie styles in clothing—are to be found among a very large number of the growing college-educated constituency. And what Roszak is articulating is the self-righteous call for such people to withdraw into their own universe, and in the name of ultra-radicalism actually reduce the opportunities for basic change.

Politically it is simply impossible to persuade the majority of the people of the advanced countries to become voluntary ascetics. They, unlike the inhabitants of the counterculture who usually come from affluent homes and live off the wealth of the society, still have material needs that are unsatisfied. Even more important, dealing with the agony of the poor in the advanced countries— and of the hundreds of millions in the Third World who are much more desperate—requires that contemporary technology be used for the creation of food, housing and clothing. It was, for instance, technological rationality—in this case, applied scientific research —that resulted in the "green revolution" of new strains of wheat and rice, making it possible to generate huge increases in the agricultural production of India. To carry out the program of the counterculture would literally threaten millions with starvation. The poetic demand to do away with machines, so compelling to young people who have never run them or realized their dependence on them, comes to seem extremely reactionary.

This is not to say that the hippie view is completely without substance. It is quite right to argue that production is not an end in itself, as the capitalist ideology of eternally increasing consumption holds. And it is right to say that once the basic needs of all the people of the earth are satisfied, man should turn to other pursuits. Marx, in his most profound definition of socialism itself, asserted that the "Kingdom of Freedom" would not emerge until compulsory work had ended. And he understood that if one dispensed with the discipline of the labor market, there would be a mutation in the psychic character of man—there would be "new" men.

But Roszak and those to whom he speaks want to pass immediately into the Kingdom of Freedom, even if by doing so, they desert that vast majority of mankind which is still forced to live in the Kingdom of Necessity. Yet it would be wrong to assess the significance of these yearnings in terms of their most extreme formulation. There are, the *Fortune* survey indicates, some millions of young people who have taken the best of these values, but who are still concerned about the actual struggle to change the society as contrasted to dropping out from it. They are the ones who followed Senators McCarthy and Kennedy in 1968 and who organized that national celebration of peace in October, 1969. And they could well respond to a socialist program for the humanization of technology, not by way of the disaffiliation of a sensitive, irresponsible minority, but through the conscious creativity of the majority. So there are trends altering the class structure of neo-capitalist society in such a way as might make it possible to build a new coalition not simply for this or that reform, but for the good society. The grandchildren of the prisoners of starvation, the technicians and the liberally educated children of affluence could come together in an alliance to transform both the quantities and the qualities of life.[7]

## III

The socialist vision, then, could be made relevant to the twenty-first century. That would mean that masses of men and women would seek to construct a society in which compulsory work and money would both tend to disappear. These ultimates are important in that they define a goal to be approximated—and also because they concern the political choices that must be made tomorrow. If, for example, one is very clear about the need to make more and more goods and commodities free, then that will affect how one designs a health insurance program.

In 1971, for instance, Richard Nixon's medical proposals were designed to leave existing structures intact by contracting out the society's responsibility to private insurance companies (although it should be noted that ten years earlier Nixon would have probably denounced his own plan as "socialized medicine"). The bill proposed by Senator Kennedy and supported by the unions, on the other hand, actually aimed at changing medical practices and relied on general government revenues for financing. The Kennedy proposal was not, to be sure, socialist, but an understanding of the socialist ideal helps greatly in making people realize that it is the infinitely preferable of the two liberal options.

So in what follows I speak of a far future which must inspire the immediate present.

In one of his most extended discussions of what socialism would be, Karl Marx was clear that it involved the abolition of compulsory work. I quote him at length not out of veneration, but because his words remain an extraordinarily accurate perception of the most desirable possibility for social change. "The Kingdom of Freedom," Marx wrote, "begins first with the fact that work ceases to be determined by need and external expediency; so in the nature of things it will be located beyond the sphere of material production in the proper sense of the word. As the savage must wrestle with nature to satisfy his needs and to maintain and reproduce his life, so must civilized man do the same thing under all social forms and possible modes of production. With his development, man expands the realm of material necessity and his own needs; but at the same time, he expands the productive forces that satisfy them. In this sphere, freedom can only emerge if socialized man [*vergesellschafte Mensch*], the associated producers [*assozierte Produzenten*] regulate their relation to nature rationally and bring it under communal [*gemeinschaftliche*] control rather than being ruled by it as by a blind power; and if this is accomplished with the least expenditure of effort and under conditions worthy and adequate to human nature. But this remains always as the Kingdom of Necessity. Beyond that there exists the true Kingdom of Freedom where the development of man's powers becomes an end in itself, a realm which can only bloom on the basis of the realm of necessity. The shortening of the working day is its fundamental premise."

Essentially, Marx is saying that in the fullness of socialism, all men will work like artists, out of an inner need and satisfaction, and not because they are forced to earn their daily bread. In arguing that even in the planned, socially controlled society work is still unfree as long as it is compulsory, Marx was anticipating that passionate anti-socialist, Friedrich Nietzsche, who wrote, "Phew! To speak as if an increase in the impersonality inside a mechanized plant will make a new society and turn the scandal of slavery into a virtue."

By now we have become so accustomed to the regimen of compulsory (in an economic sense) labor that we have lost even the memory of the precapitalist period when leisure was more common. For as Marx documented in his brilliant history of the bourgeois struggle to lengthen the working day and week, the limit Massachusetts law set on the labor of children in the nineteenth century defined the normal working day for an adult in the seventeenth century. In the Middle Ages the working year was only 150 to 200 days. So Nietzsche's insight reflected, if from a reactionary point of view, an instinctive understanding of working people whose lives had been subjected to the calculation of clocks and the division of labor. A hundred or so years later we have "progressed" to the point where we have forgotten how natural it is not to work.

What Marx understood and Nietzsche did not was that the application of science to technology would make it possible—even necessary—to change the very nature of work. Social productivity, he understood a hundred years before the actual advent of automation, was increasing so enormously that it was coming into conflict with the very structure of capitalist society itself. An economy whose productive system expanded geometrically paid wages in arithmetic increments, and that fact contains within it the potential for crisis. Neo-capitalism, as has been seen, "solves" this difficulty by creating a number of new phenomena: the poverty of affluence, the government-generated jobs in the war sector, the liberal arts as a dumping ground for the children of the middle class. Precisely because this system follows commercial priorities even when it acts governmentally, it cannot cope with its own genius and even the hint of abundance threatens its most cherished values because it brings unemployment, ecological ruin, aimless universities and many other crises.

This is the key to that paradox presented by the National Commission on the Causes and Prevention of Violence: that after the most prosperous decade in American history, this country is in danger of building a hate-ridden, strife-torn anti-utopia.

But socialism would be free of exactly those constraints that make it structurally impossible for capitalism to make a truly social use of its own productivity. In the immediate future a democratically socialized society could use its enormous economic power to meet its own needs and to aid in the industrialization of the world. There is so much work that needs to be done within America and internationally that the next several generations at least must put the "socialized individual" to work to meet basic needs. Yet in the more distant future it is not only possible but necessary for society to enter the Kingdom of Freedom. Once the basic needs of all of mankind are provided for, and productivity still grows, men may be forced to live without compulsory work. The sentence decreed in the Garden of Eden will have been served.

I would not suggest that a psychic transition of this character will be easy. It is a familiar phenomenon that some people are crushed by retirement, bewildered when the compulsion of work is removed from their lives. At a conference sponsored by *Dissent* in 1969 Meyer Schapiro, a brilliant art critic and socialist, placed this kind of crisis in a thoughtful context. The ideal of the artist, of freely chosen and loving work, Schapiro said, is problematic even for the artists themselves and would be infinitely more difficult to apply in the lives of the masses of people. For every successful painter or sculptor there are many others whose hopes are disappointed. And even those who do succeed often require tremendous sacrifices from their family and friends in order to develop their genius.

I suspect that Schapiro has touched upon one of the fundamental social-psychological issues of the twenty-first century: whether, in an economy of abundance, men can find within themselves and their relations with one another, rather than in external necessity, a reason for living. Strangely enough, the problem with this aspect of the ultimate socialist projection arises because Marx's vision was so thoroughly aristocratic. He hoped for nothing less than that every citizen become a Renaissance man. "In a Communist society," he and Engels wrote, "there will be no painters but only highly developed men who, among other things, paint."

But among the great Marxists it was Trotsky whose optimism was the most audacious: "Man will become immeasurably stronger, wiser and subtler; his movements more rhythmic, his voice more musical. The forms of life will become dynamically dramatic. The average human type will rise to the heights of an Aristotle, a Goethe, a Marx. And above this ridge, new peaks will arise."

This soaring vision is, in part at least, an expression of that dangerous messianic socialism I described earlier. Yet if one understands it as the statement of a limit toward which mankind strives but perhaps will never reach, it serves to free the mind from the narrowness of the present. The human body has been changing under capitalism: in the United States Selective Service exams show that height is increasing in the twentieth century; and, of course, athletic records, and presumably biological prowess, have been dramatically extended. A higher living standard, with good diet and medical care, certainly can make people more beautiful, as the rich discovered a long time ago. In the realm of the intelligence there are no comparative statistics, but the qualitative growth in the number of scientists, and educated people generally, must mean that some of man's genetic potential has been saved from the savage fate scarcity and starvation used to visit upon it.

It is certain that we are on the eve of psychic mutations, that our unprecedented man-made environments are going to produce new kinds of people. The question is not whether this will happen, but how it will take place: under commercial priorities (Marcuse's pessimistic vision); under totalitarian control (Orwell's fear); or consciously chosen and shaped by a free political and social movement.[8]

The end of compulsory labor is one socialist ultimate; the abolition of money is another.

As many economists have recognized, money is the basis of a system of "rationing by the purse." In a society of maldistributed incomes it is obviously unjust that an elite should enjoy luxuries while the masses are denied necessities. Long before the socialist movement will even be in sight of its final aims it can ameliorate this outrage by the redistribution of income, for then the rations will at least be more justly shared. But that is a reform that might even be assimilated into an Adam Smithian model of the economy. As Paul Samuelson remarks, Smith would now agree that dollar wealth has to be distributed "in an 'ethically optimal' manner—and kept so by non-distorting, non-market intervention" in order to get the most efficient production and "to give people what they really deem is best for them."

Socialists should propose to go well beyond such a change and eventually to challenge the principle of money itself. In a discussion of property that produces unearned income John Strachey argued that given such a phenomenon, "a moral poison is bound to permeate the society." And Ernest Mandel has rightly remarked that as long as access to goods and pleasures is rationed according to the possession of money, there is a pervasive venality, an invitation to miserliness and hostility to one's neighbor. Particularly in the area of necessities no one should be required to choose between needs or the sacrifice of them in order to get luxuries—and that choice is what money makes inevitable.

Socialism should therefore work toward making more and more goods and services free: medicine, housing, transportation, a healthy diet, etc. The standard response of many economists to such a proposition is that cliché of Economics I: there is nothing that is really free. All commodities cost something to produce and if the individual does not pay for them directly, someone does indirectly. But this is to miss the enormous social gain that would occur if society were to decide to pay for all the collectively fundamentals of life. The change in moral atmosphere such a new mode of distribution would portend would be profound.

The other standard criticism of free goods is the charge that they invite waste. People, one is told, will lavishly misuse their new rights and a socialist society will therefore be the least efficient in human history. That prediction is partly based on the parochial assumption that man will act in a radically new environment exactly as he did in the old, that the greed and acquisitiveness of several hundred years of capitalism are of the human essence. It is not even necessary to become particularly visionary in responding to this proposition for the theory and practice of recent years has provided a basis for the socialist hope as many of the most intelligent of the affluent young have turned against consumption for consumption's sake.

In his famous essay on the economics of socialism Oskar Lange argued that those goods and services for which demand is relatively inelastic can be made free without running the risk of wastefulness. Salt is a classic example. The amount of it consumed in good times or in bad is relatively invariable. If it were made free it is doubtful that individuals would suddenly vastly increase their use of it. The situation would be different in the case of transportation within a city. If that were made free there would unquestionably be a large increase in the use of transit facilities since people would be much more likely to visit one another, to go on outings, etc. Yet who can say that such an increase in sociability and recreation is "wasteful"? And who could care to ride a subway simply because it is free?

There is some experience to go by. In California there is a private medical plan run by the Kaiser Company. It has succeeded in sharply reducing the cost of care while improving the service. According to the thesis about the inherent greediness of men, the people who subscribe should use their rights more than the citizen who pays a higher cost. In fact, the Kaiser patients go to the doctor less than the patients of the expensive fee-for-service system. As an article in *Fortune* put it, "Kaiser's experience refutes the widely held belief that if medical services are 'free,' or virtually free, the public will stampede to them."[9]

Socialism, then, is not simply a program for socializing investments, ownership and redistributing wealth, important as all those goals are. It retains the notion of a truly new order of things and it asserts this through the vison of seeking in the distant but conceivable future to abolish compulsory work and the rationing system of money as far as is humanly possible. And perhaps I can sum up this vision by retelling a famous socialist parable.

In desert societies—including the American Southwest—water is so precious that it is money. People connive and fight and die over it; governments covet it; marriages are even made and broken because of it. If one were to talk to a person who has known only that desert and tell him that in the city there are public water fountains and that children are even sometimes allowed to turn on the fire hydrants in the summer and to frolic in the water, he would be sure one were crazy. For he knows, with an existential certitude, that it is human nature to fight over water.

Mankind has lived now for several millennia in the desert. Our minds and emotions are conditioned by that bitter experience; we do not dare to think that things could be otherwise. Yet there are signs that we are, without really having planned it that way, marching out of the desert. There are some who loathe to leave behind the consolation of familiar brutalities; there are others who in one way or another would like to impose the law of the desert upon the Promised Land. It may even be possible that mankind cannot bear too much happiness.

It is also possible that we will seize this opportunity and make of the earth a homeland rather than an exile. That is the socialist project. It does not promise, or even seek, to abolish the human condition, for that is impossible. It does propose to end that invidious competition and venality which, because scarcity allowed no other alternatives, we have come to think are inseparable from our humanity.

Under socialism, there will be no end to history—but there may be a new history.

# Notes

## CHAPTER I

1. Lenin: *Collected Works* (Moscow: Foreign Language Publishing House, 1963), Vol. XXVIII, p. 180 (hereafter cited as Lenin: *CW*). Bismarck in 1882: Hans Muller, *Ursprung und Geschichte des Wortes "Sozialismus"* (Hannover: Dietz Verlag, 1967), p. 137. Crédit Mobilier: *Marx-Engels Werke* (Berlin: Dietz Verlag, 1960–), Vol. XII, pp. 24 and 33. (Hereafter all quotations from Marx and Engels will be taken from this edition and cited as *MEW*, with roman numerals for the volume numbers and arabic for the pages. However, in those cases in which a significant and/or lengthy passage is quoted from a work originally written in French or English, that text will be noted rather than the German translation of the *MEW*.) "False Brothers": *MEW*, XXIX, p. 573. *The Communist Manifesto: MEW*, IV, pp. 482 ff. Karl Kautsky on state socialism: *Die Neue Zeit*, Vol. 10, No. 49 (1891–1892), pp. 705 ff. Zbigniew Brzezinski, *Between Two Ages: America's Role in the Technetronic Era* (New York: The Viking Press, 1970), p. 112. Barrington Moore, *Social Origins of Dictatorship and Democracy* (Boston: Beacon Press, 1966), p. 410.

## CHAPTER II

1. Marx to his father: *MEW, Ergänzungsband*, Pt. I, pp. 4–5.
2. Utopia in India, Persia, and China: Iring Fetscher in

*Sozialismus: Von Klassenkampfe zum Wohlfahrstaat,* Iring Fetscher, Helga Grebing, and Gunter Dill, eds. (Munich: Verlag Kurt Desch, 1968), pp. 13 ff. Max Weber, *Ancient Judaism* (New York: The Free Press of Glencoe, 1952), p. 156. Eighth-century crisis: John A. Wilson, *The Intellectual Adventure of Ancient Man* (Chicago: The University of Chicago Press, 1946), pp. 337–338. Isaiah: *The Complete Bible,* J. M. Powis Smith and Edgar Goodspeed, trans. (Chicago: The University of Chicago Press, 1948), pp. 635 and 637. Ernst Bloch, *Das Prinzip Hoffnung* (Frankfurt: Suhrkamp Verlag, 1959), Vol. I, p. 582.

3. Marx on Plato: *MEW,* XXIII, p. 388. On Plato's times: A. B. Winspear, *The Genesis of Plato's Thought* (New York: S. A. Russell, 1956), passim. Iambulos: Ernst Bloch, op. cit., pp. 566 ff.; David Winston, *Iambulos: A Literary Study in Greek Utopianism,* Ph.D. Dissertation (Columbia University: 1956; microfilm). Cockaigne: Winston, op. cit. Stoic utopias: Bloch, op. cit., pp. 569–572. "Productive misunderstanding": Bloch, op. cit., p. 566. Plato and Anabaptists: Ernst Bloch, *Thomas Münzer* (Frankfurt: Suhrkamp Verlag, 1962), p. 69.

4. Kautsky: quoted, Fetscher et al., op. cit., p. 25. Émile Durkheim, *Le Suicide,* Nouvelle Édition (Paris: Librairie Félix Aléan, 1930), p. 282. Joachim and Francis: Fetscher et al., op. cit., p. 26. Michael Freund, *Propheten der Revolution* (Bremen: Schunemann's Universitäts Verlage, 1970), p. 44. Heretical movements of the twelfth to the sixteenth century: Fetscher, et al., op. cit., pp. 26 ff.; Friedrich Engels, *The German Peasant War: MEW,* VII, pp. 327 ff.; Michael Freund, op. cit.; Ernst Bloch, *Das Prinzip Hoffnung und Thomas Münzer.* Kautsky on Münzer and More: *Thomas More und seine Utopie* (Stuttgart-Berlin: Dietz Verlag, 1922), p. 1. Engels on Münzer: *MEW,* VII, pp. 400–401.

5. Anabaptists: H. N. Brailsford, *The Levelers and the English Revolution* (Stanford: Stanford University Press, 1961), p. 31. Sheep eat men: Thomas More, *Utopia* (New York: Penguin Books, 1965), pp. 46–47. Christopher Hill, *The Reformation to the Industrial Revolution* (New York: Pantheon Books, 1967), p. 51. Michael Walzer, *The Revolution of the Saints* (New York: Atheneum, 1969), pp. 20 ff. Marx on Communist parties: *MEW,* IV, p. 341. Levelers and Diggers: C. B. Macpherson, *The Political Theory of*

*Possessive Individualism* (New York: Oxford University Press, 1962), Sect. III; Christopher Hill, op. cit., p. 101; Brailsford, op. cit., pp. 656 ff.; Eduard Bernstein, *Sozialismus und Demokratie* (Stuttgart: Dietz Verlag, 1919). New Law as *Communist Manifesto:* Brailsford, op. cit., p. 659. Three principles: Ibid., p. 660.

6. Babeuf: *Textes Choisis,* Claude Mazauric, ed. (Paris: Éditions Sociales, 1965), p. 209. Babeuf's plan: ibid., p. 193. Manifesto of the Equals: Buonarrotti, *Conspiration pour l'égalité dite de Babeuf* (Paris: Éditions Sociales, 1957), Vol. II, p. 95. Alexander Gershenkron, *Continuity in History and Other Essays* (Cambridge: Belknap, 1968), p. 274. Marx and Terrorism: Schlomo Avineri, *The Social and Political Thought of Karl Marx* (Cambridge: Cambridge University Press), Chap. VII; *MEW,* I, p. 402; *MEW,* VI, p. 107.

7. Saint-Simon, *Doctrine de Saint-Simon, Exposition, Première Année, 1829* (Paris: Marcel Rivière, 1924), C. Bouglie and E. Halévy, eds., passim; G. D. H. Cole, *History of Socialist Thought* (London: Macmillan and Co., 1953–1965), Vol. I, p. 41; Alexander Gershenkron, *Economic Backwardness in Historic Perspective* (Cambridge: Belknap-Harvard, 1966), pp. 23–24. On Saint-Simon's use of the word *association:* Bouglie and Halévy, op. cit., p. 203, n. 201. George Lichtheim, *The Origins of Socialism* (New York: Praeger, 1969), p. 43. Owen: V. A. C. Gatrell, "Introduction" to *Report to the County of Lanark,* by Robert Owen (Baltimore: Penguin Books, 1970); G. D. H. Cole, op. cit., pp. 90 ff.

8. Marx on preconditions: *MEW,* III (*The German Ideology*), pp. 24–35 and 68. C. B. Macpherson, op. cit., Sect. II. Leszek Kolakowski, *The Alienation of Reason* (New York: Doubleday and Company, 1968), pp. 34 ff. Kant, *Prolegomena to Any Future Metaphysics* (Manchester: Manchester University Press, 1953). Hegel on the French Revolution: quoted in *MEW,* XX, p. 605. *Geschichte und Klassenbewusstssein* (Berlin: Der Malik Verlag, 1923), p. 134. *Phenomenologie des Geistes* (Hamburg: Felix Meiner, 1952), p. 15. Cunning of Reason: Hegel, *Recht, Staat, Geschichte* (Stuttgart: Alfred Kroner Verlag, 1955), p. 432. On Hegel and Adam Smith: Georg Lukacs, *Der Junge Hegel* (Berlin: Aufbau Verlag, 1954); Jean Hypolite, *Études sur Marx et Hegel* (Paris: Marcel Rivière, 1955), p. 89. Marx on history: *MEW,* II, p. 98.

# CHAPTER III

1. G. D. H. Cole, *History of Socialist Thought,* Vol. I, p. 245. On Weitling: George Lichtheim, *The Origins of Socialism* (New York: Praeger, 1969), pp. 170–171. Blanqui, *Textes Choisis* (Paris: Éditions Sociales, 1955), pp. 71, 101, and 166. Engels on British working class: *MEW,* II, pp. 225 ff. E. J. Hobsbawm, *Labouring Men* (New York: Basic Books, 1964), Chaps. 5–7. Marx on conspiracy: *MEW,* VII, p. 273. Engels on Blanqui: *MEW,* XVIII, p. 529. Marx on Feuerbach: *MEW,* III, pp. 5–6. Marx in 1843 (*Zur Kritik der Hegelschen Rechtsphilosophie*): *MEW,* I, p. 385. Economic-Philosophic Manuscripts: *MEW, Ergänzungsband,* Pt. 1, pp. 535, 517, 514. Althusser, *Lire le Capital* (Paris: Maspéro, 1968), Vol. I, p. 79; and *Pour Marx* (Paris: Maspéro, 1968), passim. Daniel Bell, *The End of Ideology,* rev. ed. (New York: Collier Books, 1961), p. 365. Karl Korsch, *Karl Marx* (Frankfurt am Main: Europäische Verlagsanstalt, 1967), p. 181.

2. All quotations from *The Communist Manifesto: MEW,* IV, p. 459. Engels in 1845: *MEW,* II, p. 613. Marx in 1847: *MEW,* IV, p. 202. Engels in 1847: ibid., p. 317. Cole on definition of socialism: op. cit., Vol. I, pp. 4–5. English Artisans: George Lichtheim, *A Short History of Socialism* (New York: Praeger, 1970), p. 35. Working-class opposition to industrial rationality: Carl Landauer, *European Socialism* (Los Angeles and Berkeley: University of California Press, 1959), Vol. II, p. 1657. Jean Jaurès, *L'Esprit du Socialisme* (Paris: Éditions Gonthier, n.d.), p. 35. Cole, op. cit., Vol. I, p. 246. Engels in 1893: *MEW,* IV, p. 589. Franz Mehring, *Karl Marx* (London: Allen and Unwin Ltd., 1936), p. 148. Riazanov, *Marx et Engels* (Paris: Éditions Sociales Internationales, n.d.), pp. 88 ff. Marx on economics and politics in 1848: *MEW,* VI, p. 397. E. H. Carr, *Studies in Revolution* (New York: Grosset and Dunlap, 1964), pp. 22 ff. and p. 36. Marx on proletariat and bourgeoisie in Germany: *MEW,* IV, p. 397. Marx in December, 1848: *MEW,* VI, p. 108. Marx and Engels in March, 1850: *MEW,* VII, pp. 421 ff., p. 440.

3. On Marx and Engels' use of "dictatorship of the proletariat":

Hal Draper, "Marx and the Dictatorship of the Proletariat," *New Politics* (Vol. I, 1962) p. 73. The World Society: *MEW*, VII, p. 553. Marx and Engels' denunciation of the World Society: ibid., p. 45. Class Struggles in France: *MEW*, VII, pp. 33 and 84. Sidney Hook, *Towards the Understanding of Karl Marx* (New York: The John Day Company, 1933), pp. 300 ff. Engels in 1874: *MEW*, XVIII, p. 529. Engels on the Paris Commune: *MEW*, XVII, p. 624.

4. Marx and Engels on the ultra-Left in the Communist League: *MEW*, VIII, pp. 412–413, 575, 589–90. Antonio Gramsci, *Quaderni del Carcere*, IV, *Note sul Machiavelli, sulla Politica e sullo Stato Moderno* (Milan: Einaudi, 1966), p. 84.

## CHAPTER IV

1. Lenin on Plekhanov: *CW*, VIII, pp. 467 ff. General trends in 1860s: Arthur Rosenberg, *Democracy and Socialism* (New York: Alfred A. Knopf, 1939), pp. 154 ff.; British Socialism: G. D. H. Cole, *History of Socialist Thought,* Vol. II, p. 379; David Riazanov, *Marx et Engels* (Paris: Éditions Sociales Internationales, n.d. [originally 1923]), pp. 110 ff. French and English workers in 1850s: Cole, op. cit., pp. 133 ff. Marx and the British trade unionists: George Lichtheim, *A Short History of Socialism* (New York: Praeger, 1970), p. 167. Marx's "Inaugural Address": *MEW*, XVI, pp. 10 ff. Engels in 1850 on the Ten Hours Law: *MEW*, VII, pp. 226 ff.

2. Robert C. Tucker, *The Marxian Revolutionary Idea* (New York: W. W. Norton, 1969), pp. 194–196. Marx on the Paris Commune: *MEW*, XXXV, p. 160; see also Michael Harrington, "The Misfortune of 'Great Memories,'" *Dissent* (October, 1971). Lenin on Commune: *CW*, VIII, pp. 207 ff.; Frits Kool in *Die Linke gegen die Parteiherrschaft*, Frits Kool, ed. (Olten: Walter Verlag, 1970), pp. 42–43. Bakunin, *Archives Bakouniennes* (Leiden: E. J. Brill, 1957), Vol. II, p. xxix; Vol. III, pp. 177–178 and 352; *MEW*, XVIII, p. 401. Frantz Fanon, *The Wretched of the Earth* (New York: Grove Press, 1963), p. 104. Herbert Marcuse, *One Dimensional Man* (Boston: Beacon Press, 1964), p. 256. Marx on the lumpenproletariat: *MEW*, XXIII

(*Das Kapital*), pp. 670 ff.; *MEW*, VII (conspiracy), pp. 272 ff.; *MEW*, VIII (*18th Brumaire*), p. 161. 1871 IWMA resolution: *MEW*, XVII, p. 422. Marx on universal suffrage (1852): Marx and Engels, *On Britain* (Moscow: Foreign Language Publishing House, 1962), p. 362.

3. Germany in 1850s and 1860s: Carl A. Landauer, *European Socialism* (Berkeley and Los Angeles: University of California Press, 1959), Vol. I, p. 222; Gustave Mayer, *Radikalismus, Sozialismus und bürgerliche Demokratie* (Frankfurt: Suhrkamp Verlag, 1969), pp. 108 ff. Marx on Lassalle: *MEW*, XXX, p. 432. Schulze-Delitzsch: Landauer, op. cit., pp. 237–238. Lassalle: *Ferdinand Lassalle's gesammelte Reden und Schriften* (New York: Wolf and Hoehne, n.d.), Vol. I, pp. 263, 322–323; Vol. II, pp. 227, 223 ff. Marx and Engels on Lassalle in 1863: *MEW*, XXX, pp. 345 and 356; Franz Mehring, *Karl Marx* (London: Allen and Unwin, 1936), pp. 309–310. Engels in 1885 on Lassalle: *MEW*, IV, p. 83 n. Lassalle and Bismarck: Arthur Rosenberg, op. cit., pp. 159 ff.; *MEW*, XVI, p. 76. Marx to Schweitzer: *MEW*, XXXII, p. 570. Barrington Moore, *Origins of Dictatorship and Democracy* (Boston: Beacon Press, 1966).

4. German Socialism in the 1870s and 1880s: Wolfgang Abendroth, *Sozialgeschichte der Europäische Arbeiterbewegung* (Frankfurt: Suhrkamp Verlag, 1965), pp. 51 ff. Louis Blanc, *L'Organisation du Travail*, 5th ed. (Paris: Société de l'Industrie Fraternelle, 1848), pp. 103, 149, 161. Karl Marx on bureaucracy owning the state: *MEW*, I, p. 249. *Anti-Dühring*: *MEW*, XX, p. 259 and n. Karl Kautsky on state socialism: *Die Neue Zeit*, Vol. 10, No. 49 (1891–1892), pp. 705 ff. Engels to Bernstein: *MEW*, XXXV, p. 170. Engels to Bebel: ibid., p. 323. Gabriel Kolko, "The Decline of Radicalism in the Twentieth Century," in *For a New America*, ed. James Weinstein and David W. Eakin (New York: Vintage Books, 1970), p. 203.

5. German socialist progress: Landauer, op. cit., pp. 365–366; Abendroth, op. cit., pp. 52–53. Nineteenth-century economic trends: Fritz Sternberg, *Capitalism and Socialism on Trial* (New York: Greenwood Press, 1968), pp. 56 ff.; p. 97. Engels on crisis: *MEW*, XXV, p. 506 n. Austrians in 1901: Norbert Leser, *Zwischen Reformismus und Bolschewismus: Der Austro-Marxismus als Theorie und Praxis* (Vienna:

Europa Verlag, 1968), pp. 224–225. German real wages:
Abendroth, op. cit., pp. 68–69. President of State Insurance:
quoted in Sidney Hook, *Towards an Understanding of Karl
Marx* (New York: The John Day Company, 1933), p. 19.

6. Lichtheim on "Marxism": *Marxism: An Historical and Critical
Study* (New York: Praeger, 1961), p. 235. Engels at Marx's
funeral: *MEW*, XIX, p. 335. Engels on his division of labor
with Marx: *MEW*, XXI, p. 328. Antonio Gramsci: *Quaderni
del Carcere, Il Materialismo Storico*, Vol. I (Milan:
Einaudi, 1966), pp. 12–14. Kautsky to Adler: Friedrich
Adler, ed., *Victor Adler Briefwechsel mit Karl Kautsky*
(Vienna: Verlag der Wiener Volksbuchhandlung, 1954), p.
375. Lenin: *CW*, V, p. 375. Kautsky to Adler: Adler, op. cit.,
p. 501. Bebel: ibid., p. 531. Jean Jaurès: *Sixième Congrès
Socialiste Internationale, Amsterdam, 14–20 Août* (Brussels: 1904), pp. 578 and 58. Robert Michels, *Political Parties*
(New York: Hearst International Library, 1915), passim
and p. 408.

## CHAPTER V

1. Wassily Leontiev, "The Significance of Marxian Economics for
Present-Day Economic Theory," in *Marx and Modern Economics*, ed. David Horrowitz (New York: Monthly Review
Press, 1968), p. 94. Paul Samuelson, "Wages and Interest:
A Modern Dissection of Marxian Economic Models," *Amer-
ican Economic Review* (December, 1957, Vol. XLVII, No.
6), pp. 884 ff.; Marx as minor: ibid., p. 911; natural re-
sources: ibid., p. 894. Gotha Program: *MEW*, XIX, p. 15
(see also *MEW*, XIII, p. 618, and *Das Kapital, MEW*,
XXIII, p. 218). Critique of Samuelson: Fred M. Gottheil,
*American Economic Review* (September, 1960); reply by
Samuelson: ibid. Marx in 1843: *MEW*, I, pp. 231 and 370.
Max Adler, *Die Solidarische Gesellschaft* (Vienna: Europa
Verlag, 1964), p. 12.

2. *Theories of Surplus Value: MEW*, XXVI, Pt. 1, pp. 12 ff.; p. 366.
Labor theory of value as pro-capitalist: George Lichtheim,
*A Short History of Socialism*, p. 40. C. B. Macpherson, *The
Political Theory of Possessive Individualism* (London-New
York, Oxford University Press, 1962), p. 48. Robert L.

Heilbroner, *Between Capitalism and Socialism* (New York: Vintage Books, 1970), p. 140. Ben Seligman, *Main Currents in Modern Economics* (New York: The Free Press of Glencoe, 1963), p. 48. Alexander Gershenkron, *Continuity in History and Other Essays* (Cambridge: Belknap Press, 1968), p. 20.

3. Marx on method: *MEW*, XIII, pp. 631–632. Joan Robinson, *An Essay on Marxian Economics* (London: Macmillan and Co., 1949), pp. 18–19. Ralf Dahrendorf, *Society and Democracy in Germany* (New York: Anchor Books, 1969), p. 162. On definition of capital: Joan Robinson, "The Relevance of Economic Theory," *Monthly Review*, Vol. XXII, No. 8 (January, 1971), pp. 29 ff.; see also Pierro Sroffa, *Production of Commodities by Means of Commodities* (Cambridge: Cambridge University Press, 1960). Marx on living labor in capital: *MEW*, XXVI, Pt. I, p. 365. The "sixth chapter" of *Das Kapital:* Roger Dangeville, ed., *Un Chapitre inédit du "Capital"* (Paris: 10/18, 1971), p. 249. Ben Seligman: op. cit., p. 49. Clark Kerr, *Marshall, Marx and Modern Times* (Cambridge: Cambridge University Press, 1969), pp. 64 ff.

4. Christopher Hill, *Reformation to Industrial Revolution* (Baltimore: Penguin Books, 1969), p. 15 (*note:* this reference does not occur in the hard-cover edition published by Pantheon). *Grundrisse der Politische Oekonomie* (Berlin: Dietz Verlag, 1953), pp. 592 ff. Paul Sweezy, *The Theory of Capitalist Development* (New York: Monthly Review Press, 1968), pp. 142 ff. Samuelson: op. cit. Joan Robinson, *An Essay on Marxian Economics*, pp. 32 and 36. Karl Kautsky, *Bernstein und das Sozialdemokratische Programm* (Stuttgart: Dietz Verlag, 1899), pp. 115–125. Lenin: *CW*, IV, p. 201. Henryk Grossman, *Das Akkumulations- und Zusammenbruchgesetz des kapitalistischen Systems* (Frankfurt: Verlag Neue Kritik, 1967), pp. 580 ff.; Jürgen Habermas, *Politica* (Neuwied: Luchterhand, 1967), pp. 190 ff., see also Thomas Sowell, "Marx's Increasing Misery Doctrine," *American Economic Review* (March, 1960), pp. 112 ff. Rudolf Hilferding, *Karl Marx and the Close of His System, by Eugen Von Boehm Bawerk and Boehm Bawerk's Criticism of Marx* (New York: Augustus Kelley, 1949), pp. 193–195.

# CHAPTER VI

1. Werner Sombart, *Warum gibt es in den Vereinigten Staaten keinem Sozialismus* (Tübingen: Moher, 1906); Werner Sombart, *Socialism and the Social Movement* (London: J. M. Dent, 1909), p. 276. Phillip Taft, *The AF of L in the Time of Gompers* (New York: Harper and Brothers, 1957), p. vii. Lenin, *Lenin on the United States* (New York: International Publishers, 1970), p. 57.

2. Robert Owen speech: Albert Fried, ed., *Socialism in America: A Documentary History* (Garden City, N.Y.: Doubleday and Company, 1970), pp. 105–106. Stow Persons, "Christian Communitarianism in America," in *Socialism in American Life*, ed. Donald Drew Egbert and Stow Persons (Princeton, N.J.: Princeton University Press, 1952), Vol. I, pp. 127–129. Frances Wright: quoted in Phillip Foner, *History of the Labor Movement in the United States* (New York: International Publishers, 1947), Vol. I, p. 102. Marx and Engels on the United States: *MEW*, II, pp. 534–535; *MEW*, IV, pp. 10 and 341; *MEW*, XXX, p. 287; *MEW*, XXXVI, p. 624. Marx and Kriege: *MEW*, IV, pp. 3 ff. On the failure of the Homestead Act: Stephen Threnstrom, "Urbanization, Migration and Social Mobility," in *Towards a New Past*, ed. Barton J. Bernstein (New York: Vintage Books, 1969), p. 160; Richard Hofstadter, *The Age of Reform* (New York: Vintage Books, n.d. [originally 1955]), p. 54. Agrarian militancy: Seymour Martin Lipset, *Agrarian Socialism* (New York: Anchor Books, 1968), p. 17. On Claflin and Woodhull: *MEW*, XVIII, pp. 99 and 102; *The General Council of the First International, 1871–1872, Minutes* (Moscow: Progress Publishers, n.d. [1964?]), p. 206. On the Marxists in the labor movement: Ira Kipnis, *The American Socialist Movement, 1871–1912* (New York: Columbia University Press, 1952), pp. 8 ff. Selig Perlman, *Theory of the Labor Movement* (New York: Augustus Kelley, 1949 [originally 1928]). Joseph Schumpeter, *Capitalism, Socialism and Democracy* (New York: Harper and Row, Publishers, 1950), p. 336. Leon Samson, *Toward a United Front for American Workers* (New York: Farrar and Rinehart, 1933), p. 21.

3. Phillip Taft and Phillip Ross, "American Labor Violence: Its Causes, Character and Comparative Perspectives," in *Violence in America: Historical and Comparative Perspectives*, ed. Graham and Gurr (Washington, D.C.: Government Printing Office, 1969), Vol. I, pp. 226 ff. Hardacker: quoted in Gerald N. Grob, *Workers and Utopia* (Chicago: Quadrangle, 1969), p. 36. Lipset, *The First New Nation* (New York: Doubleday and Company, Anchor Edition, 1967), p. 205. Great upheaval figures: Foner, op. cit., Vol. II, p. 54; Grob, op. cit., p. 87. Marx on Henry George: *MEW*, XXXV, pp. 198 ff. Engels on George: *MEW*, XXXV, pp. 579, 588, and 589. Howard Quint, *The Forging of American Socialism* (Columbia: University of South Carolina Press, 1953), p. 71. German-American socialists: Fried, ed., *Socialism in America*, p. 180. Engels in 1890: *MEW*, XXXVII, p. 353. Henry Pelling, *American Labor* (Chicago: University of Chicago Press, 1960), p. 89. 1893–1894 debates: Taft, op. cit., pp. 71 ff.; Quint, op. cit., p. 71.

4. Voluntarism: Marc Karson, *American Labor Unions and Politics* (Boston: Beacon Press, 1965), p. 135; J. David Greenstone, *Labor in American Politics* (New York: Alfred A. Knopf, 1969), p. 26 and n.; William Appleman Williams, *The Contours of American History* (Chicago: Quadrangle, 1966), pp. 360 ff. Gompers and Wilson: Bernard Mandel, *Samuel Gompers* (Yellow Springs: Antioch Press, 1963), pp. 297 ff.; Thomas Brooks, *Toil and Trouble* (New York: Delacorte Press, 1971), p. 133. AFL after World War I: Taft, op. cit., pp. xix and 369; Irving Howe and Lewis Coser, *The American Communist Party: A Critical History* (Boston: Beacon Press, 1967), pp. 109 ff.; James Weinstein, *The Decline of Socialism in America* (New York and London: Monthly Review Press, 1967), p. x.

5. Engels on Two Factors: *MEW*, XXI, p. 253. John R. Commons, ed., *History of Labor in the United States, 1896–1932* (New York: The Macmillan Company, 1935), Vol. II, p. 60. On capitalist crisis and "the long-term factors": E. J. Hobsbawm, *Labouring Men* (New York: Basic Books, 1964), pp. 128 ff. On violence: Jerome C. Davis, "The J Curve of Rising and Declining Satisfaction as a Cause of Some Great Revolutions and a Contained Rebellion," in *Violence in America*, Vol. II. Immigration: Oscar Handlin, *Immigration as a Factor in American History* (Englewood

Cliffs, N.J.: Prentice-Hall, 1959); Nathan Glazer and Daniel Patrick Moynihan, *Beyond the Melting Pot* (Cambridge: Massachusetts Institute of Technology and Harvard University Press, 1963), pp. 181 ff. Selig Perlman, op. cit., pp. 168–169. Catholics: Karson, op. cit., p. 255. 1910 Census: W. S. Woytinsky, *Labor in the United States* (Washington, D.C.: Social Science Research Council, 1938), p. 237. "New recruits": Hobsbawm, op. cit., p. 142. Hourwich quotation: Handlin, op. cit., pp. 58–59.

## CHAPTER VII

1. Marx to Engels, October 8, 1858: *MEW, XXIX. Das Kapital,* Vol. I, 1867 Introduction: *MEW, XXIII,* p. 12. Paul Samuelson, *Economics,* 7th ed. (New York: McGraw-Hill, 1967), p. 700. E. H. Carr, *The Bolshevik Revolution* (Baltimore: Penguin Books, 1969), p. 55. Gunnar Myrdal, *The Challenge of World Poverty* (New York: Pantheon Books, 1970), pp. 43 and 517, n. 28. Antonio Gramsci on *Das Kapital:* quoted in John M. Cammet, *Antonio Gramsci and the Origins of Italian Communism* (Stanford: Stanford University Press, 1967), p. 61. Marx on English colonialism (originally written in English): Shlomo Avineri, ed., *Karl Marx on Modernization* (New York: Doubleday, Anchor Books, 1969), pp. 94, 133, 137, and 139. Marx on the Revolutionary Class: *Philosophie de la Misère* (Paris: 10/18, 1964), p. 491. Myrdal on spread effects: *An Inquiry into the Poverty of Nations* (New York, Pantheon Books, 1970), Vol. I, p. 189; *The Challenge of World Poverty,* p. 28.
2. Friedrich Engels, Note to the 1888 edition of *The Communist Manifesto: MEW, IV,* p. 462 n. Marx on the Asiatic mode of production: Avineri, op. cit., p. 132. Engels on the Asiatic mode: *MEW, XXVIII,* p. 259. Marx's letter to *Otetschestwennyje Sapiski: MEW, XIX,* pp. 107 ff. George Lichtheim, *The Origins of Socialism* (New York: Praeger, 1969), p. 216. Russian populism: Karl Landauer, *European Socialism* (Berkeley and Los Angeles: University of California Press, 1959), Vol. I, p. 399; E. H. Carr, *Studies in Revolution* (New York: Grosset and Dunlap, 1964), p. 69. Marx on Bakunin: *MEW, XVIII,* p. 633. For the development of Marx's interest in Russia: *MEW, XXXII,* pp. 42,

197, 649, 659. Engels on Russia: *MEW*, XVIII, p. 563. Marx and Engels: Preface to the Russian edition of *The Communist Manifesto, MEW*, IV, p. 576. On Bernstein and the Russian scenario: Leonard Schapiro, *The Communist Party of the Soviet Union* (New York: Random House, 1959), p. 10, n. 2; E. H. Carr, *The Bolshevik Revolution*, Vol. II, pp. 384 and 387. For Engels' late views: Engels to N. F. Danielson, October 17, 1893, *MEW*, XXIX, pp. 148 ff.; Engels to G. W. Plekhanov, ibid., pp. 416 ff.; Nachwort zu "Soziales aus Russland," *MEW*, XXII, pp. 421 ff. Engels to Kautsky: *MEW*, XXXV, pp. 357–358.

3. London Congress resolution: J. Braunthal, *Geschichte der International* (Hannover: Dietz Verlag, 1961), Vol. I, p. 311; for a general history, Braunthal, ibid., and Haupt and Reberioux, eds., *La Deuxième Internationale et l'Orient* (Paris: Éditions Cujas, 1967). E. Ferri and J. B. Justo, *El Partido Socialista en la Republica Argentina* (Buenos Aires: Partido Socialista, 1909); see also G. D. H. Cole, *History of Socialist Thought*, Vol. III, Pt. 2, p. 830. Shaw: Braunthal, op. cit., pp. 311–312; Cole, op. cit., Pt. 1, p. 191. Bernstein on colonies: Braunthal, op. cit., p. 313. Van Kol in 1904: *Sixième Congrès Socialiste Internationale, 1904* (Brussels: Internationale Socialiste, 1904), p. 44. Van Kol Stuttgart resolution: Haupt and Reberioux, op. cit., p. 94. Bernstein speech: ibid., p. 97. Kautsky on colonies: "Sozialistische Kolonialpolitik," *Die Neue Zeit*, Vol. 27, Bd. II (1909), pp. 33 ff. Lenin: *CW*, XIII, "The International Socialist Congress at Stuttgart," p. 77. Marx and Engels on colonies: Avineri, op. cit., p. 71; *MEW*, XXIX, p. 358; *MEW*, XXI, p. 197. Congo: Braunthal, op. cit., pp. 321 ff.; Haupt and Reberioux, op. cit., pp. 105 ff.; Cole, *History of Socialist Thought*, Vol. III, Pt. 2, pp. 641 ff. Vandervelde: Haupt and Reberioux, op. cit., p. 107. Lenin, *CW*, XXIII, pp. 338 and 145.

## CHAPTER VIII

1. Fritz Sternberg, *Capitalism and Socialism on Trial*, trans. Edward Fitzgerald (New York: Greenwood Press, 1968 [originally 1951]), p. 120. Lenin: 1908 Introduction to *The*

*Development of Capitalism in Russia, CW*, III, p. 33. On Stolypin: Alexander Gershenkron, *Continuity in History and Other Essays* (Cambridge: Belknap, 1968), p. 240. On Russian economic development before World War I: Charles K. Wilber, *The Soviet Model and Underdeveloped Countries* (Chapel Hill: University of North Carolina Press, 1969); Gershenkron, op. cit., pp. 127–147; G. D. H. Cole, *History of Socialist Thought*, Vol. III, Pt. 1, p. 411. Y. Varga, *Le Testament de Varga*, ed. Roger Garaudy (Paris: Grasset, 1970), p. 36.

2. Marx in 1867: *MEW*, XXIII, pp. 14–15. Engels on Italy: *MEW*, XXII, p. 439. 1898 Program: E. H. Carr, *The Bolshevik Revolution, 1917–1923* (Baltimore, Penguin Books, 1969), Vol. I, p. 15. Karl Kautsky, "Triebkrafte der Russische Revolution," *Die Neue Zeit*, Vol. 25, Bd. I, No. 10 (1906), pp. 331–333. Lenin on Engels: *CW*, II, p. 25. Lenin on the Russian Revolution: 1908 Introduction to *The Development of Capitalism in Russia, CW*, III, pp. 32–33; for the American model, see "The Agrarian Program of the Liberals," *CW*, VIII, p. 319. 1905: L. D. Trotsky, *Results and Perspectives* trans. M. J. Olgin (Ceylon: Lanka Samasamaja Publishers, 1954 [originally 1906]). Carr on Trotsky's scenario: *The Bolshevik Revolution*, p. 71.

3. Lenin, "Farewell Letter to Swiss Workers," *CW*, XXIII, pp. 271–273. Trotsky in 1905: Trotsky, *Results and Perspectives*. Lenin in 1919: "Achievements and Difficulties," *CW*, XXIX, pp. 68 and 87. Varga, op. cit., pp. 47–48. Lenin on the dictatorship of the proletariat in 1905: *CW*, IX, p. 133. 1905 articles: *CW*, VIII, pp. 468 ff., 472. *State and Revolution: CW*, XXV, pp. 412, 415, 416. Engels to Kautsky, June 29, 1891: *MEW*, XXII, p. 234. Lenin in 1919: *CW*, XXX, pp. 262 and 267. *State and Revolution, CW*, XXV, p. 449. Julian Martov, "Dictatorship of the Minority" in Irving Howe, ed., *Essential Works of Socialism* (New York: Holt, Rinehart and Winston, 1970), p. 125.

4. Lenin 1920 speech: *CW*, XXX, p. 418. E. H. Carr on 1917 and Europe: *The Bolshevik Revolution*, Vol. III, p. 224. Antonio Gramsci: *Quaderni del Carcere*, Vol. IV, p. 68. Lenin on the conditions: *CW*, XXXII, p. 215. On Kronstadt: *CW*, XXXII, p. 358. Lenin in 1921 on the European revolution: *CW*, XXXII, p. 180. For Lenin in 1923, see Moshe Lewin,

*Lenin's Last Struggle* (New York: Vintage Books, 1970), passim. "Better Fewer, But Better": *CW*, XXXII, p. 488. "On Cooperation": ibid., p. 474. Lenin's letter to the Communist Party: *CW*, XXXVI, p. 597. "Our Revolution": *CW*, XXXII, p. 478. "On Cooperation": ibid., pp. 474–475. "Better Fewer, But Better": ibid., p. 500. Roger Garaudy, *Pour un Modèle Français du Socialisme* (Paris: Gallimard, 1968), p. 303. Marx on rights: "Kritik des Gothaer Programms," *MEW*, XIX, p. 21. Editorial note: *CW*, XXXVI, n. 653, p. 712.

5. Stalin, 1924: *CW*, VIII, p. 65; 1926: ibid., pp. 67–68. Lenin in 1915: *CW*, XXI, p. 342; 1916: *CW*, XXIII, p. 59. E. H. Carr, *Socialism in One Country* (Baltimore: Penguin Books, 1970), Vol. II, p. 50, n. 2. For Trotsky and Bukharin: Isaac Deutscher, *The Prophet Unarmed* (New York: Vintage Books, 1965), passim. *The History of the CPSU (B)* (New York: International Publishers, 1939), p. 305. On the revolution from above: *cf.*, Engels, "Die 'Krisis' in Preussen," *MEW*, XVIII, pp. 290 ff.; *Herr Eugen Duhrings Umwälzung der Wissenschaft: MEW*, XX, p. 259 and n., Nachwort zu "Soziales aus Russland," *MEW*, XXII, p. 433. Lenin, Preface to the Russian translation of Marx's letters to Kugelmann (1907), *CW*, XII, p. 107. IWMA Statutes: *MEW*, XVI, p. 14. Stalin, "Once More on the Social Democratic Deviation in Our Party," *CW*, IX, p. 33; on self-criticism: *CW*, XI, p. 32. Deaths in the thirties: Zbigniew Brzezinski, *Between Two Ages* (New York: Viking, 1970), p. 126 and n. Poland in 1970–1971: dispatch by K. S. Karol, *Le Monde* (February 20, 1971). Livestock destruction: Charles K. Wilber, op. cit., p. 48. Engels on agriculture: "Die Bauernfrage in Frankreich und Deutschland," *MEW*, XXII, pp. 499–504.

6. E. Preobrazhensky, *The New Economics*, trans. Brian Pearce (Oxford: The Clarendon Press, 1965), pp. 72 and 73. Marx on Gotha Program: *MEW*, XIX, p. 21. Engels in 1891: *MEW*, XXII, p. 209. Engels to Bebel: *MEW*, XXXVI, p. 88. Stalin's interview with Ludwig: *CW*, XIII, p. 121. Varga, op. cit., p. 71. Social class and Soviet education: Brzezinski, op. cit., p. 163 n. Gramsci: *Quaderni del Carcere*, op. cit., Vol. III, p. 134. Iring Fetscher, *Karl Marx und der Marxismus* (Munich: R. Piper and Co., 1967), pp.

17 and 89. Wilber, op. cit., p. 233. Khrushchev and de-Staliniization: Wolfgang Leonhard, *Die Dreispaltung des Marxismus* (Dusseldorf: Weign, 1970), pp. 200 ff. K. S. Karol on Russia: *Le Monde Hebdomadaire* (September 17–23, 1970). Varga, op. cit., p. 65. Sakharov: *The New York Times* (July 22, 1968).

7. Edda Werfel: Leonhard, op. cit., p. 360; Kosik, op. cit., p. 450; Stojanovic, op. cit., p. 448. Stojanovic, *Kritik und Zukunft des Sozialismus* (Munich: Hanser Verlag, 1970), p. 62. Deutscher, *The Prophet Unarmed,* pp. 130–131; *The Prophet Outcast,* p. 32. Marx on state as private property: *MEW,* I, p. 249. Bukharin: *A Documentary History of Communism,* ed. Robert V. Daniels (New York: Vintage Books, 1960), Vol. I, p. 85. Workers' Truth: Robert V. Daniels, *The Conscience of the Revolution* (New York: Simon and Schuster, 1969), p. 161. Rakovsky, *Essential Works of Socialism,* ed. Irving Howe (New York: Holt, Rinehart and Winston, 1970), p. 371. Charles Bettelheim, *Calcul Économique et Formes de Propriété* (Paris: Maspéro, 1970), p. 87. Deutscher on "bourgeois restoration": *The Prophet Unarmed,* p. 462.

## CHAPTER IX

1. Guesde: quoted in James Joll, *The Second International, 1889–1914* (New York: Harper Colophon Books, 1966), p. 101. Germany after World War I: Cole, *History of Socialist Thought,* Vol. IV, Pt. I, pp. 136 ff.; Helga Grebing, "Der Sozialismus in Deutschland," in *Sozialismus,* ed. Iring Fetscher (Munich: Kurt Desch, 1968), pp. 168 ff. Rosa Luxemburg, *Ausgewahlte Reden und Schriften* (Berlin: Dietz Verlag, 1951), pp. 645 ff.; p. 694. Paul Levi, *Zwischen Spartakus und Sozial-Demokratie* (Frankfurt: Europäische Verlagsanstalt, 1969), pp. 37 ff. On German socialism: Cole, op. cit., pp. 136 ff.; pp. 635 ff. Wissell: Carl Landauer, *European Socialism* (Berkeley and Los Angeles: University of California Press, 1958), Vol. I, p. 843. Independent Labour Party in 1924: Adolph Sturmthal, *The Tragedy of European Labour* (London: Gollancz, 1944), p. 88.

2. Hilferding in the twenties: Fetscher, op. cit., p. 173. Hilferding

on banks: quoted in Henryk Grossman, *Das Akkumula-tions- und Zusammenbruchgesetz des kapitalistischen Systems* (Frankfurt: Neue Kritik, 1967 [originally 1926]), p. 57. Hilferding on the depression: W. S. Woytinsky, *Stormy Passage* (New York: The Vanguard Press, 1961), p. 471. Naphtali: quoted in Sturmthal, op. cit., p. 74. Snowden and Henderson: David Marquand, "The Politics of Deprivation," *Encounter* XXXII, No. 4 (April, 1969), pp. 37 ff. Harold Macmillan, *Winds of Change* (New York: Harper and Row, 1966), p. 253. Labor and Socialist International Program: Sturmthal, op. cit., p. 76. Mosley: Marquand, op. cit. Skidelsky: ibid. Tarnow: Sturmthal, op. cit., p. 71.

3. Blum: *L'Oeuvre de Léon Blum, 1945–1947* (Paris: Éditions Albin Michel, 1968), pp. 284 and 273. André Philip, *Les Socialistes* (Paris: Seuil, 1967), p. 90. Faure: quoted, ibid., p. 76. Cole on De Man: *History of Socialist Thought*, Vol. V, p. 189; Landauer, op. cit., p. 1405. Henri de Man, *Cavalier Seul* (Geneva: Éditions du Cheval Aile, 1948), pp. 163 ff. Déat and Marquet: Philip, op. cit., p. 74. Lichtheim on Déat: *Marxism in Modern France*, 2nd edition (New York: Columbia University Press, 1968), p. 41, n. 12. Epitaph: Sturmthal, op. cit., p. 5. Ralph Miliband, *The State in Capitalist Society* (London: Weidenfeld and Nicolson, 1969), p. 99.

4. Nationalizations after World War II: Michael Kidron, *Western Capitalism Since the War* (Baltimore: Penguin Books, 1970), pp. 24 ff. Kautsky, *Das Erfurter Programm* (Stuttgart: Dietz Verlag, 1892). Jaurès on state: quoted in Philip, op. cit., p. 45. 1910 resolution: ibid., pp. 36–37. Jaurès and nationalization, 1894: *Jaurès et le Socialisme des Intellectuels* (Paris: Georges Lefranc Aubier, 1968), p. 31. Otto Bauer, quoted in Norbert Leser, *Zwischen Reformismus und Bolshewismus* (Vienna: Europa Verlag, 1968), p. 147. British mines: Cole, *History of Socialist Thought*, Vol. IV, Pt. I, p. 416. Geneva Conference: ibid., p. 328. Sidney Webb, *Fabian Essays in Socialism* (Gloucester, Mass.: Peter Smith, 1967 [originally 1889]), pp. 68–69. Engels on Fabians: *MEW*, XXIX, p. 8. Clause Four: quoted: Paul Foot, *The Politics of Harold Wilson* (London: Penguin Books, 1968), p. 123. Ralf Dahrendorf, *Society and Demo-*

*cracy in Germany* (New York: Doubleday and Company, 1963), p. 167. André Philip, *La Gauche, Mythes et Réalités* (Paris: Georges Lefranc Aubier, 1964), p. 71. *The Accidental Century* (New York: The Macmillan Company, 1965), Chap. III. Post-1945 British nationalization: C. A. R. Crosland, *The Future of Socialism* (London: Jonathan Cape, 1956), p. 484. Steel renationalization: Paul Foot, op. cit., p. 189; *The Economist* (January 31, 1970). Macmillan and nationalization: Macmillan, op. cit., p. 232; Foot, op. cit., p. 341, n. 1. Douglas Jay, *Socialism in the New Society* (New York: St. Martin's Press, 1963), p. 278.

5. Wolfgang Abendroth, *Sozialgeschichte der Europäische Arbeiterbewegung* (Frankfurt: Suhrkamp Verlag, 1965), p. 182. SPD working-class percentage: Kidron, op. cit., p. 119. André Gorz, *Réforme et Révolution* (Paris: Seuil, 1969), p. 34. Raymond Williams, ed., *May Day Manifesto* (London: Penguin Books, 1968), p. 183. Crosland, op. cit., pp. 35 ff.; pp. 92, 417, 439. Crosland in early sixties: *The Conservative Enemy* (New York: Shocken Books, 1962), p. 139. Jean-Jacques Servan-Schreiber, "Entre Pompidou et Poher," *L'Express* (May 12–19, 1969). *Protokoll, Ausserordentlicher Parteitag, Bad Godesberg, 13–15 November, 1959* (Bonn: Vorstand der SPD, n.d.), pp. 17 ff. Heinrich Deist, ibid., p. 183. John Kenneth Galbraith, *The New Industrial State* (Boston: Houghton Mifflin Company, 1967), p. 99. Deist: *Protokoll*, op. cit., pp. 213 ff. SPD 1970 Congress: *Der Spiegel* (May 11, 1970). Young Socialists: Bremen Congress: *Vorwarts* (Bonn: March 18, 1971); Party reply: ibid; Schiller: *Der Spiegel* (March 22, 1971); Poll: *Der Spiegel* (March 1, 1971); Vogel: *Der Spiegel* (May 3, 1971). British white-collar percentage: Kidron, op. cit., p. 122.

6. Thomas Balogh, *Planning for Progress*, Fabian Tract 346 (London, 1963); Richard Titmus, *Commitment to Welfare* (New York: Pantheon Books, 1968), passim and p. 133. Harold Wilson, *Purpose in Politics* (Boston: Houghton Mifflin Company, 1964), p. 18. Titmus, op. cit., p. 125. Andrew Schonfield, "Stop-Go Dilemma," *Encounter* XXVI, No. 6 (June, 1966), p. 7. George Lichtheim, "Devaluation," *Commentary* (February, 1968). Michael Shanks: quoted, ibid. John Hughes, "The Increase in Inequality," *The New*

*Statesman,* Vol. 76 (November 8, 1968), p. 620. British poverty, 1970: *The Economist* (December 19, 1970). Daniel Singer: *Prelude to Revolution; France in May, 1968* (New York: Hill and Wang, 1970), p. 277.

## CHAPTER X

1. John Kenneth Galbraith, *Economic Development,* Sentry ed. (Boston: Houghton Mifflin Company, 1964), p. 4. Iran: see Walter Z. Laquer, *The Struggle for the Middle East* (New York: The Macmillan Company, 1969), pp. 31 ff. Raul Prebisch, *UNCTAD, Second Session, New Delhi, 1968* (New York: United Nations, 1968), p. 417; see also Fernando H. Cardoso, "The Industrial Elite," in *Elites in Latin America,* ed. Seymour Martin Lipset and Aldo Solari (New York: Oxford University Press, 1967), p. 95. Russia in 1913: Charles K. Wilber, *The Soviet Model and Underdeveloped Countries* (Chapel Hill: University of North Carolina Press, 1969), p. 14 and Table 1–2, p. 15. Gunnar Myrdal: *Asian Drama: An Inquiry into the Poverty of Nations* (New York: Pantheon Books, 1968), Vol. II, p. 717. Alexander Gershenkron, *Continuity in History and Other Essays* (Cambridge: Belknap, 1968), p. 137. On Weber: Seymour Martin Lipset, "Values, Education and Entrepreneurship," in Lipset and Solari, op. cit., p. 4. Gunnar Myrdal, *The Challenge of World Poverty* (New York: Pantheon Books, 1970), p. 83.
2. Mao Tse-tung, *Selected Works* (hereafter cited as *SW*) (London: Lawrence and Wishart, 1954), Vol. III, p. 215. *Hong Hong Weekly* quoted in Ygael Gluckstein, *Mao's China* (London: Allen and Unwin, 1957), p. 193. On the 1928–1937 period and the Kuomintang, cf. Barrington Moore, *The Social Origins of Dictatorship and Democracy* (Boston: Beacon Press, 1966) pp. 187 ff.; and Michael Harrington, *Communist China: A Socialist Analysis* (New York: Young People's Socialist League, 1962 [mimeo]). On inflation in China in 1949: Gluckstein, op. cit., p. 103; Chang Kia-ngau, *The Inflationary Spiral* (New York: John Wiley, 1958), passim. Mao on classes in the Chinese Revolution: *SW,* III, p. 220. On China in the 1920s, see Harold Isaacs,

*The Tragedy of the Chinese Revolution,* rev. ed. (Stanford: Stanford University Press, 1951). Communists and workers: Benjamin Schwartz, *Chinese Communism and the Rise of Mao* (Cambridge, Mass.: Harvard University Press, 1952), p. 97. Mao on peasantry and proletariat (1939): *SW*, III, pp. 87 ff. Engels on the peasants (1892): *MEW*, XIX, p. 58. Marx, *The Eighteenth Brumaire: MEW*, VIII, p. 198. Karl Kautsky, "Triebkrafte der Russische Revolution," *Die Neue Zeit,* Vol. 25, Bd. 1, No. 10 (1906), p. 330. *Manifestes, Thèses et Résolutions des Quatres Premiers Congrès Mondiaux* (Paris: Bibliothèque Communiste, 1934 [reprinted, Paris: Maspéro, 1969]), pp. 78–79. Sultan-Galiev: Leonard Schapiro, *The Communist Party of the Soviet Union* (New York: Random House, 1960), p. 348. Harold Isaacs, op. cit., p. 312. Roger Garaudy, *Le Problème Chinois* (Paris: 10/18, n.d.), p. 86. Mao (1928): *SW*, I, p. 66; 1935: ibid., p. 156; 1937: ibid., p. 265. 1939: ibid., III, pp. 88 and 220. "On Coalition Government": *SW*, IV, p. 294. On Tientsin, see M. Y. Wang, "The Stalinist State in China," *New International* Vol. XVII, No. 2 (March–April, 1951), p. 101. Leon Trotsky, "Peasant War in China," translation in *Bulletin of Marxist Studies* (New York: Socialist Workers Party, 1957), p. 15.

3. On cooperatives in 1952: Richard Lowenthal, "Development versus Utopia in Communist policy," *Survey* (Winter–Spring, 1970), p. 13. For a general account of the 1953–1955 period, see "Collectivization in Retrospect: The 'Socialist High Tide' of Winter–Autumn, 1955," by Kenneth A. Walker, *China Quarterly* (April–June, 1966). Central Committee in 1953: quoted in Michael Harrington, "Despotism's Fortress in Asia," *New International* Vol. XXIV, Nos. 2–3 (Spring–Summer, 1958), p. 92. Mao's July 31 speech: ibid. Paul A. Baran, *The Political Economy of Growth,* 2nd ed. (New York: Monthly Review Press, 1968), pp. 226–227 and 255. Shenyang teachers quoted in *Saturn* (Paris: December, 1957), p. 87. Garaudy, op. cit., p. 133. Text of the Central Committee Resolution of August 29, 1958, ibid., p. 288. 1962 Central Committee: ibid., p. 136. Mao's April 15, 1958, speech quoted, Charles Johnson, "The Two Chinese Revolutions," *China Quarterly,* No. 39 (July–September, 1969), pp. 22–23. On the 1959 reorienta-

tion of party policy, cf. Philip Bridgham, "Mao's 'Cultural Revolution': Origins and Development," *China Quarterly*, No. 30 (January–March, 1967) and Dwight H. Perkins, "Economic Growth in China and the Cultural Revolution," ibid. Joan Robinson: *The Cultural Revolution in China* (Baltimore: Penguin Books, 1969), p. 35. Richard Hughes, "Mao Makes the Trials Run on Time," *The New York Times Magazine* (August 23, 1970), p. 67.

4. Central Committee text of August 8, 1966, in Garaudy, op. cit., pp. 289 ff. On Shanghai, 1966–1967: ibid., pp. 164–165; and Philip Bridgham, "Mao's Cultural Revolution in 1967: The Struggle to Seize Power," *China Quarterly*, No. 35 (April–June, 1968), pp. 8–9. On Liu: Robinson, op. cit., p. 148. Anibal Quijano Obregon, "Contemporary Peasant Movements," in Lipset and Solari, op. cit. Russian Communists on Maoism: Wolfgang Leonhard, *Die Dreispaltung des Marxismus* (Dusseldorf-Wein: Econ Verlag, 1970), pp. 329 ff. A. Gramsci in Franco De Felice and Valentino Parlato, eds., *La Question Méridionale* (Rome: Editori Reuniti, 1969), pp. 64–65. 1926 article: ibid., p. 127. Lin Piao, *"Long Live the Victory of People's War!"* (Peking: Foreign Language Press, 1965).

5. Gramsci on cities: *Quaderni del Carcere* (Milan: Einaudi, 1966), Vol. III, *Il Risorgimento,* p. 95. Barbara Ward, "The Poor World's Cities," *The Economist* (December 6, 1969). Marx on the lumpenproletariat: Eighteenth Brumaire, *MEW*, VIII, p. 161. Bakunin: quoted in George Lichtheim, "Imperialism," *Commentary* (April, 1970), p. 72. Peter Worsley, "Revolutionary Theories," *Monthly Review* (May, 1969), p. 36. Glaucio Ary Dillon Soares, "Industrialization: The Brazilian Political System," in *Latin America, Reform or Revolution,* p. 196, n. 12. Samir Amin: *The Maghreb in the Modern World* (Baltimore: Penguin Books, 1971), p. 222.

6. The German Ideology: *MEW*, III, pp. 34–35. Marx and Engels on "self": *MEW*, IV, p. 15. Robert Heilbroner, "Socialism and the Future," *Commentary* (December, 1969). *Venceremos! The Speeches and Writings of Che Guevara,* ed. John A. Gerassi (New York: The Macmillan Company, 1968), pp. 403–404. Ibid., p. 301. Guevara letter: ibid., p. 412. Edward Boorstein, quoted in Leo Huberman and Paul

Sweezy, *Socialism in Cuba* (New York: Monthly Review Press, 1969), p. 199. *The Economist* (August 1, 1970). René Dumont, *Cuba, est-il socialiste?* (Paris: Seuil, 1970), p. 40. Ibid., p. 96. *The Economist* (August 1, 1970). Agricultural brigades: Dumont, op. cit., p. 144. Democracy: ibid., pp. 101, 178, and 191. "Parasites" Law: Associated Press dispatch (March 18, 1971). Huberman and Sweezy, op. cit., pp. 200 and 219. K. S. Karol, *Guerillas in Power* (New York: Hill and Wang, 1970), pp. 328, 478, 481, 482. Yugoslavia: Stojanovic, op. cit., pp. 93–94; Dominique Rouvre and Jean Morin, *Esprit* (February, 1970); Albert Meister, *Esprit* (September, 1970); Roger Priouret, *L'Express* (January 18, 1971); Robert A. Dahl, *After the Revolution* (New Haven: Yale University Press, 1970), p. 130; Daniel Chauvey [pseud.], *Autogestion* (Paris: Seuil, 1970), pp. 59–60.

7. Mexican Socialism: René Dumont, *L'Afrique Noire est mal partie*, p. 209; Irving Louis Horrowitz in Lipset and Solari, *Elites in Latin America*, p. 167. Peru: dispatch by Malcolm W. Browne, *The New York Times* (June 29, 1969). Dumont: *Cuba, est-il socialiste?* p. 228. Gunnar Myrdal, *The Challenge of World Poverty*, pp. 485–487. Victor Alba, "New Alignments in Latin America," *Dissent* (July–August, 1970). Egypt: Iring Fetscher, ed., *Sozialismus, vom Klassenkampf zum Wohlfahrstaat* (Munich: Verlag Kurt Desch, 1968). Bassam Tibi, "Der Arabische Sozialismus"; Laquer, *The Struggle for the Middle East*, pp. 229 ff.; René Dumont and Marcel Mazoyer, *Développement et Socialismes* (Paris: Seuil, 1969), pp. 179 ff. 1964 Russian analysis: *The Struggle for the Middle East*, pp. 175–176. Bakadash: ibid., pp. 177 and 304 ff. Sudan: Dispatch by Eric Rouleau, *Le Monde Hebdomadaire* (August 13–19, 1970). *Vorwarts* on Sudan: Dispatch by Walter Osten, February 25, 1971. Richard Lowenthal, "Development versus Utopia in Communist Policy," *Survey* (Winter–Spring, 1970), pp. 9–11. *Le Monde Hebdomadaire* (July 9–15, 1970). Dumont and Mazoyer, op. cit., p. 193. Samir Amin quoted, Dumont, *L'Afrique Noire est mal partie*, p. 215.

8. Bevan quoted, Gunnar Myrdal, *Economic Theory of Underdeveloped Regions* (London: Ducksworth, 1957), p. 48. Elites: *Asian Drama*, Vol. I, p. 275. Nehru and Gandhi: ibid., Vol. II, pp. 788 and 852. "Socialism": ibid., Vol. II,

p. 808. Congress in 1955: ibid., Vol. II, p. 800 and n. 3. Public enterprises: ibid., Vol. II, p. 819. "Green Revolution": Myrdal, *The Challenge of World Poverty*, pp. 125 ff. and pp. 401 ff.

## CHAPTER XI

1. Engels on socialist and social democrat: *MEW*, XXII, pp. 417 ff. Socialist Party statistics: James Weinstein, *The Decline of Socialism in America* (New York and London: Monthly Review Press, 1967), pp. 27, 84–85, 93, 103, 115. Daniel Bell, *Marxian Socialism in the United States* (Princeton, N.J.: Princeton University Press, 1967), pp. vii and x. Ira Kipnis, *The American Socialist Movement, 1897–1912* (New York: Columbia University Press, 1952), p. 429. Debs quote: Marc Karson, *American Labor Unions and Politics* (Boston: Beacon Press, 1965), p. 160. IWW policies: Foner, *History of the Labor Movement in the United States* (New York: International Publishers, 1947—), Vol. IV, p. 77. Groups Socialist Party appealed to: David A. Shannon, *The Socialist Party of America: A History* (New York: The Macmillan Company, 1955), pp. 68 ff. Weinstein: op. cit., passim. Socialists and the labor party: Foner, op. cit., Vol. III, p. 377; on Walling position: Shannon, op. cit., pp. 64–65; the twenties: Weinstein, op. cit., pp. 76 and 325.

2. Urbanization: Irving Bernstein, *The Lean Years* (Baltimore: Penguin Books, 1966), p. 49. Matthew Woll and Depression: Arthur Schlesinger, Jr., *The Coming of the New Deal* (Boston: Houghton Mifflin Company, 1958), p. 90. Socialist Party in the thirties: Shannon, op. cit., pp. 224 ff. Kentucky leaflet: Schlesinger, *The Coming of the New Deal*, p. 139. "Most old-line AF of L leaders . . .": ibid., p. 140. 1936 FDR campaign: Arthur M. Schlesinger, Jr., *The Politics of Upheaval* (Boston: Houghton Mifflin Company, 1960), p. 292. Hofstadter, *The Age of Reform* (New York: Vintage Books, n.d. [originally 1955]), p. 308. Leftist historians: William Appleman Williams, *The Great Evasion* (Chicago: Quadrangle Books, 1968), p. 153; James Weinstein and David W. Eakins, eds., *For a New America* (New York: Vintage Books, 1970).

3. Original Communist movement: Max Shachtman, "A Re-Examination of the Party," *New International* (Fall, 1957); Max Shachtman and Theodore Draper, "An Exchange of Views," *New International* (Winter, 1958). Theodore Draper, *The Roots of American Communism* (New York: The Viking Press, 1963), p. 395. Earl Browder, *The People's Front* (New York: International Publishers, 1938), p. 232. Arthur McDowell: *Socialist Review*, Vol. 7 (July–August, 1938), p. 3. Norman Thomas in 1938: Bernard J. Johnpoll, *Pacifist's Progress* (Chicago: Quadrangle Books, 1970), p. 203. Communist Party in 1939: Irving Howe and Lewis Coser, *The American Communist Party: A Critical History* (Boston: Beacon Press, 1967), pp. 385–386.

4. Schlesinger on New Deal: *The Politics of Upheaval*, p. 651. Employment Act of 1946: Stephen Kemp Bailey, *Congress Makes a Law* (New York: Vintage Books ed., 1964). Kennedy tax cut: Arthur M. Schlesinger, Jr., *A Thousand Days* (Boston: Houghton Mifflin Company, 1965), pp. 648–649. AFL-CIO Conventions: Gus Tyler, *The Labor Revolution* (New York: The Viking Press, 1967), p. 111; *The Federationist* (January, 1966, and January, 1968). UAW Convention: *Washington Report*, Vol. 10 (May 4, 1970). Theodore H. White, *The Making of the President, 1968* (New York: Atheneum Publishers, 1969), p. 365. On interest groups: J. David Greenstone, *Labor in American Politics* (New York: Alfred A. Knopf, 1969), pp. 16 and 351. George Meany on socialism: *Hearings on Unemployment Compensation* (Washington, D.C.: House Ways and Means Committee, 1959), pp. 458 ff. American labor and European social democracy: Greenstone, op. cit., p. 7.

## CHAPTER XII

1. André Gorz, *Réforme et Révolution* (Paris: Seuil, 1969). Alvin Schorr, *Explorations in Social Policy* (New York: Basic Books, 1968), p. 275. Dispatch by Allan Otten, *The Wall Street Journal* (February 25, 1969). *Report of the National Commission on Civil Disorders* (Washington, D.C.: Government Printing Office, 1968), p. 28. *Report and Recommendations of the Council, White House Conference on*

*Civil Rights* (Washington, D.C.: Government Printing Office, 1966), p. 67. Rudolph Oswald, "The City Worker's Budget," in *The Federationist* (February, 1969). *Building the American City: Report of the National Commission on Urban Problems* (Washington, D.C.: Government Printing Office, 1968), p. 67. Violence Commission: *The New York Times* (November 24, 1969).

2. *Economic Report of the President* (Washington, D.C.: Government Printing Office, 1969), p. 175. *Building the American City*, p. 153. *Report of the National Commission on Civil Disorders*, pp. 140 and 458. Charles Schultz, "Budget Alternatives after Vietnam," in *Agenda for the Nation*, ed. Kermit Gordon (Washington, D.C.: Brookings Institution, 1968), p. 44. John Kenneth Galbraith, *The New Industrial State* (Boston: Houghton Mifflin Company, 1967), p. 245. Christopher Jencks and David Reisman, *The Academic Revolution* (New York: Doubleday Anchor Books, 1969), p. 111. Peter M. Blair and Otis Dudley Duncan, *The American Occupational Structure* (New York: John Wiley and Sons, 1967), p. 79. *Manpower Report of the President, 1969* (Washington, D.C.: Government Printing Office, 1969), p. 26. Jencks and Riesman, op. cit., pp. 175, 125, 147, 148, 150.

3. National Committee on Urban Growth Problems, *The New City* (New York: Praeger, 1969), pp. 3 ff. Andrew Schonfield, *Modern Capitalism: The Changing Balance of Public and Private Power* (London: Oxford, 1965), p. 115. Abraham Ribicoff, "The Competent City," address, *Congressional Record*, Vol. 113, No. 8 (January 23, 1967). Lawrence A. Mayer, "The Housing Shortage Goes Critical," *Fortune* (December, 1969). Romney quoted: The National Urban Coalition, *Counterbudget* (New York: Praeger, 1971), p. 149. David Marquand, "May Day Illusions," *Encounter* (August, 1968), p. 56. Raymond Fletcher, "Where Did It All Go Wrong?" *Encounter* (November, 1969), p. 9.

4. Robert Dorfman in *Measuring the Benefits of Government Investment*, ed. Robert Dorfman (Washington, D.C.: The Brookings Institution, 1965), pp. 4–5. Robert Dorfman, *The Price System* (Englewood Cliffs, N.J.: Prentice Hall, 1964), p. 140. Gardner Ackley, *The Wall Street Journal* (May 1, 1967). Karl Kaysen, "Model Makers and Decision Makers" in *Economic Means and Social Ends*, ed. Robert

Heilbroner (Englewood Cliffs, N.J.: Prentice Hall, 1969),
p. 149. Yankelovich poll: *Fortune* (September, 1969), p.
95. Nat Goldfinger, "A Trade Union View of Anti-Inflation
Policies in the 1960s" (mimeo) (Washington, D.C.: AFL-
CIO, October 21, 1971).

5. "From each according to his ability . . .": *MEW*, XIX, pp. 20 ff.
Stalin on equality: "New Conditions, New Tasks in Eco-
nomic Construction," *Works* (Moscow: Foreign Language
Publishing House, 1955), Vol. XIII, p. 59. John Strachey,
*Contemporary Capitalism* (New York: Random House,
1965), p. 243. Paul Douglas: *Building the American City*,
p. 182. Anthony Downs, "Moving Toward Realistic Hous-
ing Goals," in *Agenda for the Nation*, p. 175. *The Academic
Revolution*, p. 111. Dan Cordtz, "Change Begins in the
Doctor's Office," *Fortune* (January, 1970).

6. *Fabian Essays in Socialism*, p. 67. Keynes quoted: Strachey,
*Contemporary Capitalism*, p. 56. A. A. Berle, *Power* (New
York: Harcourt, Brace and World, 1969), pp. 258–259.
Robin Marris, "The Truth about Corporations," *The Public
Interest*, No. 11 (Spring, 1968), p. 45. Hayek, in Melvin
Anshen and George Bach, eds., *Management and Corpora-
tions, 1985* (New York: McGraw-Hill, 1960), p. 107. Swed-
ish social democrats: Gunnar Adler-Karlson, *Functional
Socialism* (Stockholm: Bokforlaget Prismen, 1969). Arlen
J. Large, "Technology in the Mindless Market," *The Wall
Street Journal* (October 17, 1969) (contains report on the
National Academy of Science panel). *Economic Report
of the President, 1967* (Washington, D.C.: Government
Printing Office, 1967), p. 133. "Corporate Profits and the
Wage Gap," *The Federationist* (July, 1968). On corporate
reforms: Andrew Schonfield, "Business in the Twenty-First
Century," *Daedalus* (Winter, 1969), p. 202; C. A. R. Cros-
land, *The Conservative Enemy* (New York: Shocken Books,
1962), p. 48; Douglas Jay, *Socialism in the New Society*
(New York: St. Martin's Press, 1963), pp. 281–282.

7. TVA: *Annual Report of the TVA* (Washington, D.C.: Government Printing Office, 1968); Tellicoe Newtown, "Draft
Study," TVA mimeo (June, 1969). Robin Marris, *The Economic Theory of "Managerial" Capitalism* (New York: Free
Press, 1964), p. 101. Sir John Eden: *The Economist* (January 9, 1971). *The New Industrial State*, pp. 103–104. Berle:
*Power*, pp. 211 and 213.

8. Wealth: Herman Miller, *Rich Man, Poor Man,* rev. ed. (New York: Crowell, 1971), pp. 156–157. Tax policy: *The Wall Street Journal* (July 23, 1969). Retained profits: Berle, *Power,* p. 203. Joan Robinson, "Socialist Affluence," in C. H. Feinstein, ed., *Socialism, Capitalism and Economic Growth* (Cambridge: Cambridge University Press, 1967), p. 177. Joseph Pechman, "The Rich, the Poor, the Taxes They Pay," *The Public Interest* (Fall, 1969), passim.

## CHAPTER XIII

1. *Das Kapital,* Vol. III: *MEW,* XXV, pp. 345–346. Engels in 1848: *Karl Marx on Modernization,* ed. Shlomo Avineri (New York: Doubleday Anchor, 1969), p. 69. Engels in 1894: *Das Kapital, MEW,* XXV, p. 506, n. 8. Karl Kautsky, *Sozialismus und Kolonialpolitik* (Berlin: Verlag Buchhandlung Vorwarts, 1907); Rosa Luxemburg, *The Accumulation of Capital,* trans. Agnes Schwarzchild (New Haven, Conn.: Yale University Press, 1951). Kautsky on "ultraimperialism": "Der Imperialismus," *Neue Zeit,* Vol. 32, Bd. 2, No. 21 (September 11, 1914). Lenin, *Imperialism: The Highest Stage of Capitalism, CW,* XXII.
2. Lenin (Chap. VII), *CW,* XXII, p. 266. Imperialist super-profits: ibid., p. 241. *Toward a Democratic Left* (New York: The Macmillan Company, 1968). Fritz Sternberg, *Capitalism and Socialism on Trial,* trans. Edward Fitzgerald (New York: Greenwood Press, 1968 [originally 1951]), p. 27. John Kenneth Galbraith, *The Great Crash* (Boston: Houghton Mifflin, Sentry ed., 1961), pp. 180 ff. Henryk Grossman: *Das Akkumulations- und Zusammenbruchgesetz des kapitalistischen Systems* (Frankfurt: Neue Kritik, 1967), pp. 444–446. Trade figures: *UN Conference on Trade and Development, Second Session, New Delhi (1968)* (New York: United Nations, 1968), Vol. I, p. 8. On the new trend in the sixties and seventies: Sanford Rose, "The Poor Countries Turn from Buy-Less to Sell-More," *Fortune* (April, 1970). Oil cost-price gap: Michael Tanzer, *The Political Economy of International Oil and the Underdeveloped Countries* (Boston: Beacon Press, 1969), p. 6. Oil in world trade: S. M. Miller, Ray Bennett, and Cyril Alapatt, *Work-*

*ing Paper of the Center of International Studies of New York University* (February 11, 1970). A. Emmanuel, *L'Échange Inégal* (Paris: François Maspéro, 1969), pp. 49–50.

3. Harry Magdoff, *The Age of Imperialism* (New York: Monthly Review Press, 1969), pp. 16 and 38. Ernest Mandel: *Inter-Continental Press* (May 17, 1971), pp. 450 ff. Gabriel Kolko, *The Roots of American Foreign Policy* (Boston: Beacon Press, 1969), p. 89. Y. Varga, *Political Economic Problems of Capitalism* (Moscow: Progress Publishers, 1968), p. 167. Gunnar Myrdal, *The Challenge of World Poverty*, p. 406. Kolko, op. cit., p. 49; Miller et al., op. cit.

4. *Toward a Democratic Left*, Chaps. VII–IX. Capital outflows, 1965–1966: *UN Conference on Trade and Development, Second Session*, p. 9. Gabriel Valdes: *Le Monde* (June 13, 1969). Charles K. Wilber, *The Soviet Model and Underdeveloped Countries*, Table IV–1, p. 56. Zambia: Robert A. Wright, *The New York Times* (August 17, 1969); *The New York Times* (August 26, 1969); "A Stake in Zambia," *The Economist* (August 23, 1969). Mossadegh: Tanzer, *The Political Economy of Oil*, pp. 321 ff. Brazil: *The Economist* (August 15, 1970); *The Wall Street Journal* (August 20, 1970).

5. Marx on compensation: quoted by Engels, *MEW*, XXII, pp. 503–504. Sanford Rose, "The Poor Countries Turn from Buy-Less to Sell-More," *Fortune* (April, 1970), p. 93. Emmanuel, op. cit., p. 209. William Bywater, President, District 3, IUE (AFL-CIO), "Why Free Trade is Unfair to U.S. Workers," *The New York Times*, January 3, 1971. International unionism: *Christian Science Monitor* (March 27 and April 12, 1971).

6. *The Economist: The Growth and Spread of Multinational Companies* (London: The Economist Intelligence Unit, 1971), p. 28. Lester B. Pearson, Chairman, *Partners in Development: Report of the Commission on International Development* (New York: Praeger Books, 1969), p. 88. Job displacement: Rose, "The Poor Countries," op. cit., p. 170. Charter of Algiers: *UN Trade and Development Conference, Second Session*, p. 421. Gross domestic product figures for the Third World: *Towards Accelerated Development: Report of the Committee for Development Plan-*

*ning* (New York: United Nations, 1970), p. 1. Birth control research: *Partners in Development,* p. 199. NICB estimate: Sanford Rose, "The Rewarding Strategies of Multi-Nationalism," *Fortune* (September 15, 1958). Ibid., p. 101. World GNPs: *War Peace Report* (October, 1968), p. 5. Rumanian transaction and the "takeout" tactic: "The Rewarding Strategies," p. 101. Ambassador George W. Ball, "Making World Corporations into World Citizens," *War Peace Report* (October, 1968), p. 10. Jean-Jacques Servan-Schreiber, *The American Challenge,* trans. Ronald Steel (New York: Atheneum, 1968).

7. *Toward a Democratic Left,* Chapter IX. Marshall Plan and oil: Gunnar Myrdal, *Challenge to World Poverty,* p. 337. World Bank, 1956–1957: *May Day Manifesto,* pp. 78–79. Lima meeting: *The Economist* (May 22, 1971), p. 92. Nixon aid message: *The New York Times* (April 22, 1971). Jerome Levinson and Juan de Onis, *The Alliance that Lost Its Way* (Chicago: Quadrangle Books, 1970), p. 159. World Bank and oil: Tanzer, *The Political Economy of Oil,* p. 27. Thomas Balogh, *The Economics of Poverty* (London: Macmillan, 1966), p. 29. Copenhagen Meeting: *The Wall Street Journal* (September 28, 1970). Aid percentages: *Partners in Development,* pp. 145–148. Paul Rosenstein-Rodan, in *Disarmament and Economic Development,* Vol. 4 of *Strategy and World Order* (4 vols.), ed. Richard A. Falk and Saul H. Mendlovitz (New York: World Law Fund, 1966), pp. 520–521.

8. World Bank interest rate: *The Challenge of World Poverty,* p. 39. Brzezinski, *Between Two Ages: America's Role in the Technetronic Era* (New York: Viking Press, 1970), p. 51. Celso Furtado, "Les USA et L'Amérique Latine," *Esprit* (Juillet–Août, 1966), p. 47. Taiwan: "State Enterprises Pace Taiwan's Growth," *The New York Times* (January 18, 1971). Ernest Mandel, *Traité d'Économie Marxiste* (Paris: Julliard, 1962), Vol. II, pp. 293–294. *Asian Drama,* Vol. II, p. 1000. Indian statistics: *Patterns in Development,* p. 286. Labor-intensive agriculture: *Challenge of World Poverty,* pp. 96–97; UNCTAD II, p. 418. Capitalist farming: *Challenge of World Poverty,* p. 109. Land reform: ibid., p. 113. Indian School of Political Economy: *The Economist* (March 27, 1971).

## CHAPTER XIV

1. Sidney Hook, *Towards the Understanding of Karl Marx* (New York: The John Day Company, 1933), p. 14. Stanley Moore, "Utopian Themes in Marx and Mao," *Monthly Review* (June, 1969).

2. Owen: G. D. H. Cole, *History of Socialist Thought,* Vol. I, p. 94. Keynes, *Essays in Persuasion* (New York: W. W. Norton and Company, 1963), p. vii. Crosland, *The Future of Socialism* (London: Jonathan Cape, 1956), p. 417. Kenneth Boulding, "Is Scarcity Dead?" *The Public Interest* (Fall, 1966). Richard Nixon, "Message on the Environment," *The New York Times* (February 11, 1970). Robert Heilbroner, *Between Capitalism and Socialism,* pp. 280 and 284, n. 1. John J. Wells, "Will the Earth Reach an Energy Ceiling?" *The Wall Street Journal* (January 6, 1971). Fuller, *The New York Times* (March 27, 1971).

3. Marx on consumption under capitalism: *MEW*, XXVI, Pt. 1 (*Theorien über den Mehrwert,* I) pp. 145–146; *MEW*, XXV (*Das Kapital,* III) p. 310. Weber and Veblen: S. M. Lipset, *Revolution and Counter-Revolution* (New York: Anchor Books, 1970), p. 171.

4. Marx on the middle class: *MEW*, XXVI, Pt. 2, p. 576. Kautsky, *Bernstein und das sozialdemokratische Programm* (Stuttgart: Dietz Verlag, 1899), pp. 129 ff. Bad Godesberg Congress: *Protokoll* (Bonn: SPD, n.d. [1959]), p. 29. Herbert Marcuse, *One Dimensional Man* (Boston: Beacon Press, 1964), p. 256.

5. 1965 work force: *Manpower Report of the President, 1969* (Washington, D.C.: Government Printing Office, 1969), Table E–8, p. 235. Department of Labor, *U.S. Manpower in the 1970s* (Washington, D.C.: Government Printing Office, n.d. [1970]). "Moderate Standard": Rudolph Oswald, *The Federationist* (February, 1969). Labor and 1968 elections: Theodore H. White, *The Making of the President, 1968,* p. 365. Marx on affluence: *MEW*, VI, p. 402. Rossow Report: Michael Harrington, "Don't Form a Fourth Party," *The New York Times Magazine* (September 13, 1970). John H. Goldthorpe, David Lockwood, Frank Bechhofer, and Jennifer Platt, *The Affluent Worker in the*

*Class Structure* (Cambridge: Cambridge University Press, 1969), passim and pp. 162, 190. Australia: G. D. H. Cole, *History of Socialist Thought*, Vol. III, Pt. 2, Chap. XXIII, and Vol. IV, Pt. 2, Chap. XXVIII. Michigan survey: *Washington Report* (April 12, 1971). Daniel Bell, "The Corporation and Society in the 1970s," *The Public Interest* (Summer, 1971), p. 31. AFL-CIO: Executive Council statement (August 17, 1971, mimeo). C. A. R. Crosland, "A Social Democratic Britain," Fabian Tract 404, London, 1971, p. 8.

6. 1980 Labor market: *United States Manpower Report*. Thorstein Veblen, *The Engineers and the Price System* (New York: The Viking Press, 1933), pp. 28 and 69. Serge Mallet, *La Nouvelle Classe Ouvrière* (Paris: Seuil, 1969), pp. 16–17. Alain Touraine, *Le Mouvement de Mai ou le Communisme Utopique* (Paris: Seuil, 1968), pp. 162–168. CFDT: *Le Monde* (May 10–11, 1970); *L'Express* (May 18–24, 1970). John Kenneth Galbraith, *The New Industrial State* (Boston: Houghton Mifflin, 1967). Daniel Bell, "Notes on Post-Industrial Society," *The Public Interest* (Winter, 1967), p. 27. Sweden: *Vorwarts* (Bonn) (February 25, 1971).

7. Kenneth Kenniston, *Young Radicals: Notes on Contemporary Youth*, pp. 263–264. Bruno Bettelheim, "Obsolete Youth," *Encounter* (September, 1969). "A Talk with Walter Lippmann," *The New York Times Magazine* (September 14, 1969). College statistics for the United States: U.S. Bureau of the Census, *Current Population Reports*, Ser. P–23, No. 34, "Characteristics of American Youth, 1970" (Washington, D.C.: Government Printing Office, 1971). Trotsky, "The Intelligentsia and Socialism," *Fourth International* (London) (Autumn–Winter, 1964), p. 109. Girod de L'Ain, *Le Monde Hebdomadaire* (October 30–November 5, 1969). Theodore Roszak, *The Making of a Counter-Culture* (New York: Doubleday and Company, 1969), pp. xii, 68, and 240.

8. Realm of freedom: *MEW*, XXV, p. 826. Friedrich Nietzsche: *Morgenrote, Werke* (Salzburg: Bergland, 1956), Vol. II, p. 475. Working day: *MEW*, XXIII, p. 287; Ernest Mandel, *Introduction to Marxist Economic Theory* (New York: Young Socialist Alliance, 1967), p. 13. Engels on Communist society: *MEW*, III, p. 378. Trotsky, *Literature and Revolution* (New York: Russell and Russell, 1957), p. 256.

9. Paul Samuelson: *Economics*, 7th ed., pp. 610–611. John

Strachey, *Contemporary Capitalism,* p. 140. Kaiser Plan: Edmund K. Faltermayer, "Better Care at Less Cost without Miracles," *Fortune* (January, 1970). "National Health Insurance, What It Is, What It Isn't," *Federationist* (January, 1970).

# Index

Abendroth, Wolfgang, 205
Absolute poverty, 104
Absolute surplus value, 98
*Academic Revolution, The* (Jencks and Riesman), 278–279
Accident insurance programs, 67
*Accidental Century, The* (Harrington), 202, 353
Ackley, Gardner, 287
Adams, John Quincy, 111
Adler, Max, 79, 363
Adler, Victor, 73, 74, 75
Affluence
    England, 356, 359, 360
    Marx on, 355
    U.S., 110, 128, 286, 355–356, 364, 367
*Affluent Society, The* (Galbraith), 283
*Affluent Worker in the Class Structure, The*, 356
Africa, 7, 135, 136, 139, 145, 183, 216–217, 234, 242, 245
    democracy, 337
    exploitation of, 310
    investment in, 316
    modernization of, 219, 325
    population control, 329–330
    tariffs and, 328
    urban poor, 234
    *See also* names of countries; Third World
Agnew, Spiro T., 279–280
Agrarian radicalism, 116, 254
Agriculture
    England, 22, 52
    Russia, 171–173, 179, 230–231
    Third World, 12, 238–239, 321–323, 328–329, 340–341, 366
    U.S., 81, 277, 279, 284
Air pollution, 285–287

Air Quality Act of 1967, 287
Albigensians, 18
Alexander the Great, 16
Alger, Bruce, 268
Algeria, 218, 243
    urban poor, 235–236
    *See also* Third World
Algiers, Charter of, 329
Allende, Salvador, 245
Alliance for Labor Action, 265
Alliance for Progress, 134, 219, 334, 338
"Alliance for Progress and Peaceful Revolution, The" (Rosenstein-Rodan), 217
Althusser, Louis, 41, 78
    on Marxism, 41
American Civil War, 114
American Federation of Labor (AFL), 117, 121, 123–127, 130, 131, 251, 253–255, 257, 259, 266, 357
    hostility to immigrants, 132–133
    Labor's League for Political Education, 266
American Federation of Labor–Congress of Industrial Organizations (AFL-CIO), 264–269, 289, 358
    protectionist position of, 325
American Federation of Teachers, 360
American United Automobile Workers, 327
Amin, Samir, 235–236
Amsterdam Congress, 146, 188
Anabaptists, 17, 21, 22, 28
Anarchists, 68
*Anti-Dühring* (Engels), 68, 73
Anti-socialist socialism, 6, 21, 45
    Bismarck, 6, 8, 56, 64, 66–70
    origins of, 65–70

Anti-socialist socialism (*Continued*)
    Russia, 152, 154
*Appeal to Reason,* 252
Arab Communism, 243–244
Arab socialism, 243–244
Arab Socialist Union, 243
Arabs, 7, 151
Arendt, Hannah, 178
Argentina, 144, 330
    *See also* Latin America;
      Third World
Aristocratic utopianism, 15–16
Aron, Raymond, 353
Ascetic communism, 13
Asia, 135, 136, 137, 140, 216–217,
    220, 222–223, 234
    democracy, 337
    exploitation of, 310
    investment in, 316
    modernization of, 219, 325
    population control, 329–330
    tariffs and, 328
    urban poor, 234
    wages, 316
    *See also* names of countries;
      Third World
*Asian Drama: An Inquiry into the
    Poverty of Nations* (Myrdal), 246
Asiatic mode of production, 139–
    140
*Atlantic Monthly,* 120–121
Atomic Energy Commission, 348
Attlee, Clement, 7, 188, 203, 305
Augustine, Saint, 15
Australia, 138, 220, 221, 357
Australian Labour Party, 357
Austria
    bourgeoisie, 46
    Marxism, 200
    nationalizations, 199, 200
    socialism, 200, 204–205
Austria-Hungary, 64, 188
Austrian social democrats, 72
Automation, 364
    Marx on, 100
Avineri, Shlomo, 26

Babeuf, Gracchus, 5, 22, 24, 25

Babouvists, 24, 25
Bakdash, Khalid, 244
Bakunin, Mikhail, 56, 62, 63, 68,
    69, 141, 234
    debate with Marx, 62, 63
    lumpenproletarian socialism
      and, 62
Ball, George W., 331
Balogh, Thomas, 212, 333–334
Bank of England, 199, 213
Baran, Paul, 228
Bartering, 94
Baruch, Bernard, 260
Bauer, Otto, 200, 209
Bebel, August, 69, 73, 75, 175
Belgian Congo, 146, 149–151, 187
Belgian Workers' Party, 150
Belgium, 146, 187, 192, 330
    colonialism, 146, 149–151
    imports, 314
Bell, Daniel, 41–42, 78, 252–253,
    357–361
Belmont, August, 125
Berger, Victor, 254
Berle, A. A., 264, 297
Bernstein, Eduard, 68–69, 73, 142,
    146–147, 190–191
Bernstein, Irving, 256
Berry, George L., 259
Bethlehem Steel Corporation, 298
Bettelheim, Bruno, 363
Bettelheim, Charles, 185
*Better Fewer, But Better* (Lenin),
    166, 167–168
Bevan, Aneurin, 246, 247, 249
Bismarck, Otto von, 73, 122, 157,
    172, 175
    as an anti-socialist socialist, 6,
      8, 56, 64, 66–70
    bureaucratic capitalism, 69
    welfare programs, 67–68
Black, Hugo, 257
Blacks, 151
    education, 363
    unrest of, 353, 356
Blanc, Louis, 38, 68, 264, 303
Blanqui, Auguste, 5, 38, 39, 40, 51,
    52, 62, 63, 69, 163

Blanqui, Auguste (*Continued*)
    Engels on, 39
    on proletarians, 38
    on suffrage, 38
Blanquists, 38, 50, 52, 59, 163, 172
Bloch, Ernst, 14, 17
Blue-collar labor, 353–354, 356
Blum, Léon, 188, 196–197, 212, 360
Boer Republic, 145
Boer War, 144–145
Bohemia, 18, 19
Bolivia, 334
    *See also* Latin America; Third
        World
Bolshevik Party, 171, 184, 185
Bolsheviks, 154, 155, 159, 164, 165,
    171, 179, 183–185
Bonaparte, Jérôme, 59
Boorstein, Edward, 238
Born, Stephen, 47
Boudin, Louis, 69
Boulding, Kenneth, 346–348, 349,
    351
Bourgeois democracy, 47, 48
Bourgeoisie, 26–27, 45, 46, 188
    Austria, 46
    China, 222, 226
    Engels on, 66, 351
    England, 45, 46–47, 147–148
    France, 47
    Germany, 46, 48–49, 58, 66,
        157
    Italy, 46, 157
    Marx on, 49, 351
    Russia, 156–159, 170, 185
Brabant, 17
Brahmins, 13
Brandt, Willy, 205–206, 210
    coffee, 322–323
    exports, 322–323
    urban poor, 235
    *See also* Latin America; Third
        World
British India, 314
British Miners' Union, 201
British Steel Corporation, 203
Brooks, Thomas, 126
Brophy, John, 259

Brothers and Sisters of the Free
    Spirit, 19
Browder, Earl, 261–262
Brown, George, 213
Brzezinski, Zbigniew, 9, 173, 336–
    337
Buddha, 13
Bukharin, Nikolai, 69, 171, 184–185
Buonarrotti, Filippo Michele, 22,
    24–25
Bureaucratic capitalism, 67–69
Bureaucratic collectivism, 8, 10,
    155, 169, 173–178, 182–186,
    227, 308
Burke, Edmund, 155

Canada, 138, 221
Capital
    centralization of, 88
    constant, 95
    export of, 313, 316, 317
    finance, 313
    organic composition of, 102
    ownership of, 96
    production of, 93–94
    surplus, 313, 317
    as a symbol of value, 91–92
    technical composition of, 102
    two meanings of, 93
    as unproductive, 92–94
Capitalism, 3–5, 12, 17, 109–133
    atomization, 32, 34
    automation and, 364
    bureaucratic, 67–69
    change after World War II,
        314
    China, 222–223
    commodities and, 90–98
    early, characteristics of, 271–
        272
    emergence of, 20, 21
    Engels on, 8, 46–47, 71–72,
        77–108, 128, 135–136, 143,
        147–149, 157, 194, 209,
        281, 312
    England, 203–204
    France, 27, 197, 202

Capitalism (*Continued*)
Germany, 193, 194, 195
imperialism and, 312–313
inefficiency and assimilative
power of, 75–76
intellectual life and, 32–33
as an irrelevance for mankind,
310
labor under, 83
length of working day and, 60
Lenin on, 135, 151–152, 170
Marx on, 8, 46–47, 77–108,
134–136, 138–139, 152,
156, 157, 170, 171, 174,
194, 281, 350
law of motion of, 98–108
nationalizations and, 198–204
neo-, 41, 273–291, 359, 369
overestimation of, 46
planning under, 281–284
reform of, 9
rise of, 21
Russia, 156, 170, 171
socialist, 187–215
structural changes in, 71–72
as a transitory system, 89–90
U.S., 250, 257, 263–264, 272–
307
utopianism and, 18
waste of, 27–28
the welfare state and, 270–307
the world market and, 271,
308–343
as the basis of production, 311
Engels on, 310, 311, 312
intracapitalist investment,
314–316
major development after
World War II, 314
Marx on, 310–311
neo-colonial investment,
316–317
in perpetuating economic
backwardness, 318–323
in perpetuating poverty,
318–323
planning, 332–336
restructuring of, 324–332

World War I and, 188
Carpenters' Union, 112
Carr, E. H., 48, 136, 142, 159, 164,
170, 190
Castro, Fidel, 144, 237–240
Chad, 337
*See also* Africa; Third World
*Challenge of World Poverty, The*
(Myrdal), 246, 248
Charter of Algiers, 329
Chartism, 43, 45, 50, 58, 60
Chauvey, Daniel (pseudonym),
241–242
Chernyshevsky, Nikolai Gavrilo-
vich, 167
Chiang Kai-shek, 223, 319, 339
Chicago Federation of Labor, 126
Chile, 7, 334
*See also* Latin America; Third
World
China, 6, 7, 13, 139, 141, 167, 168,
185, 217, 222–223, 245, 314, 317
bourgeoisie, 222, 226
capitalism, 222–223
collectivization, 227–228, 308
Communism, 180, 223–233,
339–340
Cultural Revolution, 231–233,
237
Great Leap, 12, 230, 231, 242
Japanese invasion (1937), 223
landlords, 226
ownership, 340
peasants, 224–231, 340, 355
surplus and, 228
People's Liberation Army, 231
poverty, 230, 308
the proletariat, 224
Red Guards, 232
strikes, 231
totalitarianism, 229, 233, 340
utopias, 13
welfare state, 13
Chinese Revolution, 222–223
compared to Russian Revolution, 223–224
Christian democrats, 210
Christian Federation of Labor, 360

Christianity, 13
  Engels on, 14–15
  revolutionary creed, 14–15
  *See also* Protestantism; Roman
    Catholic Church
*City of God* (Saint Augustine), 15
*Civil War in France* (Marx), 163
Claflin, Tennessee, 116
*Class Struggles in France* (Marx),
  50
Clayton Act, 125
Cleaver, Eldridge, 235
Co-determination principle, 201–
  202
Coffee, 322–323
Cole, G. D. H., 37–38, 44, 45, 192,
  197
Collectivization
  China, 227–228, 308
  Cuba, 308
  Egypt, 308
  future of, 4–5
  Russia, 8, 10, 155, 169, 173–
    178, 182–186, 227, 308
  U.S., 357
Colonialism, 134–154, 187, 310
  Belgium, 146, 149–151
  cost of, 148
  Engels on, 143, 147–149
  England, 137, 138, 147, 148,
    247
  France, 218, 235–236
  Germany, 148
  Lenin on, 135, 147, 148, 149,
    151–152
  Marx on, 137, 138, 143, 147,
    148, 247
  U.S., 148, 319
Colorado Labor War, 120
Commodities
  capitalism and, 90–98
  cost of, 371
  demand for, 105–106
  Engels on, 90–98
  as an exchange value, 90, 95
  free, 371–372
  labor as, 98
  Marx on, 90–98, 105–106

production of, 90–98
  supply of, 105–106
  as a use value, 90, 95
Commons, John R., 128
Communism, 4, 6, 9, 10, 18–20,
  345
  aim of, 40–41
  Arab, 243–244
  ascetic, 13
  China, 180, 223–233, 339–340
  compared to fascism, 176
  Cuba, 239–241
  Egypt, 243
  Engels on, 43, 44, 370
  England, 45, 50
  France, 41, 45, 273
  freedom movement under,
    180–182
  Germany, 45, 47, 190–192
  Iraq, 243
  Italy, 53, 176, 273
  Marx on, 36, 43, 45, 174, 370
  Peru, 243
  Russia, 154–156, 165, 169–
    186, 225, 229, 339–340
  socialism corrupted by, 154–
    155
  Sudan, 243, 244
  Syria, 243, 244
  Third World, 180, 223–233,
    239–244, 339–343
  totalitarianism and, 69, 160,
    169, 173–178, 271, 310
  U.S., 252, 254, 257, 260–263
Communist International, 225, 261
Communist League, 47, 50, 52, 57
*Communist Manifesto, The* (Marx
  and Engels), 37, 42, 43, 44, 45,
  46–47, 48, 54, 58, 61, 71, 139,
  152, 181, 187, 189, 211
  on the bourgeoisie, 351
  on capitalism, 46–47, 135
  on centralized state credit, 65–
    66
  four types of society in, 139
  Lassalle and, 65–66
  on wages, 65

Communist Party (China), 223, 233

Communist Party (Germany), 190–192

Communist Party (Italy), 53, 176

Communist Party (Russia), 179

Communist Party (U.S.), 260–263

Communitarian socialism, 113

Conference for Progressive Political Action, 119, 126–127, 255

Congregationalists, 22

Congress of Industrial Organizations (CIO), 258, 259, 262, 263, 266, 356
  Political Action Committee, 266

Congress of the Socialist International, 75, 326–327

Connally, John, 267

Conquest, Robert, 173

Constant capital, 95

Constantine, Emperor, 15

Consumers' cooperatives, 65

Consumption
  abstinence from, 96
  attitudes under socialism, 348, 350, 371–372
  depressions and, 100–101
  disparity between production and, 100–101, 104

Cooperatives
  consumers', 65
  producers', 65, 68

Council of Economic Advisors, 276, 298

Credit, centralized state, 65–66

Credit associations, 65

Crédit Mobilier, 7

*Critique of the Gotha Program* (Marx), 78, 174

*Critique of Political Economy* (Marx), 87

Cromwell, Oliver, 21, 224

Crosland, Anthony, 205, 206–207, 211–212, 346, 358

Cuba, 7, 144, 218, 236, 237–241, 242, 245, 340
  agriculture, 12, 238–239

collectivization, 308
Communism, 239–241
housing, 239–240
militarization of work, 239
poverty, 308
Russia compared to, 240–241
socialism, 237–238
sugar harvest (1970), 12
unemployment, 238–239
*See also* Latin America; Third World

Cultural Revolution, 231–233, 237

Czechoslovakia, 9, 168, 180–182, 233

Dahrendorf, Ralf, 91, 202

Daley, Richard, 267

Darwin, Charles, 73

*Das Kapital* (Marx and Engels), 41, 42, 61, 63, 71, 77–108, 137, 221
  alienation idea in, 42
  basic paradox of, 79
  on capitalism, 77–108, 135–136, 157
  on commodities, 90–98
  contemporary critics of, 6
  on global abundance, 346
  simplifications in, 87
  on socialized man, 77–108
  structure of, 86–88
  on wealth, 77, 79, 108
  on the world market, 310–311

David, 146

De Castro, Josue, 217

De Gaulle, Charles, 199

De Leon, Daniel, 124

De Man, Henri, 197–198

Déat, Marcel, 197

Debray, Régis, 245

Debs, Eugene Victor, 109, 126, 252–255, 263

Debsian socialism, 119, 125, 252–255, 257

Debsian Socialist Party, 125

*Decline of Socialism in America, The* (Weinstein), 254

Deist, Heinrich, 209

Democracy
    anti-democratic bureaucracies
        and, 75
    bourgeois, 47, 48
    as the essence of socialism, 37–
        40, 42, 48, 52–54
    Marx's commitment to, 37–40,
        42, 48, 52–54, 64, 70, 76
    Third World, 336–342
    *See also* Social democracy
Democratic Federation of Labor,
    360
Democratic Labour Party, 357
Democratic Party, 125, 255–257,
    266–269
Depressions, 129, 195
    consumption and, 100–101
    of 1837–1842, 52
    the Great, 72, 107, 130, 150,
        190, 251, 256–264, 314
Descamps, Eugène, 360
Determinism, 31–32
Deutscher, Isaac, 183–184
Dickens, James, 213
Dictatorships
    Engels on, 51
    Lenin on, 161–163, 172
    Marx on, 161, 162–163
    of the proletariat, 49–52
Diggers, the, 23
Dillon Soares, Glaucio Ary, 235
Dirksen, Everett McKinley, 267
*Dissent,* 369
Domino theory, 317
Donne, John, 30
Dostoevsky, Feodor, 155, 345
Douglas, Paul, 293
Draper, Theodore, 261
Dubinsky, David, 259
Dumont, René, 238–239, 242
Durkheim, Emile, 17–18
Dutch Indies, 314

Ebert, Friedrich, 190, 191, 192
Ecology
    socialism and, 346
    Nixon on, 285–286, 347
    *See also* Pollution

Economic backwardness, capitalism
    in perpetuating, 318–323
"Economics," use of the word, 79,
    82, 84
*Economic Theory of Underdevel-
    oped Regions* (Myrdal), 246
*Economic-Philosophic Manuscripts*
    (Marx), 40
*Economics, Peace and Laughter*
    (Galbraith), 217
*Economist, The,* 322, 327
Ecuador, 334
    *See also* Latin America; Third
        World
Eden, Sir John, 301
Education
    blacks, 363
    France, 364–365
    Russia, 175
    student unrest, 353, 364–365
    U.S., 278–279, 290, 294, 356,
        360, 362–364, 367
Egypt, 243, 244, 245
    collectivization, 308
    Communism, 243
    nationalization, 243
    peasants, 243
    poverty, 308
    *See also* Third World
*Eighteenth Brumaire, The* (Marx),
    224
    demystification, 5–6
    on dictatorships, 51
    on the Fabians, 201
    on feminist free-lovers, 116–
        117
    on free-land movement, 115
    on George, Henry, 121
    on global abundance, 346
    on importance of public irri-
        gation works, 140
    on inequality, 174
    on Kriege, 115
    Lassalle and, 65–66
    Lenin and, 57–58, 161–162
    on the lumpenproletariat, 234
    on Münzer, 20

*Eighteenth Brumaire* (*Continued*)
  on nationalization, 68–69,
    199–200
  on the Paris Commune, 51
  on peasants, 224
  period of initial political in-
    volvement, 71
  on periodic processes, 71
Eisenhower, Dwight D., 264, 276,
  282, 289
Eisenhower, Milton, 275
Emmanuel, A., 315, 325
Employment Act of 1946, 264
Energy, 348–349
Energy ceiling, 348
Engels, Friedrich, 7, 9, 35, 110,
  140, 173, 187, 188
  on the American Civil War,
    114
  on basic tenet of Marxism, 73
  on Blanqui, 39
  on bourgeoisie, 66, 351
  on capitalism, 8, 46–47, 71–
    72, 77–108, 128, 135–136,
    143, 147–149, 157, 194,
    209, 281, 312
  on Christianity, 14–15
  Cole on, 37–38
  on colonialism, 143, 147–149
  on commodities, 90–98
  on Communism, 43, 44, 370
  political beginnings of, 37–54
  on poverty, 236
  on the proletariat, 38–39
  on revolutions, 49, 51, 142,
    224
  Riazanov on, 47
  on Russia, 142
  on social democracy, 113, 251
  on socialism, 44–45, 51–52
  on socialized man, 77–108
  on surplus, 175
  on Ten Hours Bill, 60
  version of *Theses on Feuer-
    bach*, 40
  on wages, 65
  on wealth, 77, 79, 108
  on the world market, 310–312

England, 113–114, 119, 123, 129,
  131, 162, 255, 297, 305, 311,
  314
  affluence, 356, 359, 360
  agriculture, 22, 52
  bourgeoisie, 45, 46–47, 147–
    148
  capitalism, 203–204
  Chartism, 43, 45, 50, 58, 60
  colonialism, 137, 138, 147,
    148, 247
  Communism, 45, 50
  cotton industry, 52
  devaluation of the pound, 213
  English Revolution, 21–23
  exports, 314, 315
  Fabians, 145, 201, 296
  fascism, 196
  foreign aid, 333
  housing, 275
  income inequality, 211–212
  Independent Labour Party,
    123, 145, 193
  industrial monopoly of, 71, 148
  Labour Party, 193, 195–196,
    201–203, 205, 206, 212–
    214, 283, 299, 356, 358
  Levelers, 22, 23
  Lollard movement, 19
  *May Day Manifesto*, 206
  militant movements, 17
  nationalizations, 199, 201–
    204, 301
  overproduction, 310
  peasants, 21–22, 224
  poverty, 212
  the proletariat, 28, 29, 38–39,
    43, 148, 356
  social insurance, 202
  socialism, 44, 110, 188, 193,
    195–196, 199, 201–206,
    212–215, 283
  strikes, 58–59
  suffrage, 64
  syndicalist movement, 149
  Ten Hours Bill, 60
  Tories, 38, 203, 204, 205, 213

England (*Continued*)
  unions, 28–29, 58–59, 201, 327
  utopianism, 21–23, 28
  wages, 129, 313, 327
  welfare state, 7, 202, 213
  white-collar workers, 211
English Revolution, 21–23
Enlightenment, 25
Entrepreneurial radicalism, 116
Environment, *see* Ecology; Pollution
Erfurt Program, 162, 199
Erikson, Erik, 362
Essenes, the, 14
Evans, George Henry, 112
Exchange value, 90, 95
Exports
  Brazil, 322–323
  of capital, 313, 316, 317
  England, 314, 315
  France, 315
  Germany, 314
  Third World, 315
  U.S., 317
  of jobs, 326
External diseconomies, 284, 285
External economies, 284–285

*Fabian Essays*, 296
Fabians, 145, 201, 296
Fanon, Frantz, 62, 144, 235, 236, 249
Fascism, 138, 149
  compared to Communism, 176
  England, 196
Faure, Paul, 197
Feather, Victor, 327
Feminist free-lovers, 116–117
Ferri, Enrico, 144
Fetscher, Iring, 177
Feudalism, 22–23, 31, 47, 81
  end of, 17, 20, 22
  Germany, 49
  labor under, 83
  lack of, in the U.S., 111, 113
  Russia, 341
  social relationships, 84

Finance capital, 313
First International, 62–63, 116, 117, 251
Flanders, 17
Fletcher, David, 283
Ford Foundation, 329
Ford Motor Company, 287, 330
*Fortune,* 204, 281, 289, 294, 324–325, 362, 363, 366, 372
*Foundations of Leninism, The* (Stalin), 170
Fourier, Charles, 113, 300
Fourth International, 317
France, 43, 51, 52, 59, 64, 113, 114, 131, 149–150, 162, 170, 192, 213, 251, 323
  bourgeoisie, 47
  capitalism, 27, 197, 202
  colonialism, 218, 235–236
  Communism, 41, 45, 273
  education, 364–365
  exports, 315
  foreign aid, 333
  French Revolution, 23–27
    Hegel on, 33–34
    Marx on, 26–27
  length of working day, 197
  Marxism, 185
  nationalizations, 199, 200, 202, 203
  peasants, 23–24, 224
  Popular Front, 197
  the proletariat, 27, 28, 46, 164, 197, 353, 354, 360
  Radical Party, 299
  socialism, 188, 196–198, 200, 202, 205–206
  strikes, 360
  student unrest, 364–365
  unions, 360
  utopianism, 21, 23–27
  wages, 313
Francis of Assisi, Saint, 18
Franklin, Benjamin, 95
Free Democrats, 202
Free-land movement, 114–116

French Revolution, 23–27
   Hegel on, 33–34
   Marx on, 26–27
Freud, Sigmund, 285
Freund, Michael, 18
Fuller, Buckminster, 348–349
Furtado, Celso, 338
*Future of Socialism, The* (Crosland), 346

Gaitskell, Hugh, 212
Galbraith, John Kenneth, 209, 219, 264, 278, 283, 289, 296, 302, 359–362
   on income inequality, 314
   on nationalization, 209
Gandhi, Indira, 248
Gandhi, Mahatma, 247, 249
Garaudy, Roger, 168, 229, 231
General Electric Corporation, 330
General German Workers' Association, 65
General Motors Corporation, 303, 330
Generation gap, 362
Geneva Conference of European Socialists, 201
George, Henry, 115, 121
Gerassi, John, 217
*German Ideology, The* (Marx and Engels), 236, 345
German social democrats, 64, 70, 73, 74, 130, 162, 190–194, 199–202, 205, 208–210, 255, 259, 352
Germany, 17–20, 43, 52, 64–75, 113, 119, 122, 136, 142–143, 146, 156, 159, 162, 168, 170, 181, 197–199, 220, 251, 261, 314, 323, 352
   accident insurance program, 67
   bourgeoisie, 46, 48–49, 58, 66, 157
   capitalism, 193, 194, 195
   Christian democrats, 210
   co-determination principle, 201–202
   colonialism, 148
   Communism, 45, 47, 190–192
   consumers' cooperatives, 65
   credit associations, 65
   exports, 314
   feudalism, 49
   Free Democrats, 202
   Godesberg Program, 205, 208–211, 212, 352
   health insurance program, 67
   Independents, 190–191, 192, 194, 201
   Lenin on, 160, 190
   liberals, 65, 66
   Majority socialists, 190, 191, 192–193, 194
   Marxism, 56, 67, 191
   National Congress of Councils, 191
   nationalizations, 199, 201–202
   Nazis, 7, 63, 197, 198, 352
   peasants, 19–20, 22, 224
   philosophy of, 12–13
   post-World War I, 190, 193–194
   producers' cooperatives, 65
   the proletariat, 160, 164, 353
   social democrats, 64, 70, 73, 74, 130, 162, 190–194, 199–202, 205, 208–210, 255, 259, 352
   socialism, 48–49, 58, 67, 188, 190–194, 199–202, 204–205, 208–211
   *Spartakusbund,* 191
   strikes, 9, 184, 185
   suffrage, 64
   Trotsky on, 190
   unification of, 67, 172
   wages, 72, 130
   workers' education societies, 65
   Young Socialists (Jusos), 210
Gershenkron, Alexander, 26, 27, 85–86, 88, 220
Ghana, 243, 245
   *See also* Africa; Third World
Global abundance, 345–351

Godesberg Program, 205, 208–211, 212, 352
Gold
  discovered in California, 52
  as a symbol of value, 91–92
Goldfinger, Nat, 289–290
Gompers, Samuel, 110, 111, 119, 122, 123, 124, 126, 130, 133, 257, 258, 260, 265
  voluntarism, 124–125, 251, 264, 266
Gorz, André, 205–206, 273
Gotha Congress of 1875, 67
Gradualism, 60-61, 70
Gramsci, Antonio, 53, 137, 164–165, 176, 190, 192
Great Depression, 72, 107, 130, 150, 190, 251, 256–264, 314
Great Leap, 12, 230, 231, 242
Greece, utopianism, 11, 13, 15, 16–17
Greeley, Horace, 113
Green Corn Rebellion, 254
Greenbackers, 116
Grossman, Henryk, 104, 314
Ground rent, 80
*Grundrisse der Politische Oekonomie* (Marx), 99
Guesde, Jules, 73, 188
Guevara, Che, 218, 237–238, 240, 245, 249, 320

Haberman, Jürgen, 104
Handicraft industry, 71
Hanna, Mark, 125
Hardacker, M. A., 120–121
Harney, 50
Hayek, Frederick A., 296
Haywood, "Big Bill," 254
Health care
  Germany, 67
  U.S., 290, 294, 367, 372
Heath, Edward, 327, 301
Hegel, Georg Wilhelm Friedrich, 6
  compared to Marx, 4
  on the French Revolution, 33–34
  philosophy of, 33–34, 177

Heilbroner, Robert, 84, 237, 346–348, 349
Henderson, Arthur, 195
Herzen, Alexander, 141
Hilferding, Rudolf, 69, 105–106, 194, 195, 209
Hill, Christopher, 22, 98
Hillman, Sidney, 259
Hillquit, Morris, 131
Hindoos, 137
Hippies, 365–366
*History and Class Consciousness* (Lukacs), 32
*History of Labor in the United States* (ed. Commons), 128
*History of Socialist Thought* (Cole), 37–38
Hitler, Adolf, 7, 67, 197, 198, 226, 261
Ho Chi Minh, 218, 355
Hobbes, Thomas, 31, 33
Hobsbawm, E. J., 39
Hobson, John Atkinson, 312
Hofstadter, Richard, 116, 259–260
Holland, 149–150, 330
  decline of merchant pre-eminence, 311
  imports, 314
Homestead Act of 1862, 115
Hong Kong, 326
  *See also* Asia; Third World
Hook, Sidney, 50, 345
Hoover, Herbert, 258, 326
Hoover, J. Edgar, 36
Horowitz, Irving Louis, 217
Hosiery Workers, 259
Hottentot Election, 146
Hourwich, Isaac, 132
Housing
  England, 275
  Third World, 239–240
  U.S., 274–276, 279, 281–283, 288, 292–293
Housing Act of 1949, 276
*How We Should Reorganize the Workers' and Peasants' Inspection* (Lenin), 166
Huberman, Leo, 239–240

Hughes, John, 214
Hume, David, 31–32
Humphrey, Hubert, 266–267, 336, 355
Hungary, 168, 180–181, 184, 228, 233
    uprising (1956), 9
Hus, Jan, 19
Hutcheson, William L., 257

Iambulos, 16, 17
Imperialism
    alternatives to, 312–313
    capitalism and, 312–313
    England, 136, 144–146
    five major determinants of, 313
    Lenin on, 312–313, 318
    production and, 313
    U.S., 319–323
*Imperialism* (Lenin), 312
Imports
    Belgium, 314
    Holland, 314
    Switzerland, 314
    U.S., 315, 318, 322–323, 328
Independent Labor Party, 126
Independent Labour Party, 123, 145, 193
India, 7, 139, 142, 145, 167, 168, 218, 246–249, 337–340
    agriculture, 366
    British rule in, 137, 138
    land reform, 342
    Marx on the society of, 140
    poverty, 342
    U.S. aid to, 319
    *See also* Asia; Third World
Indian School of Political Economy, 342
Indonesia, 16, 243
    *See also* Asia; Third World
Industrial Revolution, 246
Industrial Workers of the World (IWW), 131, 132, 253–254
Inheritance taxes, 306
Institute for Industrial Recovery, 199
Inter-American Development Bank, 334

International Brotherhood of Teamsters, 257, 265
International Business Machines Corporation, 326
International Coffee Agreement, 322, 323
International Companies Law, 331
International Confederation of Free Trade Unions (ICFTU), 327
International Metal Workers Secretariat, 327
International Monetary Fund, 333–334
International Petroleum Company, 334
International Union of Electrical Workers (IUE), 325–326
International Workingmen's Association (IWMA), 144, 172
    establishment of, 59
    London Conference (1871), 63
    Marx's Inaugural Address to, 59–60
Internationalizations, 332
    of foreign aid, 333
Intracapitalist investment, 314–316
Investments, 314–322, 330–333
    intracapitalist, 314–316
    Lenin on, 316–317
    neo-colonial, 316–317
    in oil, 316, 319, 322, 333
    Third World, 314–322, 330–333
Iran, 219
    *See also* Asia; Third World
Iraq, 243
    *See also* Asia; Third World
Ireland, 52
Irrigation works, 140
Isaacs, Harold, 225–226
Israel, 7, 14, 221
Italy, 17, 131, 137, 197, 234, 297
    bourgeoisie, 46, 157
    Communism, 53, 176, 273
    nationalizations, 199
    the proletariat, 353, 354
    socialism, 144

Jacksonians, 116
Jacobins, 61
Japan, 138, 183, 220, 226, 323
    invasion of China (1937), 223
Jaurès, Jean, 45, 75, 209, 360
    on nationalization, 200
Java, 175
    *See also* Asia; Third World
Jay, Douglas, 203, 299
Jencks, Christopher, 278–279
Jews
    religion, 7, 13–14, 17
    U.S., 254
    utopianism, 11–14
Joachim de Floris, 18, 20, 21
Johnson, Lyndon B., 266, 267,
    274, 276, 298
    on pollution, 286–287
Jones, Jack, 327
Judaism, 7, 13–14, 17
Junkers, 66, 68
Justo, Juan B., 144

Kaiser Company, 372
Kant, Immanuel, 32, 33
Karol, K. S., 179, 240–241
Kaunda, Kenneth, 321–322
Kautsky, Karl, 8, 17, 19, 68, 73–75,
    104, 143, 147, 162, 190–191,
    312, 313, 352, 359
    Lenin on, 158–159
    on nationalization, 199–200
    on peasants, 224–225
    on revolutions, 157–159
Kaysen, Karl, 287–288
Kennedy, Edward, 367
Kennedy, John F., 264, 266, 267,
    276, 289, 298
    on tariffs, 320
Kennedy, Robert F., 266, 366
Kennedy Alliance, 338
Kennedy Round, 320, 328
Kenniston, Kenneth, 362–363
Kentucky Federation of Labor, 258
Kerensky, Aleksandr Feodorovich,
    161, 162, 192
Kerr, Clark, 97

Keynes, John Maynard, 260, 263,
    289, 296, 346
    compared to Marx, 96
Keynesianism, 264, 285, 289, 290
Keyserling, Leon, 264, 289
Khrushchev, Nikita, 178–179, 229
    on Stalin, 178–179
Kipnis, Ira, 253
Knights of Labor, 117, 121, 122
Kolakowski, Leszek, 31
Kolko, Gabriel, 69, 317, 318
Korea, 315
    *See also* Asia; Third World
Korsch, Karl, 42
Kosik, Karel, 181–182
Kriege, Hermann, 114–115, 118
Kugelmann, 105
Kuomintang, the, 223

La Follette, Robert Marion, 119,
    251, 255
Labor, 55–61
    abolition of, 344, 345, 367–372
    absolute surplus value, 98
    blue-collar, 353–354, 356
    as a commodity, 98
    gradualist movement, 60–61,
        70
    increased productivity of, 99,
        102–103, 107
    as an increment in value, 95–96
    Marx on, 345
        abolition of, 367–368
        compulsory, 367–368
        wage, as unnecessary, 59–60
    as the measure of equivalence,
        82–83
    militarization of, 239
    protectionism of, 325–326
    relative surplus value, 99, 104
    science as an element in the
        process of, 93
    social character of, 91
    socialization of, 88
    technology and, 93, 354, 368–
        369
    theory of value, 82, 84–85, 89
    under capitalism, 83

Labor (*Continued*)
  under feudalism, 83
  unpaid surplus, 80–82
  wage, as unnecessary, 59–60
  white-collar, 211
  world industrialization and,
    325–327
  *See also* Unions; names of
    unions
Labor rent, 80
Labor's League for Political Education, 266
Labour Party, 193, 195–196, 201–
  203, 205, 206, 212–214, 246,
  283, 299, 356, 358
Land pollution, 286
Landauer, Carl, 192–193, 197
Lange, Oskar, 372
Lassalle, Ferdinand, 65–67, 117,
  122, 251, 303
    *The Communist Manifesto*
      and, 65–66
    Engels and, 65–66
    Marx and, 65–67
Latin America, 135, 136, 216–217,
  221, 234, 245
  democracy, 337
  exploitation of, 310
  family loyalty in, 221
  investment in, 316
  land reform, 341
  modernization of, 219, 325
  population control, 329–330
  socialism, 245
  tariffs and, 328
  urban poor, 234, 235
  wages, 316
  *See also* names of countries;
    Third World
*Latin American Revolution* (eds.
  Horowitz, de Castro, and
  Gerassi), 217
Lenin, Krupskaya, 166
Lenin, V. I., 6, 20, 26, 74, 111,
  134, 141, 146, 147, 155–169,
  191, 192, 194, 341
  on capitalism, 135, 151–152,
    170

on colonialism, 135, 147, 148,
  149, 151–152
on dictatorships, 161–163, 172
Engels and, 57–58, 161–162
on Germany, 160, 190
on imperialism, 312–313, 318
on investments, 316–317
on Kautsky, 158–159
Marx and, 57–58, 61–62, 161–
  162
Marxism of, 48, 161–163
Paris Commune and, 61, 62
on peasants, 224–225
Populism and, 167, 169
on the proletariat, 160
on revolutions, 160–169
on Russia, 160
on socialism, 167–168, 170
Leontiev, Wassily, 77–78, 106, 237
Leopold II, King, 150
Lescohier, Don D., 128
Levelers, the, 22, 23
Levi, Paul, 191
Levinson, Jerome, 334
Lévy, Armand, 59
Lewis, John L., 326
Libya, 244
  *See also* Africa; Third World
Lichtheim, George, 73, 140, 214
Liebknecht, Karl, 73, 191
Lin Piao, 225, 232
Lincoln, Abraham, 114
Lippmann, Walter, 363
Lipset, Seymour Martin, 120
Little Steel Massacre of 1937, 120
Liu Shao-ch'i, 232, 233
Locke, John, 82
*Logic* (Hegel), 6
Lollard movement, 19
London *Economist*, 203, 238, 239,
  298
Louis XVIII, King, 27
Louis Philippe, King, 27
Lowenthal, Richard, 245
Ludwig, Emil, 174
Lukacs, George, 32, 53
Lumpenproletarian socialism, 62–63
  Bakunin and, 62

Lumpenproletarian socialism
  (*Continued*)
    Engels on, 234
    Marx on, 62–63, 234–235
    overpopulation and, 63
    Third World, 234–236
Lunar program, 349
Luther, Martin, 18, 19
Luxemburg, Rosa, 74, 75, 191, 312
Lycurgus, 16

McCarthy, Eugene, 366
MacDonald, Ramsay, 193
McDowell, Arthur, 262
Macmillan, Harold, 195, 203, 301
Macpherson, C. B., 31, 83
Madagascar, 16
Magdoff, Harry, 317
Mali, 245
    *See also* Africa; Third World
Mallet, Serge, 360
Malthus, Thomas Robert, 103
Mandel, Ernest, 317, 339, 371
*Manifesto of the Equals*, 24, 25
Mao Tse-tung, 5, 134, 141, 144,
  222–223, 249, 340, 355
    Cultural Revolution, 231–233
    on peasants, 224, 230–231
    on the proletariat, 224
Marcuse, Herbert, 62–63, 235,
  352, 371
Maréchal, Sylvan, 25
Marquand, David, 283, 284
Marris, Robin, 296, 300–301
Marshall, Alfred, 85–86
    compared to Marx, 96, 97
Marshall Plan, 319, 332, 335
Martov, Juliy Osipovich, 163, 164
Marx, Karl, 9, 12–13, 34–35, 110,
  173, 185, 187, 188, 198, 205, 211,
  221–222, 270–271, 280, 300
    on affluence, 355
    on American Civil War, 114
    anti-democratic temptation of,
      43, 49
    on the aristocracy, 44
    on Asiatic mode of production,
      139–140

on authority, 184
on automation, 100
on the bourgeoisie, 49, 351
on bureaucracy, 68
on capital
    organic composition of, 102
    technical composition of,
      102
    as unproductive, 92–94
on capitalism, 8, 46–47, 77–
    108, 134–136, 138–139,
    152, 156, 157, 170, 171,
    174, 194, 281, 350
    law of motion of, 98–108
Cole on, 37–38
on colonialism, 137, 138, 143,
    147, 148, 247
commitment to democracy, 37–
    40, 42, 48, 52–54, 64, 70, 76
on commodities, 90–98, 105–
    106
on Communism, 36, 43, 45,
    174, 370
complexity of, 55–76
death of, 8
debate with Bakunin, 62, 63
on demand for goods, 105–106
demystification, 5–6
on dictatorships, 161, 162–163
    of the proletariat, 49–52
on disparity between produc-
    tion and consumption, 100–
    101, 104
on falling rate of profit, 101–
    102, 103–104
as the father of totalitarianism,
    48
on free-land movement, 115–
    116
on the French Revolution, 26–
    27
on George, Henry, 121
on global abundance, 346
Hegel compared to, 34
on importance of public irriga-
    tion works, 140
Inaugural Address to the
    IWMA, 59–60

Marx, Karl (*Continued*)
　　on Indian society, 140
　　on inequality, 174
　　on joint stock companies, 295–
　　　296
　　Keynes compared to, 96
　　on Kriege, 115, 118
　　on labor, 345
　　　abolition of, 367–368
　　　compulsory, 367–368
　　　wage, as unnecessary, 59–60
　　Lassalle and, 65–67
　　Lenin and, 57–58, 61–62,
　　　161–162
　　on lumpenproletarian social-
　　　ism, 62–63, 234–235
　　Marshall compared to, 96, 97
　　Marxist analysis of, 37–108
　　on Napoleon III, 63
　　on nationalization, 68
　　on natural resources, 78, 80
　　orthodox Communist interpre-
　　　tation of, 36
　　on overproduction, 147
　　on the Paris Commune, 51, 58,
　　　61–62
　　on peasants, 224
　　period of initial political in-
　　　volvement, 71
　　as a philosopher, 30
　　on Plato's *Republic*, 15–16
　　political beginnings of, 37–54
　　as a political economist, 77–
　　　108
　　on poverty, 236, 308
　　on prices, 104–106
　　on production, 217–218, 286
　　on the proletariat, 39
　　radicalism of, 61
　　on religion, 308
　　on revolutions, 29, 49, 59–60,
　　　137–138, 142, 172
　　Riazanov on, 47
　　on rights, 168
　　on Russia, 73, 140–143
　　on science, 94
　　self-change concept, 40
　　on the senses, 41

　　on social democracy, 113–114,
　　　251
　　on socialism, 44–45, 51–54,
　　　174, 351, 366–368
　　on socialized man, 77–108
　　on suffrage, 64
　　on taxes, 121
　　on technology, 99–100
　　on Ten Hours Bill, 60
　　use of the word "economics,"
　　　79, 82, 84
　　on wages, 65
　　on wealth, 77–79, 107, 108
　　on the world market, 310–311
Marxism, 8, 40, 157–158, 193–194
　　Althusser on, 41
　　analysis of Marx, 37–108
　　Austria, 200
　　basic tenet of, 73
　　deradicalization of, 61
　　Engels on basic tenet of, 73
　　first elaboration of, 73
　　France, 185
　　Germany, 56, 67, 191
　　of Lenin, 48, 161–163
　　mechanistic notion of, 26
　　most significant failure of, 74
　　Russia, 48, 57–58, 161–163,
　　　224–225
　　of Stalin, 48
　　state socialism and, 69
　　Third World, 325
　　U.S., 117, 121–125, 252–253
Mathematics, 32
Maurer, James Hudson, 254
*May Day Manifesto*, 206
Meany, George, 265, 266, 268–269
Mehring, Franz, 46, 65, 73
Men of the Land, 14
Mensheviks, 163
Mercantilists, 85, 91
Messianic socialism, 345, 370
Metaphysics, 30, 31, 32
Mexico, 155, 326
　　investment in, 315
　　*See also* Latin America; Third
　　　World

Michailowski, N. K., 140–141
Michels, Robert, 75
Migration, 71, 256
Miliband, Ralph, 198
Military socialism, 89
Millenarians, 38
Model Cities Program, 276
*Monde, Le,* 181, 245, 364
Money, 83–84, 91–98
    abolition of, 344, 345, 367,
        371–372
Monotheism, 13–14
Monroe, James, 111
Moore, Barrington, 67
Moore, Stanley, 345
More, Thomas, 16, 19, 22
Morgan, J. P., 125
Morgan, Thomas J., 123
Morocco, 235–236
    *See also* Third World
Moscow University, 175
Mosley, Oswald, 196
Mossadegh, Mohammed, 322
Multinational corporations, 330–
    331, 332
Münzer, Thomas, 21, 22, 26
    preaching of, 19–20
Muslims, 236
Mussolini, Benito, 145, 176
Mutualists, 68
Myrdal, Gunnar, 136, 138, 220, 221,
    246–249, 318, 329, 336, 337,
    339, 341

Nader, Ralph, 299, 303–304
Naphtali, Fritz, 195
Napoleon I, Emperor, 27
Napoleon III, Emperor, 7, 27, 56,
    59
    Marx on, 63
*Narodniks,* 141, 142
Nasser, Gamal Abdel, 243
National Academy of Science, 297–
    298
National Civic Federation, 125, 260
National Commission on the Causes
    and Prevention of Violence, 275–
    276, 369

National Commission on Civil Dis-
    orders, 274
National Commission on Urban
    Problems, 293
National Committee on Urban
    Growth Policy, 280, 281–282
National Congress of Councils, 191
National Educational Association,
    360
National Industrial Conference
    Board, 330
National Industrial Relations Act,
    258
National Labor Party, 126
National Labor Union, 116
National Recovery Administration
    (NRA), 258, 259
Nationalization, 68–70, 332
    Austria, 199, 200
    capitalism and, 198–204
    Egypt, 243
    Engels on, 68–69, 199–200
    England, 199, 201–204, 301
    France, 199, 200, 202, 203
    Galbraith on, 209
    Germany, 199, 201–202
    Italy, 199
    Jaurès on, 200
    Kautsky on, 199–200
    Marx on, 68
    socialism and, 198–204
    Taiwan, 338–339
    Third World, 243, 321–322,
        338–339
    U.S., 300
    Zambia, 321–322
Natural resources, Marx on, 78, 80
Nazis, 7, 63, 197, 198, 352
Nehru, Jawaharlal, 247
Nemiery, Gafar El, 244
Neo-capitalism, 41, 273–291, 359,
    369
Neo-colonial investments, 316–317
*Neue Rheinische Zeitung* (Marx),
    47
New Deal, 260, 261, 263, 265, 303,
    326
New Harmony, Indiana, 111, 113

*New Industrial State, The* (Galbraith), 209, 302, 360–361
*New Law of Righteousness, The* (Winstanley), 23
*New York Times, The,* 321
*New York Tribune,* 113
New Zealand, 138–139, 221
Nietzsche, Friedrich, 368
Nigeria, 217
    *See also* Africa; Third World
Nixon, Richard M., 274, 280, 282, 290, 293, 298, 321–323, 333–335, 356
    on ecology, 285–286, 347
    medical proposals, 367
    Population Message, 280
    wage-price freeze, 358
Nkrumah, Kwame, 243, 245
North American Central Committee, 117
North Vietnam, 218
*Notes on Machiavelli* (Gramsci), 176

Oil, 316, 319, 322, 333
    profits from, 316
*On Coalition Government* (Mao), 226
*On Cooperation* (Lenin), 166, 167
Onis, Juan de, 334
*Origins of Totalitarianism* (Arendt), 178
Orwell, George, 371
*Otetschestwennyje Sapiski,* 140
*Our Revolution* (Lenin), 166–167
Owen, Robert, 27, 111–112, 346
    interpretation of, 28, 29
Owen, Robert Dale, 112
Owenism, 111–112
Ownership, 92–93, 297–303, 307, 340
    absentee, 338
    of capital, 96
    separation of, 295–296

Padilla, Huberto, 239
Pakistan, 217
    *See also* Asia; Third World

Palestine, 314
    *See also* Asia; Third World
Palme, Olof, 212, 361–362
Paris Commune, 58, 61–62, 162, 163
    Engels on, 51
    Lenin and, 61, 62
    Marx on, 51, 58, 61–62
Pearson Commission, 328, 330, 335
Peasants, 355
    China, 224–231, 340, 355
        surplus and, 228
    Egypt, 243
    Engels on, 224
    England, 21–22, 224
    France, 23–24, 224
    Germany, 19–20, 22, 224
    Kautsky on, 224–225
    Lenin on, 224–225
    Mao on, 224, 230–231
    Marx on, 224
    Russia, 57, 141–142, 156, 159, 165, 171–173, 179, 190, 230, 231
    Third World, 222, 224–231, 243, 340, 355
    Trotsky on, 224–225
Pelling, Henry, 123
P'eng Teh-huai, 230
*People's Daily,* 180
People's Liberation Army, 231
Pereire, Isaac, 27
Perlman, Selig, 117, 131
Persia, 314
    *See also* Asia; Third World
Peru, 243, 334
    Communism, 243
    U.S. aid to, 319
    *See also* Latin America; Third World
Petty, William, 82
*Phenomenology of Spirit* (Hegel), 33
Philip, André, 197, 202, 203, 215
Physiocrats, 82, 85, 91
Pickard, Jerome C., 286
*Plan du Travail* (De Man), 197–198

Planning
capitalism and, 281–284
socialism and, 281–284
Third World, 332–336
world market, 332–336
Plato, 15–17, 28
Plekhanov, Georgiy Valentinovich,
57, 73
*Po Prostu*, 180
Poland, 168, 180–181, 184, 228,
233
strikes, 9, 185
uprising (1956), 9
Pollution, 303–304
air, 285–287
Johnson on, 286–287
land, 286
Nixon on, 285–286, 347
water, 286
Polytheism, 14
Poor Men of Lyons, 18
Popular Front, 197
Population control, 329–330
socialism and, 348, 349–350
Populists, 116
Lenin and, 167, 169
Port of New York Authority, 302–
303
Poverty, 314, 366
absolute, 104
capitalism in perpetuating,
318–323
China, 230, 308
Cuba, 308
Egypt, 308
Engels on, 236
England, 212
India, 342
Marx on, 236, 308
Russia, 308
social, 104
socialization of, 30
Sweden, 212
Third World, 230, 308, 318–
323, 342
U.S., 266, 274–279, 354, 358
Pragmatism, 119
Prebisch, Raul, 219–220

Preobrazhensky, E., 174
Presbyterians, 21, 22
Price controls, 298–299
Prices, 83–84, 85
Marx on, 104–106
Producers' cooperatives, 65, 68
Production
Asiatic mode of, 139–140
of capital, 93–94
of commodities, 90–98
disparity between consumption and, 100–101, 104
imperialism and, 313
Marx on, 217–218, 286
powers of, 29–30
socially exploited means of, 88
supply and demand in, 84, 85,
96–97, 105–106
surplus concept, 80–81
world market as the basis of,
311
Profits, 206–207
control of, 298
falling rate of, 101–102, 103–
104
from land, 80
length of working day and, 98,
107
from oil, 316
retained, surplus as, 96
*Prolegomena to Any Future Meta-
physics* (Kant), 32
Proletariat, the, 74, 164, 355, 359
Blanqui on, 38
China, 224
dictatorship of, 49–52
Engels on, 38–39
England, 28, 29, 38–39, 43,
148, 356
France, 27, 28, 46, 164, 197,
353, 354, 360
Germany, 160, 164, 353
immiserization of, 72
Italy, 353, 354
Lenin on, 160
Mao on, 224
Marx on, 39
Russia, 158, 161, 163, 172

Proletariat, the (*Continued*)
    Spain, 353
    U.S., 353–360
Protestantism, 18, 19, 20, 131
Proudhon, Pierre Joseph, 7, 59, 62, 63, 68, 121, 138, 300, 303
Prussia, 49
Pythagoras, 16

Quint, Howard, 124

Racism, 138, 183, 266, 275, 278, 332, 353
Radical Party, 299
Radicalism
    agrarian, 116, 254
    all-or-nothing, 60
    entrepreneurial, 116
    of Marx, 61
Radio Corporation of America, 326
Rakovsky, Christian, 185
Rapp, Father George, 111
Recession of 1970–1971, 364
*Red Flag,* 180
Reid, Ogden, 321, 322
Reive, Emil, 259
Relative surplus value, 99, 104
Religion, 18–20, 146, 345
    English Revolution, 21–23
    Marx on, 308
    monotheism, 13–14
    polytheism, 14
    *See also* names of religions
Rent
    ground, 80
    labor, 80
*Report to the County of Lanark, The* (Owen), 29
*Republic* (Plato), 15–16
Republican Party, 280
Research needs, 329–330
Reuther, Walter, 262–263, 265, 266
*Revolution Betrayed, The* (Trotsky), 183
Revolutions
    Engels on, 49, 51, 142, 224
    Kautsky on, 157–159
    Lenin on, 160–169

    Marx on, 29, 49, 59–60, 137–138, 147, 172
    unions and, 55–56
Riazanov, David, 47, 73
    on Engels, 47
    on Marx, 47
Ribicoff, Abraham, 281
Ricardo, David, 29, 83, 85
Riesman, David, 278–279
Risk-taking, 96
Robens, Alf, 301
Robespierre, Maximilien, 26
Robinson, Joan, 85, 87, 92, 93, 103, 231, 305–306
Robinson, Paul, 6
Rockefeller, David, 282
Rockefeller Foundation, 329
Roman Catholic Church, 15, 18, 19, 131, 357
    on usury, 94
Romney, George, 281
Roosevelt, Franklin D., 119, 196, 251, 258–264
Rose, Sanford, 324–325, 330
Rosenstein-Rodan, Paul N., 217, 336
Rossow, Jerome M., 356
Roszak, Theodore, 365, 366
Royal Dutch Shell Company, 330
Royalists, 21
Rumania, 330–331
Russia, 6, 7, 9, 53, 137, 139, 149, 154–186, 220, 240, 341, 345
    agriculture, 171–173, 179, 230–231
    animal population (1928–1933), 173
    anti-socialist socialism, 152, 154
    Arab Communism and, 243–244
    backwardness of, 170
    Bolsheviks, 154, 155, 159, 164, 165, 171, 179, 183–185
    bourgeoisie, 156–159, 170, 185
    bureaucratic collectivism, 8, 10, 155, 169, 173–178, 182–186, 227, 308

Russia (*Continued*)

capitalism, 156, 170, 171

collective farms, 171–173, 179, 230–231

collectivization, 8, 10, 155, 169, 173–178, 182–186, 227, 308

Communism, 154–156, 165, 169–186, 225, 229, 339–340

Cuba compared to, 240–241

education, 175

Engels on, 142

feudalism, 341

foreign aid, 333

industry, 156, 220

Lenin on, 160

Marx on, 73, 140–143

Marxism, 48, 57–58, 161–163, 224–225

Mensheviks, 163

New Economic Policy, 165

peasants, 57, 141–142, 156, 159, 165, 171–173, 179, 190, 230, 231

personal privileges in, 175, 179–180

poverty, 308

the proletariat, 158, 161, 163, 172

purges, 173, 178

the rising at Kronstadt, 165

socialism, 57–58, 167–168, 170, 171, 229, 237

strikes, 176

surplus, 81, 175, 178

totalitarianism, 160, 169, 173–180, 182–186

Stalin, 173–178

Trotskyists, 170–171, 174

wages, 179

Russian Revolution of 1905, 160

Russian Revolution of 1917, 8, 12, 48, 49, 142–143, 145, 152, 154–155, 158, 159–167, 185, 217, 222, 224–225, 261

compared to Chinese Revolution, 223–224

Stalin on, 171–172

Russian Social Democratic Workers' Party, 157

Saint-Simon, Claude Henri de, 27–28, 300, 306

Sakharov, Andrei D., 180

Samson, Leon, 118, 268

Samuelson, Paul, 6, 78, 80, 102–103, 136, 371

Scanlon, Hugh, 327

Schapiro, Meyer, 369–370

Schapper, 52

Scheidemann, Philipp, 190, 191, 192

Schiller, Karl, 210

Schlesinger, Arthur M., Jr., 259, 263

Schonfield, Andrew, 213, 281

Schorr, Alvin, 275

Schulze-Delitzsch, Hermann, 65

Schumpeter, Joseph, 118, 187

Schwartz, Benjamin, 224

Schweitzer, Johann Baptist von, 66–67, 68

Science, 4, 31, 32

as an element in the labor process, 93

Marx on, 94

Seattle General Strike of 1919, 120

Second International, 70, 143–144, 153, 161, 166–167

Seligman, Ben, 85

Senior, Nassau, 60

Servan-Schreiber, Jean-Jacques, 207, 331

Shachtman, Max, 178

Shanks, Michael, 214

Sharecropping system, 81

Shaw, George Bernard, 145, 146

Shen Tsung, Emperor, 13

Silver as a symbol of value, 91–92

Simons, A. M., 255

Singapore, 315

*See also* Asia; Third World

Singer, Daniel, 215

*Situation of the Working Classes
    in England* (Engels), 38–39
Six Day War, 243
Skidelsky, Robert, 196
Slavery, 81, 151
Smith, Adam, 82–83, 85, 105, 198,
    282, 289, 350, 371
Smith, Al, 256
Snowden, Philip, 195
Social democracy, 111, 113–115,
    119, 130, 133, 146, 188, 250–269
        Engels on, 113, 251
        Marx on, 113–114, 251
        rise of, 55–56
Social Democratic Federation, 145
Social Democratic Party, 208–209
Social poverty, 104
Social Security, 265, 266
Socialism, 344–373
        abolition of labor, 344, 345,
            367–372
        abolition of money, 344, 345,
            367, 371–372
        absolutist view of, 345
        anti-socialist, 6, 21, 45
            Bismarck, 6, 8, 56, 64, 66–
                70
            origins of, 65–70
            Russia, 152, 154
        Arab, 243–244
        Austria, 200, 204–205
        communitarian, 113
        consumption attitudes, 348,
            350, 371–372
        corrupted by Communism,
            154–155
        Cuba, 237–238
        Debsian, 119, 125, 252–255,
            257
        democracy as the essence of,
            37–40, 42, 48, 52–54
        ecology and, 346
        economic growth and, 207–208
        Engels on, 44–45, 51–52
        England, 110, 188, 193, 195–
            196, 199, 201–206, 212–
            215, 283
        finite character of, 344–345

France, 188, 196–198, 200,
    202, 205–206
Germany, 48–49, 58, 67, 188,
    190–194, 199–202, 204–
    205, 208–211
global abundance and, 345–
    351
ideal form of, 344
Italy, 144
Latin America, 245
Lenin on, 167–168, 170
limitations of, 345
lumpenproletarian, 62–63
    Bakunin and, 62
    Engels on, 234
    Marx on, 62–63, 234–235
    overpopulation and, 63
    Third World, 234–236
Marx on, 44–45, 51–54, 174,
    351, 366–368
messianic, 345, 370
military, 89
most basic premise of, 344
nationalization and, 198–204
new definition of, 206–207
planning under, 281–284
population control, 348, 349–
    350
precondition of, 41
Russia, 57–58, 167–168, 170,
    171, 229, 237
Stalin on, 170
state, 38, 68–69
Sweden, 196, 204–205
technology and, 346–349, 351,
    353
Third World, 221–222, 237–
    238, 245, 342–343
    lumpenproletarian, 234–236
    preconditions for, 308–309
U.S., 106, 109–133, 251–263,
    268, 269, 272, 281–284
    attitude toward, 109–110
the welfare state and, 270–307
World War I and, 56
*Socialism As It Is* (Walling), 69
Socialist capitalism, 187–215

Socialist International, 146, 195–196
  Amsterdam Congress, 146, 188
  Stuttgart Congress, 146–147
Socialist Labor Party, 123, 124
Socialist Party (Italy), 144
Socialist Party (U.S.), 106, 126,
  131–133, 251–255, 257–262,
  269
Socialist Trades and Labor Al-
  liance, 124
Socialized man, 77–108
Sombart, Werner, 109–110, 119, 132
Sorge, 114, 121, 122, 123, 201
South Korea
  Gross National Product, 316
  U.S. aid to, 319
  *See also* Asia; Third World
Spain
  fascism, 138
  the proletariat, 353
*Spartakusbund,* 191
*Spiegel, Der,* 210
Stalin, Joseph, 5, 7, 25, 36, 47, 134,
  136, 137, 142, 145, 146, 166,
  169–186, 217, 223, 225, 226,
  228, 237, 291–292, 340
  anti-Hegelianism of, 177
  defense of inequality, 174
  Khrushchev on, 178–179
  Marxism of, 48
  on Revolution of 1917, 171–
    172
  on socialism, 170
  totalitarianism, 173–178
Standard Oil of New Jersey, 330
Stans, Maurice, 282
*State and Revolution* (Lenin), 161,
  163
State socialism, 38, 68–69
*Statehood and Anarchy* (Bakunin),
  234
Sternberg, Fritz, 71, 156, 313
Stockholders, 296, 299, 305–306,
  361
Stojanovic, Svetozar, 182, 241
Stolypin, Pëtr Arkadyevich, 156
Strachey, John, 292, 371
Straser, Gregor, 7

Strikes
  China, 231
  England, 58–59
  France, 360
  Germany, 9, 184, 185
  Poland, 9, 185
  Russia, 176
  Sweden, 361–362
  U.S., 117, 119–120, 122, 126,
    253, 258, 353
Student unrest, 353
  France, 364–365
Students, Trotsky on, 363–364
Sturmthal, Adolf, 198
Stuttgart Congress, 146–147
Subsistence wages, 82
Sudan, 217, 243
  Communism, 243, 244
  *See also* Third World
Suffrage
  Blanqui on, 38
  England, 64
  Germany, 64
  Marx on, 64
  U.S., 129
Sukarno, Achmed, 243
Sultan-Galiev, 225
Supply of commodities, 105–106
Supply and demand, 84, 85, 96–
  97, 105–106
Surplus, 228
  capital, 313, 317
  Chinese peasants and, 228
  concept of, 80–81
  Engels on, 175
  relative value, 99, 104
  retained profits as, 96
  Russia, 81, 175, 178
  Third World, 81, 228, 337
  totalitarian extraction of, 81
  unpaid labor, 80–82
Surplus value, 95
  absolute, 98
Sweden, 297
  income inequality, 212
  poverty, 212
  socialism, 196, 204–205
  strikes, 361–362

Sweezy, Paul, 101, 239–240
Switzerland, 314
Syria
    Communism, 243, 244
    *See also* Asia; Third World

Taborites, 19
Taft, Phillip, 111, 126
Taft, Robert A., 276
Taft-Hartley Law, 266
Taiwan, 326
    Gross National Product, 316
    investment in, 315
    nationalizations, 338–339
    U.S. aid to, 319
    *See also* Asia; Third World
Tariffs, 72, 325, 328
    Kennedy on, 320
    Third World and, 325, 328
    U.S., 320, 323, 328
Tarnow, Fritz, 196
Taxes, 81, 335–336
    inheritance, 306
    Marx on, 121
    U.S., 121, 274, 277, 290, 304–
      306
Technocrats, 27
Technology, 7, 134, 220, 284, 359–
    360
    control of, 297–298
    future of, 4–5
    labor and, 93, 354, 368–369
    Marx on, 99–100
    socialism and, 346–349, 351,
      353
    Third World, 347
    U.S., 132
Ten Hours Bill, 60
Tennessee Valley Authority, 300,
    301
Tessier, Gaston, 360
*Testament* (Varga), 179–180
*Theories of Surplus Value* (Marx),
    81, 93, 205, 351
*Theory of Capitalist Development,
    The* (Sweezy), 101
*Theses on Feuerbach* (Marx), 39–
    40

Third World, 6, 8, 9, 20, 22, 30, 36,
    108, 134–154, 168–169, 185, 216–
    249, 271
    agriculture, 12, 238–239, 321–
      323, 328–329, 340–341, 366
    collectivization, 227–228, 308
    Communism, 180, 223–233,
      239–244, 339–343
    democracy, 336–342
    economic levels, 216, 217
    exports, 315
    foreign aid, 319–321, 332,
      335, 338
    housing, 239–240
    investments in, 314–322, 330–
      333
    Marxism, 325
    modernization of, 325
    nationalizations, 243, 321–322,
      338–339
    peasants, 222, 224–231, 243,
      340, 355
    planning, 332–336
    population control, 329–330,
      349
    poverty, 230, 308, 318–323,
      342
    research needs, 329–330
    socialism, 221–222, 237–238,
      245, 342–343
      lumpenproletarian, 234–236
      preconditions for, 308–309
    surplus, 81, 228, 337
    tariffs and, 325, 328
    technology, 347
    urban poor, 222, 233–236
    wealth, 337–338
Thomas, Norman, 252, 257, 262
Tinbergen, Jan, 327
Titmus, Richard, 212, 213
Totalitarian utopianism, 12
Totalitarianism, 6, 36, 41, 43, 53
    China, 229, 233, 340
    of Communism, 69, 160, 169,
      173–178, 271, 310
    Marx as the father of, 48
    Russia, 160, 169, 173–180,
      182–186

Totalitarianism (*Continued*)
　Stalin, 173–178
　surplus extraction, 81
Touraine, Alain, 360
*Toward a Democratic Left* (Har-
　rington), 289, 313, 319, 332
*Towards the Understanding of Karl
　Marx* (Hook), 50
Trades Union Congress, 123, 327
Trotsky, Leon, 49, 53, 157, 159–
　160, 166, 169, 170–171, 183,
　184, 226–227, 370
　on Germany, 190
　on peasants, 224–225
　on students, 363–364
Trotskyists, 170–171, 174
Truman, Harry S., 276, 333
Tucker, Robert C., 60–61
Tugwell, Rexford G., 264
Tunisia, 235–236
　*See also* Third World
Turkey, 314
Twentieth Party Congress, 228
Tyler, Wat, 19

Unemployment
　automation and, 364
　Cuba, 238–239
　U.S., 126, 128, 263, 289, 290
Unions, 58–62
　England, 28–29, 58–59, 201,
　327
　France, 360
　gradualism movement, 70
　revolution and, 55–56
　U.S., 9, 112, 116, 117, 119,
　121–132, 250–269, 325–
　327, 353–360
　world industrialization and,
　325–327
　*See also* Labor; names of
　unions
United Automobile Workers, 265,
　267
United Mine Workers, 326
United Nations, 332, 335
　Committee for Development
　Planning, 336

United Nations' Conference on
　Trade and Development
　(UNCTAD), 219–220
United States of America, 58, 69,
　109–133, 138, 149–150, 162,
　213, 220, 221, 228, 251, 256–
　264, 298
　affluence, 110, 128, 286, 355–
　356, 364, 367
　agriculture, 81, 277, 279, 284
　air pollution, 285–287
　automobiles, 285–287
　capitalism, 250, 257, 263–
　264, 272–307
　the Civil War, 114
　collectivism, 357
　colonialism, 148, 319
　communal living in, 350
　Communism, 252, 254, 257,
　260–263
　Conference on Progressive Po-
　litical Action, 255
　Democratic Party, 125, 255–
　257, 266–269
　democratization of power in,
　353
　education, 278–279, 290, 294,
　356, 360, 362–364, 367
　exports, 317
　of jobs, 326
　foreign aid, 319–321, 332,
　335, 338
　free-land movement, 114–116
　gold discovered in California,
　52
　Green Corn Rebellion, 254
　health care, 290, 294, 367, 372
　housing, 274–276, 279, 281–
　283, 288, 292–293
　immigrants, 122–123, 129–
　133, 253, 256
　AFL's hostility to, 132–133
　imperialism, 319–323
　imports, 315, 318, 322–323,
　328
　income in, 304–305
　inflation, 354

United States of America (*Continued*)
    investments, 316, 317, 319,
        321, 330–333
    Jews, 254
    lack of feudalism in, 111, 113
    land pollution, 286
    liberalism, 205, 211, 254
    lunar program, 349
    Marxism, 117, 121–125, 252–
        253
    migration in, 256
    National Guard, 120
    nationalizations, 300
    neo-capitalism, 273–291, 359,
        369
    New Deal, 260, 261, 263, 265,
        303, 326
    ownership, 297–303, 307
    in perpetuating economic
        backwardness, 318–323
    in perpetuating poverty, 318–
        323
    poverty, 266, 274–279, 354,
        358
    the proletariat, 353–360
    racism, 266, 275, 278, 332,
        353
    railroads, 277–278
    recession of 1970–1971, 364
    Republican Party, 280
    sectarianism, 117, 122–124,
        253
    sharecropping system, 81
    social democracy in, 111, 113–
        115, 119, 130, 133, 146, 188,
        250–269
        Engels on, 113, 251
        Marx on, 113–114, 251
        rise of, 55–56
    social mobility, 278
    Social Security, 265, 266
    socialism, 106, 109–133, 251–
        263, 268, 269, 272, 281–284
        attitude toward, 109–110
    standard of living in, 128–130,
        132, 350, 370
    strikes, 117, 119–120, 122,
        126, 253, 258, 353
    suffrage, 129
    tariffs, 320, 323, 328
    taxes, 121, 274, 277, 290, 304–
        306
    technology, 132
    trade policies, 319–323
    transportation, 277–278, 285–
        287, 292–293
    unemployment, 126, 128, 263,
        289, 290
    unions, 9, 112, 116, 117, 119,
        121–132, 250–269, 325–
        327, 353–360
    urban poor, 234
    utopianism, 110–118, 121,
        123, 250, 253
    Vietnam War, 218, 269, 276,
        317, 364
    violence in, 120, 275–276, 369
    voluntarism, 124–125, 251,
        264, 266
    wage-price freeze, 358
    wages, 128–129, 132, 357, 358
    water pollution, 286
    wealth, 304, 358
    welfare state, 271–307
    welfare system, 277
    working day, 368
    World War I, 254
    World War II, 260, 263
    youth discontent, 353, 362
U.S. Bureau of Labor Statistics, 354
U.S. Department of Labor, 354, 359
U.S. Internal Revenue Service, 305
U.S. International Development In-
    stitute, 334–335
U.S. Post Office, 301, 302–303
University of Michigan Research
    Center, 357
Urban Land Institute, 286
Urban poor, 222, 233–236
    Third World, 222, 233–236
    U.S., 234
Urban Problems Commission, 276
Use value, 90, 95
Usury, 94
*Utopia* (More), 22

Utopianism, 11–35, 38, 134, 365
   aristocratic, 15–16
   beginning of, 11
   capitalism and, 18
   China, 13
   England, 21–23, 28
   France, 21, 23–27
   Greece, 11, 13, 15, 16–17
   Jews, 11–14
   16th–19th century, 21–29
   totalitarian, 12
   12th–16th century, 17–21
   U.S., 110–118, 121, 123, 250,
     253

Valdes, Gabriel, 320–321
Value
   capital as a symbol of, 91–92
   commodity exchange, 90, 95
   gold as a symbol of, 91–92
   labor as an increment in, 95–96
   labor theory of, 82, 84–85, 89
   land as a symbol of, 91–92
   of natural resources, 78
   silver as a symbol of, 91–92
   surplus, 95
     absolute, 98
     relative, 99, 104
   use, 90, 95
Van Kol, 146–147
Vandervelde, Émile, 150, 151, 152
Varga, Yevgeny Samoylovich, 156–
   157, 161, 174–175, 179–180,
   317–318
Veblen, Thorstein, 350, 359–361
Velasco, Juan, 334
Venezuela, 337
   *See also* Latin America; Third
     World
Vietcong, 218
Vietnam, U.S. aid to, 319
Vietnam War, 218, 269, 276, 317,
   364
Vogel, Hans-Jochen, 210–211
*Volks-Tribun, Der,* 114
Voluntarism, 124–125, 251, 264,
   266

Wage controls, 298
Wage-price freeze, 358
Wages, 71, 81, 100, 324
   Asia, 316
   Engels on, 65
   England, 129, 313, 327
   France, 313
   Germany, 72, 130
   Latin America, 316
   Marx on, 65
   real, 313
   rising, 103–104
   Russia, 179
   subsistence, 82
   U.S., 128–129, 132, 357, 358
Wagner, Robert, 259
Wagner Act, 259
Wald, Pierre, 18
Waldensians, 18
*Wall Street Journal,* 274, 287, 298,
   305
Walling, William English, 69, 255
Walzer, Michael, 22
Ward, Barbara, 220, 234
Water pollution, 286
Wealth, 314
   creation of, 77, 107, 108
   increase in the disparity of, 329
   Marx on, 77–79, 107, 108
   natural resources as a source
     of, 78
   Third World, 337–338
   U.S., 304, 358
Webb, Beatrice, 145
Webb, Sidney, 145, 201, 296
Weber, Max, 13–14, 221, 350
Weinstein, James, 254, 260
Weitling, Wilhelm, 38
Welfare state, 6, 9, 10, 215, 270–
   307, 314
   capitalism and, 270–307
   China, 13
   England, 7, 202, 213
   limits of, 271
   socialism and, 270–307
   U.S., 271–307
Wenceslaus, Emperor, 19
Werfel, Edda, 181

Westminster Conservative Associa-
tion, 203
*What Is To Be Done* (Lenin), 74
White, Theodore, 267
White-collar labor, 211
Wiedjik, 148–149
Wilber, Charles K., 177, 321
Wilhelm II, Kaiser, 67
Williams, William Appleman, 260
Willich, 52
Wilson, Harold, 150, 203, 205–206,
212–213, 214, 305, 333, 358
devalues the pound, 213
Wilson, Woodrow, 119, 125–126
Wissell, Rudolf, 192–193
Wobblies, *see* Industrial Workers
of the World
Woll, Matthew, 257
Woodcock, Leonard, 327
Woodhull, Victoria, 116–117
Working day, length of, 60, 61
capitalism and, 60
France, 197
profit and, 98, 107
U.S., 368
World Bank, 328, 333, 334, 335,
336
World market, 271, 308–343
as the basis of production, 311
Engels on, 310, 311, 312
intracapitalist investment,
314–316
major development after
World War II, 314

Marx on, 310–311
neo-colonial investment, 316–
317
in perpetuating economic backwardness, 318–323
in perpetuating poverty, 318–
323
planning, 332–336
restructuring of, 324–332
World Society of Revolutionary
Communists, 50
World War I, 56, 72–73, 190–191
capitalism and, 188
socialism and, 56
U.S., 254
World War II, 260, 263
Worsley, Peter, 235
Woytinsky, W. S., 195
Wright, Frances, 112–113
Wycliffe, John, 19


Yalta Conference, 118
Yankelovich polling organization,
288–289
Young Socialists (Jusos), 210
Youth unrest, 353, 362
Yugoslavia, 7, 241–242


Zambia, 321–322
*See also* Africa; Third World
Zoar, Ohio, 113
Zuffelato, Tom, 131